LENIN AND HIS RIVALS

Lenin
and his Rivals

THE STRUGGLE FOR
RUSSIA'S FUTURE, 1898-1906

by

DONALD W. TREADGOLD

GREENWOOD PRESS, PUBLISHERS
WESTPORT, CONNECTICUT

Library of Congress Cataloging in Publication Data

Treadgold, Donald W   1922-
    Lenin and his rivals.

    Reprint of the ed. published by Methuen, London.
    Includes bibliographical references and index.
    1. Russia--Politics and government--1894-1917.
2. Lenin, Vladimir Il'ich, 1870-1924. I. Title.
[DK262.T74 1976]   947.08   76-28338
ISBN 0-8371-9045-2

This edition first published in 1955 by Methuen & Co., Ltd., London

Reprinted in 1976 by Greenwood Press
A division of Congressional Information Service, Inc.
88 Post Road West, Westport, Connecticut 06881

Library of Congress Catalog Card Number 76-28338

ISBN 0-8371-9045-2

Printed in the United States of America

10 9 8 7 6 5 4 3 2

To the Memory of

Bernard Humphrey Sumner

TABLE OF CONTENTS

"If thought once masters a man, he ceases to discuss whether the thing is practicable, and whether the enterprise is hard or easy: he seeks truth alone and carries out his principles with inexorable impartiality . . ."

—ALEXANDER HERZEN, *My Past and Thoughts.*

"The dialectic of history is of such a kind that the theoretical victory of Marxism compels its enemies to reclothe themselves as Marxists."

—VLADIMIR LENIN, *The Historical Fate of the Teaching of Karl Marx.*

Part One

THE REVOLUTION IN SIGHT

I

"TO THE PEOPLE"

*Without knowing the people we may oppress
the people, we may enslave them, we may conquer them, but we cannot set them free.*

*Without the help of the people they will be
freed neither by the Tsar with his clerks, nor
the nobility with the Tsar, nor the nobility without the Tsar.*—ALEXANDER HERZEN.[1]

In the summer of 1891 there appeared in the Russian press a
letter from a priest of Kazan province reporting that a large
number of his communicants were starving. Other such reports
followed swiftly. That year and the next, the worst famine in
decades swept through Central and Southern Russia, and Russia's
educated classes rose almost as one man to succor the common
people who were dying.

Alexander Herzen long before in London, far away from his
homeland, had pondered the problem of Russia's misery and backwardness, and its need for a "social transformation." Filled with
frustrated eagerness to close the stupendous gap between Russian
reality and his own ideal vision of the future, he had hurled at
his fellow intellectuals the command, "To the people!" in his
famous newspaper, *The Bell.* [2] The significance of this slogan is
rooted in the nature of the Russian social fabric as it was then and
at the time of the Revolution of 1917. The word "people"—*narod*—
meant the Russian masses, but by no means all Russians. It referred
to the millions of wretched tillers of the soil. From the peasantry
there was beginning to emerge a new class of factory workers. These
workers seemed to be living through again some of the grim chapters of England's early industrialism which had so horrified Karl
Marx, but they often retained much stronger links with their native

countryside than the workers of Western Europe. The peasants, whether or not partially displaced to urban centers, were by no means despised by the Tsardom, which regarded them as its unshakably loyal subjects, obedient to the earthly order as they had been from ancient times to the crooked cross of Russian Orthodoxy. They were by no means always maltreated by their landlords, many of whom took seriously the injunctions of Russia's eighteenth-century monarchs to care conscientiously for the welfare of their charges. Nor were they forgotten by the Russian intelligentsia, who from the time of their first progenitors under Catherine the Great had always had at least one feeling in common—pity for the plight of the serfs, joined to the firm resolve to better it somehow. Yet though not despised or forgotten, the "people" were still, perhaps even more than their ancestors, hovering on the margin of existence. Over this margin, calamities like the famine of 1891 might unopposed sweep death and ruin, God only knew when.

Separated from the "people" by an abyss of education, outlook, and language—the external marks of radically differing social and economic position—was the relatively small but influential body of respectable men who made up what was delicately called Russian "society"—*obshchestvo*. Along with the noble landlords who made up the uniquely privileged class, this group included the fast-growing nucleus of industrialists, the men of the trained professions, as highly revered though not as well paid as their German confreres, and the government officials. Among the respectable men of Russia were to be found many who lived off the toil of the poor, though some of these very "exploiters" sought to end such a system, and as a whole "society" can be said to have wrestled with feelings of responsibility for Russia's ills.

Yet it was not "society" as such which Herzen urged to take up the burden of "going to the people." It was rather the intelligentsia. Much ink has been spilt over the difficulties of this term. The intelligentsia,[3] as it stood in 1900, was a group which might be divided into two parts. One section had emerged from the social lower depths and had parted company with that mode of life while not itself entering "respectable" circles. The other part came from the nobles and professional men of "society," these men however remaining in close contact with that environment and social atmosphere. This description may help to explain why the "intelligentsia" has been termed "not a social group at all," or one which "cuts across class lines" in Russia. It was indeed a body of men and women whose distinguishing feature was not social origin or economic position, but rather a degree of education, no matter how acquired, and a deep interest in social problems. The opposite pole of the "people," sociologically speaking, was "society"; culturally speaking, it was the "intelligentsia." These two groups overlapped, and for that reason it becomes the more difficult to follow the threads of Russia's "social transformation," in Herzen's phrase. What is most interesting about the outcome, perhaps, is that in terms of the future, the intelligentsia may be viewed as an essentially extra-economic group which was openly seeking political power—however unselfishly, in however democratic a framework—while at the same time many of its spokesmen asserted that politics was a function of economics and that meaningful political activity could only be conducted in terms of economic categories. The section of the intelligentsia which insisted most strongly on this point, the Bolsheviks, was precisely that which succeeded at last in capturing political power.

2.

This book deals with the efforts of the Russian intelligentsia to "set the people free," as Herzen put it. More precisely, it attempts to describe a crucial stage of those efforts, the decade climaxed by the miscarried Revolution of 1905. The method chosen to achieve this transformation harked back to Herzen's order, "To the people!" After unsuccessful attempts to apply this admonition rather crudely, the intelligentsia of the 90's adopted a more sophisticated form of attack. In part by leading, in part by marching alongside, the mass movement of Russia's miserable millions they intended to reach their goal. The origins, character, and beliefs of the men and women who made up this intelligentsia will loom large in our story.

It was during the reign of Catherine the Great that the intelligentsia are usually said to have come into being. By that period the "dark people" had several times turned to unlettered vagabonds as their leaders in violent, desperate, and unsuccessful outbreaks against oppression, especially in the form of serfdom. Serfdom had at the time of its legal origin in the seventeenth century bound noble to serve the state with sword and pen, while it fixed peasant on the land to produce food and pay taxes. Somehow many Russians had understood the need for this kind of social contract,[4] concluded under the reign of the "good" Tsar Alexei Mikhailovich. What the "people" had not understood was why Peter III, a century later, had freed the noble of his not very onerous duties while at the same time the serf was chained ever tighter, not to his "Little Father"—Tsar but to his landlord master. Among the Cossacks, in such men as Stepan Razin in the seventeenth century and the romantic impostor Pugachov in the eighteenth, the "dark people" had found *ad hoc* spokesmen and chieftains. In 1825 the noblemen Decembrists, more sophisticated in culture, but much less adroit in gaining popular support, had tried a different kind of revolution. They and their successors, the "conscience-stricken noblemen" (of whom Herzen was one), were frantically eager to lift their brethren of the masses out of their poverty and ignorance, but had only vague notions as to how to undertake this task. By the 1860's the intellectual leadership of highborn Herzens was challenged by new and unpolished Chernyshevskys from the lower social depths, the "declassed men." Most of them, assuming that the "innate socialism" of the Russian people would speed things toward a better future, wrote and talked endlessly of whether the Tsardom could be persuaded or coerced into starting the process of social transformation.

By 1874 the period of discussion, much of it in Zurich cafes, was at an end. In the spring of that year the younger generation of intelligentsia went off in droves to the countryside, executing Herzen's injunction in the most literal fashion. What they were to do there was more puzzling. The ironic and terrible Chigirin incident, where a few young men induced peasants to rise by producing a forged manifesto of the Tsar ordering them to do so, was the ultimate achievement possible in the 1870's. The "dark people" did not want the light which the city boys and girls brought them. The youth assumed the hosility or indifference of the people to be proof of their backwardness and stupidity—an assumption, by the way, that they would have done well to examine closely at that time, for it remained in various forms until 1917 and after, as we shall observe.

Disillusioned in the Tsar by the Great Reforms of the 60's (which they regarded as fundamentally inadequate), disillusioned in themselves by the results of the movement of 1874, the "declassed" youth turned to terrorism. As a result, the Tsar-Liberator, Alexander II, was murdered by some of the highest-minded and best-intentioned assassins the world has ever seen. Another immediate result was that a revulsion of public feeling took place, and "society" looked on with mixed feelings while the Tsarist police crushed the active revolutionaries.

The subsequent history of the revolutionary movement up to

1905 is concerned with the long and painful effort of the intelligent-sia both above and below the line of respectability to prepare sound ideological ground for the active struggles to follow, and to embark on these struggles with the support of the "people." For the first time the radical intellectuals broke through on a wide front to reach the traditionally conservative, but certainly dissatisfied, un-privileged masses of Russia. Nevertheless, this break-through was not complete, and the extent of the penetration proved to be somewhat deceptive. The wall which separated intelligentsia and people, whose experiences and values were so divergent, was breached sufficiently to make combined political action possible. As things turned out, however, the intelligentsia decided too soon that they had learned to understand and be understood by the masses. The fate of the Russian revolutionary movement may have hinged on the failure of the intelligentsia to evalute the experience of 1905 adequately with respect to this very problem.

3.

In 1891, as in 1874, there was a "going to the people" in which there took part not merely a few hundred boys and girls, but men and women from all sections of the intelligentsia. This time it was a grim and urgent task they undertook, that of saving lives rather than preaching social change. The "dark people" did not need to be told why or whence these unaccustomed visitors came, but their misery did not make them enlightened, and many doctors were driven off as "poisoners." Yet it would appear that the attempt at famine relief had some educational effect on both visitors and visited. At any rate in the middle 90's the radicals made the first real inroads in the problem of organizing politically oriented peasant groups. And by this time the radicals had had conspicuous success in doing the same with the workers of the cities.

The intelligentsia which "went to the people" for the second time, minus some of their earlier illusions, were more deeply divided among themselves than ever before. In the "respectable" wing, the estranged noblemen of the Herzen stamp now began to find themselves overshadowed by professional men, lawyers like Basil Maklakov and professors like Paul Miliukov, and the two groups had their own inner controversies to settle. At the same time the "respectables" had to define their attitude to the dis-inherited revolutionaries whose profession was the struggle with autocracy and whose life had to be lived either underground in Russia or in tight little islands of Russian emigres in France or

Switzerland. The two wings found themselves in common cause, but that did not of itself bring them into harmony.

This split within the Russian intelligentsia, as has already been pointed out, was not new. Among those who worked for an ideal future, there had been for decades men who might utter the word "constitution" in an unguarded moment and get exiled to their country estates, still remaining "respectable" after their chastisement. There had also been men who hid their crude bomb plants and tiny presses where they could, and hoped for Siberia (and possible escape) rather than the scaffold, if caught. In the old days, however, these two worlds had had no direct contact, and when the squire Ivan Petrunkevich descended into the alley hideaways of Kiev to talk as an equal with some outcast terrorists in 1879, it was the beginning of a new epoch in the annals of the Russian opposition.[5]

This division remained until 1917 and later in spite of all efforts to wipe it out, but what was new in 1891 was that the respectable men and the outcasts were brought as never before to realize that the nature of the political events to come would increasingly throw them together, even catch them in the same harness, as did 1905. The experience of famine relief, along with the other experiences of the whole "Liberation Movement," forged an opposition united in certain limited objectives—many wrongly thought, united for the overthrow of autocracy and the establishment of Russian democracy, at least. Never during this long drama did the two wings disappear nor grow to love one another. Nevertheless, the social split was not the decisive factor in the final engagement in 1917. When this came, a small kernel of the disinherited, the Bolsheviks, stood over against a great body of respectable men plus outcasts (Kadets, Mensheviks, SR's) and destroyed them with scant attention to differences of social origin or status.

Extra-economic in nature, the intelligentsia behaved in an extra-economic manner. The split which was decisive was a political—an intellectual—one. On such lines was the political party leadership sundered in the Revolution of 1917; on such lines it had already split in the Revolution of 1905. Therein is the justification for the painstaking analysis we intend to devote to the growth and development of the thought and action of the Russian parties—particularly in relation to each other.

4.

The leaders of the Liberation Movement thus stood aside from

the rise and fall of Russian economic development. They were able
to do this simply because they were usually either too well off or
too poor to be greatly affected thereby. With the "people" it was
exactly the contrary. The urban workers of Russia refused to continue to suffer economic want in silence as they contemplated the
new wealth which industrial technology was bringing to the Empire in the last third of the nineteenth century—as it had earlier
been brought to England and France and Germany in a roughly
similar way. This wealth had only an indirect impact on the village,
home of the vast majority of Russians, but nonetheless a definite
one. It was not that the peasant saw his landlord growing richer;
more often the opposite was the case. Neither did the peasants
hear from their fellows who had sought subsistence in the new
factories of the city that they were now prosperous. What some of
the peasants-turned-workers in urban centers did discover was not
the road to riches or even a reasonably secure standard of living.
Instead they began to hear that the tenement poverty of their new
existence would pass in a gigantic cataclysm which Karl Marx had
predicted, and this would, if not enrich *them,* at least strip their
privileged employers of their wealth and power. From this assurance
they might derive enthusiasm which could be hazily communicated
to their farm-bound relatives. They in turn might vaguely link the
idea of this coming upheaval with the destruction of the landlords
in their midst. So there was a grain of truth in the Marxist boast
that the proletarian tail wagged the massive, inert body of the
muzhik dog and led him to inflict the fatal bite on capitalist Tsarism. Nevertheless, the Marxists were by no means alone in evaluating highly, as early as the 1890's, the potential power and importance
of the factory workers in remolding Russia's future. Other parties
saw this too, and what some of their members saw still more
clearly was that the mass of the people was still peasant and was
likely to remain so—and therefore the ultimately decisive social
issue to be faced was the peasant problem—the problem of the land.

The plight of the "grey muzhik," Russia's tattered John Doe, had
been grisly enough to excite writers, from Alexander Radishchev
under Catherine the Great onwards, to risk harsh penalties in pub-
licizing it. The Emancipation settlement which gave the serf his
personal freedom had given him land as well, insufficient perhaps,
but that was at least in part because there was not enough land
to give. There were other defects in Russia's greatest reform.[6] Often
portions of the peasant's tillage were "cut off" and left with the
landlord, and the Marxists talked a great deal about the return

of these *"otrezki"* lots before they realized the much vaster proportions of the whole land problem. Furthermore, far too little pasture land was left to the new free farmer. Since no grass crops were included in the usual three-field rotation (winter corn, spring corn, and fallow) system, few animals could be kept for cultivating, let alone raised for market. Thus the peasant's only hope of income from his land was the sale of his grain, especially wheat. Of this crop, perhaps an eighth could be spared for export; and falling grain prices in the 80's and 90's plus high transport costs served to increase the odds against the extensive-cultivation, low-productivity Russian farmers vis-a-vis foreign producers. Owing to lack of storage facilities, both peasants who produced for market and landlords were thrown almost wholly on the mercy of the current price.

Piecemeal efforts to increase productivity and acreage on the part of government and farmer alike were inadequate, especially when confronted with the pressure of a growing farm population. Both the communal and individual peasant landholders enlarged their holdings through purchase of gentry estates and the aid of the Peasant Bank after 1883, but new capital was not available and the mounting surplus of labor power in the countryside was unable to force greater yields from land too long tortured by ancient methods of culitvation.

The peasant, left to his own devices, was uncertain as to where the road to economic security lay. Many roved regions of southern Russia in search of seasonal farm labor or possibly dipped a foot in the unfamiliar waters of factory employment. Some migrated and set up new farms in the southeast and east. A steady though thin current of peasants moved over the Urals into Siberia, and often found far greater opportunity than they had ever known at home. Migration could, however, not directly transform the lot of any large proportion of the farmers. What it might have done, and eventually after 1905 began to do, was relieve the worst home pressures sufficiently to make possible a transition to improved methods of production. Until the time of Nicholas II, however, migration was viewed with suspicion by the Imperial government. More fundamental, the officialdom of Alexander III refused to consider ending the Russian village commune.

The commune, which had existed in some form or other for centuries, had been turned into an instrument of state policy for the raising of taxes and army recruits by Peter the Great. It entailed the use of the wasteful strip system and three-course tillage, and prevented the setting up of individual farms. After Emancipation, it had been preserved as a measure to ensure collection of the redemption payments from the peasants. There were however indications that the practice of redistribution of land to conserve equality of holdings was falling into disuse by the 70's and 80's. A voice here and there urged that the commune should be abolished entirely to make way for independent homesteads. The intelligentsia, for reasons mentioned below, was generally hostile to this solution, and such voices were unable to get control of state policy until the ministry of Stolypin in 1906.

The peasant might chafe at the restrictions and waste inherent in the communal system, but he often could not think of any other escape from his poverty than to demand more land. His, or his father's or grandfather's, ex-landlord had some nearby, and the state, the church, and the Imperial family might have more. "Land," as a revolutionary slogan, usually meant to him that land which belonged to the powerful. Statistics showed that even if gentry, state, and church lands were divided, he would be little better off on the average. But even if he understood statistics, he might not think of himself as "average." He seldom dreamed of a private enclosed holding, for the sufficient reason that he had seldom seen a farm. The peasant in the 90's knew he was trapped in an economic impasse. He could not manage to find a solution, but then neither could the intelligentsia.

One of the most influential who tried was Lenin. During the 90's he was eagerly combing government statistics for evidence which might give heart to the Social Democrat who was stuck in rural Russia with an urban ideology. In his study, *The Development of Capitalism in Russia,* written in Siberian exile, he firmly contended that there was developing in the countryside a fatal kind of class antagonism analogous to that on which he relied in the swollen cities. A great "differentiation," he insisted, was taking place as a result of the gradual passage of Russian agriculture to production for market rather than for home use. To the growing category of "capitalist farmers" he assigned not only landlords but "kulaks." These thrifty and cunning people, he insisted, were growing richer while the farmer working on the economic margin kept slipping down into the mire of selling his own labor. In this fashion the number of the "agricultural proletariat" was rising menacingly. Lenin cited the increasing number of peasants abandoning their Emancipation allotments, of the growing category of "horseless peasants" and the accelerating movement to urban industrial work, as evidence of the appearance of a new class which might link its own fate with that of the city proletarians in a struggle against its own rural bourgeoisie.

The old-style landlords did not worry Lenin as much as they had some earlier revolutionaries. This "feudal" element was withering as Russian capitalism grew. The former state official, Pavlovsky, gives ample confirmation of this development. In consequence of the Emancipation, he declares, most of the rural gentry "was in the course of almost feverish liquidation." [7] In the last third of the century the landlords had lost over a third of their holdings. This was proved by the government surveys; whereas in 1877 they had owned 77.8% of the land, by 1905 they held only 52.5%, while peasants and merchants purchased the lots they were unloading as fast as they could.

Lenin and Pavlovsky thus both suggested that capitalism was sweeping into Russian agriculture. The difference was that by capitalism Lenin, as a good Marxist, meant that a landowning group and a landless group of farmers were emerging, leaving no future for the independent peasant. Regardless of the actual course of events, which appears to have approximated the direct opposite of Lenin's "differentiation" analysis, his view had much prestige among the intelligentsia. Even those who rejected it with horror in whole or part were seldom impressed by the prospects for the free farmer in Russia.

In the 90's, the condition of the Russian countryside looked bleak enough. The last two Tsars had tried in vain to rescue the perishing nobility who had so long served as the bulwark of autocracy. They had only made various sideswipes at the problem of aiding the peasant, who was widely considered as firmly loyal despite his troubles. All in all the rural classes had little to thank Tsarism for at the turn of the century. Geroid T. Robinson concludes that "the period which immediately preceded the Revolution of 1905 was one of more than usual distress" for the poor peasants.[8] It was not an era to make an optimist out of anyone closely studying agricultural problems. Not until Peter Stolypin did the bureaucracy recognize the magnitude of the political peril and the economic problem in the countryside. Both high and low-born in the rural districts might thus be promising material for the opposition movement which the intelligentsia was trying to recruit.

5.

While Russia's farmers, noble and commoner alike, fought their grueling battle with economic factors, the Empire was undergoing a stupendous, if belated, industrial transformation. In the 1890's the number of industrial enterprises increased by a quarter, the total workers employed therein by half. The money value of total production doubled. In the middle 90's Russia shared to the full Europe's commercial prosperity as it began to feel the full effects of the Industrial Revolution which had taken nearly a century to creep eastward from the British Isles. The urban population was by now over a tenth of Russia's millions. If by proletariat[9] is meant factory, mine, and railway employees, then it numbered about 1,400,000 in 1890, and a decade later 2,200,000—working under conditions which made even the 11½-hour day law which the great St. Petersburg strike extorted from the government in 1897, look like the charter of a new era, rather than merely a restriction of the demands of toil to the extent of human endurance.

Curiously for a government depending for centuries on landlord support, the Tsardom had made infinitely greater efforts to accelerate economic expansion in the industrial than the agricultural field. Building from the work of his predecessor Vyshnegradskii, Sergei Witte devoted his finance ministry (1892-1903) to enacting well the role of a "delegate of the bourgeoisie in a gentry government." [10] The supply of free labor which the Emancipation had created had already made possible great strides on the new path of industrial capitalism. There remained, nevertheless, a great gap between the unexploited manufacturing possibilities of the vast Russian Empire and the scale on which the Western countries did this sort of thing. This gap Witte and his allies among the bureaucrats, enthusiastically supported by Russia's new industrialists, sought to close. The high speed of factory and railroad building in the 90's could not, of course, suffice to eliminate the gap, part of which survived the best efforts of Stolypin and Lenin and remained to threaten Stalin's hopes for the future in the 1920's. Nevertheless, Witte's exertions produced results of great magnitude. The first necessity was surplus capital. Since "industry and agriculture in Russia were locked together in a kind of vicious circle" incapable of helping themselves or one another financially, it was plainly necessary to hunt money abroad. Through guaranteeing foreign investors high dividends, protecting the industries which most needed investment by the highest tariff Russia had yet known, and stabilizing the currency on the gold standard by 1897, Witte primed the pump. In the 90's this pump gushed forth German money and brought a flood of Belgian and French investment which in the following decade surpassed Berlin's share.

Witte was not content with overseeing these financial beginnings. He sponsored a gigantic program in the field of railway building, which had the threefold aim of utilizing great amounts of steel and thus encouraging the expansion of Russian metallurgy, extending transport facilities for raw materials and finished products, and opening up some of the Empire's sparsely held frontiers to economic expansion. Railway mileage was doubled in a decade, and the desired end was reached. Tugan-Baranovskii singles out railway building as the "fundamental cause" of Russia's breathtaking industrial growth in the last decade of the nineteenth century.

As industry grew, so did it concentrate itself in a relatively small number of regions, and in factories of considerable size.[11] In the two decades preceding 1902 enterprises employing more than a thousand workers increased their proportion of total factories from one-third to one-half. The older iron-producing Ural district was by far surpassed by the Donets basin and Krivoi Rog in the new capitalist South. By 1900 the Donets was also furnishing 70% of the coal. Baku was the site of 90% of Russia's oil production. Moscow textiles, St. Petersburg metallurgy, Lodz cotton pushed forward. A few industrial regions, a few large factories, a few crucial railway lines—Witte and his confreres had helped create a kind of industrial machine that was exceptionally vulnerable to industrial disorder, that is, to the dissatisfied proletarians, if they ever chose to act in concert. To make them do so was precisely the aim of the intellectuals.

6.

The direct beneficiaries of the runaway industrial upsurge included French and Belgian bankers, the Imperial government, and Russian private capitalists. Among these new financial and industrial magnates of the homeland there were many who saw the vision of a greater, happier, and reformed Russia across the route of bustling, booming capitalistic expansion—and in this respect they were not unlike many Russian Marxists. Others simply took their gold where they found it. It was through the backing of a small clique of such men, closely connected with official circles, that the Minister of Interior sought for economic and political adventure in the Far East, partly for the usual imperialist reasons, partly as a diversion from domestic troubles. By means of a "small victorious war," Plehve hoped to make the opportunity to exterminate the traitors in Russia's midst—by which he meant the revolutionary movement. Manchuria served as a convenient base for exploitative forays into Korea. The brand-new (though yet incomplete) Trans-Siberian Railroad made it possible for Russian troops which had fought the Boxer rebels in 1900 to remain in Manchuria. Thus Witte in his enthusiasm for railways had enabled his bitterest rival, Plehve, to undertake a policy he sharply opposed, that of edging the Empire onto the chute which led to the Russo-Japanese War.

Starting with a surprise attack on Port Arthur, the despised Oriental enemy completely discomfited the Russian colossus on land and sea and rendered the Tsardom momentarily helpless before its relentless enemy, the Liberation Movement, which had laid its snare for autocracy before Plehve ever thought of a war. If there is justice in the claim that the Russo-Japanese War helped precipitate the Revolution of 1905, there is perhaps equal substance in the assertion that the threat of revolution was a contributing cause of the war.

So came about the first catastrophe, 1905, the "dress rehearsal" for the denouement of 1917. For 1905, war and politics may claim partial credit, but the social prerequisites were already present. The fact is that the war with Japan opened the way for the engulfment of the ancient Russian state machinery by a series of fundamental social changes with which it was utterly unable to deal. In the ranks of "society," the regime's traditional bulwarks—bureaucracy, high clergy, army, and police—though they did not desert Tsarism, maintained an attitude of lukewarm loyalty, indifference, or hostility toward the war. While the bureaucracy in particular had long been recruited from the ranks of the gentry, in office they had tended more and more to abdicate the function of class spokesmen for the landlords. What links with officialdom the gentry did retain proved insufficient for them to keep their long-standing political predominance in Russian life, the more so as their economic basis speedily withered. Accordingly even the landlords who refused to speak in opposition to the regime had little stomach for defending it. Despite the Tsardom's aid to industrialization, the new magnates were restless under its financial tutelage and longed for the greater

15

risks and rewards of a freer system. "Society" seemed to turn its back on the old order as its year of trial began.

In the last two decades the "people" had altered a good deal. Now there was a body of urban workers, conscious of concentrated and growing strength, already battling employers for improved working conditions and beginning to respond to the intellectual's pleas to fight for political rights and power. Finally the peasants found heart again to strike a few violent, despairing blows at their landlords and gave at least sympathy to the city men who called them to a new struggle—which seemed somehow to aim at the same old goals of "land and liberty."

The odds therefore seemed heavily to favor the forces of the intelligentsia who were striving to bring down Tsarism. The old regime had the forts and the arms, but its opponents had the men. Herzen had provided the key to a successful "social transformation," by sending the intelligentsia "to the people." He saw that his confreres could never achieve anything without mass support, and conversely, that the "people" could never act until they had capable leadership and were prepared to accept it.

7.

It has frequently been pointed out that the Revolution of 1905 had no leaders in the sense of individual men and women. The deduction from this has been that the Revolution had no leadership. It has been said that the masses acted in spontaneous fashion and so were easily beaten down by superior force and organization. The deduction is erroneous. Individual leaders were indeed important in the attempt of 1905—but too many to ascribe any decisive role to any one or few. These individuals usually acted not directly but through their political organizations. Lenin acted as a Marxist, Chernov as an SR, Miliukov as a Kadet, and none of them at that time pretended to any peculiar personal gifts as leaders. The leaders were the Russian intelligentsia, divided into sharply defined political groups. Each of these of course had its own striking personalities, but they had no mass following and scarcely even political identity apart from their group membership. The intellectuals had failed in 1874 and learned much in 1891. From 1898 onwards they were to make ready the way so that in 1905 workers and peasants and townsmen would rise up to follow them to a battle which may be called either a defeat or a sacrificed victory.

II

TSARISM IS TOO LATE

"Sipiagin is a fool, but Plehve is a scoundrel."
—Konstantin Pobedonostsev's characterization of
the last two Interior Ministers before the Revolution of 1905.

The last of the eighteen Romanov autocrats who had ruled
Russia since the Time of Troubles (1613) was practically unique
in the Western world of the 20th century. He tried his level best
to be a good eighteenth century Emperor. No one can say he might
not have succeeded two hundred years earlier, if only he had had
the intelligence and strength of will which some of his ancestors
and not a few of their foreign wives had possessed. In his own era he
never fully realized the problems which faced him. His one successful political act, promulgation of the October Manifesto, was an
accident whose import and effect—it was no less than to save his
throne temporarily—he scarcely guessed. His family and court lived
in an atmosphere of simplicity, devotion, and utter lack of comprehension of the world outside which has lent itself without difficulty
to depiction by many writers as sheer fantasy. Personally he was
as conscientious as he was unapproachable—probably his English
collie Iman gave him as much companionship as any human being.
He was too densely self-assured to be very maladroit. With his family and friends, with a common Siberian hunter or with a "man of
God," he might display charm. With his own highest officials, he
might be gruff and preoccupied, and only too often any kind words
or unusual attentiveness to an official might be the prelude to his
abrupt and curt dismissal. Industrialism was beyond his understanding, revolutionaries were to him simply manifestations of evil to be
crushed at any cost, good government not an ideal to be sought but
an irrelevance compared to the fulfilment of the commands of his
ancestors and the maintenance of the loyalty of the Russian people
to his own person.

17

Politically, he was completely at sea. In his public utterances he never thought it necessary to define his policy, or to allow that there might be such a thing as his "policy." During the Revolution of 1905, an opposition publisher collected his entire public addresses from 1894 to 1906 and printed them in one thin pamphlet, with the sarcastic foreword, "not many words, but much food for thought is provided. In the speeches of the Monarch there is no place for wordiness, long rhetorical phrases; there is no place for flowery pretentious sentences: the real distinction of these speeches is their lack of artifice, completely epic simplicity, straightforwardness of argument." A typical "speech" may be quoted in full, his welcome to an army delegation on 16 August 1898:

> "I am very glad to see you again. I thank you for your service, especially the Cavaliers of St. George. I drink to your health, brothers, and happiness. Hurrah!"[1]

Nicholas II was of course not the idiot that this pamphlet made him appear to be. The notion that a twentieth-century monarch must devote some attention to politics was simply foreign to him. This might not have been fatal had he been willing to select, or let someone else select, ministers who could provide efficiency, direction or continuity of policy in the conduct of affairs. When he did happen across a Witte, he refused to trust him. When he found a Stolypin, he became gradually estranged from him. Rasputin inspired his trust not so much in governmental as in his private affairs; and if a man could heal his bleeding son and save the life of the sovereign heir, could his inspiration not be followed in the tedious realm of politics?

Politics may have been dull and tedious to Nicholas II, but there ought to have been nothing which claimed more of his attention if only to secure the survival of himself and his dynasty. Whatever economic transformation was sweeping over the ancient social structure of Russia—and we have already paid some attention to this matter—the place in which the fate of Russia was to be decided was the political arena. To this the Marxists, although they believed politics to be a function of economics, would nevertheless agree. They would of course deny, however, the contention here made that the intelligentsia, which was making a bid to become a new ruling class, was a group whose common distinguishing feature was political interests and activity rather than economic origin or status.

In the minds of all the intelligentsia, the questions which were to determine the future of Russia were political questions. What needed to be done to better the conditions of the "people"? What sort of regime was necessary to do it? What legal rights and privileges ought a citizen to enjoy if any social benefits were to be securely enjoyed? Upon what source of authority should legislative action to these ends depend?

The Tsardom never got beyond the first question, and scarcely seemed even to take that one seriously until the Revolution of 1905 was almost upon it. The actions of the government were always in the rear of the march of events. When, for a moment, the Tsar stumbled abreast of the fast-moving situation with the October Manifesto, he failed to repeat his chance success. Convinced he had already gone farther than he needed, he sulked through the period of parliamentarism which followed. Only on the very eve of his downfall had he one last flash of insight, when he confided to an anachronism of a different sort, Rodzianko, that everything he had done for twenty years had been wrong. For two decades Tsarism was consistently too late, and this was no accident. It was not that its machinery was necessarily inadequate. Its bureaucracy was no better or worse than many others. Its political assumptions were simply unrealistic.

Nicholas II assumed a normal condition for Russia in which a tranquil people were loyal to an absolute monarch, and any temporary abnormality was taken to be the work of "troublemakers." Hence the Tsardom showed an efficiency in following the traces of the revolutionaries and in penetrating their most secret plans which was quite absent in its efforts to alleviate the economic difficulties of any social class, including the gentry, its erstwhile bulwark. Once a concession had been made toward popular representation in the shape of the Duma, the autocracy still refused to normalize its relations with the parliament—not even the conservative Third Duma, under the prime ministership of Russia's ablest statesman in generations, Peter Stolypin. Before 1906, the government tried to rule the country by ignoring any direct expression of public opinion and refusing to admit any direct participation of even the more conservative "public men" from the ranks of "society." Political issues, if they could not be ignored entirely, were deemed beyond the competence of those outside government. Even during the parliamentary period following 1906, the Tsar never conceded that there was any question about the ultimate location of authority. Before and after 1906, it lay in his own Person. Any alternative he could imagine only as attaching to some universal catastrophe which he did not expect. He did not believe in the possibility of revolution enough to fear it deeply.

2.

Nicholas II hated revolutionaries, but despised liberals. He did not understand the argument that reforms might avoid revolution, for this was a political argument. He did not listen to the pleas of liberals to alter his governmental system because they had no right to speak on such matters. Their toying with Western notions of "constitutions" and so forth he regarded as un-Russian, idle nonsense, and pernicious, no matter what protestations of loyalty were used to cloak such demands. The liberals had asked his grandfather in 1878 to grant "those same blessings" to the Russians as he had already granted the Bulgarians—that is, a constitution. When he himself came to the throne in January 1895 an attempt to repeat such a plea to new, young imperial ears was sharply repulsed by an allusion to "senseless dreams of the participation of zemstvo men in legislative affairs." When at the end of the 90's the liberals decided to ignore the Tsar and refuse to talk to him further about public improvement, they were only recognizing an accomplished fact. It was not that they were dissatisfied with his replies; he had made none. He had simply refused to carry on a discussion. He drove the Right Liberals into the camp of the revolutionaries; many of the Left Liberals were there already.

As Emperor, his policy was accordingly nonexistent. He took what his father bequeathed to him, including the institutions of Autocracy, and assumed their suitability and permanence. What governmental policy there was emanated from his ministers, and often there was not much. Soon after his accession he appointed, to replace a Minister of Interior who displeased his strong-willed mother, the Dowager Empress, an inconspicuously endowed bureaucrat named Ivan Logginovich Goremykin. The Interior Minister was then the official who, more than anyone else, was in charge of domestic policy. The other two candidates Nicholas considered for this important post in 1895 were Sipiagin and Plehve, who were stigmatized by even his ultra-reactionary old counsellor, Pobedonostsev, as "fool" and "scoundrel" respectively. That did not prevent the Emperor from appointing precisely these two men successively to the post following Goremykin. Both were assassinated in office. By the time Nicholas had to choose another man, in the summer of 1904, the Russo-Japanese War had begun and the revolution was about to break out. In fact the Emperor was never close to any of these men, and he had no scruples about finding grounds for dismissing any of his ministers. It is not certain he understood the function of a minister, but it is probable that as far as he did, he disapproved the notion.

3.

Always uncertain as to how far the Emperor stood behind them, never able to interpret his approval of one particular measure as general support for their policies, the Imperial ministers undertook to contend with a growing strike movement which within a decade turned into a movement of mass political opposition. Goremykin was at once confronted with the problem of dealing with the growing pains of industrialism, Russia's first large-scale strikes, which swept the factories of St. Petersburg. The aims of these strikes were chiefly better working conditions. Some Marxists who took part wished the strikes had broader aims and said they ought to have, but the political element in them was so far negligible. The government therefore was not making any concessions as to its own power when it passed a maximum-hours law under pressure of the strikers. After this minor victory the workers hesitated, debating the question of what strikes could do for them. The question was shelved, however, by the depression which overtook Russia's booming industry in 1899.

Now and only now did the workers begin to listen seriously to their would-be leaders among the revolutionaries, but mass strikes were for the moment out of the question. The initiative which the factory workers were forced to drop was taken up vigorously, however, by university students. Their organized protests were sometimes nominally directed against restrictions on academic freedom, but their political character was apparent to all. The students were the vanguard of the intelligentsia, and it was they who began the "Liberation Movement."[2]

Goremykin, who had an early reputation for liberalism of a sort, was by the time of his interior ministry at least as lazy as liberal. He did declare his support of the territorial extension of the zemstvo.[3] Witte opposed the measure, and declared the zemstvo to be fundamentally incompatible with Autocracy. He later hinted that this was "Aesopean language" meaning "down with Autocracy" rather than "down with the zemstvo," but the effect of the argument in 1899 was quite the reverse. Goremykin's stand in favor of the zemstvo was enough to bring about his replacement by Sipiagin. This pliant tool of the gentry, no less "foolish" than he had been in 1895, once distinguished himself by falling on his knees drunk in a Petersburg club and praying aloud: "O God, it is not I who am guilty as to our household expenses . . ."[4]

The student demonstrations of 1899 were suppressed only to recommence in a year. When the government issued restrictive "temporary rules" for the universities, one student, acting alone, retaliated by killing the minister of education in February 1901. The recrudescence of terrorism was met by a concession. General Vannovskii replaced the dead Bogolepov with instructions to exert "heartfelt care" over the Tsar's obstreperous student subjects. The movement, nevertheless, was already out of hand. The students were now joined by workers in their fiery meetings in favor of "freedom" and "justice." A great strike in the Obukhov factory of Petersburg really alarmed the government, which was this time itself the owner-employer. In the autumn and spring, worker demonstrations were almost continual. The problem of how Sipiagin was to meet all this was solved by his assassination on 2 April 1902, this time not an act of an isolated individual but the result of a systematic plan of the Socialist Revolutionary Battle Organization.

The "scoundrel," Viacheslav von Plehve, a completely unprincipled but clever man, now replaced Sipiagin the "fool." He had already made himself unpopular as secretary of State for Finland during the period of attack on Finnish liberties, and as head of the police. While holding the latter post in 1901 he conceived the unique experiment of allowing one of his agents, Zubatov, to organize a union of mechanics in Moscow to work for improved working conditions. Zubatov tried to head off political discussion and tried to convince his membership that revolution was unnecessary by urging them to read Eduard Bernstein. This venture in "police socialism" soon became entirely too popular to manage. When the Zubatov agent in Odessa was discovered to be an actual leader of the great strikes of 1903 the whole scheme was hurriedly abandoned.

Plehve entered the interior ministry to find that an ancient bugaboo of Tsarism had after long disuse reappeared—peasant revolt, which began to send wisps of smoke curling up from Kharkov and Poltava provinces. The revolutionaries hoped—and the government feared—that although these spontaneous outbreaks had no political aims, it might be possible to graft politics onto them.

Politics, the government reasoning ran, was originated by "trouble-makers," and the agency to deal with such gentlemen was the police. Police methods, after all, were the forte of Plehve. He not only repressed the peasant riots with severity, but punished the governor of Poltava for being insufficiently harsh. Of course the governor of Kharkov, who was severe indeed with the insurgents, was promptly assassinated, but this merely provided an opportunity to punish someone else—the assassins. The Tsar himself appeared before a council of village elders at Kursk, sternly admonishing them to remember their duty to God and the state, which meant ignoring the seductions of "troublemakers."

Sergei Witte, whom we already discussed as chief stoker of Russia's burgeoning industrial machine, by this time had realized something of the danger threatening the regime and understood that police methods—even as ingenious as those of the Zubatov movement—could not ward it off. He now endeavored to win the support of the moderates in the zemstvos by a Special Council on the Needs of Agriculture, and was able to push through an edict abolishing the mutual guarantee which still bound the members of the communes for payments and recruits. It was just at this point that his influence was collapsing, however. Plehve was close to winning his long personal feud with the Minister of Finance. Using Witte's opposition to a forward policy in the Far East as a lever, in August 1903 he succeeded in prying him out of his ministry and into the chiefly honorific job of chairman of the Committee of Ministers. By this time another great strike movement had broken out in southern Russia, touched off by a walkout of the Baku oil workers.

Plehve's methods failed utterly to halt unrest. He refused to admit that arresting disorder was anything but a sort of vermin-killing operation which the agencies of state could handle. He saw no need for enlisting public support, for that ought to be forthcoming by right. Therefore he even snubbed the extremely moderate zemstvo group which, under the leadership of the conscientiously loyal Dmitrii Shipov, attempted to indicate what reforms were needed without venturing to ask any law-making powers for themselves.[5] When the zemstvo men held a cautiously conducted congress in May 1902, Plehve not only rebuffed its proposals but in retaliation forced Shipov out of his post as president of the Moscow zemstvo. Plehve's only potential collaborators were thus silenced for the duration of his ministry. On the other hand, professional men and more radical zemstvists spoke out the more sharply against him. In January 1904 a congress of physicians startled the public by denouncing the government as responsible for a multitude of evils up to disease itself. A few days later, the Japanese sank much of the Russian fleet in Port Arthur and the Russo-Japanese war had begun.

From Plehve's viewpoint this was no calamity. Since all else was of no avail, he had decided on a "small victorious war" in which mighty Russia would swiftly and gloriously whip her Oriental neighbor. This would divert attention from the siren calls of the troublemakers and rally the nation round its duty to the Tsar which it seemed inexplicably to be forgetting. However, instead of transmuting revolutionary energies into patriotic ones, the war had exactly the opposite effect. Leaders of all branches of the "Liberation Movement" preached open defeatism. Possibly a military victory or two would have rallied some of the opposition to support the government, but at any rate the war turned out to be the kind opposite to that anticipated, with a string of crushing defeats instead of one smashing triumph. After each successive defeat the opposition spoke out more sharply. Port Arthur fell after a long siege, and then came "Bloody Sunday." The Russian army was sent reeling at Mukden, followed by spring zemstvo congresses. The Baltic fleet was sunk on arrival in Tsushima Strait, and the July zemstvo congress at once began to talk like a revolutionary assembly. The Peace of Portsmouth in August was too late to reverse the trend of events.

Plehve did not live to see the end of his military venture. He was murdered on July 15 by a revolutionary plot in which one of his own agents, Azef, was involved. Police methods had not only killed their own author. They had failed to check the multiplication of the radical vermin, who proved impervious to Plehve's cleverest poisons. Worst of all, their use had consumed priceless months in which the opportunity to embark on serious reforms had been sacrificed.

Nicholas II now, as in the case of the Vannovskii appointment in 1901, appeared to give ground to terrorism. He replaced Plehve by the mild-mannered Mirskii, who at once spoke of having "confidence in society"—i.e., obshchestvo. To buttress itself the regime would deign to trust some of the enlightened aristocrats. The need of inspiring the trust of the public in the regime was still ignored. Relieved of their bitterest enemy, Plehve, the zemstvo men convened a congress at which they adopted what Miliukov called looking for an English parallel) "the famous Petition of Right," demanding sweeping reforms including an all-Russian legislative assembly.[6] The nation's intelligentsia responded to this call with even sharper demands in a "banquet campaign" on the model of the French in 1848. Not merely a parliament, but a "Four-Tail Constituent Assembly" became the universal slogan, shared by all sections of the opposition from moderate liberals to revolutionaries. The drawing together of these disparate groups, crossing the line of social respectability between the "underground" and "society," was symbolized by an inter-party opposition congress in Paris which recognized the common task of struggling for a "democratic regime."

Thus not suddenly as mere protest at the Port Arthur defeat, but amid an engulfing wave of public agitation, came the tragic procession of St. Petersburg workers of 9 January 1905. Organized by the police agent Father Gapon, these unfortunates marched peacefully and loyally to the Winter Palace to present a gigantic petition to their Sovereign, only to shed their loyalty along with their blood as the police massacred them. This catastrophe, dubbed "Bloody Sunday," was widely recognized as the "beginning of the revolution." A new wave of strikes, initiated by Baku oil workers in December, spurted abruptly. Students left universities. Peasant riots began again in Oriol.

Once more the Tsar seemed to yield at the appearance of violence. The commission of Senator Shidlovskii was set up to investigate the workers grievances, and on 18 February the Tsar issued three acts of strangely contradictory substance. This habit of hedging on the market of revolution was one established even earlier. In December the Tsar had issued an ukase ordering his ministers to consider reforms giving the peasant equal rights with the other classes, the worker more secure labor conditions, the zemstvos added independence, and so forth. Yet only two days later there followed an Imperial reprimand threatening the zemstvos for considering questions outside their competence—echoing the "senseless dreams" rebuke of a decade before. Now, two months after that, Nicholas issued, first, a manifesto sternly summoning the people to rally around the Autocracy of their fathers; second, a rescript to A. G. Bulygin (the nominal interior minister, actually fronting for D. F. Trepov who had the Tsar's trust) directing him to work out a plan for a consultative assembly of "men worthiest of the people's trust"; third, an ukase to the Senate, ordering the consideration of any new projects for reform submitted by loyal citizens. The Russian citizen contemplating these three contradictory acts might well have felt puzzlement as to the Tsar's intentions. Many just seized on the third as official sanction for the broadest kind of public discussion and agitation. Maklakov declares, "from the time of this ukase . . . the autocracy's fate was sealed." [7] The offer of a consultative assembly was ignored. The zemstvo leaders, already in the forefront of the "respectable" opposition, pushed ahead with congress after congress throughout 1905 in which they steadily increased their pressure on the Tsardom for reform. Members of the professions (and some skilled trades) organized "unions" which in turn joined to form a Union of Unions. A section of the peasantry banded together in an All-Russian Peasant Union. Even big industrialists met publicly to demand constitutional reform. Most vocal and definite of all were of course the opposition parties, whose activities form another part of our story.

More disturbing even than these unruly but peaceful assemblies were the spreading strikes, riots, and even mutinies in the armed forces—notably the temporarily successful uprising on the cruiser Potiomkin in June, the rebellion of the Kronstadt sailors in October, and the Sevastopol mutiny in November.

Again the Tsar retreated a pace. Faced by the disloyalty of almost the entire vocal population, he was unable to delay any longer publishing an act establishing a State Duma of the kind foreshadowed in the Bulygin rescript. It was to be an assembly of estates, with landowners, townsmen, and peasants voting in curias, while 27 cities were on a separate franchise. Deputies were to be chosen in from two to four stages, depending on the curia. Urban workers and lower middle classes had no vote, and the Duma itself was restricted both in its own powers and by being designated as the lower of two legislative houses, as the existing Imperial Council was transformed into an upper chamber.

Jeers and curses greeted this act of 6 August. Public clamor mounted despite the signing of the Peace of Portsmouth, ending the war with Japan, for which the Russian negotiator, Witte, was made a count. The peace, as with every other act of the Tsar in the revolution, came too late to have any effect on public opinion. It did, however, free troops for the eventual repression of the revolution.

The fate of the country now in effect passed out of the hands of the authorities, and descended into the hands of the striking workers. Numbering 200,000 in May, they had diminished in September only to grow sharply again.[8] On 7 October the workers on the

Moscow-Kazan railroad struck, and in about a week transport and communication throughout the country were paralyzed. On 12 October a Council (*Soviet*) of Workers Deputies was organized in St. Petersburg, dominated by Mensheviks but officially non-partisan, a political body which announced a general strike with the purpose of compelling the Tsar to summon a Four-Tail Constituent Assembly. Russia's workers responded by bringing economic life to a dead halt.

After four days of this impasse, the Tsar appeared to have surrendered. His famous October Manifesto, ambiguous as it was, had a tone very different from his previous half-measures. Count Witte, back from Portsmouth, had persuaded him to promise freedom of speech, press, and assembly, and to convert the Duma into a legislative body whose consent was necessary to enact any law. Witte himself became Russia's first Prime Minister.

Was the October Manifesto, likewise, too late? Much of the burden of our story lies here, and is not to be told till later. Briefly the Manifesto was the moment when the Tsar overtook the onrushing revolution, when he for once, in spite of himself and only on the urging of the ever afterwards unforgiven Witte, stepped out of the role of the divine Autocrat and into the unaccustomed realm of politics. How the politicians who were leading public opinion reacted, we will see later. For the moment we will confine ourselves to the headline-making events.

The St. Petersburg Soviet, which for the time being was the nearest thing that existed to a revolutionary general staff, declared immediately after the Manifesto that the objective was still a democratic republic, and that the fight would go on till the objective was taken. However, public jubilation blunted the edge of the strikers' former unity and determination. Four days later the strike was called off—happily for the purpose of saving face, this day coincided with the issuance of a partial political amnesty, a particularly crucial measure to the leaders of the Soviet. Then they waited for another pretext to resume the use of the weapon of the political strike which had had such dazzling, if partial, success. A second strike took place the first week in November, with the immediate aims of saving from field courts-martial the Kronstadt mutineers and ending martial law in Poland. These demands were substantially met by Witte's government, and the Soviet leaders again paused to lick their dry lips and wait for events to give them another chance. They had lost the initiative and they knew it.

Witte now set in motion the last act of the revolution proper by first arresting the shadowy figure who was the Soviet's president, Khrustaliov-Nosar, and then all of its members. The direction passed to Moscow, where in late November another Soviet had been organized. This body attempted a third strike on 7 December, which in three days had developed into an armed uprising. Crack army regiments brought in from the West were rushed into action, closed the insurgents off in the Presnia district, and crushed them by the 18th. Other armed uprisings, as in Novorossiisk and Nikolaev, were put down with less difficulty though in much of the Russian Empire violence of vast proportions occurred. By the end of December the country enjoyed an uneasy peace.

During the Moscow uprising the Tsar had yielded once more to the pleas of Witte and had issued a new electoral law for the Duma. The law of 11 December left intact the system of indirect voting by curias, but it enormously extended the franchise. Left outside it were only workers in factories employing under fifty, the poorer craftsmen, and one or two other minor categories. Suffrage became practically universal, but because of that fact, the radicals who compared the law to the demands of their old Four-Tail slogan saw only the more clearly its undemocratic elements—suffrage was almost universal and it was secret, but it was neither equal nor direct. But the opposition was powerless to turn its dissatisfaction into action. The government ruthlessly stamped out the last lingering revolutionary sparks, making no effort to adopt the external niceties of a "new," constitutional regime. On the heels of the October Manifesto counterrevolutionary mobs of extreme Rightists known as the Black Hundreds carried out bloody pogroms against Jews, intellectuals, and other "undesirables." Government troops grimly carried out so-called "punitive expeditions," showing especial harshness against the national minorities.

Was there to be a Duma? There was. It was a question not of political wisdom but personal honor to the Tsar who evidently had no thought of retracting his promise—in the sense he interpreted it. In February it was announced that the assembly would convene on 27 April and the electoral campaign began at once. Only four days before the opening of the Duma, the Tsar issued the Fundamental Laws which were supposed to implement the promises of the October Manifesto. But the "freedoms" were found to be hedged about by limitations, and the Duma was discovered to have an unwelcome partner in legislation—the Imperial Council (the upper chamber as in the Bulygin project). This body was to be henceforth half nominated by the Sovereign, half elected by certain privileged bodies. As if this was not enough to hamstring the Duma, the Tsar retained a veto power over legislation not to mention complete control of the armed forces and foreign policy. Secure in his still autocratic authority, as he thought, Nicholas II now found courage to dismiss the importunate Witte. He appointed a new cabinet headed by the indolent Goremykin, but distinguished by a new, strong personality: Peter Stolypin, ex-governor of Saratov, as interior minister.

The "Duma of people's hopes" convened on schedule. Boycotted by most of the revolutionaries, it was dominated by the liberals, and the Right was scarcely perceptible. This kind of body was of course anathema to the Emperor, who nevertheless managed to bring himself to receive the deputies on 27 April in the Winter Palace and deliver them a short, moderately phrased address.[9] The Speech from the Throne, as men with a fondness for English methods dubbed it, might have been given to a Bulygin-type Duma had one ever convened. He spoke of the deputies as those "very best men whom I gave my beloved subjects the order to elect," whom he had called upon for "cooperation" in the work of legislation. A "new regime" was hard to divine behind such phrases, among which there was to be found no mention of "constitution" or "parliament" and in which "freedom" was carefully coupled with "order." The angry address which the Duma composed in reply to this Speech was entrusted for delivery to a deputation which the Tsar flatly refused even to receive. Goremykin was sent to chastise the assembly on 13 May. The liberals retorted by declaring no confidence in the ministry, and for the rest of the session government and Duma were openly hostile to each other.

Nevertheless the majority of deputies, believing they could rely on the country's support, resolutely advanced to "legislate"—to push through reform laws which the Tsar would not dare to veto. The chief issue, that of land reform, was the object of several radical proposals by Leftist deputies; the government's own drafts on the subject were simply ignored. The legislative impasse, in view of the riotous impatience of the peasants, was anxiously considered from both sides. From the side of the government, D. F. Trepov and Stolypin tried to persuade the liberals to enter a ministry which had so far remained entirely composed of bureaucrats, despite the institution of a "constitutional" system. The liberals refused to share the power and the talks failed.[10]

From the side of the Duma, the majority, faced with government warnings against a radical land bill, adopted in the beginning of

July an open appeal to the people for support of their agrarian project. Such a "disloyal" act was taken by the Tsar as pretext for abruptly dissolving the First Duma—therein acting quite constitutionally. On the same day, 8 July, the Goremykin cabinet retired and Stolypin became Prime Minister. The government was obviously determined on firmness.

Forthwith many Duma deputies fled to Finland and issued the "Vyborg Manifesto" to the people of the Russian Empire, exhorting them to support the Duma by refusing to pay taxes or furnish recruits. The lack of response was a great disappointment to the "legislators" who had regarded themselves as popular tribunes. Isolated mutinies in Sveaborg and Kronstadt and scattered strikes took place, but the Revolution of 1905 was for all practical purposes at an end. Realists saw clearly that the summer of 1906 had put an end for the time being to hopes for ending Autocracy by mass action. The next year, 1907, there was returned a "Duma of people's wrath" with large revolutionary representation, but a sizeable Rightist group as well, and the percentage of deputies who opposed the government remained the same as in the First Duma. Stolypin sat firmly in the saddle of power, and he used it not only to dismiss the Second Duma, but to alter the suffrage law in such a manner that he would not have to dismiss the Third.

For one fateful moment Autocracy had tottered on the edge of oblivion. At that moment the Emperor was pushed, not into the abyss by the revolutionaries, but into the use of a political weapon by his new prime minister. The publication of the October Manifesto, inadequate in itself but so clearly out of character with Nicholas's previous conduct that it inspired false hopes in the widest circles, gave the regime the breathing space it needed to regroup its forces for the only kind of campaign which the Tsar found congenial: police methods. So Nicholas was saved from destruction, but never understood why. His reformists, Witte and Stolypin, were not liberals, but that did not preserve them from his profound suspicion to the degree that they insisted that police methods were insufficient to calm the revolutionary storm. The October Manifesto might have been too late even if it had marked a shift to a course of political action—we cannot be sure. What we can be sure of is that the Emperor Nicholas II never realized that only politics could save him from the attack of the politically-minded intellectuals, and this realization came only after the deluge had overtaken him in the Great Revolutionary Year of 1917.

III

THE YEAR 1898

*"At last Russia is approaching the stage of
political development enjoyed by the Western
European countries at the end of the 18th century and the first half of the 19th and by England
more than two centuries and a half ago."*
—PAUL AXELROD, 1902.[1]

As we see how Russia's millions in their abject misery were
brought to listen more attentively to their intellectual would-be
saviors, and how the political activity of these latter was first
ignored and then incompetently opposed by a Tsardom which
thought politics superfluous and irrelevant, we must feel puzzlement at why the struggle for freedom and self-government failed
as we have just described.

Unless one is to give the Marxist answer of "insufficiently developed contradictions of capitalism" or refer to some "level of progress" which predetermined the failure of the 1905 Revolution,
he may find in his story much illumination for later generations.
In backward Russia, half a century ago, a political battle was fought
in which the most strangely assorted groups took part. Here was
a Tsardom avowedly resting on the traditions of Catherine the
Great, with a few uneasy officials like Witte who were willing like
Bismarck to compromise on social problems and political externals
if they could preserve the essence of power. On the other hand
there was a number of political parties, all bitterly opposed to
Autocracy but sharply divided against each other. Of these the
chief ones were the radical Kadets, the revolutionary Social Democrats (who themselves split nominally in two and later actually
into fragments, yet finally provided the faction which seized and
kept the power in 1917), and the Socialist Revolutionaries. The
Russian political scene, as we have said, was curious in its absence

of leading personalities, compared with the heroic epochs when England and France solved political questions by violent mass participation. This is one aspect of the story which misleads those Americans who see politics in terms of Theodore Roosevelts and Woodrow Wilsons who led their own parties down unaccustomed paths by force of personality or popularity. This is not to say that Russian political leaders were absent; rather that they operated within a different framework, with a more limited range of maneuver, among party members who nearly made vocations out of their membership and whose raison d'etre was political principle. In a word, the Russian parties were ones not of men but of ideas. Ideas for them did not connote impracticability or passivity. The parties were composed of men who believed that their analysis gave them the answer to the nature of reality and how to act to change that reality. The fact that they were parties of ideas did not entail the dangers of inaction, but rather the chance that action should be taken which was based on an erroneous view of reality.

Two other features of Russian pre-revolutionary politics may likewise surprise Western readers. A common picture of the Russian who opposed the government in those days is an unkempt, hunted bomb maker who may, from time to time, close his eyes for a moment of meditation on the sufferings of the poor peasant and the iniquity of the court, but is ignorant of all else. Archetypes like this are of little use in understanding the Russian opposition. The parties were generally made up of men who had broad learning, carried the vision of Western (European and American) experience and achievement before them quite as much as their picture of Russian miseries, and on the basis of their study and comprehension of the West constructed the most careful rational plans for improving the lot of their native land. The two characteristics of Westernism and apriorist rationalism provided the common element in all the Russian opposition parties.

Russian political activity (in our sense of the competition of opposing groups) had such a short duration that it is natural that many should discount its depth and importance for that reason. Some Russians, in order to persuade foreigners of its significance, have tried to push back the moment of origin, like Miliukov when he gave 1863 as the year when the "continuous history of Russian political parties now [1903] in action" began.[2] On the contrary, not only were there no organized groups continuously in action after the Emancipation, but the different currents of political thought underwent important alterations. These currents cannot be traced in terms of individual leaders or thinkers. The names of the early emigres, Alexander Herzen and Michael Bakunin, and those of the early *raznochintsy*, Nicholas Chernyshevsky and Dmitrii Pisarev, remained talismans for the whole opposition, men whom any party could safely quote, but as prophets rather than leaders. This tendency to regard personalities—once past their peak of political activity—as possessions of the whole nation did not cease, as is illustrated by the standing ovation given the old revolutionaries Plekhanov, Chaikovsky, and Breshko-Breshkovskaia (one Menshevik and two SR's) by the entire Council of the Republic in the autumn of 1917.

The origins of the later parties are discernible enough during the 1860's and '70's. There appear the beginnings of the zemstvo constitutionalist movement among the liberals, and the organization of the revolutionary Land and Liberty group, which underwent schism into two wings which were distant antecedents of the Social Democrats and Socialist Revolutionaries, with some permutations. However, it was not until the late 90's that the three or four currents which became the parties of the three Revolutions took permanent and clear form.

The year 1898 seems to have been the crucial one in this respect. Both Socialist Revolutionaries and Social Democrats made serious, though abortive attempts to organize a party. The first contacts were being made between the two infant liberal groups, the *Beseda* circle and the newly-formed Zemstvo Union. The sharp but short fight between orthodox Marxists and "Economists" was just beginning, obscuring for the moment the more basic cleavage among Social Democrats, that between Bolsheviks and Mensheviks—a cleavage, incidentally, which can with little difficulty be traced to 1898. The counterpart of German Revisionist socialism was just sprouting in Russia, and its adherents, the "Legal Marxists," ceased to be orthodox in their Marxism not very long after they became "legal" (that is, began to write in the legal, censored press), some of them going over to the liberal camp. Most of these major groups—Socialist Revolutionaries, Bolshevik and Menshevik Social Democrats, Left and Right liberals—existed continuously to 1917, and even the Revisionists maintained an extra-party formation.

What were these currents and how did they spring into life at a time when there was no possibility at all of legal political action in Russia, and only a limited one for expressing political views?

Their antecedents are to be traced not so much to early organizations as to the schools of social thought which Russian thinkers at home and abroad had developed since the 1840's. What was new in the 1840's in Russia was neither Western influence nor social thought. Western influence on Russian thinking should properly be traced in a continuous line beginning as early as the fifteenth century. It is what was new in German, French, and British thought in the early nineteenth century, not the question of the newness of Russian acquaintanceship with that thought, which ought to attract our close attention. Thinking about what should be the nature of the state, the organization of society, the ideas which shape a culture, was no innovation either in the West or in Russia. In recent decades Russia had had its rationalists in men like Radishchev and Novikov, its liberal constitutionalists in the Decembrists, its romanticists in the Slavophiles, its philosophical idealists in the early Westernizers.[3]

The social thought of the Russian intelligentsia emerged in programmatic form with Alexander Herzen as he recorded and reacted to his experiences as the first notable Russian political exile. Along with the contemporary generation of European intellectuals, the Russians were casting aside the habits of religious thinking and sought to base their dreams of an ideal society to be realized on earth upon the findings of nineteenth-century science. Socialism, in the teachings of St. Simon and Marx, linked its precepts to the findings of British political economy. "Science" itself taught, however, that one ought to study the facts of each given case rather than applying the results of experiments on different material. Herzen and his fellows found the industrial and commercial results of Smith and Ricardo inapplicable to their peasant country, and they undertook to examine Russia themselves. Their values, however, were borrowed from the West—they were "science," or more accurately, positivism, and socialism. In consequence of their borrowing they rejected the notion of eternal values held by the Christian religion, to which the mass of the Russian people adhered, and substituted a secular humanitarianism, in which the greatest good of the greatest number took precedence over the fate of any Tsar or terrorist, any class or generation. They rejected the idea that change might be sought within the framework of existing institutions and substituted the postulate that Tsarism was doomed to be violently overthrown by a socialist revolution. They rejected the idea of economic development based on individual action and substituted the doctrine of socialism.

As they looked at Russia through positivist and socialist eyes, the populists seemed to find grounds for their new political beliefs. In the primitive village community, the *mir*, they saw the seed of socialism in the countryside; in the old craftsmen's association, the *artel*, they discerned its urban counterpart. In the peasantry as a whole they saw "communists by instinct and tradition," the mass support for a future social transformation. Not in themselves directly, but in heroes of the future, they saw the needed leadership. If the "heroes" and the populists overlapped in their thinking, one ought not to be overly scornful. Herzen might well have concluded that the elemental uprisings of the peasantry in the past had failed for want of direction either by able personalities or coherent programs. Herzen was not a man consumed by personal ambition, and neither were the populist leaders of his or later times—they could have used more qualities of leadership than they proved to possess.

In the varying pronouncements of Herzen, Lavrov, and Mikhailovsky, populism shared these common precepts. At its side emerged groups like the Nihilists, who emphasized positivism; the Petrashevtsy circle, who emphasized socialism; Bakunists, who emphasized the evils of the state; Tkachovists, who emphasized the importance of "heroes". None of them was in the mainstream of populism, but they all lay on the fringes of its teachings.

During the 1860's, when these groups were forming, there was also a reformist liberal current which flourished among the gentry of Tver and other provinces. It had no fully worked out political program, but demanded the extension of the zemstvo principle of local self-government to the nation as a whole, which implied a modern, "liberal" state for which British patterns seemed more applicable than any other. As no all-Russian parliament appeared, the liberals began to concentrate on the same immediate issue which concerned the populists, namely, the inadequacies of the Great Reforms of Alexander II, or, more broadly, the shortcomings of the whole existing order.

It was in fact only a few months after Emancipation that the first revolutionary proclamations printed in Russia appeared. They were addressed to the university students, who provided the reserve and immediate support for the handful of populist leaders. The first revolutionary circles followed swiftly; the early Land and Liberty organization of Serno-Solovevich, populist groups on Russian soil like that of N. V. Chaikovskii, Bakunist groups like that of A. Dolgushin. After the passionate crusade to the countryside of 1874 mentioned earlier, a new Land and Liberty group was formed including the kernel of Russian populists. The doctrine of "heroes" now took terrorist shape, and gained more and more prestige within the new organization.

In 1879 at a conference at Voronezh the group, which had borne the name Land and Liberty for only a year, split in two over the terrorist issue. Withdrawing from the conference, George Plekhanov organized the Black Partition group, while the terrorists took the name of The People's Will. Their central objective of assassinating the Tsar-Liberator was realized in 1881. The effort was self-defeating. Public apathy or revulsion at this deed facilitated the task of the police in smashing the plotters.

2.

The year 1883, after Plekhanov and others of the Black Partition group had for two years pondered the fate of Land and Liberty, was an important landmark in the development of revolutionary thinking. Plekhanov and his friends concluded that the main tenets of populism had been erroneous, and sought to make the necessary corrections. Land and Liberty had relied on the peasants, and they had proved a poor combustible for revolutionary sparks. Populism had scorned political action, assuming that alteration of the framework of the State would leave untouched the fundamental social problems. The populists had placed great stock in the deeds of "heroes," and in practice relied on their activity rather than the expectation of any spontaneous historical changes to give it depth and force.

In 1883 Plekhanov produced the book which he believed contained the answer to these populist errors. It was the first Russian Marxist work, entitled *Socialism and the Political Struggle*. It proclaimed a fight for free political institutions, based on the organization of the budding Russian proletariat. The industrial workers were, however, still few in number. Marxism itself was still an unfamiliar intellectual tool to the new Russian converts, and was utterly unknown to its intended proletarian vehicles. Therefore Plekhanov recognized that a long period of preparation and planning must precede any success along the lines to which he pointed. Ultimate victory, nevertheless, would be secured not by the fate of a few populist daredevils, nor of a few Marxist adepts, but by the inexorable march of capitalism across the Russian border, the predestined movement of history itself.

At the same time the revolutionaries who remained wedded to

populism were counting casualties and totting up a balance sheet for The People's Will. They likewise were willing to recognize mistakes. In 1887 the old terrorist Kravchinskii ("Stepniak") and others published letters in the emigre journal *Self-Government,* which charged their fellows with neglecting "the political idea." If populism too were going to embark upon "political" action, that course would entail a substitute for the pilgrimages of isolated intellectuals through the villages. The populists would have to seek an ally.

Thus there was raised from the side of the revolutionaries one of the most explosive issues of the whole Russian opposition movement. All possible recruits were needed for the battle. An obvious source was available in the liberals of "society" who knew about constitutions and had experience in self-government via the zemstvos. When Stepniak in 1895 prepared a draft constitution for Russia, he remarked, "Neither the liberals nor the revolutionaries will overturn autocracy alone. The pledge of victory is in mutual support by both factions of the opposition in the name of that extra-class feeling of civic solidarity, which exists in all advanced countries to a greater degree as they are more cultured." [4] The London group of emigres, like Vladimir Burtsev, who lived to become the man who probably knew the revolutionary movement best of all, shared these views. They were bitterly criticized, however, for this united-front talk which was regarded by the older generation as selling out to the liberals. Populists had long feared that a "political revolution" (as opposed to a "social" one) would merely put the liberals in power, leaving their own radical objectives for the village as far from realization as ever. Some of them now decided that this was one of the "mistakes" of the 70's, to be repaired by joint political action with liberals, but their willingness to support the liberals did not mean any liking or trust for them. The Stepniak-Burtsev school was dubbed "revolutionary constitutionalism." It did not give rise to a lasting organization, although the Party of People's Right, which existed briefly in 1894 inside Russia, owed much to its ideas.

3.

During the 80's the Marxists and new-school populists achieved no perceptible backing inside Russia. The 90's, however, saw a marked change. During the strikes of the middle of the decade, Marxist groups called Unions of Struggle for Emancipation of the

Working Class were organized in industrial cities. Lenin's active career, for example, began in the St. Petersburg Union. Yet it was only as the strikes began to fail, toward 1898, that the industrial workers began to pay much attention to the intellectuals, either to the noisy and insistent Marxist intellectuals who were pressing in on them with their pamphlets, or to the new politically-minded populists who were beginning to call themselves Socialist Revolutionaries and were striving to organize worker support. As already noted, both Marxists and populists had a much easier time of it among the university youth. During the 90's it was a rare student who professed openly to be "liberal," and the accepted form of behavior included taking part in the student strikes which began in 1899.

The year 1898 of course marks no sharp break in Russian history. A year of political realignment, it followed rather than coincided with a period of broad popular agitation. In this respect it can be compared with 1883, when "lessons" of the past were being mulled over as plans for the future were hatched. Between 1883 and 1898, however, a great deal had happened in Russia. The country had witnessed the power of a mass movement, the St. Petersburg strikes, to extract concessions from the government. Some drew the conclusion that Plekhanov had been right when he insisted that factory workers would serve as the core of successful mass action.

The most obvious difference from 1883 was that by 1898 the necessity of political action, based on a mass movement, was no longer questioned. It was now an article of faith with the whole Russian opposition—neo-populists, Marxists, and liberals. It was further assumed that such mass action stood in need of guidance. A party elite must lead, though less by virtue of its "heroic" qualities than by the soundness of its political analysis and doctrine.

Having decided how to go about the job of transforming Russia, the opposition exhibited a profound impatience. It was not an expectation of immediate success which agitated them, but an uncompromising dedication to total victory, even though it should be delayed by decades. Anyone who said, "Let us be patient and try to reform one thing at a time," was regarded as a reactionary or a fool. A fool, if he did not understand the onrush of history, a reactionary, if he tried to oppose or divert it. History was on their side—in this the opposition was unanimous—and had already doomed Tsarism to extinction. The development of Russian society, as Axelrod had said, was overtaking that of the West, and therefore a revolution for Russia in the Western tradition was certain.

The fact that the radicals believed themselves to be riding a relentless wave of the future did not stop them from willing, straining towards the inevitable. They saw no inconsistency in striving with all their might to take the initiative in their predeterminedly successful struggle. Therefore the man who said, "One thing at a time," was guilty not merely of weakness or cowardice, but of stupidity—unless he was committed to a defense of the old order, in which case he was regarded as intelligent but vicious.

Each party had its more or less precisely formulated expectations of the future, based on its understanding of the political and social past and present projected against its vision of the ideal state. Discussion of these matters was no parlor game. Since party programs were regarded as not only statements of objectives but actual blueprints of the Russian future, every word and phrase in them was vital, a matter to fight and lose friends over if necessary—and it often was. No one dared urge, "Let us leave that point and see how things develop." No such empiricism was acceptable. A stern, apriorist rationalism governed the temper of Russian politics. Anyone looking for misty, amorphous effusions of a "Russian soul" will find none among the deadly, even dully serious politicians of the "Liberation Movement." That is one reason why tactics caused such dissension among and within the parties. Tactics were so often at issue because in regard to overall strategy, in respect to the shape of things to come, there was so little to argue about.

By 1898 the notion thus was firmly held that a new order was attainable through political action by masses of people who were guided by leaders capable of correct analysis. This notion was of course the Western concept of political party, although the Western parties had only developed when parliaments had come to their countries, and Russia had no parliament. Each of the competing groups assumed it would win and dominate the government, because it would have majority support. Each deemed the others wrong, but very possibly essential as temporary allies in the assault on Tsarism. Tsarism, founding its reason for existence on tradition, could not withstand political rationalism. The new order would be built systematically, not because this or that feature was justified either by being found venerable or workable, but because it conformed to human reason. And, as Hegel had asserted, history was bringing the rational to pass; the rational was becoming real.

These keys had been struck in both philosophy and politics before. No Western revolutionaries had devoted quite so much time to ideological preparation, had worried quite so deeply about philosophical grounding or had been quite so fully convinced of the certainty of victory. Yet it was they who had taught the Russians how to take their political precepts seriously. The Russian opposition leaders intended to play the same tune as the West had already heard, one of course with Russian harmonies and overtones, but after all the same tune because Europe was one, and Russia was part of Europe. In conformity with this Western orientation the Russian opposition did succeed in creating several great parties which possessed organization, continuity, and fully worked out programs. One of these, the Bolsheviks, finally attained power.

4.

The last decade of the nineteenth century saw the revival and transformation of the Russian opposition movement. Recalling the impetus given by the famine of 1891, the disappointed hopes in the new Tsar when he acceded in 1894, and the great strikes of 1895-6, we can see how events served the cause of revolution. The radicals were not abashed at utilizing these events to the utmost. After all, they expected history to work for them, and they desired only to return the favor as best they could.

Disillusioned with the failure of terrorism and direct action by 1881, the populists had scarcely the heart to try to rebuild their shattered circles. Many confined themselves to journalism, and eschewed politics. Nicholas Mikhailovsky inveighed against the horrors of capitalism on the premise that Russia had the free choice of accepting or avoiding them. V. P. Vorontsov, better known as "V. V.," declared that capitalism in Russia was a historical impossibility, and predicted that Russia's bourgeoisie would play only a secondary role as compared with Western Europe. In brief, history did not press for capitalism in Russia, but rather for the strengthening of the peasantry and its communal institutions, "the chief possible social basis" of Russia's future. Such writers as these tried to spread the conviction that the old populist analysis was still correct, but the fatally precipitate action of 1881 had simply been premature—inexpedient, but not wrong in principle.

Other populists, however, could not wait for history to act unaided. The "revolutionary constitutionalists," whom we have already mentioned, were the first to try to find a way out of the tactical impasse by admitting to their bosom unaccustomed allies, the liberals. Who were the most prominent "liberals" of the moment? None other than the progressive zemstvo men, chiefly landlords—and how could peasant-oriented populists have anything to do with the oppressors of the muzhik? The answer of the "revolutionary constitutionalists" was logical: an ally was essential. The factory workers were still weak, and destined to remain so for a time; there was to be no sizeable capitalist bourgeoisie. These two deductions stemmed from the prediction that Russia could substantially avoid capitalism. Therefore, the existing "society," composed of gentry and middle class, might be used as supporters without fear of their becoming so strong as to overshadow their revolutionary partners. Mark Natanson and others tried to organize a party based on alliance with "society" in the Party of People's Right, which foundered almost at once on the fury of police repression. That was the end of this current in Russia. Abroad Vladimir Burtsev could still declare, "Now we are all liberals, now we are all revolutionaries, and no one has the right to refuse the duty and honor to be both liberal and revolutionary."[5] Most Russian populists refused nonetheless.

During the 90's the idea of cooperation with the liberals thus flashed only briefly through populist minds. Meanwhile another tack was proving more popular in reviving spirits dampened by 1881. Old methods of peasant agitation and terrorism were taken up once more in scattered urban circles. Though crippled by recurrent waves of arrests, they somehow managed to rebuild their secret organisations time and time again. Along with the old methods, however, these circles adopted a new viewpoint. The factory workers attracted their attention, and propaganda among them began to be considered at least as important as the traditional work among peasants. In 1892 a Group of Narodovolists on the new lines appeared in Petersburg. Moscow and other cities soon followed this example, despite angry protests from the still unregenerate older generation of populists in Paris, grouped around Peter Lavrov. The charge against the new line, significantly enough, was "selling out to Social Democracy," that is, to Marxism. The charge had some justice, as we shall see.

The most important of the new groups were not in the capitals but in Saratov and Minsk. In 1896 Andrei Argunov's group in Saratov took the name Union of Socialist Revolutionaries, better known as the "Union of the North." A year later a woman named

Liubov Rodionova succeeded in organizing a circle in Minsk which found a fertile field for its work among the small artisans and Jewish intellectuals of that Western city. Here both the "little grandmother of the Russian Revolution," Ekaterina Breshko-Breshkovskaia, and Grigorii Gershuni, probably the most promising popular leader of all the SR's, were prominent. The man who did more than anyone else to give the SR party a coherent doctrine, and its leader up to 1917, Victor Chernov, was just coming to the fore in Tambov. Abroad the new tendencies toward a renovated and revised populism found support in Berne, where Chaim Zhitlovskii and the notorious police spy, Evno Azef, organized a Union of Russian Socialist Revolutionaries.[6]

By 1897 these disparate groups were ready to attempt to form a central organization. Delegates from groups inside Russia, maintaining contact with the emigres meanwhile, held three conferences, in Voronezh and Poltava in that year and in Kiev in August 1898. The third meeting actually decided to found a party, but the police foiled this attempt in much the same way as they had frustrated the Social Democrats' effort to organize earlier that year. Actual consolidation of the SR party was to be postponed for three years.

5.

The Marxists fared better during the 90's in respect of party unanimity. Orthodox Marxism was a doctrine which one could accept or reject, unlike populism which remained a fairly nebulous collection of traditional attitudes and methods. It based itself somewhat on the ambiguous "subjective sociology" of Lavrov and Mikhailovsky. In this teaching the role of the "critically thinking individual," that is, the well-intentioned intellectual, was given much emphasis, but the course of history was still determined by objective forces. Populists were accordingly left with the option of "transforming the objectively inevitable into acts of personal will."[7] This seemed to the Marxists to be unscientific, and not wholly clear to many populists.

The Marxists thus started with an advantage over their ex-fellow populists of *Land and Liberty*. The gifted Plekhanov, Paul Axelrod, and Vera Zasulich, chief lights of the Group for Emancipation of Labor, had found in Marxism a doctrine which nearly met the requirement of negating the "errors" of the 70's, but which also had a more positive appeal. Marxism embodied a complete theory of history, philosophical method, and a definite blueprint for revolutionaries to follow. Its chief defect from the standpoint of adaption to Russia might have seemed to be its low evaluation of the peasant's future role. At that moment, however, it appeared as a virtue to the Marxist emigres, since they were fighting the populists' belief that the peasants could lead the revolution. The importance of this defect was indeed not to be fully grasped until Lenin came to grips with the agrarian problem.

To be sure, in *Socialism and the Political Struggle* Plekhanov had to recognize the agrarian nature of Russian society, and one of his arguments for political work among the proletariat was the effect it would have on the peasantry. Still, his chief emphasis, as already noted, was in preaching a political struggle for socialism to be planned through "years of sojourn abroad and thorough examination of the social problem" rather than through "going to the people" at once.[8]

Part of the planning stage on which he placed much stress was the search for an ally. The workers would be the major revolutionary force, but they were not yet strong enough to act alone. Therefore, "other progressive and opposition elements" were to be taken into temporary partnership. This phrase meant nothing else than the liberals. But how could revolutionaries, filing the "Red phantom" for future reference, cooperate with moderates? The answer was that the first task for both groups was a political revolution which must precede the creation of a socialist order. After the political revolution, the liberals could go their own way.

This dualist view of the coming upheaval was not a new idea—even in Russian thought, remembering the early radical Tkachov—but was simply good Marxist doctrine. Russia, in Marxist eyes, was still in the throes of a dying feudalism, and the birthpangs of the onrushing capitalist order would include a "bourgeois revolution" of the 1688-1789 type. The "socialist revolution" which all Marxists sought must await the first one. In other words, Social Democrats had to help history make a bourgeois revolution before they could make their own. The application of this idea of "dual revolution" was to plague the radicals right down to 1917 and later. For the moment Plekhanov meant quite simply that during the "bourgeois" stage the class forces represented by the liberals could be signed up for the fight in which they above all ought to be interested.

As in the case of the "revolutionary constitutionalist" wing of populism, Plekhanov exhibited no fondness for liberals, for capitalism, or for any kind of "bourgeois" phenomena. Summoning the Russian opposition to form a broad front of struggle against Nicholas II, he expected no group, least of all Marxists, to submerge its own identity or forget its own class interests. To do so, as certain populists were doing, Plekhanov charged, was to display unmistakably bourgeois features. Of course whatever the populists did they were already branded in Marxist eyes as petty bourgeois, since they relied on the peasantry to achieve the revolution and ignored the leading historical role of the proletariat. This was to become a familiar Marxist tactic: to attack this or that man or group for doing something which by the Marxist analysis he was bound to do anyway.

In "the first Social Democratic work" as Lenin dubbed it, a book called *Our Differences*, Plekhanov two years later struck hard at the populists while they were still down. "Bakunism and populism as revolutionary teachings have outlived their time," he wrote, and now found acceptance only in the literary field. Since populist organizations were still prostrate, this was only too true. The theories of revolutionaries might after all not be revolutionary theories, he taunted. There was currently only one such and that was the scientific socialism of Marx. Marx had proved the inevitability of the triumph of world capitalism, and from this fate Russia could not hope to escape. Whether or not Russia should enter the school of capitalism was a dead issue. It had already done so, supported by all the dynamics of life, opposed only by inertia. The advent of capitalism would exterminate the peasant commune and all such pre-capitalist institutions, so revolutionaries could base no plans upon them. Furthermore, they must forsake terrorism under prevailing circumstances, and abandon work in secret underground circles in favor of mass workers' organizations. Upon the revolutionaries devolved the task of leadership, since Russian workers were deprived of the bourgeois leadership Western workers had possessed.

Over and over Plekhanov rang changes on his central theme, the key, as he saw it, to the future and the scientific answer to the errors of the past. This theme was: only the working class could lead the struggle for liberty. Either the workers would attain political freedom, or it would not be achieved in Russia. At the Paris socialist congress in 1889, the first Congress of the Second International, he thundered, "The Russian revolution will triumph as a workers' revolution, or else it will not triumph at all." To

European Marxists, this was a commonplace. To Russians, it sounded very bold indeed.

And yet Plekhanov continued to invite other classes to struggle together with the workers against the government. He excluded only capitalists, kulaks, and bureaucrats from his call for a united front to work for a Russian Zemskii Sobor or parliament. As authority for such an appeal by a Marxist, he cited the Communist Manifesto itself. Only two opposition currents would count in the future: liberalism and Social Democracy. On one hand there was the ideology of the young Russian proletariat, on the other the school of the liberal intelligentsia, with lingering tinges of populism yet in fact becoming the "ideologue" of the rising industrial bourgeoisie. Populism only cluttered up the political picture with its attempt to represent the peasantry. This was the clear deduction, and one which would be drawn pointedly by Lenin.

From the sufferings of the 1891 famine, Plekhanov drew the lesson of the futility of relying on the peasants, while others thought the task of saving lives should supersede political polemics. Plekhanov recounted how the peasants in their uncomprehending misery repulsed attempts to help them and even killed doctors as "poisoners." He pointed sternly to these incidents as proof of the peasants' present unfitness for political action. Only political freedom, to be attained by the workers, could avert *All-Russian Ruin*—as Plekhanov called his pamphlet.

The call of the emigre Marxists for mass organization on the basis of the new "scientific" doctrine was heeded by intellectuals at home. By 1890 circles were springing up in Petersburg, where Leonid Krassin became prominent, in Vladimir, Tula, Vilna, and elsewhere. In Vilna, where the Jewish workers' movement was fast developing, there was a heated debate about "circle" methods versus "agitation" designed to arouse a mass movement about 1893. The "agitators," one of whose leaders was Julius Martov, were successful, and their methods were quickly adopted by Social Democrats in Moscow and Petersburg in 1895.[9] After Vladimir Lenin and Martov had both arrived in the capital, they had time only to organize a Union for Struggle for Emancipation of the Workers before the police arrested most of the leaders. Lenin, Martov, Theodore Dan and A. N. Potresov were among those exiled. Just before the condemned men departed they carried on talks about future tactics. They did not bother to lament the fate of individuals, including themselves; the important thing was the "movement." Lenin's story is that the differences between "political" and "economist" tendencies in the Union were the focus of these conversations, though Martov recalls no such preciseness of viewpoints. At any rate such an argument did develop in the course of the great strike movement of 1896-7.[10]

At the very moment that Social Democrats first became an influential factor in the workers' movement during the great strikes, the first major doctrinal heresy arose in the ranks of the Russian Marxists, in the shape of Economism. By 1897 the orthodox emigres in the Group for Emancipation of Labor were belaboring the Economist sympathizers who had acquired the ascendancy among Russian Marxists. There were only scattered defenders of orthodoxy left inside Russia. An open split over Economism was not long in coming.

Without attempting to settle this argument, some Social Democrats in Russia undertook in March 1898 to organize a central party apparatus. The so-called "Bund," a recently founded Jewish workers' union, was instrumental in calling a secret meeting in Minsk which called itself the I Congress of the Russian Social Democratic Labor Party. Peter Struve was called upon to write the party manifesto.[11] "The farther to the East we go in Europe, in political relations the weaker, the more cowardly, the meaner become the bourgeoisie, and the more the cultural, political tasks fall to the lot of the proletariat," he wrote. Political freedom was the goal of the Russian worker, it was announced, and of the new party. The Minsk Congress set up a central committee, designated a Kiev journal as official party organ and the Union of Russian Social Democrats Abroad as its emigre representative. The organization it founded was, however, almost at once destroyed by arrests, and it had no permanent effect on the growth of Social Democracy.

Its failure was a tragedy to the Marxists. In the conditions of underground activity, it was essential that there be a recognized directing center—a central committee—and for men who regarded sound theory as the first, indispensable prerequisite to sound action, a party journal to solve problems of doctrine and tactics was likewise a matter of first importance. A central committee might be a handful of hunted men, a "party organ" might be a puny, thin rag which appeared sporadically to be seized by the police as often as it found its way into the hands of a few bewildered workers. Such details did not trouble men whose eyes were on the future and were convinced their first steps were right.

6.

While Marxism was having trouble striking organizational roots in the workers movement, a heated doctrinal dispute was going on in the literary arena. The Russian intelligentsia was rent by a great debate in which the future of capitalism in Russia was the issue, the Marxists and the populists were the contending parties. For radicals who expected history to work for them, this issue was by no means academic. If capitalism was growing, would not the bourgeoisie and proletariat soon be strong enough to affect politics? If it was not, might not the peasantry still serve as a vehicle of political change? If the appearance of capitalism in Russia was recognized to be a fact, did that prove Marxism was right? These questions produced a ferment among Russian intellectuals comparable to that of the 1840's, when lifelong friendships were shattered over the interpretation of Hegelian philosophy. The difference was that practical political consequences were obvious from every stage of the argument of the 90's. Young men and women posed the perennial question of the Russian intelligentsia, "What is to be done?" in a new context with compelling urgency.

Plekhanov set off the fight with his broadside in *All-Russian Ruin* with his "slurs" on the political capacity of the peasantry. The populists on the magazine *Russian Wealth*, who called themselves "the friends of the people," shrieked outraged retorts. They accused the Marxists of actively desiring the coming of capitalism, of preaching the "immutability of an abstract historical scheme."

The Marxist rebuttal came from Lenin in his pamphlet *What the 'Friends of the People' Are.* He was outspoken in his reply. Some might say he was passionate, though he might regard his own statements as scientific deductions from Marxist teaching and his own feelings as irrelevant. "Scratch a 'friend of the people' and you will find a bourgeois," he wrote. The Russian peasant socialism of the 70's, which he valued, "has completely decayed and has begotten that vulgar middle-class liberalism" which welcomes "progressive trends" in agriculture, forgetting that they are accompanied by wholesale expropriation of the peasantry. Lenin in his ire was finally reduced to implying that Mikhailovsky was a ". . ." Later he became more cautious in his polemics, though never any less intense than he was in this, his earliest substantial work.

Lenin's pamphlet was illegal, but other Marxists were for the first time advancing their arguments in public and in the legal press. Most of the advanced young Russian intellectuals had become embroiled in the Marxist-populist debate. Interest was high enough so that the Imperial Free Economic Society, whose charter dated from Catherine the Great, invited some of the Marxists to discuss economic questions in its privileged sessions during the winter of 1893-4. This helped to attract the attention of the liberals to the debate. Curiously enough the government considered that Marx's economic doctrines did not present any immediate threat to its security and at first ignored this phenomenon of Marxism-in-public.

So it was that with one eye on the government, Social Democrats stepped gingerly into the stream of legal publication. Peter Struve achieved the first success in 1894 with his *Critical Remarks*. In this work he affronted populist esteem for the intelligentsia by writing the latter off as a "negligible quantity." Terming capitalism "a powerful factor for cultural progress," he concluded, "Let us recognize our own uncultured state and go to school to capitalism." Herein the populists had proof that, as Mikhailovsky asserted, Marxists actively desired the coming of capitalism. Plekhanov was moved to slap Struve's hands with the remark, Struve "did express himself very carelessly, whereby he probably led into temptation many simpletons and rejoiced the hearts of some acrobats." [12] Lenin thought Struve's offense more serious and attacked him directly, calling his book a "reflection of Marxism in bourgeois literature." For the moment, however, most of the orthodox Marxists were themselves too much interested in experimenting with the new-found medium of the legal press, to push the issue of orthodoxy.

Plekhanov in 1895 managed to pass an exposition of Marxian historical materialism under the censor's nose by giving it the forbidding title, *Towards the Question of the Development of the Monist Interpretation of History*. The next move was into the field of the periodical press. A shortlived Samara journal was soon followed by the more important *New Word* in Petersburg in March 1897, and Social Democratic articles began to be accepted by established magazines like *Russian Thought* and *Scientific Review*. In early 1899 *Beginning* and *Life* began to be issued under Marxist editors.

By this time there had taken shape a recognizable group of "legal Marxists," which did not include all of those who published legally, for Plekhanov was among the latter.[13] The group was made up of those who had moved far enough away from orthodoxy to attack Marxism from a frankly Revisionist standpoint. A literary heresy thus took its place beside the political heresy of Economism among the targets of orthodox Marxists. The signs of apostasy which had been visible as early as Struve's book of 1894 had been generally overlooked, because Plekhanov and his friends believed the greater danger was still populism. Lenin explained it later in this manner. "It is no secret that the brief period in which Marxism blossomed on the surface of our literature was evoked by an alliance between people of extreme and of extremely moderate views," in fact, "bourgeois democrats"—that is, Struve and his fellows. But Lenin defended this "first really political alliance contracted by Russian Social Democrats" because "thanks to this alliance, an astonishingly rapid victory was obtained over populism and Marxian ideas (even though in a vulgarized form) became very widespread." [14]

After all, the hegemony of the proletariat depended on the victory of capitalism—much as antibodies cannot develop until disease germs attack. This victory was predicted by both orthodox and "legal" Marxists in opposition to the populists. Though Struve welcomed capitalism, which was bourgeois, he still correctly noted its advent, and this, from the viewpoint of even the uncompromising Lenin, could be of service. Thus during the Free Economic Society debates,[15] held while Lenin and Martov were in exile, Struve plumped for high prices against populist speakers who desired low prices as benefiting the peasants. Peter Maslov and other Marxists termed Struve's position scandalous, an apologetic for capitalism. But Lenin supported Struve, declaring that high prices by shattering "serf relations" hastened the day of revolution. It was this incident, by the way, which led Lenin into the study of the agrarian problem which produced the book *The Development of Capitalism in Russia*.

When 1898 came, bringing a temporary calm in the "social movement," the many intellectuals who had been attracted to Marxism turned their attention to problems of economics and philosophy undisturbed by the distractions of political struggle. If "the sharp knife of Marxism was the instrument by which the bourgeois intelligentsia cut the Populist umbilical cord and severed itself from a hated past," as Trotsky[16] wrote later, the knife was soon returned to its chest in favor of gentler tools.

The red tints of the Marxist legal magazines were already fading. Martov, comparing the *Beginning* of 1899 with *New Word* of two years earlier, laments the evident change for the worse—that is, for the more moderate.[17] Potresov noted that the earlier anti-populist, optimistic dynamic had lost its strength. The Revisionists began to be more blunt, anticipating or following the line being taken by German followers of Eduard Bernstein.[18] In May 1899 Tugan-Baranovskii, one of the outstanding Marxist economists, criticized the Marxian theory of capitalism as "abstract."[19] A few months later, Struve rejected Marx's economic formulation of surplus value in favor of a sociological idea of surplus labor and jettisoned entirely the theories of "impoverishment" and "catastrophe" as inevitable products of capitalism.

Of course Struve had lain under his colleagues' suspicion for some time. Others found their apostasy harder to justify to their Social Democrat comrades. Tugan-Baranovskii wrote to Potresov, "I cannot blindly believe in dogma—although I prize dogma highly and know that 'without dogma' no social movement is possible."[20] Sergei Bulgakov undertook to write a learned study of *Capitalism and Agriculture* from a Marxist viewpoint and found its doctrine "disproved" in the course of his research before his very eyes.[21] S. Prokopovich in writing *The Workers' Movement in the West* underwent a comparable disillusionment.

As these "legal Marxists" lost their faith that history was on Marx's side, they felt free again to emphasize the role of the individual in social development. Berdyaev and Bulgakov led the way to "neo-Kantianism" and idealist philosophy. Not only had the "legal Marxists" abandoned Marxism, but to a large extent their interest in political matters—with one important exception, Struve, who soon became an active liberal. The orthodox shed few tears at the voluntary exit of the heretics, casting the epithet "bourgeois" at their retreating backs and murmuring "good riddance" under their breaths. Having served the purpose of helping defeat the populists, Struve and his fellows were no longer useful.

For no one could doubt that the populists were defeated, at least in the literary debate over the crucial issue of the future of Russian capitalism. An anonymous populist, who attacked the Social Democrats in an article of 1896, could only berate his foes for exaggerated faith in the printed word. What were words, he asked, when compared in their efficacy with even "one act" in the fight against Tsarism? The populist did not attempt to discuss the content of the "words" on which Plekhanov and his friends relied. Plekhanov retorted sharply against the whole populist position.[22] Of course, said he, some "so-called socialists" would still try to retard the growth of capitalism by reliance on outmoded economic formations. True revolutionary socialists, on the other hand—that is, Marxists—simply tried to reduce to a minimum the suffering of the masses necessarily connected with the historical development of bourgeois society. The question of allies was touched upon again. Socialists, in hastening the growth of capitalism toward its own destruction, might cooperate with the bourgeoisie as was done during the fight with absolutism in Germany in 1848. But as for the anonymous populist's hopes for another (Socialist Revolutionary) party, they were reducible to the absurdity of a *"student* intrigue against absolutism."* Plekhanov reached this conclusion by a process of elimination. The populists might win some students, but the other recruits sought were quite unsuitable. The peasants were still unfit for political action, as they had been in 1891; the intellectuals, the old populist totem, occupied no definite class position and therefore had no part in the coming class struggle. The old People's Will carriage of the populists, taunted Plekhanov, was a good vehicle in its day but only one wheel was left now and it must go into storage.

The Marxists thought they had beaten populism lifeless. As far as the old populism went, they were nearly right. But they were to meet the old adversary again. In its matured Socialist Revolutionary form they were soon to find that it had altered in vital respects which made it a much more formidable adversary. Perhaps the Marxists actually expected it to disappear entirely, since their fight in the 90's aimed, as Lenin put it, at "cleansing bourgeois liberalism of populism."[23] The bourgeois liberalism of the 60's and 70's, he wrote Potresov in the last year of the century, is "more or less consistent, but is purely derivative from the Populist movement." If liberalism could be stripped of these illusions, the residue, he said, would be bourgeois liberalism of the type of Skaldin, and not pretending to be socialist.

Skaldin himself had been an avowed spokesman of the peasantry, which in Marxist eyes fell in the category of "bourgeois" liberalism.[24] The peasantry was not, after all, a "class" at all, but a section of the petty bourgeoisie. How, then, could a political party base its existence on the rural masses? There were, as every Marxist knew, only two coherent classes in an industrial society, such as was fast developing in Russia—the bourgeoisie and the proletariat. A party for each, and both to fight for the overthrow of feudal survivals—Tsarism and the old agrarian system—this was the Social Democratic view of the immediate future, and they wanted no archaic nonsense about a party supporting the "class interests" of the peasantry.

Accordingly, history must produce a bourgeois party in Russia, though it was to be destroyed by the socialists once the Tsardom was crushed. Lenin thus suggested Skaldin's ideas as a model, since they were free from what he considered populist nonsense. The bourgeois ally—enemy, as it finally took shape, proved willing enough to break with populism, but it refused to follow the Skaldin path. Perhaps this explains part of Lenin's bitter hostility to the liberal Kadets. They refused to play the role of capitalist.

7.

Liberalism as it emerged in Russia was not at all colored with Skaldinist, *laisser-faire* premises. Miliukov, Russia's greatest liberal, puts it this way. Liberalism in Russia, he wrote, "connoted the idea of state intervention," and since no developed Russian liberal thought had existed in the days when laisser-faire ideas were popular in the West, it was free to become "more democratic, without being inconsistent with a former tradition." [25] With almost no exceptions, agrees the liberal professor Kizevetter, even in the 80's the liberals, instead of demanding the state keep hands off, "ascribed great significance to state interference in economic relations in the interests of social justice." [26] Since the competitive phase of capitalism, which had fathered laisser-faire in the West, was already past, the new Russian liberals of the late nineteenth century believed slogans about "free enterprise" in economic life to imply reactionary politics.

The core of the early liberals were not capitalists, competitive, monopolist, or any other type. They were members of the gentry, and their organizational center was the zemstvo institutions. The gentry did indeed stand in need of state aid, but the kind of state interference the liberals demanded was not that designed to save the gentry. Here was a paradox for Marxists to ponder. As Miliukov points out, Russian liberalism since before the Great Reforms had been directed against the gentry, although that liberalism originated among the gentry itself. The liberals, it seems clear, were intelligentsia first and gentry second; their interests, like that of the other party intellectuals, were more political than economic.

Liberalism for the purposes of this discussion is defined simply as the thinking of those men, exclusive of the revolutionary socialists on the one hand and progressive bureaucrats on the other, who demanded sweeping political and social change in Russia. This definition is not intended to imply that "liberal" objectives were absent or rare among the policy-making officials of latter-day Tsarism, or that many of the Tsars themselves did not according to their lights act out of a deep regard for the good of the Russian people. But the "liberals," who themselves used and were referred to by this term, opposed Tsarism partially or wholly although they did not demand a social revolution.

Zemstvo constitutionalism was the first organized form that this current took. Out of the provincial and district boards and assemblies which made up the zemstvo institutions created in 1864, there emerged many members of the gentry who were not only passionately interested in local self-government, but desired to spread the principle to include the Empire as a whole. Already in 1865 the Moscow gentry adopted an address to Alexander II which contained the plea, "Crown, Sire, the political edifice you have built"; in other words, add to the local zemstvos an all-Russian zemstvo or parliament. The next year the Petersburg zemstvo assembly added its voice to the same demand, but it was rebuked severely for doing so. As a result, for the next decade the zemstvists were silent.

In those days zemstvo constitutionalists had a rather "practical," empiricist bent. The idea was simply to extend the zemstvo principle, which was justifying itself by successful operation on local levels, to the nation as a whole. This might or might not mean a legislative assembly elected on a broad suffrage to which a ministry would be responsible. There was as yet no systematic constitutionalist doctrine, but rather benevolent wishes often mingled with populist and Slavophile notions depending on the individual concerned. There were indeed isolated voices, such as that of Ivan Petrunkevich, who spoke out boldly for a logical constitutional democracy at an early date. In 1882 he wrote that "we must not be actors in a constitutional comedy, but, rejecting any kind of constitution granted from above, we will insist on the calling of a Constituent Assembly"—which Herzen had been the first to demand for Russia.[27]

Petrunkevich, the dean of the future Kadets, remained in the forefront of Russian liberals the rest of his career. He lived to see the logical-minded minority to which he belonged become the vast majority among the liberals. In the 80's he was interrupted in a speech to a zemstvo meeting by the cry, "That is a call to revolution!" and there were no voices raised to defend him. The same charge was flung at him at the July 1905 zemstvo congress, a quarter-century later, but by then he was able to speak confidently for the liberal majority. He was among the first of the zemstvo liberals to advance the slogan of a Constituent Assembly, which became the watchword among all opposition factions who feared the Tsar might dupe the people with a false parliament which would veil his own retention of the real power. To prevent this, the democrats called for a freely elected representative body from all classes and regions of Russia, which would, like the American Constitutional Convention, decide once for all how Russia was to be governed. This was the kind of body Petrunkevich demanded in 1882, and which did finally meet thirty-six years later, to be driven out by the Bolsheviks after sitting only one day.

Petrunkevich not only raised the standard of democratic government in the liberal camp, but tackled the vital tactical issue of allies in the struggle for freedom. It was he also who established a new precedent for liberals by endeavoring to establish links with the underground revolutionaries. Accompanied by another zemstvist, he paid a rather melodramatic visit to Kievan terrorist leaders in order to try to persuade them to cooperate with the liberals. He urged them to suspend their "direct action" methods while the zemstvos organized their own opposition to the Tsar. The attempt failed, but the meeting was an amicable one.

Petrunkevich was on the far Left of the zemstvo constitutionalists, but he was not alone. In 1879 a Zemstvo Union representing several different Russian provinces was founded. Two years later at a Kharkov conference it adopted demands for a legislative assembly and universal suffrage. But 1881 was the year of Alexander's assassination, and the infant movement succumbed along with its more radical competitors. For the second time the zemstvists had to be silent, but ripples of agitation continued. The word "constitution" which had frightened Nicholas I so thoroughly when used by the Decembrists in 1825, still remained anathema to Nicholas II. Substitute terms had to be found, such as "self-government" and "legal order." The boldest even dared to hope aloud that the Russians "would be granted those same blessings" that the Tsar had given the Bulgars—referring to the Bulgarian constitution which followed the Russo-Turkish War of 1878. However, in general the decade of the 80's was a period when the zemstvo radicals, aside from a few bold spirits, were silent and the more moderate zemstvists pessimistic.

The shock of the 1891 famine ended this placid interlude. The same year a society calling itself *Beseda* (Conversation) was founded.[28] It included radicals like the Kokoshkins, Dolgorukovs, and Shakhovskois as well as staunch defenders of an autocracy which would operate on the idealized lines of Slavophile thought, like Khomiakov, Stakhovich, and Shipov. The requirement for membership was that all engage in some kind of "practical" work in town council or zemstvo organizations. An exemption had to be made to admit the "nonpractical" V. A. Maklakov, who was a lawyer. The purpose was to discuss social problems, not to indulge in political agitation or, until 1901, even to raise political questions. It was nevertheless an important step in Russian liberal organization.

Meanwhile the Zemstvo Union idea was being revived.[29] Sharply repulsed by the Tsar at his accession in January 1895 for "senseless dreams of zemstvo participation in the general direction of internal affairs of State," the zemstvists did not take their whipping with a good grace. At once the Imperial Free Economic Society demonstratively elected the reformist Count P. A. Heyden president. The Samara zemstvo president tried to form another Zemstvo Union to consist of a permanent council of heads of zemstvos. Interior Minister Goremykin balked at giving permission for such a group, but he finally allowed it to meet "privately and unofficially."

Thus by the end of the 90's two liberal organizations of a sort had been founded. As yet only embryonic forms of the type of overtly political groups which followed in a few years, they nevertheless helped to crystallize liberal opinion and attract public attention to the problems of Autocracy and reform. In both bodies radicals and moderates were beginning to line up. The one faction was impatient for strict constitutional democracy, the other confined itself to urging the Sovereign for the good of all to follow the reformist path of Alexander II. The moderate group was anxious lest its loyalty be compromised or suspected by the Tsar. Such an attitude aroused the radicals' contempt, as, writes Maklakov resignedly, "soldiers always deride diplomats."[30]

The new "soldiers" of the liberal movement did in fact carry the day eventually, but in the late 90's they were only appearing on the scene. Most of them were not radical squires like Petrunkevich, but professional men, most of whom were specialists employed by the zemstvos. These people came to be designated by the term, "the third element," a term which was used for the first time in 1899.[31] The term means those who were neither officials nor gentry, but made up a third social group in the field of local government. It was these professional men, along with others of the intelligentsia of "society," who led the fight of the radical gentry against those liberals who still placed "loyalty" above their sincere wishes for reforms. But this is the story of the years following 1898.

The rise of the zemstvo liberal movement was partly determined by the zigzags of Tsarist policy in the 90's because the "loyal" moderates were still predominant. Some of the "public men" offered cooperation towards the enactment of reforms intended to save Autocracy, not destroy it. They were repeatedly rebuffed, and their failure had a double-barrelled impact. First, the moderate leaders like Shipov were driven some distance towards an opposition position—reforms were essential; if the government would not willingly undertake them it must be forced to do so. Second, the "loyalists" were discredited and lost their position of leadership to the radicals.

The bureaucrats around Nicholas II had seldom shown any disposition to extend the competence of the zemstvos, let alone "crown the edifice" in any way whatsoever. Goremykin, it is true, had supported the territorial extension of the zemstvos, provided that it was dominated by the bureaucracy. Moreover, he had permitted a Zemstvo Union to form, although he had shown no disposition to consult zemstvists about state affairs. Witte's report to the Tsar, published as *Autocracy and Zemstvo* by the hostile Struve, ought to have been entitled "Autocracy or Zemstvo," for he declared the two incompatible. In consequence of Witte's report, Goremykin was removed from the interior ministry.[32] Under Sipiagin the zemstvists were completely quiescent. Under Plehve they did pluck up courage to approach the government, but Plehve rebuffed them sharply. There was little use for zemstvo men to offer the hand of cooperation to a government which only brushed it aside. The radicals chafed, the moderates sat idle in embarrassment.

So the situation stood in 1898. The liberals as yet had no defined program, no plan, no organized party. They were however unanimous in the conviction that the evolution of the State in Russia lagged far behind social and economic development, that fundamental reforms were essential. The debate, however, still continued as to how the necessary changes were to be attained. Ought the liberals to continue to urge the Tsar to enact limited reform, or ought they to demand a constitutional regime? If the latter alternative was chosen, another question arose. It was assumed by many that the Tsar would never voluntarily grant constitutionalist demands. Therefore an open struggle against Tsarism was inevitable, and in such a struggle allies had to be sought. Who were to be these allies? The Left Liberals were already looking toward the revolutionaries for help. Though they disdained violent methods and doctrinaire principles, they had already begun to talk of mutual support. For decades even among the highest circles of Russian society the memory of the early revolutionaries had been revered and their sincerity respected, even when their conduct was disapproved. From the time of Petrunkevich's brief descent into the underworld, the idea of some kind of cooperation with the revolutionaries had been mulled over by impatient reformers. There was a wall between men who lived their economically secure lives in the open and men who lived miserable lives in fear of arrest, but the wall did not look so high in 1898 as it had even five years earlier. If all the intelligentsia could cooperate, they might confidently expect to attract mass support for the revolution which already in 1898 appeared in sight.

8.

As the Liberation Movement got under way in earnest with the formation of political groups, the Western and highly intellectual orientation of Russian political activity became the more plainly marked. The Western origin of the doctrines held was reinforced by the circumstance that many of the opposition leaders were in emigration in the West during this period, and constantly relayed to Russia the impact of developments there in reformist and revolutionary thought and action. The very concept of political parties which guided the action of the whole Russian opposition, was taken direct from the West. No wonder political objectives were being framed in purely Western terms like "constitution," "legislative assembly," "universal suffrage," and the "freedoms," concepts with whose embodiment Russia was almost wholly unacquainted. As for intellectualism, although it had in fact become unfashionable to emphasize or even to mention the function of the "intelligentsia," in reality intellectuals made up the leadership of all three parties. In populist ranks, the intellectuals maintained their long-standing predominance, though they ceased to stress this fact and were turning more and more to mass propaganda and agitation among peasants and workers. In Social Democracy, the efforts of "practicals" to divert the movement in the direction of "Economism" were soon to be defeated. In the liberal camp as well, the zemstvist employees and professional intelligentsia were gradually to tighten their control until the Kadet Party could be formed under their unchallenged leadership.

Not only were the intellectuals as a social group in a commanding position, but their approach to politics remained one governed by the rational faculty of the intellect. Notions of a policy which depended on what was "practical," what worked best, were simply unacceptable among opposition circles. Even in the case of the populists who prided themselves on freedom from "dogmatism" and the often frankly opportunistic liberals—to say nothing of the doctrinaire Marxists—their conduct of political action was founded almost wholly on a priori principles, the attempt to realize predetermined goals conceived in terms of reason rather than experience. No such overriding rational motives are to be found in the actions of the leaders of the great classic revolutions of the West. The Revolution of 1905 (and also that of 1917) in Russia, the alleged home of Byzantine mysticism, thus in a certain sense marked the greatest triumph of Western rationalism in politics.

The differentiation among revolutionary groups, and the germination of a stable liberal faction, virtually complete by 1898, took place not primarily in terms of immediate goals. Political aims were almost indistinguishable in the party programs of Socialist Revolutionaries, Social Democrats, and the liberals who were to form the Union of Liberation. All parties aimed first of all at a democratic order; the two first-named, at socialism later. The first step, for all, was the more or less forcible overthrow of Tsarism followed by the convening of a representative assembly which would simultaneously determine how Russia should be governed and institute important social reforms.

What then did differentiate these groups? It will be found that the differentiation took place in terms of the various rationalist constructs of an ideal polity which the intellectual leaders of all parties had worked out, and the degree to which they were willing to pursue these uncompromisingly. What this meant in practice, and how this affected the chances for success of the Liberation Movement, will appear in subsequent chapters. Here we need only notice the tremendous practical importance of the decisions each party would make about acceptable allies, decisions which usually proved deductions from the respective a priorist premises held. As long as no party held power, how it behaved during the struggle was of vital importance. No single aspect of this behavior was so important as the choice of political groups with which each was willing to cooperate. What is most important in determining the success of a coalition army is whether the coalition can operate harmoniously. The Russian Liberation Movement was a coalition army, in which harmony was on the whole retained to a remarkable degree until the events of October 1905. '

Part Two

STORM CLOUDS GATHERING

IV

THE POPULISTS REFURBISHED

"In the realm of economics Marx is our great common teacher, although we do not feel constrained to make of him an idol."
VICTOR CHERNOV, 1906.[1]

If Victor Chernov in the 90's could have foreseen that he would preside over an All-Russian Constituent Assembly with an SR majority in 1917, he might well have felt assured of complete victory. Of course the triumph was to be an empty one, marking the beginning of the swift and total obliteration of Socialist Revolutionism in Russia rather than the eve of ascent to power. The Mensheviks never came close to power. The Kadets achieved a working majority in the First Duma, but only in the face of a still powerful Tsardom. The SR's practically held the power in their hands when the Romanovs had already fallen and the future of Russia was wide open—and had it torn away by the Bolsheviks. Their party might well feel itself one of the most unfortunate victims of the unexpected in history. Today only a deliberately distorted memory of their existence survives in Soviet Russia, while the outside world has largely forgotten their immense strength and potentialities.

In 1898, however, their prospects looked bright indeed. Populism had taken a long time to recover from the shock of 1881 and the crushing of The People's Will. It was years before the populists could bring themselves to realize that The People's Will current was dead. When they swallowed this bitter medicine, during the 90's, the revival of populism in a new form was swift.

The old vagueness of doctrine, the old reliance on "action" for its own sake, the old hope for a Utopia which would avoid capitalism—all these things were jettisoned by the new generation of populists. Capitalism had arrived. There could be no more argument about that. The question remained, did the coming of industrial capitalism mean that the Marxists were right? Did the old populism, rooted as it believed itself to be in Russian traditions, have to surrender unconditionally to the new Marxism of the industrial West? No, indeed, said Chernov and his friends.

The Socialist Revolutionary leaders, who came into prominence in the 90's and led their party in the First Revolution, were unlike the Marxist chieftains in several ways. They of course refused to accept Marxism in its entirety, though neither did they reject it wholly. They were not, as a group, passionate men of letters, like the *Iskra* group. They were not as homogeneous as the Marxists, either. Their three most outstanding men, Gershuni, Chernov, and Gotz, were men of different interests, different abilities.

Gershuni was a leader of men, a magnetic personality, a man of action who was a successful and enthusiastic terrorist, a hero. Oliver Radkey, student of the SR's, once speculated as to whether Gershuni might have overshadowed Lenin had he lived till 1917.[2] Yet Gershuni lacked the doctrinaire, intellectual turn which gave Lenin such unshakable confidence in action, yet permitted him to indulge in ruthless self-criticism and adjust his tactics swiftly.

The doctrinaire of the SR's was Victor Chernov, son of an official who had been ennobled, like Vladimir Lenin. He was the man who more than any other put the SR party on doctrinal ground it could hold against the sharpest Marxist attack. It was also he who guided his party's tactics up to 1917. Yet this intellectual sometimes had to be locked in his editorial office by Gershuni to produce a needed article, and was capable of forgetting everything in his passion for fishing. His defects, which he himself ascribed to his "broad Slavic nature," included a fondness for behind-the-scenes intrigue, an adaptability and an imperturbability which sometimes meant weakness at the crucial moments and unwillingness to exert leadership which the party so desperately needed. When 1917 came, he allowed Kerensky to violate party discipline and lead the SR party to ruin without challenging him until it was too late. Still he was capable of carrying the business of formulating party principles almost alone, as the I Congress openly acknowledged. His prestige, despite the Azef affair and his stand on the World War, was immense when he took the podium for that fateful single day's session of the Constituent Assembly. By 1917 both Gershuni and Michael Gotz, the man who cared for the party funds and organization, were dead, and Chernov admitted he felt the loss. He was a man who worked well in harness to a team, but lacked the attributes of a universal leader.

One can follow the revival of populism in its new Socialist Revolutionary form in Chernov's own uncompleted memoirs. In the 90's he belonged to a student circle in Tambov, along with his wife and his brother-in-law, S. N. Sletov. Here he examined the facts of the Russian situation and pondered them. "We did not doubt," he declares, "that capitalism was developing in Russia; we sought only the typical national peculiarities" of its development.[3] Not doubting the ruin of the ancient patriarchal village economy, he did believe this process would strengthen the unity of the village laboring class. This in turn would facilitate the growth of solidarity between the urban proletariat and the independent peasant. On these two groups would be based the "socialist people's party" for which Chernov was already composing a program. The theoretical section of this program, Chernov himself states, was nine-tenths composed of the very words of Marx, Engels, Kautsky, Liebknecht, and Bebel.[4] He had studied German and French socialism, and there was much of interest to him to be learned in both.

2.

In Marxian eyes, the small producer in any branch of economic life was necessarily the most backward. It was not large-scale production to which they objected, but its ownership by capitalists. Their analysis was that the increasing bigness of the productive unit would bring about the destruction of the capitalists themselves by creating more, and more miserable, proletarians who would end it all. Yet the small producer in agriculture, the peasant, did not fit easily into this analysis. Among Western Social Democrats only the boldest, Bebel for example, were willing to be consistent enough to declare for the expropriation of the smallest peasant farms before the large estates. In both German and French Social Democracy voices were to be found defending the interest of the agricultural smallholder. In 1894 Vollmar, in Germany, declared it was useless to try to reassure the peasant, doomed by Marxism, with "the promise of a better life in the Socialist afterworld," and he induced the Frankfurt party congress to support the peasant's economic position in terms which shocked orthodox Marxists deeply. According to one of these orthodox, Kautsky, Social Democrats must favor the peasant as little as the Junker.

Nevertheless, some party spokesmen in the Reichstag clamored for reforms benefiting the peasants. They were urged on by the South Germans and Eduard David, who wrote a book[5] to prove that maintenance of the peasant class under conditions of intensified agriculture was necessary and desirable. For the South German socialists, "the issue was never clouded: it was either a modified Socialism with the peasants, or without the peasants no Socialism at all."[6]

This was a basic conviction of the Russian Socialist Revolutionaries as well. Practically, to convince the peasants to support orthodox Marxism was impossible. More than that, however, the SR's did not believe history was out to destroy the peasants and cited evidence to that effect. It is not in order for the Marxists to sneer that the SR's sought the truth of history in the region of their own desires, unless they themselves are able to deny that not only, by their doctrine, does socialism come—but that they happened to want it that way. Capitalism of course was to be crushed; but meanwhile it would bring large-scale production to Russia, in agriculture as well as industry. The early orthodox Marxists, at least, shed no more tears over the prospective disappearance of the peasant than of the small urban producer. On the other hand the SR's "from the very beginning accepted only with great reservations the Marxist idea of the positive 'historical mission' of capitalism," as Chernov puts it.[7] He declares that capitalism has a constructive and a destructive side, and that the latter is especially evident in the realm of agriculture. The SR's wanted to save the peasants, and so sought scientific proof that this was economically practicable. History was put to work for the SR's, but the element of human will, always a strong element in populism, was not eliminated. Lenin himself, in talking about a choice between two capitalist paths, "American" and "Prussian," for Russian agriculture, tacitly admitted that the SR's in seeking to guide history were not wholly fatuous.

The SR's knew above all that the Russian peasantry made up the overwhelming majority of the people, not merely an imposing proportion as in Germany. They never forgot this as they delved into their studies of Marx. The populists, says Mitrany, "sat humbly at the feet of Marx when it was a matter of theory, but when it came to applying it they clung to the belief that the peculiar conditions prevailing in Russia and the southern-Slav countries placed them in a category of their own."[8] The old populists had cherished an almost mystical faith in the Russian peasant commune, the mir; but Mitrany declares this was not the crucial factor. Commune or not, where there were more peasants, there was more Marxian heresy. The essential point for the SR's was that small peasant farming was economically viable under the right conditions, and they found confirmation of this in the results obtained by Russian zemstvo statisticians. As for the commune, the SR's could flaunt in the faces of orthodox Marxists an unequivocal text of Marx himself. In the famous letter to Vera Zasulich, Marx had written that the commune was the obvious point d'appui for the social regeneration of Russia, provided its defects were first removed. This, wrote Chernov, was exactly the program of the SR's.[9]

Chernov and his Tambov circle took eager part in the great debate of the 90's between populists and Marxists. By now they were prepared to meet the Marxists on their own ground of scientific argument. When a populist of the old school, goaded by Marxist demands to know what their program was, cried, "It is propaganda, agitation, terror!" Chernov and his friends only smiled at such naivete.[10] They knew better ways of attacking the Marxists, and used them. They saw that some of their cohorts were incapable of dealing with theoretical problems, while they observed other populists wavering before the appeal of monolithic Marxism. Chernov says one had only to point out to these people, "standing in doubt before the intellectual seductions of Marxism, corrupting by its symmetry, the first shoots of [populist] revolutionary muzhik organizations, with developing perspectives of the great agrarian revolution of the future," and they would scurry back to the fold for good.[11] The element of activism, the thrill that rose in the populist breast on seeing their ideas practiced on however small a scale, was thus still retained. When in 1898 Chernov emigrated, seeking more theoretical enlightenment from the West, he chose to carry in his shoe no doctrinal tracts but instead the constitution of the first peasant revolutionary group (of Pavlodar) for the encouragement of the long expatriate populists of London and Paris.

It may be that Chernov was too accurate. It may be that in declaring that Marxism's valuable insights did not exhaust human reality he forfeited a useful self-deception. Appealing to Marx's slogan of his youth, "a union of those who think and those who feel," he declared that both Utopian and "scientific" socialist currents had failed to unite the two elements, while his own "constructive socialism" (of which Socialist Revolutionism was an example) synthesized them. Feeling, passion, was for him a necessary mainspring to the will which the Men Who Knew needed to carry out a revolution. Furthermore, it was part of the real make-up of the human being. For him, it was not being "scientific" to ignore emotion. It was part of sound theory to include it. The paradox is that the rigidly rationalist Marxists somewhere found a passionate devotion to the predetermined achievement of their goals which surpassed that of the equally determined, but gentler, SR's.

3.

At the end of the 90's the refurbishing of populism was thus nearing completion. Chernov outlines the views of the new school in this fashion: the coming revolution was to be based on the mass movement of the people, with terror only a prelude, revolutionary intellectual circles conducting only preliminary skirmishes. "To the proletariat was allotted the role of vanguard; to the peasantry, the role of the fundamental, main army."[12] As for the liberals, he discounted their influence, among the peasants in particular, remembering how they proved "such hopeless strangers" to the people in the work of famine relief in 1891. Nevertheless, he now proclaimed the slogan of international socialism for the proper attitude toward them: "March apart, strike together,"—against autocracy. The liberals would thus attain a temporary triumph, after which the populists would break with them. The revolution, in other words, would have two phases, as the Marxists thought. Such were the new tactics of the SR's, and the ones upon which the party was to base its action. The new tactical plan was based on one important theoretical proposition not shared by Marxists: the identity or close similarity of economic interest of the industrial worker and "toiling" peasant. The populist journalist, Peshekhonov, defended this point in his brochure of 1898, *Peasants and Workers in their Mutual Relations,* and Chernov and others zealously propagandized the idea of such a partnership. Yet notice that although Plekhanov disagreed with Chernov about peasants, Chernov wholly agreed with Plekhanov about workers. Workers were not only to be important, they were to take the lead. Industrial capitalism was not merely accepted; it now lay at the base of the SR plans, for its proletarian offspring were to carry those plans to realization. At this point populism—peasant socialism—is no longer the accurate word for Socialist Revolutionism, and we shall occasionally call the SR's neo-populists.

Something has been said about the renovation of populism from the standpoint of orthodox Marxism. Here is the place for a word about SR relation to "Revisionism." It is apparent that Chernov's teachings were by now similar to those of the South German followers of Vollmar in vital respects. However, it was not the "heresy" of Vollmar that the SR's imitated—their own reliance on the peasantry was far older. It was certain elements of Marxian orthodoxy—adopted only so far as possible without sacrificing the peasantry—which distinguished Socialist Revolutionism from the old populism. This orthodoxy came from Marx, Engels, and the others whom Chernov used in drawing up his program of the 90's, not Vollmar and his cohorts. The populists started with practice based on reliance on peasants and later acquired their rationalist theory, wholly Western in origin. The South Germans did precisely the reverse. The end result was similar, but Vollmar never captured German Social Democracy. That party's lapses from orthodoxy were rather in the direction of Eduard Bernstein's "Revisionism" than in the direction of modifying their peasant program.

If Vollmar did not influence the SR's, then, what of Bernstein? Here the difference is clear. Bernstein attempted to defend the progressive role of capitalism and to safeguard its gains from the threat of violent revolution. On the contrary, the SR's shared with Bernstein's orthodox critics a deep hatred of the bourgeoisie and a belief in violent revolution as the only salvation of the "exploited" classes. If Bernsteinism was revisionism to the Right, says Chernov, then Socialist Revolutionism was revisionism to the Left.[13] Its theoreticians began "completely from the other end; not from the factory, not from industry, but from the village, from agriculture." In regard to industrialism, they had no quarrel with Plekhanov.

The question, then, on which SR's and SD's broke their sharpest lances was the peasant problem. Aside from this, there were other disagreements. One was the question of terrorism, which the Marxists connected with anarchism and which they abhorred as a useless attempt to apply shock treatment to the march of history. The old view of terrorism—that is, political murder—had been to force concessions from the government. This view had however been altered. Now Zhitlovskii in Switzerland and Argunov in Russia defended political killing along different lines, as merely one weapon out of many leading to overthrow of Tsarism, not "compelling" it to do anything. As an instrument for this different purpose, terrorism even gained adherents in Social Democratic circles, for example, the group which published the journal *Freedom*. Chernov and his followers did not reject terrorism, but they minimized its role in party tactics. This unfortunately did leave the Marxists with a handy stick with which to beat their opponents as "unscientific," when other weapons failed.

4.

While SR doctrine was being prepared for public display, a new effort was made to complete a central organization for the party. After two unsuccessful tries, a number of SR bands in South Russia managed to found an "SR Party" at a Kharkov conference in the summer of 1900, adopting the program of the 1897 meeting. This program said nothing about terrorism at all, but provided for support of the bourgeoisie and other classes against Autocracy and relied for success on the mass movement which strikes, propaganda, and agitation were expected to produce. This "Party of the South," as it was called, was carrying on talks with the Saratov-centered "Union of the North" and the Minsk nucleus, the two main SR groups, and was also in touch with the Paris emigres. In July 1901 the "Union" reached agreement with Rusanov in Paris that he should publish with their support a theoretical organ, *Messenger of the Russian Revolution*. New arrests in the autumn broke off contacts among Russian groups, so in November Maria Seliuk and Evno Azef on behalf of the "Union" and Gershuni for the "Party" went abroad and as a result of their talks practically all neo-populists in Russia and out agreed to unite. They set up a Central Committee and an official organ, *Revolutionary Russia,* to be published in Switzerland by Chernov and Michael Gotz. There remained outside the party for the moment an Agrarian Socialist League, founded in February 1900 by Chernov and some, like Shishko, from the older generation. The League finally joined the party in the summer of 1902.

From its third number, in January, 1902, *Revolutionary Russia* officially became the organ of the united party, and it continued as such until the October Manifesto. In view of the fact that no party congress was held until the end of 1905, an astounding degree of SR unity prevailed until then. The thorny question of terrorism was solved by giving the terrorists "autonomy" within the party. Their so-called "Battle Organization" was composed of men living a kind of life which fits the classic picture of hunted underground revolutionaries. Its first thunderously successful achievement was the killing of Sipiagin in 1902. Gershuni headed the Battle Organization until he was arrested in the spring of 1903, when Azef, the provocateur in the employ of the secret police, actually became its chief and carried out the killing of his own superior, Plehve, a year later. There were other victims in 1905, including the Grand Duke Sergei, governor-general of Moscow. In most cases the assassins were caught and executed. What is surprising is that the SR's succeeded in making of the assassins more effective martyrs, in the eyes of public opinion, than the Tsardom could make of their infinitely more illustrious victims.

The newly united party, leaving the terrorists to fend for themselves, went ahead at full speed to organize local committees inside Russia. To the new SR banner there flocked students and intellectuals offended by Marxist "onesided" concentration on the proletariat—that is, forgetting the peasants—and considerable numbers of factory workers as well. The party devoted much effort to distributing propaganda literature among the peasants, despite strenuous efforts of the Ministry of the Interior to cut off this subversive flow as early as 1902.

As local committees were formed, they often maintained close relations with Social Democrat groups. In Saratov and Perm, for example, the SR committees formed part of "United Groups of SR's and SD's" and in 1903 Ekaterinburg followed suit. At the end of 1902 the Kiev *Workers Flag* group, earlier considered Social Democratic, was admitted to the SR party. The Marxists never shed tears over the departure of heretics, whose apostasy was enough proof of unfitness, but they had to take into account these SR gains at their expense.

Meanwhile agitation among the peasants was intensified. Propaganda in Poltava had some effect on the peasant risings of spring 1902, and they were followed up by formation of a Peasant Union of the SR Party (not to be confused with the nonpartisan All-Russian Peasant Unions of a later date). The SR Peasant Union worked chiefly in the Volga and Ukraine. The Marxist Maslov sneers[14] at its activities as agitation "of a primitive sort" corresponding to the level of thought of peasants "who had no conception either of class struggle or of the structure of the present order." The SR's however were undeterred by these jeers. They recognized that the peasant psychology was "not positively socialist," but determined to make it that way by their efforts. In fact, the Social Democrats were carrying on agitation in the villages on very similar lines. Maslov claims they outstripped the SR's in influence in Western Russia and Georgia while admitting that the neo-populists were ahead in the agricultural center of Russia, the central provinces and the Volga region. Furthermore, in most of the borderlands the SR's could make an appeal to local separatism which the Marxists could not with their strict internationalism. Especially in

Armenia, Georgia, and Latvia, SR federalist leanings made it easy for them to acquire the support of revolutionary groups among the minority peoples.

The party was finally making headway among the urban workers and took an active part, though not such an active one as the SD's, in the great strike in southern Russia at the end of 1903. The next year the SR's registered gains especially in the northwest from Belostok in Poland to Smolensk, and they organized an "SR Union" for Siberia. They also began to get a solid footing among Moscow workers and students for the first time—and this was Marxist territory. The foundation for the swift expansion of the party in 1905 had thus been laid on broad territorial lines.

5.

Isaiah Berlin states [15] that the writings of the authors of the Russian Revolution, "in contrast with the less or more lucid and coherent ideological structures of the great Western thinkers of the nineteenth century in Germany and France, present a confused mass of social and economic analysis dedicated to party . . . problems as they arose . . . in which only the most devoted attention to the events and necessities of the moment by which they were generated can discern patterns and trends." To understand the Russian parties, it is necessary to go to their journalistic organs. We find here not writing intended to beguile the reader's interest, inform him, nor, it often seems, to persuade him. The articles in the revolutionary press usually stated the party's considered position on an issue in as argumentative a fashion as possible, without bothering to identify the authors. These journals were not intended to take the place of penny papers or tabloids. Their purpose was completely serious; every article, every word of every issue was in dead earnest. Just as we find it hard to understand these men who made politics not only their vocation but their whole life, so we find it difficult to imagine the importance the opposition writers attached to every article published and its exact purport and phraseology. These ideological sallies taken individually are tedious, often badly organized and written. Taken altogether, they form an impressive pattern reflecting a world-view, a grand strategy, and a tactical plan.

The Paris emigres first undertook to provide the theoretical basis for the refurbished neo-populism in *Messenger of the Russian Revolution,* but these men, who declared themselves "theoretical

continuators" of the *People's Will* current and at the same time
adherents of "revolutionary socialism," were unequal to the task.
Only four numbers appeared in five years. As in the case of the
Social Democrats, the "theoretical organ" petered out, leaving
the "practical organ," in this case *Revolutionary Russia*, to take
on itself a double load.

The latter newspaper got off to a slow start with one number
per year in 1900 and 1901, apologizing· for the failure to publish
a program by contending that "Now is the time not to theorize,
but to act." When the united party entrusted the organ to Chernov
and Gotz, a fresh determination was at once in evidence. "All
revolutionary forces active in Russia"[16] must be mobilized; "a
main nerve center" for the developing revolution must be set up.
Like the Group for Emancipation of Labor in the rival Marxist
camp, the editors called for cooperation of all branches of the
opposition. All "dissatisfied social elements" must stand together,
led by the army of revolutionary socialists because it alone "pos-
sesses enough energy and consciousness" of political realities to
storm the enemy fortress. Who was the enemy? The plutocrats and
serf lords with the Tsardom at their head—though Nicholas II
was not mentioned by name. In Western countries the function
of leadership could be discharged by bourgeois liberal parties,
but due to their weakness in Russia, only the socialists could take
this role—this was "our pride." Readers, especially Marxists, were
reminded again of the need "to live and work, and not only to
philosophize"—but philosophize one must, and this Chernov and
Gotz did, more than their forefathers of the People's Will ever did.

Meanwhile, the Battle Organization was "living" and "working."
Terrorism was defended by the editors[17] when the killing of
Sipiagin had once focused public attention on this weapon of a
bygone generation. They believed that terrorist acts were not
only expedient "but necessary, unavoidable." Still, even in the
lurid if glamorous light cast by the death of the "imbecile" minister, terror was not allowed to step out of its allotted niche in
the SR program. Political murder was definitely subordinated to
the mass struggle, which terrorism was "not to replace but to
supplement and strengthen . . . the revolutionizing of the masses—
this is our constant, fundamental task as a social-revolutionary
party." Once having announced to the public that a Battle Organization was in existence, once having sanctioned its gruesome
methods in the name of the party, Chernov and Gotz ceased to
discuss the matter. Gone were the days when men dreamed that

the death of some individual, however repulsive, could solve Russia's problems.

When the spring of 1902 brought its welcome harvest of peasant riots for the first time in long years, the editors undertook to discuss the peasants' role in the coming revolution.[18] Not only were the disorders directed against Autocracy—as *Iskra* insisted—but they were labeled the beginning of a struggle of a great toiling class which, uniting with the already begun campaign of the urban proletariat, would form "one powerful current" flowing toward social revolution. Of course, the first stage would be political revolution and the overthrow of Autocracy, but the SR's must see to it that this triumph would not be "purely bourgeois" but be accompanied by fundamental democratic and social reforms which would lay the groundwork for the future socialization of labor and property. The liberal elements would naturally try to restrict the scope of these reforms, but the situation of Russia's toilers was too grave to permit this.

There was to be a revolution in two phases, then. In this Chernov agreed with Plekhanov. Still there remained the pressing question of the nature of the first phase. What would history and the revolutionaries make it? Or, more precisely, what would the revolutionaries permit history to make it? Not "bourgeois," said the SR's. When *Iskra* talked about a coming "bourgeois revolution" it should bear in mind that one had already taken place. A bourgeois change from below had been averted by one from above when, during the Great Reform era, the serf autocracy was replaced by the ascendancy of a gentry-bourgeois bureaucracy. These changes cleared the way for the development of capitalism. The Russian bourgeoisie—as well as the gentry—saw in Tsarism its protector and defender against the toiling classes, in the cities as in the villages. The bourgeois revolution was over, in other words; but two phases were left. The first phase, overthrowing Tsarism, would be political in nature; the second, establishing socialism, would alter the class structure. The latter would see the destruction of the bourgeois power, which would linger into the first phase. Once the bourgeois revolution has been achieved, as in Italy and Hungary, the peasant revolution does not exhaust itself but continues to move with the workers toward social upheaval. So said the SR writer.

In Russian terms, such social revolt must take the form of socialization of land. The Socialist Revolutionaries were far from idealizing the peasant commune with all its defects, but they believed it foolish to ignore how much easier it would be to proceed to socialization on the basis of the experience of communal traditions. The editors proclaimed agreement with "international socialism" that not the extension of individual freedom of action, but its limitation, was needed in the sphere of economic relations. Above all was this true in respect to the land.

Where then exactly did the SR's stand as to the prospects of revolution? They first of all accepted the orthodox socialist view that a political phase must precede a social one. Yet their distrust and hatred of the middle class led them to refuse to call the first phase-to-be "bourgeois" and made them intensely suspicious of the Social Democrats because of their fondness for the term. Since socialist doctrine bound them to recognize that every country passes through a "bourgeois" change, they suggested that in Russia this was already two generations past. A fully "bourgeois" change, however, would mean the complete victory of capitalism in Russian agriculture, and this they wished at all costs to avoid. Concentration of landownership in a few hands and utter impoverishment of smallholders was, they feared, already taking place. The neopopulists must avert the ruin of the rural masses. How to do this? By following the necessary political revolution with measures of "socialization" as soon as possible. "Stopping" the revolution after the first phase, as Plekhanov seemed to envisage, while capitalism tightened its grip on Russian society, was madness. This would redound only to the benefit of the bourgeoisie. How then could socialists, whose main objective was to crush the middle class, support *Iskra*'s position? On the basis of this reasoning, we may take the puzzlement of *Revolutionary Russia* to be genuine.[19]

From *Iskra*'s side, however, came a counterproblem. Who were the bourgeoisie? The SR's were themselves accused of forgetting the class struggle by taking the side of the peasantry as a whole which was, as Marx had said, a petty bourgeois class. This the SR's failed to "understand." The SR's, who were beginning to develop a touchy pride in their new intellectual sophistication, hotly retorted that they understood the facts well enough, but did not "admit" the Marxist interpretation. In the "peasantry as a whole" there was to be found not one homogeneous group but a whole series of groups quantitative and qualitative. Using as the determinant of class its "source of income" (distribution, not production—and this was of course not Marxism) one could divide the peasants into two groups, the toiling peasantry, who subsisted by the sale of their own labor, and the village bourgeoisie who lived on the exploitation of others. The "working class in the village" included the great mass of toiling agriculturists—not only the *batraki* or village proletariat.

The completely landless and often destitute *batraki* appeared alone among the villagers to be regarded by the Marxists as worthy of attention. V. Posse in the Social Democrat *Life* considered it "possible to rely only on the proletariat," including "of course" the *batraki*. But these village proletarians were only a small fraction of the peasantry, and moreover as Plekhanov [20] himself confessed, "the *batraki* are the most hopeless part of the village workers in the sense of receptiveness to revolutionary propaganda." No wonder Posse went on to declare that even "without a revolutionary peasant movement" of the useless *batraki*, the overthrow of Tsarism would not be impossible. That event, Posse wrote, would probably "take place much more simply than the comrade relying on the 'voice of the village' thinks." Such bland indifference to the role of the peasantry filled the SR's with rage. Did these Marxists actually think revolution "is possible apart from and even against the will of the peasantry?" Why say socialism would come most easily by relying on the helpless *batraki*, ignoring the bulk of the peasants? If the Marxists intended to bypass the masses, they were advised to think twice before condemning Blanquists who rely on a "revolutionary minority."

The problem of where to fit peasants into the schemata of scientific socialism was one which troubled both SR's and Marxists for many years. Both Chernov and Lenin used the tactic of taking the "peasantry as a whole" apart, which seemed very "scientific" indeed. However, it was found that under analysis this amorphous mass kept breaking at inconvenient seams. No particular piece, any more than the awkward whole, seemed a completely trustworthy vehicle for the future socialist Utopia.

In the moment of the 1902 riots, this question seemed urgent to the neo-populists in particular because they foresaw that this peasant insurgence was only the first of many swallows of the summer to come. When *Iskra* was reported to have ignored its own correspondents for these riots and concluded by deduction that they represented a village bourgeois-proletarian coalition against the remnants of serfdom, the SR's violently objected. [21] It was plain to them that the riots were what they at first appeared to be: a movement against the bourgeoisie and capitalism, not feudalism.

They were of course applying thereby their own preferred schemata as the Marxists had done. No one thought of taking the peasants' word for what they wanted.

By 1903 the refurbished populists, intent on passing as respectable among the ranks of international socialism in their new SR dress, were thus once more locked in close literary combat with their victorious adversaries of the 90's, the Marxists. *Iskra* denounced Socialist Revolutionism bitterly as a "socialist fog" [22] which hindered the growth of proletarian self-consciousness, since it tried uselessly to base itself on an union of proletariat, peasantry, and intelligentsia. In Marxist eyes these three groups were respectively a class, half a class, and no class at all. Anyway, said *Iskra*, only a handful of the intelligentsia were ready to cast their lot with the "stormy and turbulent" life of the revolutionary proletariat, while the peasantry still had only democratic and not socialist demands in common with the urban workers.

This warning to the SR craft to stay out of revolutionary waters provoked a counter-threat. *Revolutionary Russia* had kept the way open for close cooperation with the Social Democrats. Now, however, it declared that apparently the precondition of such unity was for the SR's to renounce their own convictions on the role of the non-proletarian groups. There must be accepted the war between the two parties which the Marxists already were preaching. The Socialist Revolutionaries would work toward socialism in their own way. They would try to see that the Russian revolution did not stop before it set fire to Western Europe and roused the proletariat of the whole world. But if it did not, the neo-populists would not permit the Russian revolt to remain within political bounds, but would urge it on to a denouement which would not be socialism—but would be a long step in that direction. Thus the revolution would "develop further and further" in the fight for all land, all freedom, all socialism. SR's would not be content with repeating that the coming revolution was "bourgeois, bourgeois, and bourgeois" and talk only about "some kind of *otrezki*." This was a sneer at the Social Democratic agrarian program which was still confined to a demand for return of the lands "cut-off" in 1861 to their former peasant owners. This plank sounded something more than modest to the SR's if regarded as a socialist demand.

In this article the neo-populist editors made one of the earliest contributions to the theory which Social Democrats later called "permanent revolution." Already Lenin's debt to the SR's becomes an interesting question, the more so since Lenin, unlike Trotsky, came to rely on the peasantry strongly. The first step of revolution in Russia would touch off a worldwide conflagration, it was hoped, but Russians would not remain passive in their own tasks if it did not.

While the SR's pointed with passion to the implications of peasant revolutionism for the future, they did not, however, forget or minimize the role of the workers. Had not Chernov in the 90's allotted them the role of "vanguard"? After the strike in Rostov at the end of 1902, *Revolutionary Russia* wrote that "the organized proletariat is indeed rising to the head of the general oppositional movement." [23] It added, nevertheless, what may have been a true fable about a peasant in a village assembly who read about the Rostov events and lamented that *they* didn't get any books telling how to revolt, or "we would also have raised a riot even better than in Rostov!" No one recalled that Pugachov's followers, for example, had needed no "little books" to tell them how to revolt; but it appeared as if intellectualism was spreading even to the propagandized portion of the peasantry. The SR contention, at any rate, was that the peasant was treading on the heels of his proletarian leader, and only needed organization to give voice to his spontaneous discontent.

The time had come when the SR's decided they could no longer delay making their agrarian objectives more precise.[24] Land reform could take either the shape of division (of large holdings to increase existing small private lots) or of "socialization" (equal landholding through the increase of "social property.") What this meant exactly will be discussed later, though in fact its meaning never became completely clear. For the time being let us follow the discussion as it appeared piecemeal in the press of the time, in order better to appreciate the bewilderment of contemporaries. How could this "socialization" be achieved? As in the case of the socialists in Holland, in Russia the SR's relied upon the communes as the agency of reform. The Peasant Union of the SR Party used the slogan "socialization" rather than "nationalization," the more popular term. They preferred it, despite the fact that *sotsializatsiia* was an unfamiliar word and the Slavonic equivalent *obobshchestvleniia* tripped even Russian tongues, since they emphasized the role of local agencies and deemphasized that of the central government. It is not clear what conditions the SR's assumed would prevail when the time came to "socialize" land, but whether or not a purely toilers' government would be in power, it is clear that the commune was regarded as the safest means of control when the lands of the gentry, church, and state were divided. Curiously enough, "socialization" of land was intended in the SR scheme to *precede*, not accompany, the coming of socialism, but this was not yet made clear.

Although the SR's did not believe their socialist aims could be instantly realized, they remained suspicious that the Social Democrats were not really socialist at all. When the SD's published a draft program declaring their ultimate end to be "social revolution" —simply repeating orthodox Marxism—the editors of Revolutionary Russia declared their skepticism once again. Lenin admitted that in their program-minimum, Marxists asked only social reforms which the bourgeoisie could grant without losing their ascendancy. To this the writer Novobrantsev[25] replied that the idea of postponing every kind of social change except purely bourgeois ones was not original with *Iskra*. Some German Social Democrats had done likewise, and as their final objectives became ever paler, they had emphasized immediate aims the more. He would not describe the *Iskra* program as entirely reformist, however. In its peasant section, he found it to be revolutionary, but this was a dubious compliment. *Iskra* aimed only at converting feudal dependence in agriculture into bourgeois dependence—thus *Iskra's* "socialism!" Then Novobrantsev found some gentler words for his Social Democratic rivals. Gentle, and condescending; and here was a new note in populist journalism. Only now that the SR's had attained a degree of scientific-socialist respectability could they use a superior tone to the orthodox Marxists, and the satisfaction this gave them was not concealed. Make no mistake, wrote Novobrantsev, these Social Democrats *are* socialists, but are simply confused by dogma. What partially misled them was the leadership of Western liberation movements by the bourgeoisie, though they ought to have seen by now that "the bourgeoisie does not think at all about its providential mission." In fact, he declared, all attempts in Russia to attract the bourgeoisie as a class to the political struggle proved in vain. Instead there were only isolated groups like that sponsoring *Liberation*—which *Iskra* treats like an organ of the bourgeois class as a whole. "There is no use talking, it has found the bourgeoisie!" taunted Novobrantsev—that is to say, the role of the bourgeois class would be no more significant than that of this lonely newspaper. What *Iskra* must realize finally is that "the political liberation of Russia is the business of the Russian intelligentsia and the Russian laboring people . . . and that no one else will take active part in it." Since this is so, to intelligentsia, workers, and peasants alone belong the social results of the future revolution—not to the bourgeoisie!

In this manner the Socialist Revolutionaries came increasingly close to charging Marxists with selling out the peasantry for the sake of the middle class, and thus confronted the question of defining their own attitude toward the nascent Russian liberal groups.

6.

When the liberal paper, *Liberation,* had first begun to appear, *Revolutionary Russia* noted that in the past Russian liberals had never achieved anything important.[26] However, it conceded it was no use eternally to repeat the old accusations; one had to take the liberals as they were. "The misfortune of Russian liberalism is that supporting it we find no definite, integral and strong class." Instead there were only the liberal professions and part of the zemstvo gentry which refused to be solaced with the sops which were thrown it by a Tsardom which protected industrialists first. Both the Social Democrats, representing wage labor, and the Socialist Revolutionaries, representing all labor, stood over against the liberals, who defended no definite social interests.

Nevertheless, the editors continued, the liberals were a force, even if absolutely not large, and could if they wished render important services to the "common task of political liberation." If they decided not to try to drive the government into concessions for their own sole benefit, and instead chose to "go hand in hand with the representatives of revolutionary socialism" against autocracy, then "mutual aid and support is possible, opportune, and desirable" for the time being—all parties realizing that when Autocracy was destroyed, the two paths would diverge. In history more than once yesterday's allies had become tomorrow's enemies, but "this did not prevent them from fulfilling honorably in relation to each other the obligations of allies." Thus did the neo-populists, shunning their older generation's traditional contempt for the liberals, approach them. They moved in a rather gingerly fashion, with the condescension proper for a self-respecting revolutionary group, but they approached nonetheless. First there must be a straightforward exchange of views on the literary level, then there might be official liberal-SR talks.

A few months later,[27] the neo-populist organ recalled the "excellent words" of Stepniak about "factional pride and *mestnichestvo*" which made revolutionaries snub liberals. It added, only "give us the organized force of Russian liberalism, sincerely and consistently following its oppositional tactics," and we will show our own readiness to go side by side wherever possible in certain questions. We will not expect their "conversion into revolutionary socialists" nor ask anything inconsistent with their own convictions, but we will demand firmness and consistency. There was still a hedge, however. *Revolutionary Russia* asserted there was as yet no liberal force in existence, only flickering and changing sparks of one.

This mildness to the liberals did not mean that the SR's, always attentive to "class basis," were ready to cooperate with the gentry— who furnished a good section of the liberals—as a class, or as a whole. How could they suddenly forget the gentry's past crimes and harsh treatment of the peasants? One rude contributor urged them openly, "Go together with your Tsar, the chief Russian pomeshchik, your protector and supporter." [28]

Nevertheless the SR spokesmen did not identify the liberals with the gentry as a class. Struve's party, said one, could not indeed repre- sent the industrialist or landlord classes as such, but only certain of their elements which had abandoned the bourgeois-plutocratic regime. [29] It was true that the liberals had not come entirely over to socialism, but "they are not hostile to socialism, they simply believe in it badly" and are not averse to adopting socialist mini- mum programs as their own final demands. Furthermore, while the industrialists and gentry in general do not yet hoist the liberal standard, as the monarchy weakens they can be expected to desert it. Meanwhile where did Struve and his group stand? Struve, it was noted, presented himself as an advocate of union with the Left, yet he was also making certain overtures to "semi-constitu- tionalists" on the Right. With such a mixed bag, "who will go to- gether with whom whither?" It would be much better if Struve would organize a reformist party on the lines of the French Socialist- Radicals, for example.

Now that they had made clear their own attitude toward the liberals, the SR's sailed into the SD's with renewed vigor for their overfondness for them. A regular columnist of *Revolutionary Russia* insulted the Marxists by attributing to them a "mid-position . . . between on the one hand the representatives of the Left wing of the revolutionary army [the SR's] and on the other the adherents of *Liberation* . . . who often came from the ranks of Social Democ- racy itself." [30] Had Marxists and liberals not joined together in the past to fight populism? Evidence was found not only in Social Demo- cratic tactics, but in their agrarian program, whose similarity to that of the liberals Lenin had admitted in the pages of *Iskra*.[31]

Nevertheless, Lenin's own special position in Marxist ranks with regard to the role of the peasantry was gradually being recognized by the SR's. When he wrote the article "The Worker's Party and the Peasantry," a neo-populist labeled it a landmark in the evolution of Marxist views on the rural masses. This writer suggested that Marxist confusion on the point was due to the mixture of their own ideas with those of the bourgeois "legal Marxists" in the 90's. It was suggested that Economism had been one product of just this mixture. Of course the Marxists did not explain Economism as the result of an amalgam of views or the effect of a reactionary period, but as an accident due to the arrest of all the "politicals," leaving only "Economists" at liberty. This account was scorned as one ludicrous coming from a "dialectical materialist." But this was an incidental point. Wherever the Marxists had gone wrong, the SR now thought Lenin had advanced to the same position as his populist opponents of the 90's, namely, that of believing the proletariat too narrow a foundation for the political revolution. "Better late than never," at any rate. Yet Lenin did not escape criticism despite his "evolution." He persisted in saying that in the immediate future the struggle of all peasants against the landlords would be more significant than the fight of village proletariat with village bourgeoisie, and therefore, that the Marxist agrarian program must be designed to introduce into the village conditions of life "adapted to bourgeois society." In Lenin's reasoning the SR's found fresh confirmation of their suspicions that bourgeois influence infected the thought of their Marxist rivals.

7.

As the mass movement swelled and swirled around the tiny islands of revolutionary journalism, the SR's took heart. It was not that they were so foolish as to believe the scattered copies of the party organ had raised a revolutionary storm among the people. That was not its function. Its function was to define the party's tactical line and its relations with its competitors in accordance with its expectations for the future, its analysis of the course of the revolution. Then when the expected mass movement appeared, the party would be ready. The opportunity seemed near at hand as Tsarism became deeply involved in a Far Eastern war.

Shortly after the outbreak of fighting, *Revolutionary Russia* finally published the draft of a party program.[32] In it minimum demands were distinguished from maximum ones from the stand-point of the orthodox socialist view of the two-phase revolution which Russia must undergo. The expropriation of capitalist pro-perty and socialist reorganization of production presupposed the complete victory of the working class, which was not immediately possible because of its weakness. Therefore in the first stage SR's could only demand limited reforms. These included political liberty, convocation of a Constituent Assembly, and the eight-hour day in factories. In respect to agriculture, they demanded first expansion of the communes through use of confiscated private and State lands, then, utilizing the "communal traditions" under which the land was supposed to be regarded by the peasants as the common property of all who worked it, there would come "socializa-tion" of all private properties on the basis of equal land use. Thus this kind of "socialization" did not mean "socialism" to the SR's. Complete nationalization of the land could only be realized, it was declared, in so far as "democratization" made progress.

What the SR's intended precisely to do with the land still re-mained unclear, but the political consequences of such a party pro-gram in general could not be doubted. The program was definitely founded on the premise that the "first," imminent stage of revolu-tion would not bring full socialism to Russia. In this basic premise—and desire—Marxists and liberals concurred. There was no obstacle to the search for allies now, and the SR's now made open overtures to their competitors.

Among the socialist parties, said *Revolutionary Russia,* "a cer-tain relative unity" would be enough for the needs of the moment. Owing to antagonism between the interests of labor and all other parties, "no sort of solid and constant union" was possible with liberal opposition groups, and SR's could accept no compromise political line which a liberal-socialist bloc would presuppose. There could be no bloc, but there could be an alliance. It would be foolish to forget that the enemy of the socialists' enemy was, if not a friend, then "a temporary fellow-traveler, an accidental ally." In such an alliance SR's together with SD's could counterbalance any undue liberal influence, any second-thoughts of backtracking or compromise.

Just such an alliance was the objective of an inter-party con-ference summoned to meet at Paris on the initiative of a Finnish opposition group, in late 1904.[33] The Socialist Revolutionaries found that this meeting not only fell short of their hopes but back-fired disconcertingly. The Social Democrats, on whom they had counted, and who had given an assurance through Plekhanov[34] that they would attend, not only absented themselves but condemned the whole venture as petty bourgeois. The Paris conference, however, did the best it could with the SR's, Liberationists and numerous groups from the minority nationalities who were present. Agreement was reached on two distinct declarations, one by the socialist parties, the other by all opposition groups present, socialist and nonsocialist. The socialists agreed that "we now unite our forces" for the destruction of autocracy and the realization of socialism. The general declaration said only that while no group "for a minute" would forget any of its own demands, all signatories united in three objectives: the end of Autocracy, its replacement by a "free democratic regime" based on universal suffrage, and the right of national self-determination. Such vexatious questions as the future of the monarchy were sidestepped, and a proclamation was arrived at which could be signed by nine parties.

Zilliacus, who was the originator of this conference, declared[35] that it made possible bringing liberals and revolutionaries "into one united party" which is in itself grossly inaccurate, though undoubtedly intended as simplification for an English-reading public which knew nothing of Russian political parties. Indeed the conference had no direct and concrete results at all. It symbolized the unity of the Russian opposition against its Tsarist opponent, and the consequent "defeatism" of the whole spectrum of parties vis-a-vis the Russian government in the war with Japan. But it did nothing more. It failed to achieve the sort of opposition front the SR's wanted and it unexpectedly embarrassed them in their relations with the SD's to be found alone in such a grouping. It did however bring the SR's as close as they ever came to understanding with the liberals.

In the Left-liberal Liberationists who came to the Paris conference, the SR journal detected an attitude that was anti-bourgeois, "though only vulgarly so." The growth of the Union of Liberation was welcomed as likely to hasten the differentiation in the liberal-gentry camp between those who wanted to use the revolution as a screen for compromise with Tsarism, and those who realized freedom could not be attained if they helped autocracy against the revolutionaries. This differentiation would be deepened, it was predicted, by the pressure of socialists from without.

This was the position of the Socialist Revolutionaries when the procession of "Bloody Sunday" heralded the outbreak of "revolution." Seeing in the Social Democrats signs of an internal disagreement which seemed to relate to the point which interested them most, the peasants' role, they still believed the Bolshevik-Menshevik split was a more or less fortuitous difference about tactics rather than principles, as Lenin himself insisted. They did not bother to consider the consequences if the split should be permanent, or to weigh the possibility of closer relations with the more peasant-minded Bolshevik wing. The two rival socialist groups, Marxist and populist, had fought bitterly in the past and probably would continue to do so. But the Socialist Revolutionaries saw this as no obstacle to their practical cooperation in the revolution, and they could cite the efforts of successful joint-party committees in Russia as hopeful portents. They were, however, shocked by the refusal of the Marxists to attend the Paris conference, and all their old suspicions were reinvigorated. In relation to the liberals, the neo-populists embarked on a kind of nose-holding, arm's-length collaboration toward what they regarded as the crucial and immediate objective: the overthrow of Tsarism.

V

TWO KINDS OF MARXISTS

> *"It* [the II Congress of the Social Democratic Party] *had been assembled to constitute a party. It would take at least ten years to realize that it had really constituted not one party but two."*
> BERTRAM D. WOLFE.[1]

In 1898 Russian Marxists seemed to be clearly on the way to achieving their goal. The revolution was in sight, that Russian revolution towards which the Cossack Pugachov had groped, which the Decembrist nobles had bungled, which the People's Will had utterly failed to set in motion; that revolution which would by eradicating the remnants of feudalism, put Russia astride the rails of the bourgeois capitalist development England and France were enjoying. But more than this. In Russia, there existed certain special conditions—the discontent of the peasants, the heavy concentration of industry, and the weakness of the Old Regime. Owing to their presence, the capitalist train would be stoked up to run not merely at full throttle, but at many times that speed. It would flash over the rails like lightning to its certain wreck, its swift self-destruction, and from its remains socialism would spring. In this way the Russian economy, the Russian people, would not only catch up with the West but using the West's political weapons would overtake it. This was the denouement for which all Russian Marxists hoped. The question which split them in two was this: who would be at the throttle? Could Marxists dare allow the bourgeois machine to run ungoverned? Could they safely sit by to await the wreck, or must they mount the engineer's seat themselves? Must the job of making certain capitalism was wrecked be entrusted to socialists? The question had not arisen before. In the West, when the "bourgeois revolutions" had taken place, there had been no Marxists. Now, in Russia, there were. What must be done?

The Mensheviks answered that capitalism must wreck itself. No spokesmen of the proletariat could take the throttle while the train ran on "bourgeois" time. The Bolsheviks said plainly that Marxists must sit in the driver's seat. The alternative, as Lenin saw it, could only be a Liberal engineer, and this had to be avoided at all costs. Lenin thus came to the original notion of a bourgeois revolution without and even against the bourgeoisie—a notion fateful for the future of Russia.

2.

In 1898, however, the Great Schism which was to split not only Russian, but international socialism wide open in the next decades was still in the future. Though signs of the opening fissure may be observed even that early, quite different problems and debates then agitated Russian Social Democratic ranks. After an ideological struggle against populism in the 90's, Marxists had emerged the apparent victors in a way which seemed to justify Plekhanov's wildest hopes in 1883. In the debates of the 90's they had gained a wide hearing among politically conscious groups of Russians at home and abroad. Their claims to present a "scientific" analysis of the forces remaking society had won for them an authoritative and respected position in all debates on current social questions. They had a number of able theoreticians with long revolutionary experience and prestige. These men and women had a confidence in the truth of their beliefs which was unequaled in the opposition movement. To this "truth" they had already dedicated their careers, their very lives. Any revolutionary had to live a perilous, shabby existence in Tsarist Russia, but these personal sacrifices were scarcely noticed by Marxists who counted the will and emotions of individual men as unimportant. Even family life readily became but an aspect of the political struggle. Revolutionists' wives had to think not about the needs and expenses of home and children, but of the party. Often the wives were revolutionaries in their own right as well. With such a dedicated cadre of leaders, the Marxists were in a position to be offensive-minded in their battle with Tsarism and in the partly friendly, partly hostile competition with other parties.

In March 1898 the Social Democrats had held their I Congress and the party—Russia's first—had been officially founded. It was hoped at that time, Martov writes,[2] that the widespread strike movement of the previous few years could serve as the foundation for creating a mass revolutionary party at once. But the winter of

1898-9 revealed the extent of that over-optimism. The workers' enthusiasm dwindled as their strikes began to fail. The retreating tide left only pools of revolutionary intellectuals, as before, who mulled over the consequences of their experience and engaged in heated doctrinal disputes as to the best way to rebuild the movement.

These disputes centered on the issue of "Economism." The temporary success of the strikes in improving working conditions had given rise to a Marxist current which stoutly defended the value of the "economic" struggle, if necessary postponing or even abandoning the fight for political liberty. The outstanding literary exponent of Economism in Russia was the organ of the St. Petersburg Union of Struggle for the Emancipation of the Working Class. This group Lenin had helped organize before he was arrested, but it had since strayed from his viewpoint. Its organ, *Workers' Thought*,[3] declared in the fall of 1899 that for the moment it believed the workers movement did not include many who were concerned with political ends, except to some extent in the two capitals, and also in the Jewish Bund—which was regarded as an exceptional phenomenon. The best means to conduct an "indirect and in part direct" struggle, allied with "all advanced strata" of Russian society, against autocracy, was considered to be the fostering of the "social and political independence" of the workers. The "advanced strata" proved on examination to be of minor importance, however, as allies. Both upper and petty bourgeoisie were divided, and it was erroneous to speak of the petty bourgeoisie as entirely opposition-minded, though the most advanced elements of both were sniping at autocratic bureaucracy. As for the peasantry, it was seen as swallowing up in its inert mass the few resistance-minded religious Sectarians, and as a group it was said to be only passively opposed to the Autocracy. The workers by default took the spotlight in Economist eyes. *Workers' Thought* could not understand those who viewed the lightening of the workers' burden as merely a sideline to the overthrow of Autocracy, or those who answered the thorny question of where to find the force to fight Tsarism with the glib answer, "emancipation of labor."[4] Such opinions were expected from the "so-called revolutionary intelligentsia" who, pursued by the political police, had often mistaken the fight with detectives for the fight against the Old Regime.

These were sharp words, but natural words when hurled by men in the midst of danger and day-to-day struggle in the direction of distant and secure pen-pushers. Lenin, who himself was pushing his pen in comfortless Siberian exile, ignored the taunts and stuck to the argument. *Workers' Thought,* he contended,[5] took much too narrow a view of the workers' movement and confused the seizure of power by revolutionaries with the overthrow of Autocracy—by which he meant, said he, the granting of a *"constitutional* form of government." Without this, the workers could never broaden the base of their efforts, build up mass organizations, and teach their members how to fight for social revolution. In fact, he wrote, the whole program of *Workers' Thought* added up simply to leaving the Russian workers in their backwardness and converting them into a "tail of the liberals."

Here we see Lenin in ambivalent transition. Clinging to the Marxist premise of dual revolution, he was nevertheless already rejecting liberal leadership—or cooperation, which meant practically the same thing to him since the liberals would always try to lead —for the first, bourgeois, "constitutional" phase. But the nature of his antipathy to Economism only becomes clear when one examines his reaction to what other Marxist intellectuals said in defense of it. The *Credo* of Kuskova, published in 1899, shocked him deeply. This document insisted that "intolerant, negative, primitive Marxism must yield to democratic Marxism," and that the Russian Marxist, adapting himself to special Russian conditions, must now "assist in the economic struggle of the proletariat, and take part in liberal opposition activity." In reply to this manifesto, Lenin organized among other Marxist exiles a *Protest*[6] which defended the struggle for political liberty as the greatest immediate task. However, this was not to mean that the workers, in carrying on their fight, must regard all other groups as a "homogeneous reactionary mass," which he termed an anti-Marxist conception. The workers must support all progressive classes and parties against reactionary groups, every revolutionary movement against the present system.

What the orthodox exiles were protesting against, it was clear, was not the fight of the workers for economic betterment, not the "Economism" as such. What alarmed them was the willingness of Economist theorists to leave politics to the middle class, even if only temporarily. The workers must take the lead; the Economists' teachings threatened this principle, and so Lenin proposed to Martov and Potresov a "serious war"[7] against the critics of orthodoxy. This "war" would be launched by the publication of a journal abroad. Only when a new type of literature and a definite party program were created could "the real comrades be differentiated from the 'camp-followers' and then only will personal caprices and staggering theoretical discoveries cease to cause confusion and anarchy." Thus the idea of the journal *Iskra* was born.

3.

In 1898 both Lenin and Axelrod had set forth the objectives of the orthodox intellectuals for the party. Lenin then seemed indeed to believe the revolution was in sight, for he referred to the passing of the period of theoretical definition within the party, and declared the question of practical activity to be the most urgent one. Such practical activity was to be solidly based on support of the industrial workers, the most capable of imbibing Social Democratic ideas, the most developed class intellectually and politically, the most important both as to numbers and concentration in important political centers. Thus situated, the urban proletariat, owing to its many ties with the countryside, came into contact with village craftsmen and the rural proletariat, thus causing an outflow of ideas into other exploited groups. While concentrating on factory workers, Marxists could also support those other revolutionary groups "who, in practice, are beginning to base their socialist work on the class struggle of the proletariat."[8] This they could do without compromising any of their own principles. The Marxists were convinced that "the only revolutionary theory which can serve as the banner of the revolutionary movement" was scientific socialism. The tasks posed by this socialist doctrine, however, were inseparably linked with political agitation for democratic objectives. The difference was that in the future socialist phase the proletariat would have to stand alone, but in the political struggle immediately in prospect all elements hostile to autocracy could be on its side. For various reasons all such elements would hesitate, look back, and waver. Only the proletariat, "singled out as the vanguard," could successfully lead the way. The conclusion was that not only all socialists, but all "consistent democrats" must accept the workers' leadership, must become Social Democrats. There could be no question, in other words, of yielding the political foreground to the liberals as the Economists seemed willing to do.

Axelrod, writing in the same year, tried to show that Social Democratic workers might not need to accept liberal leadership in order to obtain liberal assistance.[9] The alternative he posed for the Marxists was either to remain in the purely economic struggle, following along behind the liberals toward political freedom, or to organize an independent political party and take the lead themselves. The first alternative was a dangerous one. "St. Petersburg strikes," that is, the great demonstrations which preceded the 11½ hour day law, came but seldom, and were attended with many difficulties. The failure of such tactics might exhaust the workers' forces for a long period. If the second alternative was chosen, the prospect looked brighter. In the "economic" struggle the workers had to fight their capitalist employers; but in the political fight proletariat need not fight bourgeoisie, since the latter had not yet attained political power. In the fight for democracy the workers would even be aided by certain sections of the bourgeoisie. Such warfare was made easier by the growth of a liberal press, the spread of books and education, the development of the zemstvo institutions. All these beginnings of constitutional life in Russia, said Axelrod, fortunately had a more revolutionary spirit than similar manifestations in the West. Social Democrats must mold them further, converting them into "weapons for the revolutionizing of the mass of the people." The future Menshevik thus painted a hopeful perspective if the seductions of Economism were rejected by Russian workers; but he ended his exposition on a note of warning of the degree of Economist strength at the moment.

These two manifestoes, from exiles in Siberia and Switzerland, set out the objective for which the Siberian exiles now returned to Russia to fight. First of all, a plan was considered to call a second party congress to reestablish the organization destroyed by the police after the Minsk[10] meeting, but this proved impossible. Next it was proposed to publish *Iskra* as a coalition newspaper in which both Marxists and liberals would take part. In order to consider this scheme, Lenin, Martov, and Potresov had a conference in Pskov with Struve and Tugan-Baranovskii, who were by now openly in schism with their orthodox fellows and had become the more acceptable to Lenin for having cast off the Social Democratic "mask" to show their true "bourgeois" colors.[11] Struve and Tugan-Baranovskii represented the "general democracy" which Lenin thought *Iskra* should serve, though its editorial viewpoint was to be definitely orthodox. The Pskov talks failed, however. The three returned exiles then proceeded abroad to discuss the problem with the severely anti-Economist Group for Emancipation of Labor. Axelrod was cooperative, but Plekhanov, Lenin's revered master of doctrine, showed reluctance to take his allotted place in the new enterprise, and Lenin decided he was a "bad, insincere man."[12] Despite hard feelings, agreement was reached with the Swiss exiles, though *Iskra* was set up in Munich in order to be free from the interference of Plekhanov in particular.

The idea of an accord with Struve was not abandoned completely until after further unsuccessful talks at the end of 1900 and the beginning of 1901. At that time the editors of *Iskra*[13] declared that they realized the need to support the progressive movement, but that they could not unite in one party with it. To this the Struve faction replied that they likewise recognized "the primary political significance and mission of the Russian workers' movement. In it the political idea of the intelligentsia has found for itself a powerful ally." However, Lenin told Plekhanov[14] that "when we are informed with infuriating insolence that . . . [*Iskra* and *Zaria*] must not compete with the political venture of those gentlemen, the Liberals, then our pathetic role becomes as clear as day," and he saw such a prospect as incompatible with "our getting a real hegemony." Struve made a contribution or two to *Iskra* but otherwise this marked the end of friendly relations between him and the orthodox leaders.

4.

Iskra began publication when the orthodox leaders were still hard pressed by the Economist heretics. In exile Lenin and his fellows encountered the Economists' emigre representatives, who were more subtle and cautious, and therefore more formidable, than the Petersburg union leaders who published *Workers' Thought*. A Union of Russian Social Democrats Abroad had been divided from its very beginnings at the end of 1898 over the issue of Economism. The Group for Emancipation of Labor had refused to take part in the Union's organ, *Workers' Cause,* and when the *Iskra* group was organized it led the orthodox circles out of the Union entirely to form a new organization in April 1900.[15] Two conferences during the summer of 1901 failed to patch up this schism. Meanwhile *Workers' Cause,* supported by Kuskova, S. N. Prokopovich, B. Krichevskii, Martynov, and other emigres, continued to take a sympathetic line toward Economism by denying that it threatened orthodoxy, or that it even existed at all. At first this journal had made the fully orthodox declaration[16] that it would expose the difference between the interests of the working class and other non-socialist opposition groups, though it would be sympathetic towards any efforts to struggle actively for political freedom "since every kind of enemy of Autocracy is the *temporary* ally of the working class in its struggle for liberation." Soon, however, suspicious statements began to appear. When Axelrod repeated reports from some "travelers" from Russia that Economism was predominant among Social Democrats there, the editors of the *Workers' Cause* professed ignorance of who was meant. Plekhanov now delivered a broadside against the magazine.[17] He accused one writer of pretending to abjure Economism much as Peter denied Jesus, hypocritically when under fire. Lenin hailed this assault of Plekhanov as "simply a wail against Economism, against the disgrace and shame of Social Democracy." As for *Workers' Cause,* its use of the slogan "freedom of criticism" to protect Economists was equivalent to a demand for "free criticism of Marxism on the part of all sorts of direct and disguised ideologies of the bourgeoisie."

Lenin's own attack on Economism was made in the brochure *What is to be Done?*[18] Not a single paragraph was devoted to a discussion of the importance of the "economic" side of the workers' struggle. It was rather other transgressions of the men labeled "Economists" which concerned him. Their alleged theoretical looseness and defense of practical "spontaneity" evoked his strongest language. The Economists, said he, opposed "dogmatism" in the same way as did the "legal Marxists" a little earlier. They pointed to the wide range of views permitted in the ranks of German Social Democrats, ignoring the fact that the Revisionists who followed Bernstein, for example, had to be bound by the orthodox resolutions of the whole party. They minimized the force of theory, though Marx and Engels had sharply condemned eclecticism and emphasized the importance of theory very strongly. It was recalled that Engels had written of German workers that they "belong to the most theoretical people of Europe; they have retained that sense of theory which the so-called 'educated' people of Germany have almost completely lost . . . [and without which] scientific Socialism would never have passed so entirely into their flesh and blood . . ."[19] By distinguishing between the theoretical proclivities of German exploited and exploiters, Engels had avoided racialism, and Lenin as an internationalist was glad enough that the German workers displayed this theoretical trait. He himself had already asserted the same to be true of Russian workers—"the most capable of imbibing Social Democratic ideas" of any Russian class, he had written in 1898. "The role of vanguard fighter," added Lenin, "can be fulfilled only by a party that is guided by the most advanced theory."

Not only did the Economist refuse to accord systematic theory its proper place, according to Lenin, but they ignored the importance of systematic organisation for practical work. He identified his opponents' ideas with "spontaneity," which characterized the strike movement of the 90's. But "spontaneity" was nothing but "consciousness in an embryonic form." Instead of advancing to develop a mature form of "consciousness" among the workers, Economism bows to spontaneity, dragging at the tail of the movement, and preaches "tailism" and "primitive methods." By attending only to the economic struggle, the Economists "yield to liberalism, abandon the task of actively intervening *in every* "liberal" question and of defining *their own* Social Democratic attitude" towards each issue. They mistakenly dismiss as a "phantom" the existence of bourgeois democracy, which actually is only awaiting the chance to take the initiative. To counter the bourgeois democratic threat, Lenin offered clear advice. Social Democrats must build as good an organization as *Land and Liberty*, or a better one, but in contrast to it one inspired by a genuinely revolutionary theory. Moreover, it must be led by "professional revolutionaries" capable of directing the movement under conditions of absolutism, governed by rules of "strict secrecy, strict selection of members." Open, "democratic" organizational methods under Tsarism amount to a "useless and harmful toy." Lenin concluded by drawing up a scheme of periods of Social Democratic growth, in order to indicate that his Economist adversaries were both pernicious and *passé*. The periods were: 1884-94, rise and consolidation of theory and program; 1894-8, appearance of Social Democracy as a mass social movement; 1898-? "dispersion, dissolution, and vacillation," symbolized by *Workers' Cause*. The answer to "What is to be done?" was, "Liquidate the third period"—that is, wipe out Economism.

5.

The importance of *What is to be Done?* transcends the issue of Economism. The idea of the brochure which has received the most attention was that of building a highly-trained clandestine nucleus of "professional revolutionaries." The criteria of fitness for this group were neither charismatic individual gifts nor race nor even class, for children might escape the group prejudices of their parents. The important thing was training—training in the understanding and application of Marxism. Some regarded this concept as likely to lead to the domination of "intellectuals" in the party. Lenin feared no such thing because he denied that the word had any significance in the dialectics of history. He could readily enough identify the men referred to by the term "intellectual", but while he might urge some of them to alter their personal habits by having more contact with the real world, he saw no possibility of their acting as an independent historical force. They could become powerful only insofar as they could attract the support of, and thus come to "represent," economic classes. Marxism gave Lenin no other basis for evaluating the role of the intellectual, and Marxism gave Lenin's critics no solid basis for expressing the vague danger they sensed in the idea of "professional revolutionaries."

Whatever the practical effects of the idea might be, it is worth asking why Lenin set it forth. It is obviously possible that he simply liked the idea of a tight, consecrated elite. However, it seems clear that Lenin's conscious reasoning behind the development of the notion was that it was designed to meet a fundamental need for self-defense. The party's need to defend itself compelled it to have so few and so shrewd leaders. Against what must it defend itself? Lenin's answer was twofold. In the first place, he said Autocracy rendered democratic methods in the party useless. This is plain enough; no one could doubt that "democratic methods" were more difficult to practice under Tsarism than in the West. Was Lenin only interested in this truism? Evidently not. His whole exposition in *What is to be Done?* is based on the charge that Economists threaten sound theory and sound practice by "degrading our political and organizational tasks to the level of . . . the everyday economic struggle." The task of Social Democrats, he says, is "to *divert* the labor movement from its spontaneous, trade unionist striving to go under the wing of the bourgeoisie." "To belittle the socialist ideology . . . *in the slightest degree* means to strengthen bourgeois ideology." Freedom of criticism means "freedom to convert Social Democracy into a democratic reformist party, the freedom to introduce bourgeois ideas and bourgeois elements into socialism." What is it then precisely that the Economists are doing to harm the Marxist cause? The answer is that they open the doors of the Social Democratic citadel to liberals, for it is "the *liberals* [italics added] who bring to the workers the Brentano conception of the class struggle and the trade union conception of politics." Fear of the bourgeois politician, and correspondingly high evaluation of his capacity to "wreck" socialist plans, were elements which carried over into all Lenin's thought and action, and into that of the Soviet leaders after him. A tight party nucleus, therefore, was sought as a means of self-defense not only or chiefly against the Tsar's detectives, but against liberal politicians. The idea of "professional revolutionaries" was a means of safeguarding the interpretation and application of the only correct revolutionary theory from the infiltration of a dangerous competitor—the bourgeoisie.

6.

Let us then recapitulate the chief objection of the orthodox Marxists in relation to Economism. It had nothing to do with the comparative value of "economic" and "political" struggle per se. It was based on the desire to assure constant and "conscious" leadership of the revolutionary movement by the workers, a leadership which the orthodox believed Economism endangered.

The grounds on which the orthodox attacked the Economists were both Western and rationalist. The experience and teaching of the senior Western Marxists, the German Social Democratic party, were constantly cited, not only by the orthodox but also by their opponents. The editors of *Workers' Thought* referred to Bernstein in support of their own ideas, but not because he was a doctrinal deviant but because he was organizationally a German Social Democrat in good standing. The Economists roused orthodox ire, however, by relying on empiricism, or "opportunism," as it would soon be labeled. They believed that the workers' leadership must be prepared on the basis of what experience showed to be the nature of existing conditions, advancing when conditions warranted from the economic to the political arena. The orthodox retorted that whatever the conditions at the moment, whatever the temporary opportunities for "economic" struggle, the Economists by abdicating on behalf of the workers the leading political role sacrificed what reason showed ought to be and must be. Worst of all, they abdicated in favor of the most dangerous aspirant of all: the bourgeois liberals.

We should note that the Marxists had not started with the ingrained antipathy to the liberals which was part of the populist tradition and passed to the Socialist Revolutionaries as well. While the Marxists of the 90's had fought the populists with ferocity, they had hailed the liberals as open advocates of middle-class interest, in themselves a proof of advancing capitalism. The future Mensheviks continued this attitude. It was Lenin who began to display fear and hostility as he discussed the future of the liberals. He saw them as possible competitors for the leadership of the workers and of the opposition movement in general, as obstructors of the advancement of the Marxist doctrine via its only possible vehicle, the industrial proletariat. This kind of competition was not feared from the populists, even in Socialist Revolutionary form. As a group basing itself on on class exclusively, the SR party was for the moment more to be pitied than censured. The liberals, on the other hand, demanded closer surveillance. No matter whether they boasted of it or denied it they were assumed by the Marxists to be the spokesmen of the Russian bourgeoisie: for the time being the proletariat's great competitor, for the future its chief adversary. What did being a "competitor" mean? It meant that *the Russian bourgeoisie threatened to make its own bourgeois revolution—* which Lenin in the light of Marxist teaching considered a profound threat, for it seemed the most logical possibility of all. Lenin was to exert all his strength to prevent this from happening; the Mensheviks were willing to let it happen—but in 1902 this was not yet clear.

7.

When *Iskra* began to appear at the end of 1900, the Munich Marxists were not entirely optimistic as to the future of their new enterprise. Lenin wrote his wife that Potresov "falls into black melancholy" on account of "this chaos," but declared that he was not nearly so nervous because there were "however several good things as well as chaos!" [20] Lenin had other reservations about Potresov. He dubbed him and Zasulich the "pro-Struve party" for their defense of the liberals. Martov he then regarded as a "typical journalist," and his negative attitude to Plekhanov has already been mentioned. Still, according to Krupskaia, Lenin's comrade and wife, the Munich period was to be remembered as "the good-humored days," and the *Iskra* group made common cause against all forms of Marxist heresy, against "disunity and primitiveness" within SD ranks.

Plekhanov [21] was given the job of surveying the long-term prospects of the Marxist cause in the second number of the orthodox newspaper. "Political freedom will be the first great cultural conquest of twentieth-century Russia." Towards this goal bourgeois and proletarian movements are both moving, but the latter is more democratic because it is a struggle in favor of the majority to abolish exploitation, while the former benefits a minority which continues exploiting. With this analysis, Plekhanov noted, not all revolutionaries currently agreed. There were already revealed in the great socialist movement "two different tendencies, and perhaps the revolutionary struggle of the twentieth century will lead to that which may be called *mutatis mutandis* the split of the SD 'Mountain' with the SD 'Gironde.'" This apparently accurate prophecy of Plekhanov's has been misinterpreted. He was referring to Economists and (orthodox) Iskraites, not proto-Bolsheviks and proto-Mensheviks. In fact, when the latter split came in 1903, he regarded it as needless and in his perplexity was driven not into genuine Menshevism but isolation.[22] Since this forecast of his had not come true and the Economists had been reclaimed, he then wrote, there was no real obstacle to party unity. The prophecy of 1901 had been merely a warning to the Economists; *Iskra* paid little further attention to them.

Iskra found strong confirmation of its belief in the leading role of the proletariat from the events of 1902-3. In the great demonstrations of March 1901 the workers showed "in the most unequivocal fashion . . . that they are ready to fight actively shoulder to shoulder with the revolutionary elements of 'society' against the yoke of Autocracy."[23] The following January *Iskra* repeated the equivalent in connection with the new demonstrations. Summing up the "revolutionary year" just past in May 1903, the Marxist paper found the results to be that the liberal-zemstvo movement "came to nothing," the student unrest had stopped. Terrorism revealed its weaknesses, the "newest revolutionary peasantophilia, its unjustified optimism." Only the proletariat, with new strikes and manifestations, was stepping up the tempo of its movement. The moral which *Iskra* pointed was that insofar as the Russian revolutionary remained nonsocialist, he could continue in the fight at all "only by recognizing over himself the hegemony of the proletarian movement." Thus the exiles found in events justification of the program with which they had left Siberia.

The editors were not interested, however, in depicting all nonworker opposition currents as bankrupt. From the first Lenin especially, as the "agrarian expert" of the exiles,[24] paid close attention to the peasant movement. Already in *The Development of Capitalism in Russia* he had begun to develop his view of the relations of the agricultural classes. In that book he had described how Russian agriculture was increasingly assuming a commercial, entrepreneur character. As agriculture took on some of the important features of an industry, the separation of the rural producer from the means of production was swiftly advancing. Among the peasants engaged in commodity production, there were growing sharper a number of capitalistic "contradictions"—competition for market, struggle for independence, taking over the land of weaker, concentration of production in the hands of a minority, expropriation and proletarization of the majority. Thus there were arising two new classes, the village bourgeoisie and village proletariat. Of the last-named, the landless *batrak* was a typical example but by no means the only component. Among the rural proletarians must be included not less than half of all peasant households[25]—those with small strips of land and no horses, as well as most of those having only one horse. As an intermediate group stood the "middle peasantry" consisting of more or less self-sufficient small producers, who could survive only under optimum conditions. Lenin regarded this group as one which capitalism doomed to more or less rapid extinction.

It was on the character of Russian capitalistic development, wrote Lenin, that his differences with the populists centered. Their error was to ignore the capitalistic contradictions in peasant economy. They failed to understand the complex of material relations which determine the trend of economic development; worst of all, they added moralizing conclusions to their socio-economic views. What Lenin meant was that the populists, observing the impoverishment of the peasantry, "moralized" that this was bad and wished to stop it. Lenin had no such desires. They would have to be founded on hopes which Marxist history deemed completely illusory. He did, however, wish most strongly to use the "objective situation" in the village for revolutionary purposes.

So, starting from his 1898 analysis, Lenin in *Iskra* proceeded to draw revolutionary conclusions.[26] He did not deduce, however, that the "village proletariat" he saw emerging would simply join that of the city in a fight for socialism. Social Democrats, themselves combating "senseless and harmful" semi-feudal institutions, like the "mutual guarantee" of individual payments by the commune, must "bring the class struggle to the countryside." In the village Lenin saw a twofold conflict, one between rural workers and employers and one between the whole peasantry and the landlord class. The first of these struggles was becoming sharper; the second was less fierce, yet it had the more vital significance for Social Democrats. In other words, the first task was destruction of the remnants of feudalism; the bourgeois revolution in the village, as elsewhere, must precede the socialist one. The peasantry as a whole must participate in the opposition movement until Autocracy and feudalism were wrecked. To try now to encourage antagonisms between the bourgeois and proletarian segments of the peasantry was to put the cart before the horse. There was a struggle for socialism to come in the village as well as the city; but for the time being the struggle was against feudalism. Lenin wrote that Social Democrats might advance only bourgeois demands for the village, such as the abolition of redemption payments, the restoration of the "cut-offs," the establishment of "peasant committees," and equality before the law of peasants with other classes. The way out of the peasants' troubles, Lenin concluded, was to summon a representative assembly to put an end to Tsarism. The significance of this move the peasant "will understand."

Here we see Lenin tackling the problem of how to fit peasants into his revolutionary calculations in a gingerly, doctrinaire manner. He still was careful not to overstep the "bourgeois" bounds of the first phase of the movement, and cautious of elevating the village proletarian to the exalted status of a full-fledged ally of the urban worker. He had, nevertheless, taken an important step in the direction of gaining an ally to replace the liberal one which he had so categorically rejected. More steps were to follow speedily.

No sooner had *Iskra* outlined the basis for a Social Democratic appeal to the peasantry than an old competitor for their support reappeared in strength. Lenin and his confreres had, they saw, only scotched, not killed, the snake of populism. It now emerged in its refurbished Socialist Revolutionary guise. The "determined and relentless war"[27] which Lenin now preached against the SR's was motivated by the fact that they merely "make noise," as do many revolutionary-minded people who are aroused by the sweep of events yet have "neither theoretical nor social foundations." The SR's failed to understand the class struggle. They lacked the solid foundation of a class, which of course any party must have. They preached terrorism, which was "nothing more than fighting in single combat." They had a faulty agrarian program. They attempted to rely on the intelligentsia—not a class, but a shifting group.

As the SR's continued to make gains, Lenin brushed off their success as due to "revolutionary adventurism."[28] They had taken clever advantage of the Economist-Iskraite split in Social Democrat ranks, the terrorists' assassination of Sipiagin, and above all the recent peasant risings. This despite the fact that they had no adequate theory at all, and furthermore denied outright the value of theory. On these grounds they charged that the Marxist belief that the proletariat alone could be a genuinely revolutionary force was a dogma—although all scientific socialists had affirmed this ever since the Communist Manifesto. The SR spirit in a nutshell was, in its theory, "revolutionary phraseology" instead of an integral viewpoint; in practice, the haphazard resort to any kind of tactical measure whatsoever instead of resolute participation in the class struggle.

When *Revolutionary Russia* did publish a series of theoretical articles, Lenin found in them merely objects for detailed ridicule.[29] From these articles Plekhanov singled out for closer examination SR views on the peasantry. He was willing to admit a similarity between the SR's and certain Western socialists in respect of their claim that socialists could support the interests of the peasantry as a whole—but Plekhanov also saw in the views of both groups the same lack of clarity in explaining how this was possible. The SR's had charged that the Marxists regarded the peasants as a negligible quantity. Plekhanov did not even bother to reply but confined himself to quoting the SR press to show that the SR's likewise considered revolutionary work in the village useless for the moment. In a word, *Iskra* simply refused to take its neo-populist rivals seriously.

Nevertheless, it may have been partly due to SR pressure on the peasant issue that Lenin in 1903 set about to compose a direct appeal[30] to the poor peasants, the writing of which gave him much satisfaction. He set forth in the simplest language Social Democratic aims, and undertook to explain to the *bedniaki* their own best interests. He now found that they included almost two-thirds of all peasant households in Russia, the middle and the rich peasants the remainder. The last category numbered but one-sixth of the total, yet owned half of all the horses! Great economic inequality was a proved fact; the great need was to give the poor peasants more land. This land must come from great gentry holdings, since the state had relatively very little. Moving toward the satisfaction of land hunger, the establishment of peasant committees, in order to wipe out vestiges of serfdom and to achieve the return of the "cut-offs," would be only a "door," a first step, in a broad struggle. In this struggle, the middle peasants must also join in, safely for them for the Social Democrats "will never take the property of the poor and middle peasants who employ no laborers." I do not know if anyone recalled this statement during the collectivization of agriculture in 1930.

Thus the men of *Iskra* appealed to the peasants to aid proletarians in achieving the bourgeois revolution, and dismissed as hopeless the alleged efforts of the Socialist Revolutionaries to summon them to the task of moving straight to socialism. In the meantime they had been watching closely the beginnings of political organization in the "bourgeois" camp.

The potential disagreements between the Iskraites about the liberal role were first highlighted by the controversy over Witte's memorandum to the Tsar. Witte, as already noted, had declared the principles of Autocracy and the zemstvos incompatible. Struve agreed about the incompatibility, but deduced from this not that the zemstvo must be restricted, as Witte did, but that Social Democrats must not be indifferent to the struggle between them, that they must be "for all who to whatever extent oppose the absolute power of officialdom, that is, the Autocracy of the Tsar." Struve's slogan, however, was not "Down with the Tsar!" but "Down with Autocratic bureaucracy!"

To these articles, Struve's sole contribution to *Iskra*,[31] Lenin retorted in a tone so critical of the liberals that Plekhanov and Axelrod forced him to make some alterations in his reply. He pointed out the paradox that Struve, though a liberal, underestimated the importance of the zemstvo in the current situation. The zemstvos played a definite part in the struggle. They gave rise to conflicts between an elective institution (themselves) and the bureaucracy and thus they "unconsciously march towards" a constitution. Yet while the zemstvo might even be called "a piece of a constitution," it is a piece used to cheat Russian "society" out of a real one. Lenin declared it was this aspect of the zemstvos, their service to Autocracy, which Struve failed to understand. Struve failed to see how his slogan, "Rights and a Zemstvo with Authority," rendered Autocracy a service by indicating a way of postponing or averting revolution. Struve, it was clear, desired an illegal liberal party. Whether he achieved this or not, Lenin declared he would go on fighting the illusions of the moderates that the zemstvos were the germ of a constitution (somewhat different from a "piece" of one, apparently), that dealings with Autocracy were possible, that adherents of the "Hannibalic oath" could remain patiently peaceful in their search for liberty.[32]

In seemingly paradoxical fashion, Lenin followed up this sharp criticism of a liberal close to his own camp with praise for a man who certainly would not have made any contributions to *Iskra* as Struve had done. Applying the "class point of view," he found some good things to say about a Marshal of Gentry[33] who had made a mild speech advocating "liberty of conscience," and thus defended "bourgeois democracy." Lenin was here looking for a stick to beat Economists. They failed, wrote Lenin, to see the danger of "criticism of Marxism" because they failed to understand the divergence of interests between the Russian bourgeoisie and Autocracy, and did not perceive the growth of liberal opposition to the absolutism which obstructed the development of education and the processes of production. The Economists did not understand that "criticism of Marxism" had taken root so fast "precisely because it is one of the elements of the bourgeois . . . democracy that is growing up in Russia." The political demands of the workers, Lenin continued, differed not in principle, but only in degree, from those of the bourgeois democrats, and therefore Social Democrats must intervene in every liberal problem. In the political struggle the Marxists have "many allies towards whom we simply cannot remain indifferent," but these liberals will waver and hesitate unless constantly prodded on by Social Democrats.

As we read these words, among the mildest Lenin ever used in regard to "liberals," we may be unprepared for the reaction of the Marxists to the appearance of a liberal newspaper edited by Struve called *Liberation*.[34] *Iskra* now carried an article attacking the liberals for desiring to stay outside the class struggle, for leaving the liberal bourgeoisie in the same spot where they floundered unsuccessfully for forty years, for failing "to push them forward." Rejecting class war against Tsarism, the liberals were instead actually preparing class war against those social groups who fought Autocracy. "Neither the working class nor revolutionary democracy in general can give such a party any kind of political confidence."

Why did the men of *Iskra* speak so mildly of Stakhovich and so harshly of Struve in their evaluation of the political role of liberals? The answer is plain. Stakhovich, as spokesman for the obvious economic interests of the landholding class, could be depended upon to follow a line which could not be confused with worker demands, though useful to the workers because it opposed absolutism. Struve, on the other hand, as an intellectual familiar with Marxist doctrine, and a direct representative of no apparent class interest, always threatened to contend for the support of the masses, to sing a perverted siren song which might divert the workers from their only true objectives—as outlined by the Social Democrats. This was no minor danger to Lenin; in the very first number of *Iskra* he had written: "separated from Social Democracy, the workers' movement degenerates and becomes inevitably bourgeois."[35] The sin of the Economists was to open the door to precisely this danger, which now took concrete form in the Liberationist group, of which Struve's newspaper was the organ. Stakhovich represented only a parallel line of action, one which would be temporarily helpful to the Marxists, though later his whole class was to be liquidated! Struve offered a converging line of action plus a rival theory, no matter how eclectic, how erroneous. The "Economists," despite their eclecticism and error, were at least still subject to party authority; Struve was an apostate on the loose.

8.

Aided by events inside Russia, *Iskra's* fight for orthodoxy within Social Democrat ranks was finally successful. The "practical" side of Economism was discredited by Plehve's experiment in police unionism and the growing number of *political* demonstrations (especially the Rostov outbreak in November 1902). Copies of *Iskra,* smuggled into Russia in mounting quantities,[36] strongly influenced the local committees. The adherents of *Workers' Cause* felt their ascendancy shaken. At the Belostok conference, April 1902, they tried to set up a committee to summon a new party congress which would complete the work of the ill-fated Minsk Congress of 1898. This committee likewise was depleted by arrests. Not *Workers' Cause,* but *Iskra,* led the reconstitution of an Organization Committee which convened a II Congress in Brussels and London in July 1903.[37]

On the eve of the opening of the congress, *Iskra* triumphantly announced that it "considered Economism finally buried,"[38] and orthodox ascendancy was apparent as the congress started business. Open Economism had no defenders. The Jewish Bund, which evinced sympathies in that direction, withdrew from the party.[39]

Scarcely did the Iskraites have time to realize the extent of their triumph when a new disagreement came to light. There was a debate on the criteria for party membership—the celebrated question of Point One of the rules. Lenin proposed that a party member should be defined as one "who recognizes the Party's program and supports it by material means *and by personal participation in one of the party organizations.*" Martov proposed to substitute for the italicized phrase: "*and by regular personal assistance under the direction of one of the party organizations.*" Lenin's formulation, which of course was bound up with his whole idea of the function of the Social Democratic party, was rejected as what Martov called later a "hypertrophy of centralism."[40] Martov's broader definition was adopted, and thus on one of the most crucial issues the Mensheviks-to-be won. It was this decision which led Lenin to the most feverish attempts to convert his outnumbered faction into an organized majority. After the withdrawal of the Bund, a new division took place over the make-up of the editorship of *Iskra*. By a narrow margin Lenin's demand for a new board was carried, and the majority and minority of delegates who voted on this resolution took the name "Bolshevik" and "Menshevik."

The congress did accomplish some important tasks aside from the bitter debates, which were to outlive the London Congress by a generation or more. It adopted Martov's wording of Point One of the rules, it passed as the official party program the draft published in No. 21 of *Iskra*, as well as Axelrod's resolution on relations with the SR's and both Plekhanov's and Potresov's resolutions as to relations with the liberals. Both SR's and liberals were condemned as anti-democratic, but Potresov's resolution, contradicting at least the spirit of the Plekhanov one, set forth certain conditions which, if satisfied by the liberals, would open the way to a limited degree of cooperation with them. In substance these conditions were the rejection of any negotiated peace with Autocracy, the refusal to advance any demands hostile to the interests of the workers, and the open demand for a Four-Tail Constituent Assembly. Finally, the congress removed from the editorship of *Iskra*, Axelrod, Zasulich, and Potresov, leaving Lenin, Plekhanov, and Martov. Martov, however, refused to continue to serve; Lenin too resigned. Plekhanov, after publishing one number alone, coopted back the Menshevik editors, and the party organ thus fell into Menshevik hands.

Plekhanov was deeply disturbed by the split in the party,[41] and more than a little embarrassed by his own position on *Iskra*. He wrote plaintively: although "we must all" fight Revisionism, does that mean that "we must always and everywhere show enmity to *Revisionists?*" He urged the party to remember that the lost Economists had been reclaimed and by inference recommended that the two new factions suspend judgment. For a flowering of the workers' movement, political freedom was essential; but it was still lacking in Russia, and one of the most harmful consequences of this was a "sectarian spirit of exclusiveness . . . consistent Marxists cannot be, of course, Utopianists of centralism." Though he thus criticized the Bolsheviks sharply, still Plekhanov emphasized above all the need of avoiding deepening the schism which would be bound to harm the cause. Lenin also minimized the issues behind the division.[42] He declared that only organizational questions, not tactical ones, separated the two wings, and that even among these there was but one difference in principle, that over Point One of the rules.

9.

Despite hopeful talk about its casual and accidental nature, the split between Bolsheviks and Mensheviks was permanent. On the surface, there was no reason to suppose that the Social Democratic party had any fundamental disagreements remaining in 1903. There was no more discussion about the value of orthodox Marxist doctrine; "Economism" was a ghost which had been forever laid. There were no more debates about the primacy of political struggle; this was accepted without reservation throughout the party. It was not doubted that the Russian revolution was close at hand, and that the workers, whose party the SD's laid claim to be, would lead it. Obviously whatever issue which now might disturb Marxist unanimity must arise through divergent interpretation of these apparently unequivocal propositions.

The immediate dilemma was overtly organizational: who should be accorded the title of party member? This question had rightly been brushed aside as minor by both factions. In actual fact, the immediate issue was tactical: how should the revolution be made? In more concrete terms, with whom should the Marxists make it? Should the small "workers' party" try to achieve the revolution alone, or with some more numerous group or groups as allies?

The idea of the workers' leading the revolution practically unaided was later to be defended by Trotsky. But for the time being Trotsky was a Menshevik (he was later to recognize that he had never really been a Menshevik, but refused to admit what was equally true, that he had never really been a Bolshevik either) and he had not yet set forth this idea clearly. Among the remaining Social Democrats, there was a sharpening difference of opinion as to who was the most useful ally, between those who relied on the peasants and those who relied on the middle class as the auxiliary which would enable the workers to overthrow Autocracy and set up a "democratic republic"—the program-minimum adopted at the II Congress. This line coincided with the Bolshevik-Menshevik schism.

In 1898 the split on this basic tactical point had already been foreshadowed, though in terms of analysis rather than tactics. Lenin, in *The Development of Capitalism in Russia,* had described the advent of a village proletariat which would presumably fight for socialism some day, though it was to its immediate interests to join the rest of the peasantry in shaking off the feudal survivals preventing the necessary growth of capitalism in rural economy. Axelrod, on the other hand, had written a brochure,[43] *The Historical Position and Mutual Relations of Liberal and Socialist Democracy in Russia,* which outlined the appearance of a potentially strong opponent of Autocracy, between which and the proletariat the historical situation "requires a common objective and compels them to energetic, constant mutual assistance." This ally was the liberal bourgeoisie. Though the industrial capitalists were protected by the government, side by side with them in the middle class were other "not inconsiderable" elements whose interest coincided less and less with the financial and repressive cultural policies of the government. The center of these elements was the liberal professions, along with the intelligentsia, which was hampered by the state in its work in zemstvo and other activities, and even a certain part of the bureaucracy as well. The landed gentry too had an interest in the faster economic development of the country, lower tariffs, and so forth. In contrast to the industrialists and their "plutocratic city councils, the zemstvos in their meetings, activities, and debates are proving themselves progressive and even democratic." In Russia, where the "privileged classes" are weaker and stand in a different economic position from that of their Western equivalents, instead of there existing a general antagonism of the masses, intellectuals, and industrial classes against the nobility, the popular hatred is directed against the capitalists, and in this gentry, intelligentsia, and proletariat share. It was true that the gentry sought the help of the Tsar against the threat of peasant revolt, but nevertheless the chief trend in the zemstvos was impregnated with the spirit of capitalism. Russia was being penetrated, despite the dead weight of the Tsarist regime, by the influence of Western cultural and political forces which were laying a foundation for the political awakening of the proletariat despite the hindrances of absolutism. This, on the formal side, was the "revolutionary significance" of Russian liberalism. In contrast with the West, the Russian proletariat found in the circle of bourgeois society a *point d'appui* for its revolutionary development. Plekhanov had written that the Russian workers were deprived of the bourgeois leadership which the West had possessed. Axelrod agreed; he found in the Russian bourgeoisie not a leader, but a supporter, of the workers. This was the essential tactical premise of Menshevism. At the time of the appearance of this brochure, even the future Menshevik leader, Martov was "shocked" by it.[44] Its ideas came into play, however, less in 1898 than in 1903.

10.

After the II Congress, though this tactical disagreement hovered in the background, and was in fact graphically illustrated by the contradictory resolutions about the liberals passed at London, it did not at once clearly appear. The schism was open and deep; "Down with all soft-heartedness!" Lenin cried in pretending to disown Martov. The organizations of the Bolsheviks and Mensheviks were completely separated. The Bolsheviks had the Central Committee and no organ, the Mensheviks *Iskra* but no committee until 1904. But it was not yet fully clear what the schism was about.

To Trotsky, the brilliant young orator just returned from Siberian exile, the issue of this tragic quarrel was simply centralism. Much later he wrote apologetically that he "did not fully realize what an intense and imperious centralism the revolutionary party would need."[45] What is more, he did not seem to realize the reason for this centralism or what it was directed against in the thought of Lenin. His chief desire was the reunion of the party, since he did not see the gravity of the matter which divided it. In a brochure entitled *Our Political Tasks*, written in 1904, he called for an end to "scholastic organizational debates" in order to concentrate on the questions of political tactics to which the ultimate fate of the party was linked. He saw the recent history of the party as divided into two phases, that of "Economism" when it fought for the workers' support, and that of *Iskra*, when it strove to capture the revolutionary intellectuals. In the former, there was work directed at the proletariat, but not Social Democratic work; in the latter, work which was Social Democratic but not aimed directly at the proletariat. The two sides of the coin must be fused in the period ahead, the period Axelrod had already opened by his articles in the new post-London *Iskra* on party unity. Our "organization of professional revolutionaries" must not simply develop a coterie of subterranean propaganda smugglers, but real political leaders who would resolutely oppose the proletariat to the bourgeoise. The proletariat must be made "self-sufficing," and then it would come out as the vanguard of the political movement. Marxists must reject "Jacobinism"; a Jacobin "can only be a chief of revolutionary bourgeois democracy," not of a workers' party. The Mensheviks had been accused of opportunism, but "an opportunist inside out does not at all necessarily mean a revolutionary Social Democrat." Trotsky was then a Menshevik.[46] When he left the faction in November 1904, he may well have decided that it was made up of "opportunists" just as Lenin said, but Lenin was to him still an opportunist inside out.

Trotsky had attacked Lenin's organizational ideas. The real Mensheviks of the new *Iskra* board also attacked the "bureaucratic centralism" and "Bonapartism" of the Bolsheviks, but this was the extent of their agreement with Trotsky.[47] They did not believe the proletariat could be made self-sufficing for the struggle ahead, and their conception of the "vanguard" role the proletariat would play differed from his. They were in earnest, however, in criticizing the ideas of Lenin's *What is to be Done?* Those ideas represented "new opportunist tendencies," wrote Axelrod, "though no longer of an economic, but of a *political* character." Lenin was, it seems, an Economist turned inside out! Lenin's "conspiratorial" groups would presumably work toward an armed uprising by smuggling weapons and drawing up plans of attack, but true Social Democrats (read Mensheviks) would prepare their forces for the moment when a mass uprising becomes possible, subordinating the *technical* aspect of preparation to the political side. They would reject the caricature of Social Democracy embodied in "the cult of the professional revolutionary."[48]

However, before long *Iskra* gave up the attempt to charge Lenin with, and dissuade him from, "Blanquist" plotting, no doubt realizing that their differences went farther than that. Meanwhile they were developing their own tactical line with unmistakable clarity by stretching a hand in the direction of the liberals. When the Tsardom closed the Russian Technical Congress in January 1904, *Iskra* asked if the zemstvists would miss this opportunity to come to the defense of a liberal body.[49] Evidently the Tsardom and the reactionary wing of the gentry were trying to destroy contact between the propertied classes and democratic elements, in particular by striking at the important link between them which comprised the Third Element. But the government's attempt to "smoke out" these democratic intellectuals would simply hasten their liberation from the dying influence of the liberal bourgeoisie and their rapprochement with the masses. The workers, said *Iskra*, must aid the movement of Third Element men, intellectuals nurtured in the zemstvos, as they entered the arena of independent political action and employed slogans borrowed from the proletariat. The workers must apply "political pressure" to this movement to advance ever more radical demands. Remember, said the writer, the Social Democratic politics of the working class is "not identical with the political movement of the proletariat" whihc was led by Social Democrats—that is, the former was broader and included other opposition elements.

This sympathetic attitude toward liberal intellectuals had been foreshadowed by some future Menshevik journalists of *Zaria*. Potresov had examined the intelligentsia and concluded that "the mixed-rank intelligentsia is democratic, the mixed-rank intelligentsia is revolutionary," and called upon this group to lead the workers' movement in a manner consonant with its "glorious past." [50] Martov had pointed out that though the intelligentsia as a rule adhered to bourgeois society, part of it renounces its privileges to pass over to heretical, socialist doctrine.[51] The Russian representatives of this "part" of society would find in the scientific world-outlook of Marxism "the support which will make possible consciously breaking the chains" which bind them to the ideology of bourgeois society. Potresov and Martov of course were talking about intellectuals who were potential Social Democrats, but the Mensheviks' high evaluation of the intelligentsia, pre-Marxist and non-Marxist as well as Marxist, is clear. The Third Element, for example, was praised; but it was regarded not as a potentially Social Democratic force but as the best candidate to lead the liberal, petty bourgeois movement of town and country in a manner which would make possible cooperation with Social Democrats. The populist intellectuals received little attention. The Mensheviks believed them to represent a dying phenomenon without much current relevance.[52]

Yet in spite of this inclination to assign the intellectuals a significant political role (of course only as the leaders of "classes"), the Mensheviks condemned Lenin's tendency to emphasize the individual "conspiratorial" revolutionary for reflecting a proud, self-sufficient "intellectualism." The kind of intelligentsia approved by Minority Social Democrats was that which submerged its own interests in those of the masses it led. Notwithstanding the hindrances absolutism imposed on open political activity to which Lenin pointed, they believed a true political party must base itself firmly on mass support. This could never be secured by "underground" work, they said, and therein they remained loyal to their Western political models.

The new *Iskra* had exhorted Marxists to put "pressure" on the

Third Element. Now they broadened their front to include the zemstvists as a whole. A Menshevik writer warned in 1903 that if the zemstvists "do not want to go with the people, then the people will know how to conquer freedom without them and against them."[53] However, the proletariat could make them go farther than their class bourgeois interest would dictate. Only by demanding the Four Tails "can the liberal zemstvists count on meeting in the organized proletariat an ally in the business of achieving its immediate objectives." After the November 1904 zemstvo congress, *Iskra* declared that while its resolutions might play an important role in the attack on Tsarism, their realization depended not upon their authors but on the revolutionary proletariat.

On November 22 there was reported for the first time in the legal press a case of the adoption by a legal meeting of the demand for a Constituent Assembly. This, in the eyes of *Iskra*, was a notable example of the influence of Russian Social Democracy on the march of the bourgeois revolution. The Menshevik writer seized the chance to state the viewpoint of his own faction on the nature of the revolution (already or nearly begun). SD's and SR's agreed the revolution would have two phases; all SD's agreed the phases would be "bourgeois" and "socialist"; all Mensheviks, it was implied, believed, as Plekhanov had written in 1901, that "the triumph of socialism cannot coincide with the fall of absolutism. These two moments necessarily will be separated from one another by a significant interval of time."[54] Accordingly, since the two phases were to be distinct, during the first "bourgeois" phase, Social Democrats were right to show that "their own interests at the present time coincide with the interests of the free-thinking portion of our 'society'." Of course this coincidence of interests would not be complete because the Marxists would demand much more than merely social reform desired by liberals. Still, continued Plekhanov, the liberals must realize that at this stage the success of the Social Democrats would be of great aid to them.

Now, three years later, *Iskra* wrote that the Russian proletariat, "chief actor and central figure in the developing bourgeois revolution," could not stop en route to the shattering of all semi-feudal, pre-bourgeois relations. Struve, editor of *Liberation*, wanted to halt before the revolution was carried to its "logical conclusion." The inference was that Struve did not clearly understand his own class interest, and it was part of the job of the proletariat to make him do so.

By this time the basic dilemma of the Mensheviks was apparent.

They believed that there lay ahead a "bourgeois" revolution, then a "significant interval of time," then the social revolt. The role of the proletariat in a bourgeois revolution, and the bourgeois state which it would create, was a thorny problem indeed. He must be the "chief actor and central figure," he must have "hegemony"—this was well and good, but it did not answer the question of how the proletariat was to behave, how he was to safeguard his interests, in a bourgeois society. He might assemble, organize, and speak with freedom. He might plot the overthrow of his middle-class "oppressors." But he was only a small minority, and if he awaited the increasing proletarianization of the masses, which Marxists considered inevitable, to give him the necessary strength, not he, but only his sons or grandsons, might hope to see the "socialist" kind of revolution which after all was a Marxist party's only specific excuse for existence.

There were indeed certain ways out of this dilemma. The socialist revolution might come sooner than Plekhanov thought. Or, the "bourgeois" revolution might not mean the conquest of power by the bourgeois at all—certainly an ingenious solution, and the one Lenin used. But for the moment no way out was indicated for the Mensheviks. Their theory merely gave added cause for horror to the SR's (who feared all along that the SD's meant exactly what the Mensheviks now said when they talked of "bourgeois" revolution), aid and comfort to the liberals (who wanted some kind of "bourgeois" revolution but nothing more), and very little consolation to the Mensheviks themselves.

The Minority Social Democrats continued, however, to try to "push" the Russian middle class to do their revolutionary job, and to find evidence that the pressure was becoming effective. The Paris interparty congress, on the very eve of "Bloody Sunday," was welcomed, not as what it purported to be—a strictly limited understanding between socialists and moderates for purposes of attack on Tsarism—but as a bloc of bourgeois parties. Furthermore, said *Iskra*, this "bloc" represented merely an extension of moderate zemstvism, the whole forming one spectrum which ranged from the pale rose of Count Heyden (Right zemstvist) to the bright red of Chernov (SR).[55] Bourgeois liberalism was dressing ranks and might now be expected to fight effectively; this was the unspoken conclusion of the Mensheviks from observing the Paris conference. The fact that the SR's had taken part gave them much satisfaction. *Iskra* was glad to see that the SR's had abandoned all of their "nonsense" about socialism and perhaps would now stop causing confusion in the workers' ranks (an ill-disguised tribute to their success) and unite with forces "kindred to them." The Paris conference had marked a definite step forward in the unification of bourgeois democracy, but nevertheless was still inspired by hopes based on subjective idealism. Not only on that account had SD's refused to go to Paris, but because unity with the bourgeois opposition meant sacrificing "democratism of program and revolutionariness of tactics." As the Party Council officially replied to its conference invitation, "fruitful revolutionary acts" were possible for Social Democrats only on the basis of class struggle, not the mingling of heterogeneous groups, some of whom speculated on the victory of the Japanese bourgeois state in the war. The last charge might have been regarded as grimly ironic by the liberals who had provoked the wrath of conservatives by espousing "defeatism."

By "Bloody Sunday" the Mensheviks had a considerable advantage over their rivals. Not only were they gaining adherents in Russia at an accelerating rate, but they had the only party newspaper and by means of it had developed and publicized a tactical line to which its opponents had no literary voice to reply. It is no wonder that the Socialist Revolutionaries did not grasp the significance of the split among Russian Marxists. Lenin, the Bolsheviks' only outstanding thinker and writer, did not acquire an emigre newspaper until December 1904, and most of what writing he did during the gloomy year and a half following the II Congress was devoted to intra-party matters. He was by no means sure of the best way to end the Schism. In December 1903 he was insisting with all his might on the immediate convening of another party Congress, but a year later he wrote that "only the most hopeless fools" could place all their hopes in a Congress now, that the main thing was to get money and above all a literary organ, and quickly.[56]

In the spring of 1904 he blasted the Mensheviks with his brochure *One Step Forward, Two Steps Back*. According to Zinoviev[57] the title implied Social Democrats had taken a step forward from Economism to Iskraism, then two steps backward to the liberal ideas of "legal Marxism." No such accusations, however, were made in the brochure. Lenin still declared the division in the party was chiefly due to questions of organization, not program or tactics; even the opportunism of the new *Iskra,* he said, was limited to organizational matters. The implications of the pamphlet, nevertheless, indicated that this was but a small part of the truth.

Relations of the party to the proletariat it claimed to represent received his close scrutiny. The Social Democratic party was the party of a class, and therefore "almost the entire class (and in times of war, in the period of civil war, the entire class)" should adhere closely to the party. However, it would be "tailism" to think that under capitalism the entire class could rise to the level of consciousness of its party vanguard. Of this Martov was guilty in his formula for party membership, which, ostensibly defending the interests of the broad strata of the proletariat, *"in fact . . . serves the interests of the bourgeois intellectuals,* who fight shy of proletarian discipline and organization." *"Tailism in matters of organization* is a natural and inevitable product of the mentality of the *anarchist individualist."* As opportunism in doctrine slips through the stages of sneering at orthodoxy, to "criticism," to bourgeois democracy, so does opportunism in organization slide from sneering at discipline to "autonomism," to anarchism, and "helplessly surrenders to bourgeois psychology, uncritically adopts the point of view of bourgeois democracy, and blunts the weapon of the class struggle of the proletariat."

There remained no doubt as to whose "tail" Lenin accused the Mensheviks of straggling behind. It was the tail of the liberals, who were not even organized yet, though Lenin showed by his fixed attention to the newspaper *Liberation* where he quite correctly expected their organization to appear. If the Social Democratic party was not well-organized and disciplined, the liberals were sure to wrest the initiative from it—this was the key idea of the brochure, this was the chief deduction from the proceedings of the II Congress.

Lenin paid specific attention to the Potresov resolution there adopted in relation to agreement with liberals. Its defect was "political vagueness"; it did not "define the class meaning of Russian liberalism." It confused two problems, that of exposing the "anti-revolutionary and anti-proletarian" features of "all liberal democratic trends," as against the *"conditions* for temporary and partial *agreements* with any of these trends." In fact it was absurd to prescribe any conditions at all. It was much better to leave the matter for the central Party machinery to deal with. Lenin's objection to the Potresov resolution was not that its "conditions" were too mild. He even suggested it might be expedient to make an agreement with some liberal group which fell short of them—one which did not, for example, demand a Constituent Assembly. Actually he never proved willing to conclude any sort of agreement with any liberal group at any time; the essential point is that if he had thought it expedient, he would have done so with equal distaste whether the group was Right or Left liberal, and nothing could have made him like it. Even if liberal spokesmen were to "declare clearly and unambiguously" (Potresov's words) that they would resolutely side with Social Democracy, said Lenin, "we, the party of the proletariat, *would be obliged not to believe them.* Being a liberal and resolutely siding with the Social Democrats are two mutually exclusive things."

Lenin's attitude to the liberals was elaborated in his attack on the Menshevik plan to support[58] the zemstvo congress of November 1904. The plan was for workers in each Russian province to organize mass demonstrations in conjunction with each local zemstvo as it debated the congress's resolutions, demonstrations which would then proceed to enter the halls and present their own demands. Lenin ridiculed this plan in scathing detail. *Iskra,* he charged, turned the question of relations with liberals upside down when it talked of "pressure" on zemstvists. The pressure must be applied to the government, not liberals. The bourgeoisie is "notoriously an ally with reservations, a problematic and unreliable ally, a semi-ally." He might have added, in practice not an ally at all.

He taunted *Iskra* with the terms of the Potresov resolution, which he himself had opposed but which they approved. What had become of these terms, when *Iskra* claims that the liberals by merely coming out against absolutism "have in fact become our allies"? Though liberals may occasionally speak in the name of the people, they cannot do this consistently—they will always waver. Some of them, like Prince Eugene Trubetskoi in his recent article in *Law,* become panic-stricken at the specter of proletarian victory.[59] The workers could only conquer by force for themselves what the bourgeoisie promised to give them as charity.

At last the tactical disagreement between Bolsheviks and Mensheviks was in the open. The Mensheviks placed their hope in the liberals as an ally in the bourgeois revolution just beginning, and Lenin branded these hopes as harmful and illusory. His own candidate for a workers' ally had not yet been clearly nominated, but already, as we have seen, there could be little doubt that it would be the peasantry. So far, however, he had not even had an instrument to present his views systematically. Now he acquired one, the newspaper *Forward,* and wrote to a friend in jubilation, "Hurrah! Do not lose heart, we are all reviving now and will revive." [60] In the struggle to reunite the party and to restore the "Majority" faction to real control over it, Lenin saw as the crucial weapon the newspaper which he had just succeeded in setting up. Some might have regarded it as mad to think of breaking the back of Tsarism with a newspaper. But this newspaper, like the other party organs, was nothing but incarnate politics, and it was through politics that the Russian intelligentsia were to win their fight eventually. First recapture the Party, then capture the government—this was Lenin's aim. It was not his fault that the Revolution of 1905 would not wait for these objectives to be attacked in that order.

VI

RUSSIA GETS A LIBERAL PARTY

> *"We accept the political jargon of our opponents and remind them that the political victory of the bourgeoisie, by their own teaching, is all that can be achieved in the present moment."*
>
> PAUL MILIUKOV, 1905.[1]

The impact of Paul Miliukov on the Russian liberal movement was comparable to that of Lenin and Chernov on their respective revolutionary parties, in the sense of increasingly intellectualizing and rationalizing liberal ambitions. At the beginning of the twentieth century, both existing liberal organizations, the *Beseda* group and the Zemstvo Union, were still dominated by a "practical" bent. In *Beseda* this principle was written into the rules of membership; no one could be admitted to the group unless he was currently engaged in work in the rural or urban self-government bodies. The Zemstvo Union likewise consisted only of the presidents of the guberniia zemstvo boards, who were almost wholly preoccupied with their zemstvo duties. Until 1901 neither group was considering questions of overall political reform, and even then they put the problem in terms of "improving" or "perfecting" the state system to which they remained loyal.

The gradualist leanings of the 90's may not well represent Russian liberalism, if we remember the determination of the zemstvo constitutionalists of the 60's and the stern consistency of Petrunkevich from the 80's onward. Furthermore, this gradualism did not necessarily mean empiricism. One strong current of the liberalism of the 90's was not at all interested in experimenting with political forms as such, but instead was guided by a mystical vision of the ideal state which was inherited from the Slavophiles. In fact, this current still used the name "Slavophile." The outstanding man of this current was Dmitrii Shipov, one of the most appealing figures of the whole Liberation Movement, personally upright, conscientious, and thoroughly admirable. It was no accident that, as he himself admitted, no "attempt to present any definite, reasoned system" of political thought was to be found in his memoirs. We can trace his beliefs in outline from a 1901 draft of a sort of credo which he sought to persuade Russia's foremost "public men"[2] to accept, for presentation to the Tsar, as an expression of their own convictions. Here he declares that ideally a state would best be governed by an hereditary monarch, since he should be above all conflicting group interests. In practice, he confessed, absolute sovereigns had often forgotten their duty and infringed both law and the rights of citizens. The fundamental prerequisite of his ideal state was that the sovereign should strive for union with the people. Other countries had found some sort of representative assembly to be a "necessary condition" of such a union. In Russia this role was fulfilled, he asserted, by the Zemskii Sobor of the days before Peter the Great, wherein interests of people and monarch blended. In contrast to it, the assembly of a constitutional state inevitably *opposes* these interests to each other. The old Slavophile maxim, "the power of authority to the Tsar, the power of opinion to the people," was still present in the thought of this eminently practical epigon of a school of mystical thinkers. What was important to the welfare of the State was not forms of government but mutual trust between Tsar and people, exchange of views between the Imperial throne and the nation's natural (not elected) spokesmen, the educated men of "society." Thus Shipov[3] regarded the crux of the political problem. As immediate tasks he mentioned curbing the power of bureaucracy, extension of local self-government, and establishment of a consultative assembly of "public men" to help in lawmaking. Shipov, the moving spirit of the Zemstvo Union, wanted to attack Russian backwardness through inner, moral reform, as had the Slavophiles before him, but was eager to see external manifestations of this—the essential point was, however, that not fine-spun rational formulations nor some assumed legal right could serve as justification, but mutual confidence of ruler and ruled, both partaking of the inner Russian tradition, the *sobornost* of pre-Petrine times.

2.

When he examined Shipov's draft memorial, Prince S. N. Trubetskoi[4] refused to accept its principles, much as he might approve the noble motives of its author. Such a notion of ideal Autocracy, he retorted, was "Utopian." Arbitrariness could only be removed by legal limitations on the sovereign; the notion was absurd that a few gifted, experienced "public men" could under twentieth-century conditions represent the whole of Russia. The mystical premises of Shipov's neo-Slavophilism were rejected, and such liberals as Trubetskoi proceeded in a more matter-of-fact direction. The position here defended by Trubetskoi was probably best represented by Basil Maklakov, whose personal disagreement with Miliukov, carried over into literary polemics of their emigre old age, well symbolized the split between the Right and Left of Russian liberalism as it eventually took form. Curiously enough, Maklakov, while a lawyer and no mystic, nevertheless spoke in terms not fundamentally dissimilar to Shipov's. The very title of his memoirs, "Government and 'Society' in the Decline of Old Russia," shows what factors he thought should decide the political future. He quoted Herzen[5] to illustrate his own line of thought, "What can stand in the way when 'sovereignty and freedom,' the educated minority and the people, *the Tsar's will and social opinion,* are together?" This was no aristocratic attempt to circumvent the popular will. It was the statement of a belief that Russia's masses plainly were not ready for unlimited democratic government, that their educated spokesmen, who understood their needs, must be trusted to take the first steps toward the necessary reforms—trusted both by the people they were assumed to speak for and the Tsar who would, if he saw reason (Shipov would say, if he heeded the inner voice), turn to them for advice. It was a statement not of ultimate, rationalist goals, but of the necessary first steps; not of the end in view, but the direction, which Bernstein had revised Marxism to emphasize. It was the voice of empirical liberalism, as the Economists had given voice to empirical Marxism. Maklakov said, let us do what can be done at the moment; Miliukov was to say, let us proceed to construct the liberal order. Maklakov himself well saw the rigorous apriorist cast of the Left-liberal thought of the turn of the century. The Left-liberals, said he, wished to give the vote to those who knew nothing of how to use it. They rejoiced the worse the government behaved since the faster would come its overthrow in consequence—"the worse for them, the better for us," *chem khuzhe, tem luchshe.* With this phrase the pre-SR populists had taunted their rationalist SD competitors; and Maklakov used it against Miliukov for analogous reasons.

Fixing their eyes on the future, the Left-liberals had a "mystical faith" in constitutions, Maklakov charged.

What offended him was not "mystical faith"; we must take this as metaphor. The mystical bent of the neo-Slavophiles did not provoke criticism, since despite their different points of departure, Shipov and Maklakov hoped for the same practical palliative: that the Tsar would choose to save himself by accepting the proffered hand of the "public men." Of course among these "public men" were Shipov and Maklakov themselves; and they were unquestionably among the best. Nevertheless it is curious that Miliukov had been criticized for personal ambition when the effect of his doctrine, contrary to that of his competitors in the liberal camp, would have been exactly to minimize his own importance on the political scene in comparison to the aims of Maklakov and Shipov who were seeking power for a small group of men to which they themselves happened to belong. One need not, by the way, accuse these two enlightened and admirable men of self-interest in order to make this comparison.

What did displease Maklakov about Miliukov was his uncompromising rationalism and Westernism. The Left-liberals' use of "untried" political slogans, their "ignoring" of the peculiarities of Russian development, their fixed attention to the future at the expense of the immediate, "practical" needs of the present—this provoked Maklakov's suspicions. Suspicion turned to alarm when Miliukov's Westernizing rationalism led him to search for an ally which should, according to the calculations of reason, permit the liberals to achieve their objectives. Miliukov chose as his ally, as we shall see, the revolutionary parties. This was not because Russian liberals and revolutionaries had ever been able to work together in the past, not because they were basically like-minded, but because their apriorist immediate aims were taken to be the same, and furthermore, because moderates and revolutionaries had cooperated up to a point in the great Western revolutions. Maklakov had already criticized the Leftists for turning to the untutored masses and for ignoring empirical data about their lack of political experience. Even worse, to him, was that they turned also to the revolutionaries for aid, and deformed the old Russian liberalism into a "struggle directed toward the overthrow of Autocracy *at any cost* in union with *any allies whatsoever.*"[6]

3.

In 1898 there were accordingly three groups of liberals: those who, like Shipov, based their moderate approach on the mystique of the Slavophiles; those who, like Maklakov, were moderate because they were empiricist; and those who, following Miliukov, were radical on rationalist and Westernizing grounds. In the years preceding 1898 the Slavophiles, through their chief representative, Shipov, had the ascendancy in the liberal movement. Like all other Russian political factions, they too sought allies to achieve their objectives, but the ones they sought were members of the government who would put their trust in "society." They were to find that this was a totally vain search. But although they could find no bureaucrats to cooperate with them, they kept trying. It was their willingness to follow not only the orders, but the wishes, of the unfriendly bureaucrats, which led them to lose the initiative to the Miliukovites, the future Liberationists, at a critical time—in 1898.

The newly reformed Zemstvo Union, after being sanctioned uncordially enough by Goremykin, met once only, at Nizhnii-Novgorod in August 1896. The next meeting, planned for the following March, never took place. Goremykin evidently found the pressure of Pobedonostsev and his kind too much for him and sent word that the Union must be dissolved completely. Shipov, though wholly disillusioned in Goremykin, yielded. When the presidents of the zemstvo boards met in Moscow in August 1898 to celebrate the dedication of a memorial to the Tsar Liberator, Alexander II, they listened to mild speeches favoring "liberal autocracy" and dispersed, even rejecting the overtures of the Imperial Free Economic Society looking towards joint publication of a zemstvo organ. However, the idea of such a journal was discussed by various circles during the year 1899, and on 20 December the Society announced it was going ahead with publication—only to be forestalled by imperial suppression of the group in April 1900.

The idea of some kind of liberal organ, preferably political, remained alive notwithstanding. Struve, the apostate Marxist, consulted with the radical zemstvist, Ivan Petrunkevich, in February 1900, about the possibility of putting out an emigre liberal newspaper. However, since plans for *Iskra* were now under way, Struve turned instead to try to secure liberal collaboration in the new Marxist newspaper. His talks with the Marxists finally came to nothing, and Struve invited one of his friends in Russia to join him in Frankfurt to make final plans for an emigre liberal paper.[7] What happened to this meeting is not clear. Finally Struve returned to Russia in March 1901, but he was almost at once arrested and exiled to Tver for taking part in a student demonstration in St. Petersburg. In a short time Struve managed to make his way abroad again, leaving his (unidentified) friend in Finland to try to spread the idea of *Liberation,* the proposed name for the emigre organ. As a result of this man's efforts, the St. Petersburg "Committee of the Union of Liberation" was formed and the idea of a secret organization to include both zemstvists and intellectuals spread into other cities. At a home-crafts exhibition in St. Petersburg in March 1902 final preparations were made for financing and supporting *Liberation,* which began to appear in Stuttgart in June. The plans for a Union of Liberation were discussed at a series of "literary suppers" from the autumn of 1902 on, whose participants organized a "Culinary Committee." Under its aegis there took place in St. Petersburg in April 1903 a meeting of writers which decided to organize a Union of Liberation. This group was designed to unite all opposition elements in Russia without exception. Organization was undertaken at a conference near Constance, Germany, in July, and a follow-up meeting in Kharkov planned the First Congress for January 1904 in St. Petersburg. Into the Union went men with a broad range of political opinions: Ivan Petrunkevich, dean of the zemstvists and presiding officer at Constance; both Princes Dolgorukov, the "radical" Peter and the "moderate" Paul; the "radical" Prince G. E. L'vov, the "moderate" N. N. L'vov; the gifted Prince D. I. Shakhovskoi; Fedor Rodichev, author of the address which had excited the Tsar's "senseless dreams" rebuke; the academicians Bulgakov, Novgorodtsev, Miliukov, Tugan-Baranovskii, and Struve; the Revisionist socialists, Kuskova, Prokopovich, and Bogucharskii; the Right-wing populists, Annenskii, Peshekhonov, and Korolenko. The Union represented a truly impressive array of Russia's best political figures and thinkers, and its formation testified to the tremendous strides which Russian liberalism had made towards self-definition and organization. It also signified the victory of the radicals. Despite the fact that both moderates (of the Maklakovite faction, tho not Maklakov himself) and radicals (of the Miliukov stripe) were represented in this group, which set itself the task of bringing the entire non-revolutionary section of the intelligentsia into its purview, still the radicals, the rationalists, the uncompromising Westerners, were in firm control—of the Union, and of Russian liberalism.

4.

That the capture of the liberal movement by the radicals came about was in no small part due to the personality of Paul Niko-

laevich Miliukov.[8]. Son of a Moscow architect, he came to intellectual maturity in the 70's when the first overt opposition movement,
that of populism, was making its groping attempts toward social
salvation. Apparently he was never sympathetic to this stage of
populism, nor did he ever become identified with populism at any
point despite his later collaboration with its magazine *Russian
Wealth*. He was a student not of the Russian writers of the 60's
but rather of the Western rationalist philosophers Kant, Locke,
Hume, Comte, Spencer, and Marx. He was arrested for student
agitation, went to Italy, and returned to Moscow University. It
was as a professor that he felt the impact of the 1891 famine, and
it was in academic circles that he continued to work. In 1901 he was
arrested but the police failed to discover that he was the co-author
of a plan for an underground organization. He nevertheless spent
six months in prison. When he was freed, he was active in making
plans for an emigre liberal organ, and was offered the editorship of
Liberation, which he passed on instead to Struve. For writing the
famous lead article he contributed to its first number, he spent six
months in prison again, and Russia's greatest historian, Kliu-
chevskii, petitioned for the release of the man who bade fair to rival
his own scholarly reputation, but whose political passions he did
not share. When Plehve did release Miliukov, the interior minister
taunted him with an offer of the Ministry of Education. Miliukov
returned the provocation with a refusal which hinted that he might
accept instead Plehve's own job, the interior ministry. Each despised
the other, though it is doubtful if Plehve recognized the profound
threat that Miliukov represented to everything he stood for.

On the heels of this episode Miliukov went abroad to visit the
United States and to try to tell Americans, in a series of lectures
at Chicago,[9] what the Russian Liberation Movement was about.
He made it clear that the Russian liberal-Left he represented was
uncompromisingly democratic in political philosophy, that they
sought the support of the masses—workers and peasants—who ought
of right and who would in fact control Russia's destiny. Arguments
that only "educated" classes understood issues and were fit to govern, Miliukov brushed aside. The Right liberals who defended a
two-house legislature and limited suffrage to provide checks and
balances, he declared, assumed that the popular vote was easily
subject to manipulation either by absolutism or demagogues. But
this was always the argument of reactionaries! It was no use to talk
of waiting till the Russian people were "ripe" for self-government.
Centuries of autocratic absolutism had not ripened them, and only

in a free state could they learn to use their responsibilities wisely.

Here spoke the apriorist, the uncompromising rationalist. Just as in the case of Lenin and Chernov, Miliukov went on to say, not only ought a democratic system come to pass, but it is bound to come because history is bringing it to Russia. Certainly Miliukov did not deny that there existed "radical differences" between Russia and the West—though only those attributable to historical factors, not innate peculiarities of some kind. What he insisted was that whatever "differences" existed, Russia and the West still had in common what Bryce called the "laws of political biology," [10] the general laws of political evolution under which at a certain point a representative system was inevitable. Inevitable—yet demanding the most sustained and intense efforts of the Russian intelligentsia to bring to pass. Lenin and Chernov could understand this apparent contradiction in Miliukov's thinking much better than either Shipov or Maklakov within liberal ranks.

5.

As Miliukovite rationalism was taking the lead in the thought of the liberal movement, so were the intellectuals out in front in terms of organization. The "practical" emphasis of *Beseda* and the Zemstvo Union was absent from the Union of Liberation, and many of the old zemstvo liberals felt out of place in it. Accordingly some constitutionalists who had been reared in strictly zemstvist ranks decided to form their own organization instead of entering the Union, "in view of the unaccustomedness of zemstvists to conspiratorialness and heterogeneity." [11] In November 1903, following the Liberationists' Kharkov meeting, a Group of Zemstvo-Constitutionalists came into being and conducted a series of "Novosiltsevian" meetings, so named after Iu. A. Novosiltsev, their Moscow host. Their first Congress, in February 1904, followed that of the Liberationists by just a month.

Neither the Union of Liberation nor the Group of Zemstvo-Constitutionalists purported to be political parties, but both were plainly aiming in the direction of one. The Liberationists set themselves the task of uniting the whole non-Marxist intelligentsia, from men of the liberal professions through the Third Element to the zemstvist constitutionalists—and moreover, to win them all to the banner of militant, radical democracy. The Zemstvo-Constitutionalists set themselves a narrower goal, that of converting zemstvist ranks to constitutionalism, and specifically of dominating the national zemstvo Congresses which began in November 1904. As things turned out, it was impossible to push all zemstvists into constitutionalism. The zemstvo congresses finally split into the Right-liberal Octobrist party and the Left-liberal Constitutional Democratic (Kadet) party. Liberationists and Zemstvo-Constitutionalists both entered the latter.

6.

The radicals had the initiative in the liberal movement from the time that the neo-Slavophile leaders of the zemstvo bowed to the wishes of Tsarism in 1898. Yet the Slavophiles were still to play a role in the organization of opposition to Autocracy. In 1902, offended at being bypassed by the newly-constituted Special Council on Agricultural Needs, the zemstvists again banded together for consultation. This time the issue was not, as it was in 1896, the abstract right of the zemstvists to confer on local problems, but specific opposition to the government's refusal to invite their consultation on reform. At the home-crafts exhibition of March 1902 and a "fire-protection congress" of the same month zemstvists discussed the best way to proceed. It was decided to convene the presidents of the provincial zemstvo boards in Moscow on 23 May.[12]

At this meeting the Left (Petrunkevich, Shakhovskoi) and both Slavophile Right (Shipov, Stakhovich) and Westernizer Right (Count Heyden) were represented. The demand of all factions was not merely that Witte's council should consult the elected zemstvo assemblies, but they also set forth, as allegedly affecting "agricultural needs," a series of other demands for eliminating class restrictions on peasant rights, tax reform, strengthening of the zemstvos, and freer discussion in public assemblies and press. Maklakov approved these demands as a call for "liberal Autocracy," lamenting that they were not granted by the Tsar until his ukase of 12 December 1904 when it was "too late" to satisfy even the authors of the May 1902 demands, let alone anyone else.

In May 1902 the government, far from listening to this friendly advice, was outraged. Plehve summoned Shipov[13] to explain such an 'illegal" conference, but also used honeyed words. By virtuous declarations that he was on the side of the zemstvos and moreover, that the Russian state system might even have to be altered "in 30, 40, or 50 years," he induced Shipov to withdraw the demand that the zemstvo assemblies be consulted. Shipov talked to Witte at the same time and received analogous assurances from him. Witte explained that his memorandum to the Tsar about the zemstvos had been misinterpreted, and gave general approval to Shipov's objective of a rapprochement between the government and the "public men." These were empty words; Shipov was soon forced to confess that Plehve had duped him and was proving himself, if anything, more hostile to the zemstvists than before.

The Tsardom obstinately refused to understand Shipov's point. The vaguely well-intentioned promises of better laws contained in the manifesto of 26 February 1903 were regarded by Shipov as showing mistaken reliance on "legal" methods rather than the "moral" ones through which a Tsar ought to serve as instrument "ecumenical popular feeling." [14] He was likewise disturbed by the continued identification of the Autocracy with absolutism—and not merely the Tsar's absolute personal power but the absolutism of irresponsible bureaucracy as well. Yet Shipov was still hoping that the Autocracy would create "the conditions, growing out of recognition, peculiar to the spirit of the Russian people, of the primacy in political life of a predominantly moral tendency." On this ground he opposed the current of constitutionalism which in early 1903 was about to take organizational form in the Union of Liberation. The "moral" reform for which he hoped might still come about if the zemstvists could persuade the government to take the right path.

The zemstvo bureau whose responsibility it had been to summon yearly meetings had lapsed in 1896, but it was revived at the May 1902 conference. The governmental reprimand which followed in the summer induced the leaders to postpone the 1903 meeting. Instead, on finding themselves together in St. Petersburg for consultations by the Interior Ministry over insurance reform, the zemstvists held an *ad hoc* conference on 25 April 1903. Here a proposal by K. K. Arsen'ev, to ask the government to summon zemstvist representatives as a part of the state machinery which considered legislation, was narrowly defeated by a 15-13 vote. By this time Plehve, who blamed the zemstvists' increasing boldness on the unflinchingly loyal Shipov, lost patience. He refused to confirm Shipov's election as Moscow zemstvo board president in the spring of 1904 and thus succeeded in removing him from the zemstvo movement.

One of the reasons Plehve gave for this action against an obviously loyal subject of the Tsar was that Shipov had shown favoritism toward the Third Element, the professional employees of the zemstvos. It was true that Shipov thought the "future" of the zemstvos lay with the Third Element. He was indeed correct if he meant the political future of the zemstvists, for the Third Element was to make a much swifter and deeper mark in Russian liberalism than its bigger and much older brother, the zemstvo-constitution-alist group. Plehve may have seen better than Shipov the political potentialities of the Third Element, but he was unable to counter-act its influence on the gentry and more particularly the zemstvists. He was incapable of making any positive political appeal to any group, but he succeeded well enough in repulsing the advances of the Slavophiles, the only group willing to offer real support to the regime in exchange for moderate reforms. Thus by rendering the Slavophiles' political objective, cooperation of Tsardom with the "public men," impossible, he helped mightily to weaken their influence in liberal circles and strengthened the hand of their radical competitors. The bureaucrats, it was now plain, were not to be trusted. When Witte was removed from the finance ministry in August 1903, Maklakov saw that a "liberal Autocracy" was im-possible under existing conditions. As an empiricist he was at least willing to learn from the bitter experience of Shipov, though Shipov himself was not. He continued to hope for some kind of "moral" awakening. Even as late as the appointment of the mild Sviatopolk-Mirskii in the fall of 1904 he thought the Slavophile ideal might be realized. Whatever of their hopes refused to die, the neo-Slavophiles were completely isolated by 1903. Having had their faith in Autocracy pounded out of them by Autocracy itself, they still refused "to follow the tail of the Revolution," as Makla-kov says, and they found themselves politically homeless.

7.

The Slavophiles struggled valiantly against the Liberationists for leadership of the new liberal movement, though they met rebuffs from the only ally with whom they could realize their ob-jective. This struggle is clearly reflected in the pages of *Liberation*, Struve's emigre organ which appeared in the summer of 1902.

Both Right and Left liberals had their say in the very first num-ber.[15] The spokesman of Russian constitutionalists, "S. S." (Miliu-kov), declared that the liberal program must be founded on "principle and feasibility," and set out a list of political objectives including the personal freedoms, equality before the law, and classless popular representation in the government. The empiri-cism of the right was voiced by a "group of zemstvists" which

declared as its objective the abolition of "anarchy" whether owing
to the Tsardom or the masses. Struve in his editorial set the keynote of mediation and reconciliation which *Liberation* sounded
repeatedly in its early days. His organ, he declared, was committed
to "the Hannibalic oath" for the political liberation of Russia,
as Herzen had half a century earlier "sworn" not to rest till the
fall of serfdom, as Hannibal had sworn to fight till Rome fell.
Struve would aim at replacement of the "arbitrariness of Autocratic bureaucracy" by the rights of personality and society. "These
words, we foresee, will seem to one too moderate, to another too
radical," but our task is "not to divide but to unite." The reference
was to *Iskra's* slogan, "Before we unite, we must draw a line of
demarcation." Said Struve, the cultural and political liberation
of Russia cannot be exclusively the business of one class, one party,
one doctrine. Our group will be liberal and democratic, and reformist: "even the extremist Russian parties in their present demands do not go beyond broad political and economic reforms
in the democratic spirit." This half-nod in the direction of the
revolutionaries was an omen of the tactical issue on which Slavophiles and Liberationists were to clash most bitterly.

A Leftist at once challenged[16] the "group of zemstvists" of the
Right to define what was meant, in the phrase about "anarchy
of government and people," by anarchy of the people. If the revolutionaries were referred to, it did not behoove the liberals
under existing conditions to turn from them as alien and contrast
the zemstvo opposition with the revolutionary opposition. This
did not mean that liberals should adopt all revolutionary methods,
but "we must have done with timid half-measures of legal oposi-
tion . . . One does not ask for a constitution, one takes it." The
literary polemics continued, but something more dramatic had
happened which sharpened the Left's criticism of the Shipovites:
Shipov's talk with Plehve and his agreement to withdraw the
zemstvist demand for consultations. A Liberationist, Anton Staritsky-
kii, branded this whole maneuver as a "false step." If the zemstvists were courageous, he wrote, the people would stand behind
them, but this was exactly the wrong way to attract mass support.
A contributor "Senex"[17] lashed out at the "Slavophile monarchist idyll" which led Shipov into acquiescing in Plehve's ignoring
of zemstvist opinion on the needs of agriculture. "Old Zemstvist"
shrilled that bureaucracy was beating the zemstvists "like street
urchins"; would they calmly bow to such treatment?

Struve chided[18] the Slavophiles gently. The zemstvo movement, he said, represented "only one current" of the rising Russian democracy. If it should lose its tie with the broad democratic tendency, it would cease to serve the cause and merit the support of all freedom-loving forces of the extra-class Russian intelligenstia and become a simple instrument of the gentry.

Miliukov was characteristically blunt. [19] After eight months of publication, *Liberation* had shown that it had attempted to represent too wide a spectrum of opinions to present accurately any viewpoint. Despite talk about amity, disagreements within liberal ranks were a fact. It was time to think of building a liberal organization of a definite tendency, and this could only be done by working from strong cadres of "convinced constitutionalists." This statement brought Struve to pull abreast of the radical spokesman: a party must be formed, Struve declared, one that is "openly and decisively constitutionalist . . . openly and decisively democratic." This, in his opinion, entailed universal suffrage. Such criteria exclude "the possibility of bringing into the party people of the so-called Slavophile type of opinion."

This was a virtual (though not final) rejection of unity with the Slavophiles. Turning their back on them, the Liberationists found themselves face to face with the revolutionaries. They had maintained an attitude toward the Revolution ranging from benevolent neutrality to sympathetic encouragement, from the time of the founding of the liberal organ. Struve had sharply condemned government reprisals against the peasant rioters of Poltava and Kharkov.[20] He reprinted a report of the increasing sympathy of Russian "society" towards terrorism which stated that "those who condemned Karpovich now praise Balmashev." It was the government which was responsible for the conditions which gave rise to these excesses, and it had better learn at once that the only peaceful way out was the "open admission into the government of the forces of society for the radical reorganization of the state." Note, however, that Struve here merely stated Maklakovism sharply. This was not a Liberationist formulation; in fact, Struve was never to become a full-fledged Liberationist.

Struve also occupied middle ground[21] between the two liberal wings in dealing with the accusation that moderates tried to "frighten" the government with revolution. He wrote that it was not a question of a threat, for the prospect of revolution had to be analyzed not from the standpoint of will but rather that of inevitability. The Russian revolution was not yet ripe to achieve the radical political reform for which the nation cried out, but it would surely come when the crimes and sacrifices of the existing order mounted sufficiently high. Summoning Autocracy to avert revolution by swift and sweeping reforms, the liberals obeyed the voice of conscience; but depicting before Tsardom's eyes the otherwise inevitable perspective of revolution, they only expressed their scientific conviction.

In the same issue of *Liberation* in which this article appeared, Struve addressed the revolutionaries directly for the first time. There could be no compromise with "political arbitrariness" now any more than in the 50's. In order to put an end to it, "the broadest mutual tolerance" was required from all the various segments of the Russian opposition. Some said that monarchists and republicans, individualists and socialists, could never cooperate; but such men were blinded by doctrine and had lost touch with the demands of real life. The reactionary editor of the *Moscow Gazette*, Katkov, had labeled all the opposition as sedition, and from his own viewpoint he was right. Nevertheless if that was true, "that means that in Russia there is no sedition, but only opposition." Accordingly, liberalism must "recognize its solidarity with the so-called 'revolutionary' currents" in their political tasks insofar as they might lead to the strengthening of "legal order." On the other side the revolutionary camp must "recognize liberalism as its ally in the achievement of political freedom" which was the essence of the Russian revolution. Neither side could do without the other.

The question of allies, which each Russian opposition group realized to be crucial since none was strong enough to accomplish its objectives unaided, thus came forward for open discussion among liberals. Struve, who had been the author of the first official manifesto of the Social Democratic Party,[22] knew perfectly well what the only possible terms of liberal cooperation with the revolutionaries could be: an unenthusiastic, uneasy entente for a specific purpose, the overthrow of Autocracy. He knew furthermore that the socialists regarded this as merely a first step, the necessary preliminary to social revolution, while liberals believed that one convulsion would bring about a kind of polity under which the interests of all groups, conflicting as they might be, could be brought into some kind of free reconciliation.

In other words, the apriorist sociology of the liberals did not stop with the coming "bourgeois revolution," any more than did that of the socialists. However, since the succeeding phase would be one in which their desired allies, the socialists, would have to abandon the social-revolution part of their scheme, the liberals did not go out of their way to stress their view of the future. Why should they? They believed anyway that persuasion was of no use in making the socialists yield; it would be the objective historical situation which would compel a turn to peaceful methods. A broad hint of these expectations was provided when Struve appraised the results of electoral gains by German Social Democrats in 1903.[23] In Germany, he declared, the nation's liberal and democratic development depended entirely on the growth of Social Democracy. It was natural that as that party grew, it should lose much of its earlier flavor of absolute truth and unwillingness to compromise. Struve then went ahead to draw deductions from the German scene applicable to Russian liberalism. Russian liberals had not yet advanced clearly democratic political and social demands, particularly on the agrarian and labor problems. Yet no section of the Liberation Movement could bypass these questions. Every segment "must boldly include in its demands serious social reforms for the benefits of peasants and workers. It is not yet too late for Russian liberalism to take the correct political position— not against social democracy but together with and in union with it."

Thus appealing to the example of German Social Democracy, which Plekhanov and Lenin so highly respected, the liberals painted a picture of how socialists could behave respectably in a bourgeois state. Still this was treading on slippery ground. Struve knew from his own experience how bitterly the socialists resented any liberal attempts to direct their course. He therefore concentrated instead on making the bourgeois revolution—a pill the socialist doctors had already prescribed for themselves as patients— more palatable to them by assigning it social and economic as well as political objectives, and left the future to be determined by the growth of the capitalism he valued so highly. If the pill was not too disagreeable to revolutionaries, they might subsequently be less feverish about trying to force a dose of social revolution down the throats of the unwilling liberals.

Struve hastened to make his generalizations about social reform more precise.[24] After all, he began, liberalism and socialism were inseparable in their basic ideal. Socialism, instead of threatening liberalism, came "not to destroy, but to fulfil the covenants of liberalism." Thus *Liberation* was bound to advance demands, many of which socialists had first elaborated, in the interests of the working classes. The needs of labor offered no problem; they were those long ago clarified in Western countries in respect to improved working conditions. However, the agrarian problem, at least in Russia, demanded a special sort of attention. There the old Physiocratic slogan "pauvres paysans—pauvre royaume" retained a significance it had largely lost in industrialized countries. The antagonism between large-landowner and small-peasant economy, which the populist Engelhardt had described, was a real one.[25] To restore the small-peasant sector to health, not only must the privileges of the gentry be abolished as they were in the French Revolution, but in addition positive measures must be taken for "the transfer of land into the hands of the laboring masses." Such transfer moreover might involve compulsory alienation of lands by the government, as well as the more desirable "right of pre-eminent purchase at a just valuation" of lands offered for sale.

Having advanced such a "democratic" social program, the *Liberation* group felt they had sufficiently approached socialist program minima that Struve's ex-confreres, the Social Democrats, had no further reason to hold back from the kind of temporary entente they themselves had announced willingness to enter. One contributor seized the chance of Plekhanov's plea[26] to the Bolsheviks for tolerance to lament only that Plekhanov had not shelved the spirit of sectarianism in relation to the rest of the Liberation Movement as well. The out-moded faith of the revolutionaries in "some kind of street fight" which under existing conditions could bring only defeat, led them to hostility toward those who lacked such faith. Nevertheless, if the extremists were seriously interested in the political struggle and put the realization of their aims higher than the glory of their party, if they believed that from all standpoints the first and most pressing task of the Russian revolutionary movement was to attain political freedom, then they must "strive toward unification of the liberation movement" just as Plekhanov did toward the reunion of his own party.

Then, just at the moment when *Liberation* had begun to woo the revolutionaries openly and denounce the Slavophiles for consorting with the bureaucratic lackeys of the Tsar, there came an event which caused them to hesitate—the beginning of the Japanese War. Struve, after first denouncing the government which had brought on "this useless war," soon had second thoughts.[27] Still repeating that he believed the war could bring no good result, he thought it his duty to call on all good Russians to remember their patriotism and to work for the victory of the army, if that were possible. Another writer, though likewise accusing the Tsardom of war guilt, talked of a distinction between internal and external situations in Russia, the threat of "Asiatic tribes," and so on. Struve, in an open letter to Russian students, proclaimed the slogan, "Long live the army, long live Russia, long live freedom, long live free Russia!"

Miliukov, who had so far been willing to allow Struve to act as journalistic spokesman for the radicals he led, now responded with sharp retorts.[28] Such advice to the students, he said, was neither practical nor wise. He condemned "those moderates" who were being drawn into supporting the government on "patriotic" grounds. Struve replied feebly that of course Plehve as before remained the enemy, but as for himself, it was impossible to employ the same methods as before the war. To Miliukov, however, the problem was simple, and he saw it in essentially the same terms as the socialists. The liberals' aim was to overturn Autocracy; if the state was weakened by war, this would simply be achieved all the sooner. As one of his backers put it: "Let the idol Autocracy be overthrown in the waters of the Yellow Sea." [29] "And in this question," says Maklakov sadly, " 'society' followed P. N. Miliukov, and not Struve." The almost unanimous "defeatism" [30] of the Russian opposition in regard to the Russo-Japanese War forms a striking contrast to the almost unanimous (save the Bolsheviks) "defensism" or at least benevolent neutrality toward defensism displayed during the First World War. There are obvious reasons for the difference. The Far East was far away from Moscow, whose inhabitants did not fear Japanese siege. Russia in 1904 had no great democratic allies which might influence her in case of victory. But in any case the leaders of the Liberation Movement were flushed with optimism about the struggle ahead, and the unity of the opposition was undamaged by the wounds which 1905 was to inflict upon it. The intellectuals who made up the parties felt that the Russia that mattered was outside and aside from Tsardom and that Tsardom was the only enemy. After 1905 most of them knew better.

8.

The Miliukovite anti-Slavophile, pro-revolutionary line was not challenged again by *Liberation*, though it sometimes lagged behind it. In March 1904 an unsigned editorial [31] said flatly, first of all we must "sharply mark ourselves off from that visionary Slavophile liberalism, which considers it possible to achieve the reform of Russian life in alliance with Autocracy." As for the monarchist principle itself, whether one favors or opposes it, in the Tsardom it had if not the worst enemy at least the most dangerous possible ally, and was being thereby discredited. "We abandon all illusions about possible influence on the Autocratic government and—still more—possible cooperation with it." In order to liquidate the existing order, the liberals, continued the writer, put their reliance on broad influence over public opinion, and the achievement of freedom; but not that alone, for freedom was "unthinkable and impossible without a broad plan of social betterment, in which and through which freedom will find its concrete embodiment."

The formulation of the Kadet point of view was almost complete. An important question nevertheless remained: precisely through what institutional means would the new order be brought about? In July 1904 a tentative answer[32] was advanced in retort to a letter-writer who, scandalized by the "Lefting" of the Liberationists, advised them for the time being to take a "passive position." The editors accused their critic of wishing them "to be dragged on the tail of events" which they would neither bring about nor avoid. The objective must be openly stated: it was a popular representative body with full legislative power including review of the budget, to be elected on the basis of universal and direct suffrage. "Equal and secret" were of course assumed. This meant acceptance of the revolutionaries' "Four-Tail" slogan, but there was as yet no mention of a Constituent Assembly. Struve was unwilling to go that far until 1905, and when the Revolution finally began, as a result of his cautiousness his journal lost the very initiative it had preached.

On the crucial question of the liberals' allies, however, there was no equivocation. Two months before Bloody Sunday Struve attacked Prince Eugene Trubetskoi for his widely-discussed article in *Law*, in which he saw in the revolutionaries' monopoly of "free" (i.e., illegal) discussion and organization "a great danger." [33] Until Autocracy was ended, retorted Struve, every force against it was not a great danger but a "great boon." The moderates had a right to attack extremist parties from only one standpoint, "the inexpediency and insufficiency" of their methods of struggle against Autocracy. Struve advised Trubetskoi bluntly that "there is no internal enemy in Russia but Autocracy" and all that nourishes it. This was unadulterated Miliukovism: the flat assertion that no difference in principle existed between Russian liberalism and the doctrine of the Russian socialist parties in the era of bourgeois revolution, and as a result the tactical slogan, "No enemy on the Left." When it eventually appeared that there *was* at least one irreconcilable enemy on the Left, the reason was clearly not a change of mind on the part of the radicals, but a clarification of an always latent position of the Bolsheviks. Friendship, political or other, is a two-way street. Not being political pacifists, the Kadets were never under the illusion that they could kill Lenin's hostility through kindness. In terms of 1904, however, the slogan "No enemy on the Left" epitomizes the position of Liberationism and the tactic to which it led Russian liberalism.

9.

The enemy was on the Right; the enemy was the government. No attempt to change its spots, as for example when the interior minister Sviatopolk-Mirskii inaugurated his "new course," could lessen the radicals' hostility. Miliukov himself told Prince Mirskii bluntly[34] when he became minister that his appeal for "confidence" was useless, that "between Autocracy and consistent constitutionalism there is no intermediate position." When Mirskii first sanctioned, then forbade the November 1904 zemstvo congress, this wobbling was triumphantly cited as proving the "fiasco" of the new policy.

Mirskii was thenceforth ignored, in the excitement of the liberal journalists over the "banquet campaign" which followed the November congress and led directly to Bloody Sunday. The tremendous public furor of late autumn was well reflected in the pages of *Liberation*, but by December the mounting radicalism of popular opinion left the emigre organ far behind. Not incorrectly had a contributor accused it of being "not a compass, but a mirror" of the opposition movement.[35] Thus for the second time after beginning in the forefront of a political movement, Struve found himself in the rear ranks and isolated, in the constitutional democratic camp as he had been in the Social Democratic one. He was to have only negligible political influence in the actual organization of the party which owed more to his journalistic spadework than to that of any other man. Dan correctly remarks[36] that he was not radical enough to serve as a spokesman for the urban intelligentsia and lower middle class which formed the hard kernel of Liberationism.

10.

The Union of Liberation had at last held a congress in the first days of 1904, taking final form as a federation of autonomous local committees and professional organizations.[37] Since the congress was held in St. Peterburg, the utmost precautions had to be taken to avoid police interference. For example, the report on political institutions was entitled, "On the Austrian electoral reform, from the works of Gellert." The "Four Tails" were accepted by the congress, though the question of a Constitutent Assembly was sidestepped. A Union Council was set up, consisting half of zemstvists and half of "intellectuals," and this composition reflected the later make-up of the Kadet party itself.

The Group of Zemstvo-Constitutionalists, organizing officially a month later, showed itself considerably less radical. For example, it talked of finishing the war as a matter of national defense before turning to combat the internal enemy, Tsarism. Despite its less radical viewpoint, the Group did resolve to work in close unity with the Liberationists, while remaining separate from their organization.

In October 1904 the Liberationists met again and worked out a party program, though by accident it was not officially adopted until the congress of the following March.[38] In essentials the Kadet program was here complete: an outright demand for a Four-Tail Constituent Assembly, compulsory alienation of land at a just valuation for the benefit of the peasants, the eight-hour day for the workers. The Union also resolved to begin organization of "professional unions" (later to be welded into one Union of Unions) which should establish organizational links with the central committees of all Leftist parties and work out a common program with them. In November the Liberationists obtained, through the help of the wealthy Moscow industrialist Savva Morozov, a legal newspaper, *Our Life*, in St. Petersburg. This was the first open organ of the Left-Liberals in Russia, though it was soon to be followed by another, *Son of the Fatherland*. When the Paris inter-party conference was summoned in November, the Union of Liberation sent some of its foremost leaders to attend: Miliukov, Prince Dolgorukov, Bogucharskii, and Struve. These delegates reached agreement with the Socialist Revolutionaries and other smaller opposition groups, achieving what Maklakov too strongly terms a "formal union with the revolution" [39] in which the liberals adopted "not only the phraseology but the ideology" of the revolutionaries. The statement overemphasizes the results of the Paris conference. What Maklakov might call "borrowing" from, Miliukov "parallel development" with, the revolutionaries, did not result from any chance meeting but was the result of Liberationist sociology which, as Maklakov himself points out, dated from years earlier.

The October congress of the Union decided also to send delegates to the next zemstvo congress, which had been summoned to meet in Moscow in November. After a silence of a year and a half, the zemstvists had seized on Mirskii's appointment as a chance to hold another meeting in order to consider, for the first time, the general political situation. Shipov battled against the inclusion of this "point 6" [40] in the agenda of particular problems with which the congress was to deal, but since no one else on the zemstvo bureau agreed with him, he yielded. His reasons were not simply connected with his conservatism. He was impressed by Mirskii's seeming willingness at last to approach his own ideal of reform through the cooperation of Tsardom and "public men," and he desired to avoid embarrassing the new policy of "confidence." However, he loyally supported the zemstvists' decision once taken. Indeed he insisted to Mirskii personally,[41] in spite of his own previous vote to the contrary, that the situation was by now too grave for the zemstvists to limit themselves to discussion of problems of "alimentation, medical care, and the like," as Mirskii wished. A compromise reminiscent of that with Goremykin in 1896[42] was reached, and the congress was allowed to convene as a "private group" in Moscow on 6 November.

Over half of the delegates were members of *Beseda*,[43] yet even the "loyalism" of that group had weakened by this time and the majority of the men at the meeting had constitutionalist leanings. The decisions of the congress, embodied in the "Eleven Points" (which Miliukov termed "the famous Petition of Right" to an American audience[44]), still spoke in terms of mutual confidence between government and "society." However, it also demanded the classic "freedoms" and a central representative assembly which, it was agreed by a 71-27 vote, should have legislative, not merely consultative, powers. The question of suffrage, however, was left open and the "Four Tails" went unmentioned. Nevertheless, if the October Manifesto was a "constitution," then the November zemstvo congress had declared in favor of one.

The congress resolved that local zemstvo assemblies should discuss these "Eleven Points" and petition the government for their adoption, but many of the delegates were a little taken aback at the tremendous popular response to this appeal. The "banquet campaign" (as men who recalled France's 1848 Revolution dubbed it) embraced not only zemstvists but a great variety of other urban groups. The city councils, up till then largely unaffected by the opposition movement, were seized by feverish interest,[45] and occasionally workers joined in demonstrations in favor of a constitution—although the Menshevik plan for mass worker participation was not realized.[46] The restrained language of the "Eleven Points" was almost forgotten in the Liberationist-minded resolutions which poured into the Ministry of the Interior, and the slogan "Constituent Assembly" was more favored than the zemstvists' cautious "popular representation."

The Tsar was induced by Mirskii to consider accepting many of the demands of the November congress, "private" or not.[47] The ukase of 12 December actually did promise to adopt four of the eleven points, though Nicholas decided, after consulting Witte, to omit a Mirskii-sponsored provision for summoning zemstvist representatives for legislative consultation. As a result of this omission, Mirskii at once asked to resign. The same day as the 12 December ukase was published, an official reprimand sharply castigated as "mutinous" the resolutions which had resulted from the "banquet campaign," and consequently the Slavophiles virtually abandoned in despair their momentarily revived hope for "liberal Autocracy." Maklakov marks this point as the end of the "role of the loyal zemstvo," [48] even though the Shipov-led "minority" of the November congress continued to play an important part through 1905. Indeed, it was from this "minority" that came the bulk of those who founded the Octobrist party, whose program was based on "loyalty." Nevertheless, Octobrism was rather the heir of the empiricist liberal Right than the Slavophilism which hoped for "moral" regeneration of the state. The true Slavophiles such as Shipov and N. A. Khomiakov became "constitutionalists by imperial decree," because they were loyal, not because the October Manifesto agreed with their teaching. It was rather the empiricists who hailed the Manifesto as the kind of constitution Russia was "ready" for, and took the name of their "Octobrist" party from the pronouncement which pleased them so much. To complete the confusion, Maklakov, the spokesman of Right empiricism, entered not the Octobrist but the Kadet party. Of the three currents which were competing for ascendancy in the liberal movement in 1898, only one was led in 1905 to where its spokesman wanted it to go, and that was Miliukov's Liberationism.

11.

"Bloody Sunday" found the Liberationists in command of the liberal movement. The Slavophiles had been disarmed and rendered powerless by the refusal of their chosen ally, the Tsardom, to give them the slightest assistance. The Right empiricists kept silent; "be content with the possible" was not a popular gospel in time of incipient revolution. The Liberationists appeared to be marching at least in the vicinity of, if not in step with, their revolutionary allies. Their own organization had been firmly established, they had acquired two legal newspapers in addition to their emigre organ, they bade fair to take the initiative away from the Zemstvo-Constitutionalists in the zemstvo congresses themselves. Having captured the support of much of "society," they were ready to bid for the backing of workers and peasants as well on the basis of their democratic reformist program. In November Liberationist leaders entered into conversations with Father Gapon in order to arrange participation of the members of his "union" in the November-December demonstrations, and Pokrovsky hints that Kuskova, the "Economist" turned Liberationist, was herself the author of the petition Gapon tried to present to the Tsar on 9 January.[49]

The Liberationist line was apparently irresistible. Even in *Beseda* itself, as Maklakov reports, there were "people who were seized by hope in the new allies and faith in their power." [50] This was the real fear of the Right liberals, whether Slavophile or empiricist. Shipov attacked Liberationist rationalism and positivism, but what alarmed him most was not this intellectual error but the consequences, which both Maklakov and he foresaw and observed.[51] It was the rational program of the Union of Liberation, rather than common interests and experience, which drew it to the socialists.

Miliukov and his future Kadets realized this quite clearly. Between a program which tried to blunt social contradictions and one which tried to sharpen them, said he, "harmonization is hardly possible." [52] "One is 'opportunist' and works through compromise, while the other is uncompromising and works through social struggle. Competition is always strongest among the closest rivals . . ." and this was the reason that the socialists had denounced most sharply of all the article in *Liberation*[53] which had supported compulsory alienation of land. Since it was hopeless to discuss a common program of economic and social reform (though as he had just pointed out the two programs might come uncomfortably close) —and this was "tacitly admitted by the silence on the subject of such reform of the document of the Paris agreement"—it was necessary to restrict an alliance between socialists and liberals to political reform. Since both parties put this first, alliance on that basis was possible. "As soon as that political reform shall have been attained, a radical change of party lines will take place . . . But until the political freedom comes, they all . . . will make common front against the common enemy . . ." This statement embodied not only Liberationist, but orthodox socialist doctrine, which had been clearly stated in almost identical terms by the spokesman of both revolutionary parties. Concretely, the terms of cooperation with actual Liberal groups had been set forth in the Potresov resolution adopted by the II Congress of the Social Democratic Party, terms which the Union of Liberation had satisfied by its own program of October 1904.[54]

In actual fact, a kind of "common front" among all opposition groups was formed and maintained in 1905 until the issuance of the October Manifesto. Nevertheless, the necessary degree of co-operation was not attained. The explanation of this phenomenon is not to be found simply in discrepancy between theory and practice, which often sounds like the most plausible explanation to historians of political ideas. The rational concurrence upon which the alliance was predicated was more apparent than real, and the divergences between the two wings of the Russian opposition which were revealed in actual revolutionary experience were already present in theory. The fact that these divergences already existed, and the reasons they were not perceived earlier by the opposition leaders themselves, are matters which this writer has been trying to elucidate.

If the rational concurrence had been, if not complete, sufficient, probably not the October Manifesto, but the summoning of a Constituent Assembly, would have resulted from the Revolution of 1905. But it was only in the midst of the great stress and tumult of the Revolution that the lack of concurrence became clear, and by that time there was no turning back: all parties had to go on to hang separately, whereas they had been confident that by hanging together they were sure to gain victory.

Part Three

THE CLOUDBURST

VII

CHERNOV: A TOILERS' REVOLUTION

> *We must regard the Russian revolution "not as*
> *a bourgeois revolution, in the usual sense of the*
> *word, but not as a socialist revolution either; but*
> *rather as a completely peculiar sort of process . . ."*
> KARL KAUTSKY, discussing 1905.[1]

When the revolutionary storm broke at last with the massacre of
Bloody Sunday, all the opposition leaders were convinced that they
knew what sort of upheaval was in store for Russia. History or-
dained that it would be of a certain order; and there seemed to
be agreement among the party leaders as to what characteristics it
would end in the enactment of sweeping social reforms. Martov
would have and what not to call it, even though they could not
agree on a name for it. They all knew it was not to be a "socialist"
revolution. They all knew it would eliminate the absolute power
of the Tsar, and transfer the power to a democracy, that it would
inaugurate an era of personal and public freedom, and that it
would end in the enactment of sweeping social reforms. Martov
called it a "bourgeois" revolution; Miliukov accepted the term
though would not use it himself; Lenin insisted on calling it a
"bourgeois democratic" one; Chernov refused to accept or use the
word "bourgeois" at all, and spoke of a "toilers'" (*trudovaia*) or
"political" revolution. As to which emphasis was most accurate as
a forecast and most practicable as a blueprint, all were willing to
accept the verdict which history would render, when prodded and
pushed by the opposition party in question.

Chernov and the Socialist Revolutionaries started the fateful year
1905 at a disadvantage compared to the Marxists, with respect to
party organization. They had not yet held a party congress, and
were not to do so until December. Perhaps the example of the
Social Democratic congress, which had merely resulted in a deep
intra-party cleavage, suggested to them that they need not hasten

with this task. *Revolutionary Russia* had published a draft program in May 1904, but this could not be sanctioned officially until a Congress was held. The autonomous terrorist Battle Organization was apparently strong and successful, and it was soon to add the life of the Grand Duke Sergei, governor-general of Moscow, to its sacrifices. Actually it was led by a police agent, Azef, though as yet there were few in the party who had the remotest suspicions of the fact. [2]

While the central party machinery was still weak and infiltrated by the police, there was a brighter side to the picture. Inside Russia party membership was growing, as one of its leaders wrote, "from hour to hour." New committees were fast being organized, especially in the Northwest. Special organizations were formed for workers in the major cities, students in the universities, and in Odessa one was set up for soldiers. In February a Caucasian Union took shape; in March, a Union of the Volga; in May a Ukrainian organization. The party vigorously participated in urban workers' demonstrations, and its activity among peasants was sharply increased. In early June a meeting was held which replaced the old Peasant Union of the Party, dating from 1902, with a new one. In August the new Union began to publish abroad a journal for peasants. One of the party's most tireless workers in the rural areas, Breshko-Breshkovskaia, wrote an impassioned appeal for intellectuals to help in peasant agitation. At the end of July at a Moscow congress the Socialist Revolutionaries took part in organizing an "All-Russian Peasant Union." Delegates from 28 gubernias, in the ratio of four peasants to every intellectual, discussed the land question with enthusiasm and were induced to adopt a demand for a Four-Tail Constituent Assembly. The congress voted unanimously for abolition of private property in land and confiscation of state and church lands without indemnity, as well as gentry lands with partial compensation, under conditions which the Constituent Assembly would determine. In any case the land was to be the collective property of "the people."

Many writers have minimized the importance of the Peasant Union,[3] claiming it was unable to speak for the peasantry in any true sense. This criticism is beside the point, for the Peasant Union could not be anything but weak in view of the low level of education and political consciousness among the peasantry. The extent that the peasants *were* organized for political action can be credited almost wholly to the efforts of the populists who labored for two generations toward that end. That they had no greater success than they did may be partially explained by the fact that populism did not aim simply at giving the peasants their heart's desire, the land as their very own, but at "socializing" the land in a way the masses found it difficult to understand. If the SR's refused to accept the Marxist prescriptions for agricultural reform, they still clung to the Western doctrine of "socialism," however nominally "adapted" to the Russian scene via talk about building on the old Russian commune. Yet despite the fundamental unpalatability of their demands to a large part of the peasantry, the neo-populists succeeded in gaining the support of thousands of peasants for them. Viewed from this angle, the Peasant Union was a more imposing achievement of the Socialist Revolutionaries than first appears.

2.

It would seem that among the peasantry, at least, the only possible revolutionary activity would be that concerned with the mass movement. Some old-line party agitators endeavored to organize local land seizures, but they were proud of the fact that many of these took place without personal violence or destruction of property. However, one Socialist Revolutionary group was of another mind. In Geneva in 1904 there was organized a circle committed to arouse "agrarian terrorism," though such leaders as Chernov, Gotz, and Shishko opposed it sharply. The leader of the group, Sokolov, finally received party permission to return to Russia in the autumn in order to attempt to realize his program under certain agreed limitations. No sooner was he back than he violated the agreement, but further intra-party squabbles on the matter were averted when the police arrested most of the Sokolov group at a meeting at Kursk in April 1905.

The "conventional" type of terrorism had prospered in the meantime. Its most notable success had been the assassination of Plehve, which through formidable irony had been Azef's first major project as head of the Battle Organization, after he had replaced Gershuni, the imprisoned giant of the party. The next important blow after Plehve was to be a grandiose triple assassination to include the Grand Duke Sergei, governor-general of Moscow, the Grand Duke Vladimir Alexandrovich, and Kleigels, governor-general of Kiev. This plan miscarried but Sergei at least was killed on 4 February by Ivan Kaliaev. In the late summer of 1905 the terrorist group temporarily suspended activity, partly in consequence of sweeping arrests in St. Petersburg in May, an incident which the ultraconservative *New Times* overoptimistically termed "the Mukden of the Russian Revolution." Local SR groups in Nizhnii-Novgorod, Ufa, and elsewhere continued to carry out terrorist acts, but the role of planned political assassination had by this time been definitely subordinated to mass organizational work in party tactics. Socialist Revolutionaries concentrated on extending their influence among workers and peasants, and by the time of the I Congress in December, Maslov reports, there existed party committees in "almost all regions" of Russia.

3.

When the news of Bloody Sunday reached the exiled editors of *Revolutionary Russia,* they, in common with all the Russian opposition, recognized its character quickly. It was, they were sure, not a strike, not a demonstration, but a "popular uprising, this is the beginning, the threshold of revolution!" [4] It was what they had worked for, what they expected. It did not constitute an elemental, formless cataclysm, but an event for which they had an historical category ready and waiting. Immediately it became urgent to redefine this category, to prevent its perversion either in terms of scientific interpretation or political tactics. The greatest danger here was that the revolution would be "bourgeois." Shishko, an SR journalist, noted bitterly that those who regarded the impending revolution as "bourgeois" and tried to realize it on that pattern included not only liberals but Social Democrats. For the Marxists, "tightly chained to this dogma of their program," were committed merely to sharpen the bourgeois revolution instead of looking ahead to the socialist phase. Socialists must concentrate their attention, said Shishko, on the social revolution which was their only *raison d'etre.*

Of course he was willing to agree that the first phase would bring about results analogous to those of the Western revolutions: political freedom, which of course must be achieved first. The SR's had learned only too well from Tsarist repression how difficult it was to think of organizing the masses without liberty. A party which originated in the idea of the "people's will," furthermore, could not be suspected of neglecting the idea of democracy; of course the new regime must be politically democratic. Nevertheless, those who championed the class struggle of the workers could not fight for the victory of the middle class.

By now the SR's had seen from Lenin's writing that he agreed with them in respect of not desiring the victory of the middle class either. How to explain the paradox that he, a Social Democrat, could take such a position? If, as Lenin said, the middle class was not to have "hegemony" in the bourgeois revolution, in what sense would it be bourgeois? Lenin's answer appeared to be that it would be "bourgeois" in "class character," though not by the leading class forces involved. That could only mean strengthening the principle of private property—and indeed so Lenin thought. But especially in the village, the chief object of SR solicitude, strengthening property rights would make complete socialism infinitely more difficult to achieve later. If Lenin really desired socialism, how could he reason thus? The SR's were puzzled.

The SR's did in any case agree with Lenin that not only must the middle class be kept from taking the leading role, but that it should instead pass to the urban proletariat. Now if the workers took the lead, said Shishko, how could the revolution remain within bourgeois limits? The extent it would transcend these limits would depend, he continued, on the part played by the peasants. He recapitulated the growth of strength and determination of the village revolutionary movement, and noted that though it was insufficiently organized there were already some trained cadres ready for action. These would surely follow the lead of the urban workers who would, without compromising their own class demands, serve as the vanguard of the great social revolution which would come on the heels of the political, "laborist" phase.

Thus the Socialist Revolutionaries formulated a concept analogous to the "permanent revolution" of Trotsky and Lenin. The workers and peasants would seize power, establish a democratic republic, and sweep on to social revolution without a break. Capitalism, or at least private property, was not to be given a chance to grow stronger before it was destroyed. The "socialization" of land—which was *not* socialism— would give the workers and peasants a strong point from which they could advance to build a completely socialist state. Now there were still to be two phases; to mix the two was to the SR's the Maximalist heresy which they fiercely combatted. There would be, nevertheless, no "significant interval" between phases; and in this Lenin and Chernov stood together against the Mensheviks, whose position on this issue was acceptable to the Kadets for tactical purposes.

Since they held this view of the immediate future, the neo-populists were both angered and nonplussed by Marxist accusations that *they* were "bourgeois" and desired alliance with the middle class. Both their Russian traditions and Western-inspired socialism filled them with hatred for *meshchanstvo* in any form. Charges of being pro-bourgeois, wrote the Paris SR organ *La Tribune Russe*,[5] came with an ill grace from those (Lenin) who three years ago called the Marshals of Gentry their "allies of tomorrow" and who demanded dissolution of communal ownership of property to the profit of the individual. SR's, on the other hand, believed in waging class war against the bourgeoisie in the political as well as the economic sphere. They had no illusions about the revolutionary energy or democracy of Russian liberals, "the most pusillanimous and the least intelligent, perhaps, of all the world's bourgeois parties." Nevertheless, declared one writer, repeating the orthodox socialist maxim, revolutionary socialists must not reject in principle all possibility of coalition at a given moment with the most advanced elements of the liberal opposition. SR's would support liberals on condition that they adhered to the popular demand for universal suffrage. In that case both parties might work together until the political revolution was achieved. In other words, the SR's did as the Mensheviks did; they differentiated between liberals, set forth conditions for the radical wing to satisfy, and accepted temporary cooperation with it as long as it satisfied the conditions. The SR's had accepted the radicals formally on such a basis when they reached agreement with the Liberationists at the Paris conference; the Mensheviks never formally indicated their acceptance of liberal allies, but simply did so in practice. Lenin and the Bolsheviks, on the other hand, denied there was any important difference between liberal wings, in principle declared willingness to work with both, and in practice refused utterly to work with either.

The SR's thus had certain similarities of tactical appraisal with both wings of the Social Democratic party. The enemy was Tsarism. The temporary ally was the liberals, as the Mensheviks said. The leading force was the urban proletariat, as both SD wings said. The mass support was the peasantry, as the Bolsheviks said. As to party minimum-programs, they were nearly identical for all opposition groups. The difference was in the agrarian planks, and there the Socialist Revolutionaries stood alone against both the Marxists and liberals who wished to extend property in land, while they themselves wished to "socialize" it. No wonder the neo-populists felt the other two parties belonged in the same camp, as both seemed to agree in the matter which concerned the SR's most—the fate of the peasantry.

4.

A new outbreak of peasant riots in the spring of 1905 led *Revolutionary Russia* to quote with approval a journalistic enemy, the conservative newspaper *New Times*: "The wish of the peasants is one alone, and expressed briefly: the transfer of all lands to themselves." Scarcely a soul in Russia would have denied that this was what the peasants wanted. However, opinions differed drastically as to whether they ought to be granted their wish, and none of the opposition groups (nor of course the government) was willing to permit them to take the land, legally or illegally, *individually* and keep it for themselves. The Socialist Revolutionaries, for their part, wanted the "socialization" of land.

Exactly what they meant by this is difficult to say. The whole polemical struggle among the SR's ("socialization"), Mensheviks ("municipalization"), and Bolsheviks ("nationalization") was so obscured by charges and countercharges about the "bourgeois" or "socialist" character of those who advanced this or that program, that not enough attention was devoted to the task of elucidating precisely what the practical effect of the various programs was to be. We cannot know how they all would have worked out. The only one nominally put into effect was the SR program, and it was enacted by the Bolsheviks, in 1917, though not seriously nor consistently nor permanently. Since the debate was based only on the intentions of the three groups, then, it is safest to take statements of intent largely at their word instead of endeavoring to prove, as did some of the polemicists, that their execution would have produced results diametrically opposite to those desired.

By "socialization" the SR's meant chiefly two things: ownership of all land by the peasants collectively through some form of local self-governing institution, and equal rights of individuals to the use of land. They saw the root of evil in the village in private property. They thus rejected the idea of a regime of smallholders, under which the greater part of them would simply be ruined by competition and the chance factors which operate powerfully on farmers on the subsistence level. Instead, land was, as Chernyshevsky had wanted, to be not the property but the "belonging" (*dostoianie*) of all the people. "We shall make it no one's, and precisely as no one's does it become the belonging of all." [6] We may take this as an expression of the desire of the SR's to avoid turning the land over to ownership of either the state on one hand or the individual peasant on the other. The country was too vast for a land settlement to be carried out and subsequently adjusted from Petersburg. In any event there was a good deal of distrust of over-centralization in SR minds—Lenin charged, anarchist tendencies. "Nationalization", then, was unthinkable to the SR's. Individual ownership was not to be allowed to take hold; fortunately the existence of the commune had prevented that so far, and the peasant was to be preserved so far as possible from acquiring "bourgeois" attitudes—which Lenin insisted he was already doing—so that it would be easy to move from "socialization" to real socialism in the village. For "socialization" did not mean socialism to the SR's. Even Lenin[7] seemed to have failed to understand this at first, since he jeered at the juxtaposition of "socialization" and extension of farm cooperatives in the SR minimum program. Chernov, however, always made the point explicit. "Socialization" was a measure for the "first stage," a "caretaker" measure which would save the peasants from full agricultural capitalism and facilitate eventual socialism. It was not a socialist, but a democratic demand. Chernov wrote later, "socialization is nothing else but extension of the principles of democratic self-government to a new field, to the agricultural economy of the country." [8]

The SR's thus had abandoned the illusions of their predecessors that the commune was "socialist"; nevertheless, they believed the commune could serve as a powerful lever for "socialization." The existing communes ought first, in the view of Chernov, to be expanded by addition of the confiscated lands of state, church, and gentry. Still there might be left "small independent producers," presumably those existing outside the commune, though not rich enough to employ wage labor. They should be encouraged to enter the expanded, reformed communes (perhaps called by some other name), but they were not to be forcibly expropriated. The land was then to be tilled, though not owned, by individual farmers whose right to "equal land use" was to be secured by measures of taxation, and whose economic security was to be safeguarded by their membership in village cooperatives. The concrete forms of land use would depend on the free choice of bodies of local cultivators. Free from bureaucratic pressure, such bodies would still not be entirely sovereign in the matter of land reform, since the individual was to be able to appeal their decision if he thought his right to "equal land use" (based on what he could cultivate by his own labor) was being infringed.

The nature of the final "socialist" land settlement was left for future definition. Chernov sometimes referred to it as involving "nationalization," but he thought it impossible, citing Kautsky, to introduce nationalization in the bourgeois state which the political revolution would create, without in fact strengthening the bourgeois regime. The same argument was used by the Mensheviks against Lenin in 1906, and therefore they wished to "municipalize" (i.e., turn over to organs of local self-government) the expropriated large estates. Lenin, while he combatted SR and Menshevik land programs vehemently, ended by enacting the SR land program as appropriate to approximately the same social situation as the SR's had envisaged for "socialization." Lenin did so for tactical reasons connected with the popularity of the SR's in 1917; but in doing so he realized that the SR land program was not intended to bring, nor would it bring, full socialism to the village.

5.

While the SR land program differed sharply from that of the Bolsheviks in 1905-6, the part the peasants played in the tactical calculations of the two groups was not so dissimilar. Both divided the peasantry as a whole into subgroups. Chernov distinguished the middle and small rural bourgeoisie, living by the exploitation of others' labor, from the village working class which "lives by exploiting its own labor power"—a phrase which Lenin ridiculed, and indeed it was meaningless in Marxist terms, but the meaning is plain.[9] Lenin assigned two-thirds of peasant households to the "poor peasant" (*bedniaki*) category, which he seems to have expected to behave in a rather proletarian manner. By 1905, however, he speaks only of the "village proletariat" (*batraki*) as worthy of consideration in "socialist" as distinguished from "democratic" calculations. And even these persons were never completely assimilated to the "urban proletariat;" Lenin gave only the latter the unqualified badge of honor. The rural poor, nonetheless, retained a special place in Lenin's schema, whatever it was they were expected to do and whomever they were expected to fight against.

Chernov believed the "laboring peasantry" would fight the rural bourgeoisie while the urban proletariat struggled against the urban middle class; and both simultaneous clashes, like the revolution as a whole, would have two phases, bourgeois and socialist. Lenin declared that in the "bourgeois" phase, the peasantry as a whole would participate, since it was chiefly petty bourgeois and therefore merely part of one class, not a class by itself nor, as Chernov thought, parts of two classes—proletariat and bourgeoisie. Ultimately, however, it is difficult to see that Chernov and Lenin were far apart in their forecasts and desires of peasant conduct, and this is partly owing to Lenin's ambivalence on the peasantry. Even in Lenin's forecast, the urban proletariat would combat the urban middle class in the first as well as the second phase, and there was no obvious obstacle to the rural poor (whatever portion of them was really or nearly proletarian) doing likewise. The "revolutionary peasant committees" envisaged by the III Congress of the SD's (Bolshevik-controlled) could not be expected to desist from rough handling of their richer village brethren.

Thus despite divergent analyses, Lenin and Chernov reached a roughly similar end result as regards peasant tactics. The difficulty of explaining to this or that peasant how he ought to act according to one theory and not the other because of his own class character, vanished if he were expected to behave much the same in either case. (Lenin and Chernov might both declare they had been mis-understood if they read the foregoing sentence, but still might have to admit that their differing analyses led to roughly similar practical prescriptions.)

It is not surprising, in view of the fact that the SR's and Bol-sheviks shared at least a high evaluation of the peasants' role, that they moved closer to each other in the beginning of 1905. Despite Lenin's contempt and Chernov's suspicions, despite the fact that in the autumn of 1904 the Bolsheviks had refused to come to Paris to consider just such a temporary, limited agreement with the SR's as Lenin proposed in early 1905, despite the fact that each regarded the other as at least partly bourgeois in attitude or class character, they were not at all dissatisfied with finding themselves marching not on the same path, but at least on closely adjacent roads.

6.

Nevertheless, since the SR's had been rebuffed in autumn 1904 by their preferred allies, the Marxists, they turned their attention without much enthusiasm to the liberals. *Revolutionary Russia* repeated over and over—although it might as well have saved its breath so far as the Marxists were concerned—that the Paris agree-ment had nothing to do with a bourgeois-socialist "bloc" but was simply an arrangement for "simultaneous attack" on Tsarism by hitherto uncoordinated groups.[10] The government was trying its best, noted an SR writer, to divide and smash the liberal opposition. Though the Liberationists had not succeeded entirely in capturing the November 1904 zemstvo congress, their slogans of cooperation with revolutionaries were meeting with a surprising amount of support in moderate circles. During the "banquet campaign," "for the first time Russian liberals dared . . . to stand on their feet and raise their heads like a man" and their success surpassed all expectations. But since the masses remained aloof from the protest meetings of "society," the liberals then began to imagine themselves the nucleus of the whole movement. After all, Struve had expected this sort of situation; the masses were not ready, he thought, for real political initiative. The peasants, he had written, would only appear as a conscious political force once complete political liberation was achieved, and he had minimized the readiness of the workers for struggle. Struve forgot, retorted *Revolutionary Russia*, that the intelligentsia's "liberation movement" was itself evoked by revolutionary attacks on Tsarism and gave evidence of the direct effect of the growing strike and peasant movements of the masses themselves. The liberals' movement was only one part of the opposition activity. Still, it could fulfill an important role as a result of continuing "evolution and differentiation" among moderate elements. As the socialists faced non-socialist democracy with the aim of utilizing its most capable forces for the sake of the revolution, they would find their purpose would be best suited by the differentiation just appearing of "democrats" from "moderate constitutionalists."

Did the limited support SR's were willing to offer the liberals imply, as the Soviet historian Chermenskii asserts,[11] that they had abandoned their antipathy to the bourgeoisie once they moved from "rambling declarations about the bourgeoisie *in general* to the characterization of its political liberal representatives"? Not at all. On the contrary, the Socialist Revolutionaries at once condemned *Iskra's* "plan" for workers' aid to the zemstvo campaign as having the quite non-revolutionary aim of acting through the bourgeois opposition. *Iskra*, the Menshevik organ, was guilty of two-faced behavior. In fact it forgot fighting tactics and concentrated on the liberals. Officially it rejected all cooperation with them, privately it conferred with them with the objective of preventing fright at the "red phantom." The question of the moment, thundered *Revolutionary Russia*, was armed uprising, and joint action was possible only with those who declared solidarity with the aim of placing the fate of the nation in the hands of the armed populace and the Constituent Assembly. If liberal democrats refused to "take this new step," they would lose whatever vital forces they possessed to the revolutionary camp.

SR suspicions were renewed when the liberals published a draft constitution in the spring of 1905.[12] The provisions exciting sharpest criticism were those for a two-house legislature, denial of woman suffrage, and that which not only retained the Tsar but left him in control of the armed forces. Now the SR's recognized well enough that this draft was the work of the Right liberals. The Union of Liberation was not held responsible for it. Nevertheless, the SR's blamed the Liberationists for delaying their own program since October 1904 and called on them to state their own position at once. A month later, when *Revolutionary Russia* summarized the relations of the party to the rest of the opposition,[13] it still declared for temporary and limited agreement with liberals, but repeated that this depended on the degree of their readiness "to give support to the democratic movement." Once more the writer warned the laboring classes against exaggerated hopes in the liberal party, since experience had proved that the degree of its natural compliance was determined by the revolutionary action of the working class. In other words, SR's agreed with the Mensheviks that the forcefulness of liberal political action was derivative from the mass movement, not an independent variable.

When the liberals finally proposed an agrarian program envisaging "nationalization" of gentry land (with compensation), *Revolutionary Russia* responded by rather surprised outcries: "illogical, undesirable, impossible, unjust." [14] Notwithstanding the adjectives, the tone of the article was less harsh than might have been expected from those who wanted to extend communal, not individual ownership. After all, the program of Herzenstein and Manuilov, while not socialist, was certainly radical—much too radical, in fact, for many liberals. Chernov may have reasoned that defenders of nationalization could scarcely oppose "socialization" in principle; if land was to be confiscated and turned over to the state, then perhaps it might be turned over to the communes as well or instead.

7.

In August the wheels of Tsarist bureaucracy creaked, turned, and ground out a law establishing a consultative assembly, termed the "Bulygin Duma." This law was condemned by almost every vocal political group in Russia, but there were dissensions in Socialist

Revolutionary, as well as Marxist and liberal, ranks as to whether to boycott it or instead try to use it against Tsarism for the time being. Almost everyone assumed it would not last long, and in fact it never met at all. K. Tarasov hinted that the peasants might not understand the reason for a boycott.[15] The question was one not of principle, but of tactics; he thought the Duma elections might be useful for agitation, and it might be advantageous to participate in the sittings if only to demand its outright abolition from the assembly floor. The editors of *La Tribune Russe*, who published this letter, branded such arguments as "illusions," but could not fail to see that they were not limited to Tarasov alone. A Poltava group of SR's protested [16] that a boycott would simply give the victory to the reactionaries; instead a determined bloc of men ought to be sent who would show, by virtue of the support of the masses outside, that the Duma could not function. *Revolutionary Russia* agreed that bourgeois democracy would be influenced by such tactics—indeed, had SR leaders not shown at the Paris conference and elsewhere that they would never deny the possibility of revolutionizing the liberal opposition? But what if the liberals had "expended all the stock of their civic courage?" The Union of Unions, that radical organization of professional men which Miliukov himself had helped set up in 1905, had declared for outright boycott. The zemstvos had been prepared to follow suit; but then their Bureau induced postponement of debate until they were ready to reject the boycott. As a result, the liberals, instead of appearing, as they wished, to be the vanguard of the opposition, were everywhere at its tail. The Right wing was apparently still capable of swaying the liberal camp. The liberals might still be useful, but they were dragging in the wake of the revolutionaries. The tasks ahead were ones before which the liberals shrank back. According to the SR writer, the next step was not to be elections for a Duma, but a Constituent Assembly. And this must inevitably follow, not precede, an armed uprising. The most urgent problem was not any assembly, but violent action.

8.

What the Socialist Revolutionaries meant by the "political revolution" was by now clearly apparent. The word "revolution" was quite as important as the word "political." An armed uprising was openly stated to be the proper means for realizing the aims of the program-minimum for reconstruction of the Russian state.

Without an armed uprising, even a Constituent Assembly would become meaningless. And thus in still another respect Socialist Revolutionary tactics approached those of the Bolsheviks. The old order must be shattered by a powerful blow, not ground up piecemeal in a pseudo-parliament. This blow would be delivered by the revolutionary parties, relying on mass support. As for the liberals, they were not expected to join in an uprising. They might perhaps consent to stand aside while the "armed populace" destroyed Tsarism, and then join in a Constituent Assembly which would bring into being a democratic, not a socialist, regime. The Liberationists alone among the moderates, thought the SR's, would ever be willing to go along with such a course of events, even if only passively. Therefore it was to the interests of the revolution to encourage the split between the Liberationists and the liberal Right. In this respect their policy was similar to the Mensheviks'; in respect of emphasis on armed uprising, they were at one with the Bolsheviks. It should be clear by now, however, that in their overall view of the revolution to come as well as their estimate of the basic social forces involved, Chernov was much closer to Lenin than to Martov.

9.

Revolutionary Russia retained its old suspicions of the Menshevik *Iskra* in 1905. It was no longer bothered by the differences with Social Democrats in relation to program, that is, on terrorism, and the agrarian question. What was more important was immediate aims. The "plan" of *Iskra* in connection with the zemstvo campaign, and that journal's condescending attitude toward Socialist Revolutionism, confirmed all the old suspicions that pro-bourgeois attitudes were widespread in the "orthodox" Marxist camp. *Revolutionary Russia* was "deeply afflicted" [17] by the policy of *Iskra* and considered it impossible "to have any kind of relations" with it— in other words, with the Mensheviks.

On the other hand, since *Forward* and then *The Proletarian*, Lenin's new journals, had appeared, the neo-populists could no longer miss perceiving that there were now two very different kinds of Social Democrats, one of which seemed to be moving in their direction. They knew that Lenin had considered sending Bolshevik representatives to the conference which Father Gapon called in April 1905 (a meeting on the lines of the previous Paris conference) ,[18] while the Mensheviks condemned the whole plan from the first. Further evidence that Lenin was swinging round toward the neo-populist viewpoint was gleaned from the decisions of his Bolshevik-run III Congress, held in the summer of 1905.

Revolutionary Russia examined these decisions with ill-concealed glee. Orthodox Marxists believed [19] that a proletarian party could only concern itself with a peasant when he had left the land for the factory. Nevertheless, at the III Congress "the more revolutionary part of Social Democracy" demonstrated a "decisive reversal" on this matter, which was so vital to the SR's. The Bolsheviks had recognized the right of the peasant to revolutionary confiscation of gentry lands. Quite rightly the Mensheviks might accuse Lenin of backsliding from the true faith. Naturally Plekhanov told him he might soon be going over to Socialist Revolutionism! Since by Lenin's calculations nine-tenths of the peasantry was petty bourgeois, was he not risking introducing petty bourgeois forms into the developing capitalist rural economy? Still, the Socialist Revolutionaries could not afford to crow too loudly about what they saw as a conversion to their faith. The peasant question, long ignored by Social Democrats, had forced its way to the front of political events. It was hoped that Lenin could find his way out of the charmed circle in which "pseudoscientific interpretations of the orthodox try to enclose the further development of the great teachings of Marx." The writer could not resist closing with the observation that Lenin's attempts to prove his orthodoxy on the agrarian question were bound to fail. But this was no demerit in SR eyes.

The SR's did not expect Lenin, whether he proved his "orthodoxy" or not, would succeed in converting the Mensheviks to his views and compelling them to admit their errors. The neo-populists were sure that *Iskra* would cling to the notion of a "bourgeois revolution." [20] Of course, some of the inescapable deductions from this dogma might not please them. For example, as some liberals had rightly insisted in relation to the boycott question, since the Mensheviks were reconciled to the inevitability of a purely bourgeois revolution, they were also bound to accept its preliminary phase of constitutional monarchy. What the Mensheviks seemed bound to seek was not the revolutionary abolition of Tsarism but its evolutionary reconstruction through popular representation.

10.

However, if a party stood simply for a "toilers' revolution," it might advance boldly to the leadership of a mass movement, spearheaded by the urban proletariat, with the peasantry following close behind, which would destroy Tsarism and create a Russian democratic republic. Thus the Socialist Revolutionaries reasoned, and in October 1905 events appeared to be moving fast toward justifying their expectations. In the course of the opposition movement, the Liberationists had played an important role. The class interest of the portion of the bourgeoisie whose spokesmen they were assumed to be, might or might not coincide with the kind of change the neo-populists intended to bring about. Whether this class interest would be served by the establishment of what Lenin called a "revolutionary democratic dictatorship of proletariat and peasantry," was by no means clear to the Socialist Revolutionaries, and they certainly could not expect it to be to the liberals. However, if a free Russia in that image—an image the neo-populists seemed in 1905 substantially to share with Lenin—was acceptable to the liberals, their support would be welcomed. If not, as *Revolutionary Russia* had often said, the masses could do without their aid. But in relation to the last proposition, Lenin and the SR's diverged. Lenin not only expected to do without liberal aid, but to have to contend with liberal sabotage and treason, which he was determined to crush. What attitude the SR's would have taken if they, marching with Lenin, had achieved victory in 1905, we will never know. If there had been a coalition government including Bolsheviks and SR's, in 1905, it is likely that the SR's would have soon discovered that their attachment to liberty precluded any real cooperation with Lenin in administering the state. Even the Left Socialist Revolutionaries, who were considerably more radical than Chernov, found in the space of a few months in 1917-1918 that this was true.[21] The Bolshevik position was just taking shape in 1905, and it is not surprising that at that time the SR's misjudged the potentialities of Lenin.

VIII

LENIN: A DEMOCRATIC REVOLUTION

1905 "proved that the sole revolutionary-Marxist force in the country was the party of the Bolsheviks." ANNA PANKRATOVA.[1]

More workers were out on strike in January 1905 than during the whole previous decade,[2] and the two revolutionary parties increased their membership and influence to an extent almost proportionate to the growth of open popular discontent in both city and village. Social Democracy, Martov asserts, directly embraced thousands of workers and students and exerted a strong influence on hundreds of thousands of the urban and rural masses.[3] For the first time Marxist organizers invaded the village, and the immediate effect of this encounter upon the propagandists was greater than that upon the peasants they were trying to propagandize. The obvious temper of the villagers led the Social Democrats to abandon the limited scope of the agrarian program of 1903 and to demand the confiscation of gentry lands. Both the Bolshevik and Menshevik conferences of the late spring of 1905 gave the official stamp of approval to the new demands and formulated them more precisely to serve the needs of peasant agitation. The impact of the party on the peasants, however, remained negligible; even a Soviet historian confesses that "one must not exaggerate the breadth and depth of the influence of revolutionary Social Democracy on the peasant masses." [4]

Among the urban workers, however, the influence of the Social Democrats was indeed both broad and deep. Their leaders skillfully utilized the "economic" grievances of the proletariat to organize massive political demonstrations, in Baku and Ivanovo-Voznesensk in May, Lodz in June, Nizhnii-Novgorod in the autumn, and elsewhere. They took the lead in the Odessa strikes from May onwards, and their agitation undoubtedly played a role in the memorable mutiny on the cruiser Potiomkin. They were successful in organizing "self-defense" actions against many of the pogroms which were being fostered by reactionary groups, often with the connivance or support of the government. After the universities were granted autonomy in September, Social Democrats were very much in evidence in the public meetings which found refuge in academic auditoriums. Beginning in the summer, the Mensheviks in particular participated actively in the organization of "professional unions." Both wings of the party, however, were most concerned with organizing the urban proletariat.

Especially after the failure of the 1 May demonstrations, the Mensheviks believed that the workers were unwilling to risk a repetition of the massacre of "Bloody Sunday" by mass demonstrations, so tried instead to take advantage of all legal means of agitation. Thus they participated in, while the Bolsheviks boycotted, the elections of worker representatives to the Shidlovskii Commission, which was appointed by the government to investigate the grievances of the proletariat leading to the march of 9 January. The Bolsheviks concerned themselves more with establishing trustworthy nucleuses of party members at points where they might have maximum effect on manifestations of the mass movement. The Minority thus preferred to concentrate on "legal" and "open" agitation, while the Majority thought "legal" methods useless, from the standpoint of organizing the workers or of trying to build an effective political party.

2.

Since Lenin had repudiated the Central Committee of the party and organized a Bolshevik "Bureau of the Committees of the Majority" in autumn 1904, the Mensheviks had in turn organized their own Groups of the Central Committee. Lenin controlled the party committees in Petersburg, Moscow, Riga, Odessa, and elsewhere, while the Mensheviks held those in Kiev, Kharkov, Rostov, Ekaterinoslav, and others; but wherever possible each faction also organized its own members in the "other's" cities. Most of the Central Committee was arrested in February 1905, and the result was to deepen the organizational split. Thus the meeting in London in the spring which called itself the III Congress of the Party was actually Bolshevik, while the Mensheviks met separately in Geneva at about the same time.

Although it appeared that the party was now permanently sundered in two, in practice the local committees of both factions drew closer together in the course of the fall's feverish activity. By September a joint "federative" committee and the Menshevik Organization Committee, which had emerged from the spring conferences, met, along with representatives of the minor sections of Social Democracy, and the conference resolved upon the boycott of the "Bulygin Duma"—a decision, however, in which the Menshevik delegate refused to concur. Since no elections for a Bulygin Duma took place, this was of no practical importance. By this time the great autumn strikes were under way and the Soviets were being set up; and by tacit rather than formal agreement intra-party differences were shelved temporarily.

3.

While differences on a theoretical level did not become perfectly plain until 1905, Martov notes that in practice Bolsheviks and Mensheviks acted with much more similarity than would appear from the party literature of the period. After all, they started from the same orthodox doctrine. Their shared conviction that as Marxists they had the tremendous advantage of being armed with a scientific method for the study of historical evolution undoubtedly contributed to a feeling of mutual solidarity at the moment of the revolution for which they had worked so hard and waited so long. The spokesmen of both wings had after all declared after the schism of 1903 that only "organizational" differences separated them. The spokesmen of the Western socialist parties, taking them at their word, constantly urged them towards reunification.[5] Nevertheless, despite the apparent reasonableness of reunion, stoutly defended by Plekhanov, Trotsky, and others, there became clear in 1905 differences so fundamental that the two wings were unable ever to be reconciled in a union again—an alliance, perhaps, which the Stockholm "Unification" Congress momentarily concluded, but nothing more. These divergences, as we have seen, were foreshadowed in 1898 and expounded in 1903-4, but during the course of 1905 they were unmistakably brought into the open.

The nature of these divergences has been much debated. Some, like Isaiah Berlin, have contended they related to the relative "hardness" and "softness" of the men who led the Bolshevik and Menshevik factions. Others, like Andrew Rothstein, have contended that they were concerned with differences in tactics.[6] It should be clear by now that the latter view is correct as far as it goes. Personal

peculiarities of men like Lenin and Martov undoubtedly had much
to do with the amount of acrimony exchanged in the argument
over tactics; to this extent Berlin is right. However, the explanation
must be sought beyond the limits of either view as so far expressed.
Let us first summarize the tactical difference before attempting
a broader explanation.

The problem was, how should the "proletarian party" conduct
itself during the bourgeois revolution in Russia? Should it attempt
to act alone, or in alliance with other forces? All Marxists were
agreed on one point: the proletariat must be the "vanguard," in
the bourgeois as well as in its own future socialist revolution. Both
Bolsheviks and Mensheviks believed further that the success of the
proletariat·would depend on the degree of cooperation forthcoming
from another class, in both cases a section of what Marx regarded
as the bourgeoisie. Lenin and the Bolsheviks believed the necessary
ally to be the peasantry, Axelrod and the Mensheviks the bourgeois
(gentry and intellectual) liberals. In other words, both looked for
allies inside Russia. One leader, however, thought the proletariat
could not compromise itself with any such alliance—it must carry
out first the bourgeois, then the socialist revolution, while maintaining strict class independence. Its only reliable ally must be
sought outside Russia, in the international proletariat. This thinker
was Lev Trotsky, the theorist of the "permanent revolution." Let
us leave aside consideration of Trotsky for the moment, and ask
what broader implications could be found in the difference in
Bolshevik-Menshevik tactics.

Both wings maintained explicit fidelity to the Marxist analytical
framework. But the *desires* of both show clearly through the cracks
of their *expectations*. Lenin was not at all enthusiastic about a
Russian bourgeois revolution, or about the Russian bourgeoisie.
He wanted to hurry through the former, and limit the role of the
latter. He is unable to keep his fundamental detestation of the
Russian middle class out of his analysis. Of course, says he, even its
most loathsome members would be welcome allies if they oppose
Autocracy, but when liberals did just that he accused them of
hypocrisy and rejected their alliance. They would *spoil* the bourgeois revolution because they would (naturally enough) want to
run it themselves. The peasants, with whom he undoubtedly had
much human sympathy, anyway, had the advantage that they were
politically backward and could only follow—so would not disturb
the Social Democrat in the driver's seat of the bourgeois revolution.

Axelrod and his friends had a good deal less antipathy to the bourgeois phase which Marxism told them lay ahead in Russia. Lenin, was right when he pointed this out, but he turned the proposition into a charge of inertia, passivity, and downright betrayal of the workers on the part of his Menshevik confreres. What it is probably more accurate to say is that the Mensheviks feared the Russian bourgeoisie much less than Lenin, so perhaps for that reason hated them less. Evaluating more highly their culture (or the extent to which they shared the culture of the Western middle class) and ability, and considering their "class nature" to involve less actively "evil" drives than Lenin did, yet at the same time realizing their weakness as a class, the Mensheviks did not shrink from the prospect of a bourgeois government. It was tacitly assumed that this interim bourgeois government, which would supplant Tsarism, would not govern too badly, that it would be forced by the workers' pressure into granting reforms which should go to the extreme of "bourgeois" radicalism, at any rate, and should furthermore lack the strength to resist the final socialist onslaught of the proletarian party when the time for attack had come. Many Mensheviks would find this description of their expectations either too gentle or too harsh (from the standpoint of orthodox Marxism), but the common denominator might be expressed in some such fashion. A bourgeois government, in the eyes of the Mensheviks, was inevitable. Aside from that fact, it would not *spoil* Russia for a proletarian regime, but on the contrary would provide the conditions under which a Russian proletariat could grow strong in numbers and influence, in preparation for taking power in the name of socialism. Therefore, with eyes wide open as to the future consequences, the Mensheviks welcomed bourgeois support to the proletarian leadership in the first stage, the destruction of Autocracy.

One way of making clear the differences between Bolsheviks and Mensheviks is to examine a variant of Russian Social Democracy which was in essence neither. This was the conception of Trotsky. [7] It was worked out not only in accordance with his preconceived hatred of bourgeois liberals and deep distrust of the peasantry, but in terms of his practical experience in 1905. He took active part in the Soviets of the autumn and was for a few days president of the St. Petersburg Soviet of Workers Deputies. From his point of view, the revolution owed whatever success it did achieve to those purely proletarian organizations. The question of allies, which he had apparently already decided in his own mind, was, he thought, solved in any case by events. While the liberals "tolerated" the revolution only until 17 October, the main struggle came after that. Therefore, there could be no question of cooperation with the bourgeois capitalists. As for the peasants, their role had been even more nefarious. The proletariat, in its insurrection of December, was broken not on strategic errors, but on the bayonets of the peasant army. "The first wave of the Russian revolution broke on the crude political incapacity of the muzhik" who devastated the landlords' domains in order to seize the land, and who then, in uniform, shot the workers. In 1907, Trotsky wrote that the peasant "is not capable of playing an independent and spontaneous role, still less to assume a political direction."

Despite partial failure, wrote Trotsky, the October strikes were a colossal demonstration of the hegemony of the proletariat in the bourgeois revolution; what is more, the hegemony of the city over a country with a rural population. "The old power of the land, consecrated by the populist school, was replaced by the despotic authority of the capitalist city." The proletariat, in its heroic fight for eventual socialism, must inevitably penetrate the citadel of bourgeois as well as feudal property, and would thus encounter the hostility *both* of bourgeois groups which supported the workers at the beginning, and of the peasant masses. The contradictory interests which dominate the situation in a backward land where the immense majority are peasants can only end in a solution "on an international plane," in the arena of a world proletarian revolution.

This was the theory of "permanent revolution." It was a doctrine about both the spatial and temporal extent of the Marxism apocalypse. The proletariat is forced to reach across national, not class, lines for the crucial portion of the assistance he needs. In terms of a *Russian* revolutionary movement *per se,* such a doctrine was Utopian, and it never became popular so far as actual tactical calculations went, though all Social Democrats continued to speak in international terms and pay lip-service to the idea of an international revolution. The temporal part of the doctrine, however, was well adapted to the revolutionary impatience of the eager and determined young men who wanted to see a proletarian revolution in their own lifetime. For in Trotsky's theory, the "significant interval" which Plekhanov assumed would separate bourgeois and socialist phases shrank into nullity. The first phase would be followed not by social peace and a bourgeois regime, but by a continuous period of struggle in which the bourgeois phase merged into the socialist phase. There was no question of how the workers were to behave in a bourgeois state, for there was to be none. Since the victory of the workers in Russia was to be secured by the rising of the Western proletariat against their already bourgeois states, there indeed were to be no more bourgeois states at all—at least in Europe.

According to Trotsky, then, it was useless for the proletariat to search for reliable allies. Correctly foreseeing that the Russian workers would not be strong enough to achieve their own revolution alone, Trotsky put his trust in the workers of Germany and other Western nations. Making the assumptions he had about the interests of the other classes which attracted Bolsheviks and Mensheviks, he could not do otherwise. There was no logical defect in his scheme, and the whole scheme was both rationalist and Western. It was appropriate that having acquired from the West not only his rationalist conceptual framework, but the germ of the theory of "permanent revolution" (from Mehring and Parvus),[8] he looked to the material forces of the West to carry it into reality. Still, in 1905 even he can scarcely have hoped that the European proletariat would rise suddenly to save Russia. In fact he did not fully formulate his theory until the First Revolution was almost over, and was unable to gain any important adherents to it within the Social Democratic party until years later. Having broken with the Mensheviks over their reliance on the bourgeois liberals, and not sharing Lenin's hopes in the peasantry, he became isolated—literally as well as figuratively, as it happened, for after his arrest along with the St. Petersburg Soviet he was exiled to Siberia.

5.

The Bolsheviks and Mensheviks were agreed that the Russian proletariat must find an ally. They were bound by the resolutions of the 1903 Congress to support the bourgeoisie insofar as it proved itself capable of fighting Tsarism, and to the Marxist, both peasants and moderate liberals were "bourgeois." The Mensheviks unhesitatingly chose the liberals and practically ignored the peasants; Lenin chose the peasants, and devoted much energy to showing why it was impossible to choose the liberals.

During the "banquet campaign" of November 1904 Lenin had resoundingly rejected the Mensheviks' "plan" for supporting the middle class. Just before Bloody Sunday he made clear what kind of support he himself was willing to offer. The nearer the revolution approaches, the proletarian party must be all the more cautious to retain its class independence and "not permit its class demands to drown in the water of general democratic phrases." [9] The more openly "society" comes out with such phrases, the more "mercilessly" Social Democrats must expose the class character of this "society." Of course, they will remember that "the proletariat must support the constitutional movement of the bourgeoisie." By doing so, it would stir up and rally around itself the widest possible circles of the exploited masses, preparing an uprising for the moment of the greatest governmental weakness, the deepest popular turmoil. The Marxists must thus express their "support" of the constitutionalists by the most determined employment of the general ferment for agitation and organization among those workers and peasants previously untouched by the opposition movement. This is what Lenin meant by "support" for constitutionalists. "Support" in this context has nothing to do with active aid. It means something like simultaneous but independent action for parallel ends—parallel, not similar, for the Bolsheviks were by now aiming at an uprising, not a constitution.

While Social Democrats would support every kind of bourgeoisie, "even the most villainous," wrote Lenin,[10] insofar as it combatted Tsarism, the proletariat did so not in expectation of any kindness from the middle class in return, but only for the sake of its readiness to strike the mutual enemy a blow. The Mensheviks, unfortunately, seemed to see things differently, Lenin implied. He did not need to be explicit; he was well enough understood. What he said was that the "intellectual" trend in the party talks of trade: if the liberals come out on the side of the Social Democrats and not the Socialist Revolutionaries, then Marxists should be willing to fight alongside them. The Mensheviks of *Iskra* were attempting to draw a distinction between zemstvo liberalism and bourgeois democracy (in other words, separate the Left-liberals from the Right-liberals). They were suggesting that if the intellectual wing of zemstvism would separate itself from the rest of liberalism, the remainder would be fit only for "the sting of scorpions." What *Iskra* forgets is that the democracy of *all* the bourgeoisie is "limited, narrow, and inconsistent." What would happen if the radical intellectuals of Liberationism moved Left? They would simply move closer to the Socialist Revolutionaries, nothing more—the gulf between them and Marxists would remain. Potresov, asserting that understanding is possible with only those liberals who support universal suffrage, is still bemused with the notion of "irresistible paper reagents." [11] but his search for the right litmus paper is futile: "reliable democrats, bourgeois democrats cannot be." Russian bourgeois democracy reflects the interests of merchants and industrialists, especially the middle and small ones, as well as those of the masses of proprietors among the peasantry. Ignoring the peasant proprietors, the broadest layer of bourgeois democracy, is *Iskra's* chief mistake.

Thus Lenin attacked the Menshevik (and SR) notion that it was possible or desirable to separate the liberal-Left from the moderates for the purpose of making an alliance with the former. To place hopes of this kind in the Liberationists was to assume that they could jump the track, so to speak, of their class interests. The adjoining track for the Liberationists was that of the party of the radical intelligentsia, the SR's. Of course they might approach their "neighbor" if they so wished; but that would just mean approaching another slightly more radical bourgeois party (the SR's), not moving into the Marxist camp. (Therefore, by the way, the neo-populists rather than liberals were the logical Marxist allies, since their "tracks" too adjoined; and Lenin did not delay to make this clear.)

The Mensheviks' reliance on the liberal-Left was regarded as an error, the result of muddled thinking. But it was also something more serious. It could result in betrayal of the revolution itself. Lenin made the point by analogy from the French Revolution.[12] The Girondists (read Mensheviks) had not been traitors to the Revolution, but "inconsistent, indecisive, opportunistic defenders" of it and therefore the Jacobins combatted them. Consequently, the "outright traitors," monarchists, priest-constitutionalists, and so forth, "supported and exculpated the Girondists from the attack of the Jacobins." Similarly, the Mensheviks, inconsistent in relation to "the principles of organization and tactics" of the Russian Revolution, are supported by the "outright traitors" to the revolutionary cause, the Liberationists.

Lenin's denial of difference in principle between the two liberal wings was echoed by the Bolshevik Bureau.[13] True, it said, the Liberationists "officially" supported the universal suffrage which the proletariat demands, but there was evidence that this was but their "parade costume" for the edification of the masses. In reality "they are *not democrats*." When the moderates (for example, Prince Eugene Trubetskoi)[14] had compromised themselves with accusations against the revolutionaries as "internal enemies," the Liberationists had momentarily turned on them, yet did not find it necessary to continue polemics with the faction defending limited suffrage. Social Democrats could therefore not prefer one to the

other; they must support both liberal wings "without any obligations." Formal, concrete agreements were beside the point since the
Marxists and liberals simply employed different methods. This is
how the Bolshevik Bureau regarded the matter.

6.

Since Lenin was denying that Liberationists were any different
from Maklakovists in terms of class interest, he had to make the
most strenuous efforts to show that the obvious difference in the
way the two wings were behaving was only a ruse by which they
concealed their essential kinship. Evaluating the evidence as to
how they behaved was beside the point, for Lenin had already
decided that the Liberationists were false democrats. No matter how
democratic the noises they made, they were explained away in
advance. But since the public did not have the Leninist key to
liberal democracy, it might be misled and this was a profound
danger which the Mensheviks, thought Lenin, failed to observe.

In March he wrote, "at this very moment bourgeois democracy is
particularly straining its powers to seize in its own hands the workers' movement," and cited liberal leaflets appealing for proletarian
support.[15] He reminded his readers of a Russian proverb: "God
save us from our friends, and we will save ourselves from our
enemies." Furthermore, liberals were trying to delude the peasants
with bold demands for the land to be given to the farmer, but
in a manner which secured gentry and bureaucratic participation
in the distribution of holdings. Lenin asked the peasants outright:
Will you consent to this pomeshchik-bureaucrat interference, "or
will you interfere *yourselves* and build yourselves a free life,"
ignoring liberal promises?[16]

Lenin used the "Basic Law of the Russian Empire," a draft
produced by moderate liberals, as a two-edged weapon.[17] It was
too conservative, for one thing; its "political sophisms" helped expose the liberals' class character, and showed the evil of the moderates. On the other hand, it besmirched the Liberationists too, in a
curious manner. They had in fact not indorsed the draft at all. To
Lenin, however, this proved *not* that it was too moderate for them,
but just that they shied away from programs and were politically
backward—a perfectly natural feature owing to their intermediate
position, "suspended between Autocracy and the proletariat."[18]

The Bolshevik leader watched the zemstvo congresses of 1905 with
deep suspicion. When the April congress went so far as to call for

a Constituent Assembly, he discounted this Liberationist victory since the Shipovist minority among the zemstvists was only silenced for the time being. The deputation which this congress sent to the Tsar was labeled as "the first steps of bourgeois treason." Struve had accused Marxists of being conspiratorial; but this was how the liberals conspired! The Tsar and moderates were clearly ready to conclude a firm peace with each other. Would not this disgrace make true democrats turn away from the constitutionalists? Lenin, in reproaching the liberals in general, of course knew quite well that the Right, not the Left, sponsored the 6 June deputation. In practice, they were simply one and the same to him.

The advance of Liberationist radicalism changed Lenin's attitude not at all. When Petrunkevich at the July zemstvo congress formally renounced any further approaches to the Tsar and turned "to the people," Lenin brushed this speech aside.[19] More important was the fact that Petrunkevich still kept on answering governmental terrorism by peaceful methods, asking the peasant to arrange friendly purchase of land with the landlord's consent, and though disavowing the Tsar, wanted to keep the monarchy. Of course the liberal bourgeoisie must go to the people, said Lenin, for without them it is powerless to fight Autocracy. It goes to the people not as representative of its class interests, but as a trader, a broker between the two sides of the struggle. Thus Lenin wrote in May. It is clear that he thought the bourgeoisie had no real interest in fighting the "bourgeois revolution." There was no more pretense that he believed they and he were fighting on the same side.

The July zemstvo congress came close to approving a boycott of the Bulygin Duma, but the September congress declared for participation. Lenin was not surprised. Yet despite their (actually, their rightist opponents') decision to go to the Duma, the Liberationists were once more asserting that there could be no talk of compromise. Quite right, said Lenin. The liberals want freedom, but they no less passionately desire a peaceful deal with Tsarism; "therefore in words it is one thing, in deeds quite another."

When the program of the Union of Liberation was finally published, Lenin found it no more to his liking than the law on the Bulygin Duma. The Liberationists had taken the name "constitutional democrats" "in order to conceal the *monarchist* character of the party." They desired simply a "just division" of power; a third to the monarch, a third to the bourgeoisie (upper house), a third to the people (lower house). This would be achieved not by struggle, but by "honest brokership." Struve wrote long ago[20] that moderates always gain by the struggle of extremist parties. They do not forget that now as they maneuver between Autocracy and the people, using each against the other, hoping to get at least "a third!" It has now become clear that bourgeois interests lead naturally to the slogan "Four-Tail Constituent Assembly," but not at all to "provisional revolutionary government." The former has become the slogan of "the policy of peaceful agreement, trading and brokership," of the monarchist bourgeoisie who see in it their best hope for retention of the monarchy. As far as the whole Liberationist program is concerned, it is anyhow only an opening bid. The Kadet bourgeoisie will settle with Tsarism "for a cheaper price than its present program."

In reality, liberal acceptance of the traditional revolutionary slogan of "Constituent Assembly" must have come as a slight shock to Lenin. At first glance it was hard to see how a freely elected body of that type could register anything else but the "will of the people," that is, the democracy which to all good Marxists was to be a mark of the bourgeois revolution. Nevertheless, to the Bolsheviks the verbal acceptance of any slogan whatsoever (though it is interesting to imagine Lenin's reaction if the liberals *had* declared for some kind of "provisional government") could not alter the class interests of the moderates as Lenin conceived them. The bourgeoisie as a whole, he repeated, was not "capable of decisive struggle against Autocracy" because it feared the loss of its property and the revolutionary action of the workers who would carry on till the social revolution was achieved.[21]

The "middle class" had been induced by the proletariat, which was constantly pushing them forward, to demand a Constituent Assembly. Very well; Lenin recognized this as a fact. Nevertheless, in doing so the middle class merely "hobbles after the revolution," always in retard of actual events, dragging at the tail. What was more, the slogan "Constituent Assembly" was not enough for "consistent democracy," for the urgent tasks of the revolution. It was true enough that Social Democrats used the slogan in their party program—but in connection with the overthrow of Autocracy and its replacement by a democratic *republic*. Whether such an assembly would have the actual power to "constitute" would depend on full freedom for electoral agitation. This would be impossible under the monarchy, which the bourgeoisie wished to keep.

It was altogether clear by this time that Lenin had completely rejected the notion of being satisfied with any political changes at all which the liberals might institute or to which they might consent. If they demanded a constitution, Marxists must point out that they do not ask a Constituent Assembly; if a Constituent Assembly, not a republic—and so they must be firmly labeled "monarchists." If they had accepted a republic, they would still have been far from accepting a "provisional revolutionary government"—and might have conceivably been dubbed "crude republicans" or something else to indicate they would not and could never desire the kind of change which the proletariat wanted. Lenin and his Bolsheviks would of course "push forward" the bourgeoisie by forcing them to strike half-hearted blows at Tsarism to keep from entirely alienating popular support, and to compete for opposition leadership so they would be in a position to snatch some gains if the revolution did strike down the old order.

Now such a policy had very great dangers from the Bolsheviks standpoint. Liberal competition for a mass following had from the first excited deep Marxist fears. Still, by "exposing" the liberals' "treachery" at every turn, the Bolsheviks believed they could stave off this threat, prevent the moderates from carrying off any material gains from the revolution, and still keep the revolution in some sense "bourgeois." The bourgeoisie would obtain "freedom," after all, from the revolution. It was therefore bound to waddle, stagger, and hobble after the proletariat in quest of this objective. Yet this "freedom" for the middle class would be transitory. The proletariat and peasantry, said Lenin, would not stop at the first phase, but would fight on until the socialist revolution was won. The people would rise in revolt and seize power by force; the victory of the democratic revolution in Russia would be the signal for the start of the socialist revolution in all countries. In such a way Karl Marx had regarded the prospects in Germany in 1848, and he had written to Vera Zasulich that if a Russian revolution coincided with one in the West—then the commune might serve as a starting point for socialist development! The last half of this statement Lenin might have regarded as un-Marxist, but the "permanent revolution" was not a Russian Marxist invention, nor did Lenin state it first among Russian Marxists. That honor belonged to Trotsky.

But what of the bourgeoisie in this eclipse of Plekhanov's "significant interval" between the two phases? It would see its impending doom and turn to the side of reaction as soon as ever its "freedom" was gained. The masses would continue to victory; the two phases merged in time, Lenin and Trotsky arrived at a similar conclusion. Still there was a vital difference between them. Lenin hoped for and rather hollowly predicted the aid of the international proletariat, but Trotsky thought it indispensable. For Lenin, and not at all for Trotsky, the peasantry was to be the ally which secured the workers their victory.

7.

Lenin announced his choice of ally in March, as peasant uprisings mounted throughout Russia.[22] Analyzing the make-up of the peasant class, he found first the village proletariat. Between it and the urban workers it was necessary for the Social Democrat to organize the closest ties. He was the ideologue of both one and the other, and these tasks related to both the bourgeois and the socialist phases of revolution. Herein the landless peasant comes closest to winning the Marxist badge of honor. On the other hand there stood the rich peasant. He was undoubtedly hostile to feudalism, landlords, and bureaucrats, so despite his antagonism to the village proletarian, he could become a (bourgeois) democrat. Last, there was the middle peasant who stood between these two groups and partook of some features of each. Lenin drew this general conclusion: "The general traits in the position of all these subgroups render the peasantry as a whole and its whole movement undoubtedly democratic, no matter how great is this or that manifestation of lack of consciousness or reactionariness." Thus together with their long-range preparation of the elements of socialist struggle in the village, the Marxists must make clear the "real democratic and revolutionary content" which is hidden behind the peasant's desire for land and liberty, and must energetically support and push forward this aspiration as a mighty force in the democratic revolution.

Lenin had finally found a type of bourgeois whom he could conditionally, temporarily, accept. In this class alliance with the village petty bourgeoisie, he could likewise afford to cooperate with its ideologue (though Lenin did not call it that): the Socialist Revolutionary party. Just before "Bloody Sunday" Lenin had pointed out the extent of the neo-populists' evolution "from populism to Marxism."[23] Yet he set forth in detail their deviations from orthodox Marxism and still charged them with ignoring the bourgeois nature of the liberal opposition and peasant proprietors alike. Lenin did not expect the SR intellectuals, though they might think themselves socialists, to use popular communal. traditions in the interests of socialism. What would actually happen would be that the bourgeois peasant proprietors would use the socialist phraseology of the SR's in the fight against socialism. The only correct agrarian program, he reiterated, was the Social Democratic one. Notwithstanding all this, the pseudo-Marxist revolutionaries (SR's) could play an important role in the *democratic* revolution, and when Lenin learned of the events of 9 January he declared instantly: "We Social Democrats . . . must go hand in hand" with the revolutionaries of bourgeois democracy in time of uprising.[24] By this he can only have meant the Socialist Revolutionaries.

However, when Father Gapon, leader of the Bloody Sunday procession, proposed a fighting agreement between the two chief revolutionary parties, Lenin played a double game.[25] He welcomed the suggestion, declared that Gapon stated their immediate common aims correctly, and wished it success. In practice, however, the Bolsheviks refused to send delegates to the inter-party conference which Gapon summoned, for tactical reasons Lenin later explained to the II Congress.

Lenin based his formula for winning the democratic revolution on the union or *smychka* of proletariat and peasantry rather than any formal alliance between the parties who spoke for them. Together these two groups (not classes; to a Marxist they represented a class and a half) would form a revolutionary government, which, supported by the revolutionary army, would proceed on the basis of "six points."[26] These included the calling of a Constituent Assembly, the arming of the people, introducing political freedom for all citizens and oppressed nationalities, the eight-hour day for workers, and founding of peasant committees which would achieve democratic reforms in the village including confiscation of gentry lands. This procedure was sloganized as the "revolutionary democratic dictatorship of the proletariat and peasantry." It alone could secure free elections for a Constituent Assembly, which in any other context would be a sham.

Lenin's "dictatorship" slogan was an answer to the Mensheviks. They declared that the Social Democrats could not participate in the provisional government of a bourgeois revolution, for in the first stage they would be unable to realize the socialism demanded by workers, would suffer defeat and shame, and furthermore play into the hands of reaction. The provisional government could only be bourgeois, they said. Lenin retorted that Martynov and his comrades were confusing their fear of "vulgar Jauresism" (referring to the French parliamentary socialist) with the objective tasks of the proletariat in bringing about a democratic republic. Was it not clear, said he, that without union with the petty bourgeois masses, the proletariat could not think of achieving this goal? Was it not plain that without the revolutionary dictatorship of proletariat and peasantry, there was no hope of success? Through this slogan Marxists would not only win the Russian political revolution, but would make it the prologue to the European socialist revolution. Of course, success would depend upon possession of revolutionary class instinct. If there is no scientific world outlook, "then it is dangerous to take part in strikes—it may lead to Economism; and to participate in the parliamentary struggle—it may end in parliamentary cretinism; and to support zemstvo liberal democracy—it may lead to a 'plan of a zemstvo campaign.'" The danger is in reality only in the "spirit of tailism and deadness" which is exhibited in *Iskra*'s distinction between a temporary revolutionary government and the "dictatorship" slogan. *Iskra* asserted that the proletariat must exert pressure on the liberal bourgeoisie so that the more democratic lower stratum will force onward the upper. To this Lenin replies that this lower stratum consists precisely of the urban and rural petty bourgeoisie, and it is this stratum at which his own slogan is aimed.[27]

8.

By the end of April both Bolsheviks and Mensheviks had defined their positions well enough so that their respective party conferences had only to give them official sanction, not work them out in debate. The Bolshevik III Congress, held in London, declared that the first duty of Social Democrats was to combat the liberal-monarchist bourgeoisie and lead the armed uprising of the proletariat. It adopted a peasant program[28] sanctioning the seizure of gentry lands, despite some fears of compromising the proletarian character of the movement. There was no definite statement in regard to the forthcoming elections to the Bulygin Duma, though Lenin opposed unconditional boycottism.[29] The Congress rejected any reconciliation with the Mensheviks and condemned their tactics. It declared that *Iskra* was no longer the party organ, and substituted the journal *The Proletarian*, which was to replace Lenin's *Forward*—nothing more than a change of name. A new Central Committee was set up. Altogether the Congress was almost entirely dominated by Lenin and it simply sanctioned his already unquestioned position as leader and spokesman of the Bolsheviks.

Not long after the Congress, Lenin appraised its results along with the results of the Menshevik Conference in the important pamphlet, *Two Tactics of Social Democracy in the Democratic Revolution*. Lenin's view of the fundamental difference between the two factions was here clearly set forth. In his preface, Lenin declared that events had forced the Mensheviks "virtually to pass over, or begin to pass over, to the side of their opponents,"[30] owing to their rejection of propaganda for a revolutionary government in favor of the "uprising-as-a-process" theory.[31] This the revolution had taught. The real problem was, could the Marxists "teach the revolution anything," whether via the only correct doctrine and the only thoroughly revolutionary class, the proletariat, they could "carry the revolution to a real and decisive victory, not in word but in deed, and paralyze the instability, half-heartedness, and treachery of the democratic bourgeoisie." In selection of means to that end, the question of emphasis was vital. Should main emphasis be given to trade unions and legal groups, or to armed insurrection, revolutionary army, revolutionary government? If to the former, Marxists would surely please bourgeois spokesmen, as the Menshevik Akimov had (unfortunately) pleased Struve. The issue was clear: "the outcome of the revolution depends on whether the working class will play the part of a subsidiary to the bourgeoisie, a subsidiary that is powerful in the force of its onslaught against Autocracy but impotent politically, or whether it will play the part of leader of the people's revolution." In other words, we may interpret Lenin as saying that if the emphasis is legal, the worker will play second fiddle; if illegal, he will lead.

Taking full political liberty to be the objective of democratic revolution, Lenin then proceeds to analyze how to reach it. First must come the conquest of power: "in the final analysis, force alone can settle the great problems of political liberty and the class struggle." The Mensheviks, following the old Economist "theory of stages," believe the best means to use is to force the Tsar to convene a representative body which shall "decide" under popular pressure to convene a Constituent Assembly. They forget that reactionaries will never stand for this, and so the issue must still be decided by armed force. The Mensheviks, declares Lenin, can describe the struggle, but are incapable of giving a correct slogan for it; "they march with a will, but lead badly."

Uppermost in Lenin's mind is the need to *lead*, to push, to force the bourgeoisie to go farther than it is willing to go in "its own" revolution. For this purpose, only the slogans of "provisional revolutionary government" and "republic" are sufficient, "since the slogan calling for a popular Constituent Assembly has been *accepted* by the monarchist bourgeoisie."[32] The Mensheviks themselves do not go *beyond* this bourgeois-blessed slogan, they fail to accept those of Lenin, and in failing to do so merely drag at the tail of the Liberationists.

However, the fatal word "bourgeoisie" as usual stands in need of elucidation. Lenin agrees with the Mensheviks that Social Democrats must, in order to take part in politics in a bourgeois society, march side by side with the bourgeoisie. "The difference between us in this respect is that we march side by side with the revolutionary and republican bourgeoisie . . . whereas you march side by side with the liberal and monarchist bourgeoisie."[33] We are left no alternative but to interpret Lenin as speaking here not purely in class terms, but also in party terms. Social Democrats are a party, and a party cannot easily "march side by side" with a class which has no party. As a matter of fact he has already made clear that he thinks the Mensheviks march with the Liberationists, and now he states plainly enough his estimate of the SR role in relation to the Bolsheviks. Bolsheviks, says he, advance slogans coinciding with those of the revolutionary and republican bourgeoisie, who have not formed a mass party; the Socialist Revolutionaries "are more in the nature of a terrorist group of intellectuals than the embryo of such a party, although *objectively their activities are reducible*" (italics added) to achieving the aims of the revolutionary-republican bourgeoisie.

The slogan, then, on which Bolsheviks and SR's are presumed to agree (revolutionary democratic dictatorship of proletariat and peasantry), leads to one possible outcome. The other possibility consists in a deal between Tsarism and the most inconsistent elements of the middle class. In fact, any other tactic but Lenin's, he declares plainly, "plays into the hands of the bourgeois democrats" as precisely does that of the Mensheviks. Not only do they agree to renounce the leadership of the people and the fruits of victory (through refusal to join a provisional government), but further "to turn them over *entirely to the bourgeoisie*." The only possibility of "retaining power" is through a "dictatorship" which will mark the beginning of the struggle for the socialist dictatorship of the proletariat.

Lenin ridicules *Iskra* for fearing the recoil of the bourgeoisie if SD's join a provisional government, not realizing it will inevitably recoil and is recoiling as its own narrow, selfish interests are met. The middle class "is incapable of carrying the democratic revolution to its consummation, while the peasantry is capable of so doing," providing the revolution—which is enlightening the peasant and showing him that not only land reform but satisfaction of his permanent interests depends on the success of the democratic revolution—"is not interrupted too soon by the treachery of the bourgeoisie and the defeat of the proletariat."[34]

Summing up his pamphlet, *Two Tactics,* Lenin recognizes that the tasks enumerated are difficult and complex, "but whoever can deliberately prefer smooth sailing and the path of safe 'opposition' [referring to the Menshevik plan of boycotting and opposing the provisional government to come]. . . . had better abandon Social Democratic work" until the revolution is over and "humdrum everyday life starts again."[35]

Thus we can see that an unbridgeable gulf separates the "two tactics" of Bolsheviks and Mensheviks. It is a chasm determined by their widely differing views of the kind of revolution they want and the choice of allies proceeding directly from these views. The difference of views is all the sharper because both are tactical deductions from the same orthodox Marxist doctrine. This doctrine says: Russia is a semifeudal state. In a semifeudal state a bourgeois revolution must precede a socialist one. In a bourgeois revolution, the proletariat must be the vanguard. Beyond that point of agreement, the difference is deep. Lenin declares that the proletariat, allying itself with the peasantry, must seize power by force and keep it. The Mensheviks assert that the proletariat must lead the bourgeoisie to achieve democracy, possibly peacefully, and then step aside to fight for socialism against the bourgeoisie.

9.

Lenin's answers to the questions of choice of allies, of whether to use armed force, of the nature of the outcome of the first phase, must be explained not only by his rigorous theoretical analysis, but by his own motives and beliefs. They appear clearly enough through the cracks of doctrine in *Two Tactics.*

Was he determined to bring about an uprising at any cost? Was he bent on brushing aside whatever objectives of his own either the Tsar or the liberals were willing to grant, and seizing them by force? Did he believe revolution to be a beneficial exercise in which every proletariat must engage? Clearly not. By his apriori analysis of bourgeois class character and interests, he was irrevocably convinced that the middle class never would nor could allow the Social

Democrats to achieve their aims peaceably. No empirical evidence could weaken this belief, no matter if the newspaper *Liberation* accepted a Constituent Assembly, "recognized" the revolution or should claim actually "to be at the head of the revolution."[36] Whatever the liberals might say, they would in fact treacherously compete by any methods for popular support, with the aim of betraying the people and the cause of revolution itself. The peasantry (unlike the bourgeoisie) could not lead; indeed, only by constant proletarian prodding would they follow. Yet they would, thought Lenin, be capable of aiding the workers to crush both Tsarism and liberal bourgeois ascendancy in the first stage. By "class character," the first phase would be bourgeois, but the "class force" of the non-peasant bourgeoisie was never to have power in its hands even for a fleeting moment. It could only console itself with the "freedom" which would belong to it in the dubious interval which would separate the two phases, an interval unlikely to be calm or peaceful. Lenin's fundamental and implacable hatred of the middle class thus leads him, while technically remaining within the bounds of orthodox Marxism, to deny that class even the shadow of the historical role which Marxism had seemed to allot to it. A middle-class provisional government, which would reach power through peaceful middle-class means, in order to extend the sway of philistine middle-class institutions—this sort of outcome was utterly abhorrent to Lenin. It was not surprising that while continuing to champion "democracy" and "freedom" and "popular sovereignty" he made sure, once in power, that these ideals should be translated into a form quite different from that he had known them to take under middle-class power—into a form not only quite different, but their very opposite.

10.

How far had Lenin, in his novel conception of "bourgeois revolution," departed from orthodox Marxism? The Russian revolutionaries of the 70's had relied on the peasantry in their search for social revolution which would by-pass the abhorred middle class and the bourgeois-tainted state mechanism itself. Then the Marxists of the 80's had renounced faith in the peasantry as a revolutionary force, and supported the middle class in its struggle for liberty. Now Lenin had apparently moved back to the populist position of the 70's, or at least had arrived at that of his contemporaries, the Socialist Revolutionaries. These men held that while the Russian middle class had already attained power, it was power of a circum-scribed kind, so that the liberals yet might support the workers in the "political" (they refused to call it "bourgeois") phase of the revolution. Still, they deeply distrusted the middle class and prom-ised they would not permit it to seize any of the "fruits of the revolution." They relied on the poor peasants, but only as the mass army of the proletarian vanguard. The SR's, like Lenin, offered the peasantry not what it demanded, land of its own, but something else (the SR's "socialization," Lenin, "nationalization.") Both Chernov and Lenin preached a revolution by armed force, through mass uprising, and insisted that a Constituent Assembly could not successfully be convened until after victory.

Of course these apparently similar positions had been reached by different routes. Lenin first relied on workers, adding peasants later; he had always held Marxist theory, and supplied revolution-ary practice afterwards; he had first supported the liberals, then rejected them; he had first apparently accepted the old notion of "bourgeois revolution," and later had declared the bourgeoisie was to have none of its "fruits" and practically assimilated the first to the second phase, elevating the proletariat to political power at once. The SR's had first relied on peasants, then added workers—and in the place of honor; they had started with practice, then declared that sound theory must be supplied; first rejecting any kind of "bourgeois" stage in favor of immediate social revolution, they had in accordance with Marxist doctrine consented to insert a preliminary "political" phase which was "bourgeois" in a way strikingly similar to Lenin's formulation.

So it was that in 1905 both the tactics and conception of the revolution held by Lenin and Chernov appeared in practice as almost identical. It is not surprising either that under the cir-cumstances Lenin found it easy to consider the possibility of a "fighting agreement" with the SR's, or that Soviet writers sedulously avoid enlarging on the similarities of the two positions and cooper-ation of the two groups in 1905.

Nevertheless, the practical likeness is in part misleading. It was not only that Lenin and Chernov differed in several important points of theory; their parties differed in their very estimate of the value of theory in general. Although the SR's had been induced in self-defense to adopt much doctrine from their Marxist opponents, that did not mean they had entirely forgotten their old attach-ment to "deeds," their contempt for abstract theorizers. To a con-siderable extent, it is true to say that they simply desired a revolution for the benefit of the peasants and sought how best to achieve it; while Lenin desired above all the attainment of his rational scheme of human evolution—not that it is necessary to doubt his attachment to the good of the workers.

In his eagerness to translate this theory into reality, to be as complete in his action as he was in his thought, he developed a tactic which was intended to bring the workers (read Social Democrats, or perhaps unconsciously, Lenin himself) to power at the soonest possible time. This meant not only out-competing the liberal competitors for power, but opposing them directly and vigorously. It meant the choice of the peasants to fill the requirement of having a bourgeois ally. It meant the use of armed force by the workers and peasants together in order to set up the provisional government they would form.

11.

Curiously enough, after the III Congress Miliukov interpreted its Bolshevik resolutions as admitting the possibility of Social Democratic participation in a *bourgeois* provisional government.[37] Bertram D. Wolfe repeats the same error in a recent book. Not only was Kadetism incompatible with Lenin's formula for the democratic revolution, but in his view concession by the Tsar of successive political reforms to reach constitutional democracy would be positively harmful, to the extent that these reforms diverted the people from the real issue. The real issue was conquest of power, not parliamentary action of any kind this side of victory. Half-hearted legislative concessions such as the Bulygin Duma, or any other Duma, were simply regarded as signs of the approaching "peaceful deal" which the middle class was expected to make with Tsarism, and did not in the least further the aim of the proletariat except as they revealed the weaknesses of Tsarism.

Lenin in fact looked most closely at the liberals in 1905 to see what they did not say (and what, he was sure, they were really thinking) rather than what they did say. Was it not obvious, he wrote in June, that if it were not for the revolutionary masses, holding out for complete victory, "society" would settle for a Bulygin constitution?[38] The Union of Unions had made the decision to boycott this Duma, but such a decision was not enough; it had to be accompanied by the slogan of armed uprising. The liberal "Manilov" dreamers feared uprising, and so confined themselves to discussing whether or not to take part in this sham assembly. The

Iskraite Manilovs, on the other hand, with their absurd and confused blueprint for qualified boycott, simply adopted bourgeois opportunist illusions.[39]

When the Bulygin project was finally enacted into law, Lenin saw it as confirming the worst fears of "democrats." "Unity of the Tsar with the people," in terms of this law, meant simply union between the Tsar and the gentry and capitalists. He did now find more to approve of in the active-boycottist attitude of the Union of Unions, however. He declared this group capable of expressing the interests of the mass of petty bourgeoisie and peasantry, and he thought it might, on condition of rapprochement with the masses, become a "mighty force" against Autocracy although powerless of itself. In the boycottist decision he saw not a sign that the bourgeoisie might take a sharper stand against the Tsar, but the first step of the petty-bourgeois intelligentsia toward "rapprochement with the revolutionary populace," just as the same Bulygin law evoked the first step of the upper and middle bourgeoisie towards a peaceful deal with the monarch. "The radical intelligentsia has extended us a finger, seize it by the hand!" The Bolsheviks might still attract it to the side of revolutionary democracy. Nothing came of this hope of Lenin's. But the significant point is that he never envisaged any "bourgeois" alliance which would stop anywhere near Kadet objectives. What he had done here was merely to evaluate the possibility of stealing the "professional" unions from quasi-Kadet leadership.

"The first steps of bourgeois treason" were soon apparent to Lenin; this phrase he applied to the zemstvo deputation of 6 June to the Tsar. Others were not long in coming. When Professor Vinogradov declared that Russia must follow the way of 1848, not 1789, Lenin dubbed him a "typical bourgeois ideologue" already "recoiling" from the revolution.[40] Such "recoiling" was inevitable and already visible, yet the Mensheviks oriented their whole tactic toward preventing such behavior. Another case of treachery was the "meeting of friends" in which the president of the Moscow zemstvo board sought to obtain amicable permission of the Governor-General of Moscow to hold another zemstvo congress.[41] Still another was when Manuilov and Trubetskoi closed the universities to stop revolutionary agitation, in a fashion Trepov would have had to do himself not long before, had the danger arisen.[42] Here was an example of Kadet tactics *in fact* during serious political crises. This was why the Bolsheviks said it was immaterial whether there would be a Black Hundred (ultra-reactionary) or a liberal

Duma. In any case the bourgeoisie would maneuver between Tsar and people, conspiring for a "deal" which would give the power into middle-class hands. Such a trade was caricatured in an imaginary conversation between Petrunkevich and Trubetskoi, published in *The Proletarian*.[43]

> "'The strictest order we will keep
> Together with an Upper Chamber:
> Progress must ever gradual be—'
> So says the rich landowner.
> 'Don't fear, prince! The liberal has not
> Fallen from the monstrous Tsarist lie,
> I even read in *Iskra* a day or so back:
> "Power will forever bourgeois be!"'"

12.

By the autumn of 1905 there had thus become plain Lenin's tactical reversal from the previous decade in relation to the bourgeois liberals. He felt the need of elucidating his reasons for the change in a little fable.[44] If a small group is fighting a crying evil, which a sleeping mass does not recognize, then the former must first waken it, then enlighten it as to the tasks of struggle, next organize it into a force capable of victory, and last teach it how to use correctly the fruits of victory. First comes the awakening: and the small group must awaken everybody. Then it becomes clear that a part of those awakened is *"interested* in the retention of the evil" combatted. The "awakers" must accordingly turn against that portion and organize against it those who accept the idea of serious consistent struggle to the end. Thus the Social Democrats (read Bolsheviks) behaved towards liberals: they awakened them (1900-2), demarcated the "awakened" (1902-4), and then openly fought the traitors (1905).

On the very day of the October Manifesto, not knowing of its publication, Lenin wrote a sketch[45] asserting that there then existed "an equilibrium of forces." "Tsarism is no longer powerful enough, the revolution is not yet powerful enough to triumph." If a Kadet constitution is granted, it will only serve as a "deception of the people, because notwithstanding there will not be complete and real freedom of elections"—simply because, he might have added, whatever elections were held, under whatever electoral law, would be conducted while the Tsarist, not a revolutionary government, was in power. His tactics when he learned of the October Manifesto appear to be based on the belief that the Manifesto was a *"Kadet constitution,"* and sought to apply the appropriate tactical measures in terms of that belief. He thought, in a word, that the day of real "bourgeois treachery" had arrived, and "openly fought the traitors" with all his might. If his liberal competitors had paid more attention to what he had said before October, they might have been less shocked by what he did after it.

IX

MARTOV: A BOURGEOIS REVOLUTION

As unrest passed into revolt in January, 1905, the Mensheviks had reason to feel confident. On their side were to be found all of the old party leaders: Plekhanov, Axelrod, Zasulich, Martov, and Potresov—excepting only Lenin, the lone first-rank Bolshevik, and Trotsky, who had just broken with the Mensheviks without joining Lenin's faction. In addition they had some outstanding ex-Economist thinkers, such as Martynov and Akimov. They had had a clear field in party journalism through their possession of *Iskra* until in December 1904 Lenin founded *Forward*. They had maneuvered the Bolshevik-dominated (as a result of the II Congress) Central Committee to discuss reunion, thereby inducing Lenin to set up his own splinter Bolshevik Bureau in protest. When liberals or neo-populists spoke of the "Social Democrats," they usually meant Mensheviks. Western Social Democrats generally supported them over the Bolsheviks, and appeared to share the Mensheviks' own view of the Leninists as temporarily over-enthusiastic trouble-makers who would sooner or later be brought to listen to reason and rejoin the fold of what *Iskra* was proud to call "orthodox Social Democracy"—despite the fact that Lenin was at least equally jealous of his own orthodox Marxism. Finally, their party organization was expanding and thriving, while the revolution seemed every day to be nearer, more likely to succeed.

Since the circumstances were these, it is not surprising that they felt that the only need was to "unloose the revolution," and that they viewed Lenin's plans for technical preparation for insurrection as not only Blanquist, conspiratorial, and Jacobin, but unnecessary. At the news of "Bloody Sunday," *Iskra* proclaimed that the Russian proletariat, not only in St. Petersburg but throughout the land, had served a "short-term ultimatum on the house of the Romanovs."[1] The event proved that neither a revolutionary populace nor a popular uprising was a figment of Social Democratic imagination. In contemporary Russia two opposing forces had been contending for power: Tsarism against "bourgeois liberalism and *raznochinnaia* democracy, fighters for culture and citizenhood." As the opposition movement passes into a developing insurrection, "it is stupid and harmful to dream of a monopoly of the active role for Russian Social Democracy." All that was needed was political hegemony, "the politically leading role." The Marxist task was not so much to "organize" as to "unloose" the great mass rising which would destroy Tsarism. In this great, majestic victorious movement, too much talk about party factions would be out of place. "For us Social Democracy is not a trading firm, not a pawnshop, but a great historical principle." [2]

When a few weeks passed after Bloody Sunday without any major signs of cataclysm, *Iskra* lost none of its confidence. It pointed out instances of popular ferment in a dozen places, and bid Marxists forget disillusionment on the one hand and "adventurism" on the other, continuing to inevitable success.

During 1905 the Mensheviks seemed not to feel compelled to attack the Bolsheviks too sharply or directly. Lenin was right when he wrote that the Mensheviks only described instead of "giving a slogan" for the revolutionary process, in the sense that they relied confidently upon the course of history and the inevitability of victory.[3] They believed firmly in the leadership of the proletariat, but they thought it would be assured by objective historical conditions rather than an attempt to "force" events, to precipitate a premature uprising.

As for Lenin's belief in the revolutionariness of the peasantry, the *Iskra* board did not attack it as evil or tending toward eventual "betrayal" of the revolution, so much as misplaced and Utopian. If the peasant helped the worker, so much the better. But Western experience indicated that his help would be insignificant. On the other hand, the Mensheviks saw the usefulness of their would-be liberal allies as self-evident. As in the West, so in Russia bourgeois liberals were working hard to achieve democracy, and it was perfectly consonant with their interests to support a bourgeois revolution, as they were sure of obtaining power. This Martov and his colleagues thought to be historical necessity, and they thought in refusing in advance to enter a bourgeois provisional government they were bargaining away nothing that was theirs anyhow. What was necessary for the Marxists to do was to encourage, to push vigorously ahead these bourgeois elements which were capable of carrying through the destruction of Tsarism. This involved accelerating the split between Right- and Left-Liberals. If this was drawing a line through the middle of the bourgeoisie, Martov might have said, Lenin was doing the same thing. The difference was merely that he drew it in another place, between peasants and liberal intelligentsia, for the purposes of finding his preferred ally. Autocracy would be destroyed by a class and a half, the proletariat and part of the middle class—both factions were agreed on that proposition, though they did not give it the same content.

Where Lenin aroused the fears of Martov and Potresov was not in his choice of a peasant ally so much as in his uncompromising rejection of liberal aid. It was precisely this which led him into inventing a scheme (which Mensheviks regarded as un-Marxist) for arbitrary seizure of power not only without the liberals but against them. If Lenin did not abandon the orthodox conception of "bourgeois revolution," thought Martov, he surely altered it fundamentally by an apriorist denial that the liberals could participate, instead of waiting to observe whether or not they *did*. By adopting his formula "revolutionary dictatorship of proletariat and peasantry" he prejudged the question of liberal aid. And in doing so he by no means secured the ascendancy of the proletariat, for, as one Menshevik declared, "this slogan in effect must be converted into a dictatorship of the peasantry *over* the proletariat."[4] Nonetheless Lenin's efforts to "force" the course of events were mainly viewed as unavailing. The Mensheviks had much less faith than Lenin in the possibility of altering the predetermined development of the Russian revolution. To a large extent they did actually view the process *"sub specie aeternitatis,"* as Lenin charged in *Two Tactics,* but it was not owing to lack of "virility" or fear of an active role, as he charged, but to a quite different view of what voluntarism could accomplish. The Mensheviks were not, however, determinist to the extent that they denied the possibility of Lenin's "frightening" part of the liberals prematurely. Nevertheless, the restrained tone they used in dealing with such a possibility, in contrast to Lenin's passion in denouncing the conceivable effects of "erroneous" Menshevik tactics, demonstrates their much greater reliance on the inexorability of the Marxian dialectic.

Russia was on the threshold of bourgeois democracy. It would be a better sort of bourgeois democracy, not because the Russian middle class was better than that of the West, but because the Russian proletariat was more advanced by far than the Western proletariat had been at the time of the classic bourgeois revolutions. Therefore the workers' role in 1905 was crucial, central, and leading, but not to be played over the footlights. Miliukov was to play Trilby to Martov's Svengali.

In February, Plekhanov laid down[5] the basic Menshevik line in relation to tactics for 1905. While in the West from time to time the proletariat had found itself isolated (1848?) in Russia it was the Tsardom which had been deserted by all. The support of "society" was not only possible for the Russian proletariat, since the next objective was not a socialist overturn but the conquest of democratic institutions, but it was also necessary. For one thing, success depended in large part on the army, which in turn depended on the officer corps—linked closely with society. There was no need to hide the Marxist flag in one's pocket, nor to unite with any other parties—and yet it was clear, said Plekhanov, that "the success of an armed uprising depends on the rapprochement of the revolutionaries with 'society'."

Not only the educated class, but also other revolutionary groups, he continued, could now be of assistance in the common struggle. The aim was to disorganize the enemy forces. Among other methods, terrorism had this result. Therefore in view of the changed situation, in which terrorism would not as in the past disorganize the revolutionaries themselves, Social Democrats could afford to alter their attitude toward "terrorist groups" (read Socialist Revolutionaries). Since success was only possible with the cooperation of these various strata, it was unthinkable that the revolution should appear to be the work of a small band of conspirators. "An armed uprising will conquer as the uprising of the broad masses or will never conquer under any kind of preliminary conditions . . . Without the masses, we are nothing."

Plekhanov's overture to the SR's came to nothing. They were not primarily terrorists, after all, but peasant revolutionists, and Plekhanov's distrust of the peasantry was still deep-seated. The SR's did not respond. On the other side, the hand of amity extended to the liberals was welcomed. The liberals, as we shall see, tried to deport themselves with restraint, knowing their overt friendship was the kiss of death to Martov, especially with Lenin peering through the curtains. Neither did *Iskra* fling itself incautiously into liberal embraces.

It was made quite plain that the role of the Liberationists was to be assistance, not leadership, of the proletariat. "As a *workers'* revolution, the Russian *bourgeois* revolution attains its victory."[6] In previous European revolutions the workers had gone to painful school under bourgeois guidance, but in Russia the workers were teaching the middle class. Liberal "society" was "borne on the crest of the proletarian struggle." It must willy-nilly sharpen the democracy of its program and the revolutionariness of its deeds, under Social Democratic pressure.

Nevertheless, the Mensheviks saw the "liberal spirit" as tragically divided. The tragedy was the moderates' compulsion to put out the flags of Four-Tail suffrage, balanced by a "secret fear, of necessity carefully concealed, of this electoral system." One Menshevik wrote that the liberals constantly wavered between confidence in *representatives* of the people and in *all* the people. This statement had Leninist overtones. The difference between *Iskra* and Lenin in this respect, however, was that *Iskra* believed the political schizophrenia of the liberals was due to the presence of two contrasting groups in their movement, while Lenin thought the liberals as a whole suffered from this psychological malady, compelling them to be in general unreliable. *Iskra* had already defined these two parts of liberalism as "bourgeois liberalism and *raznochinnaia* democracy," and it was upon the second that it rested its confidence. For the time being, however, they were chiefly interested in the influence of the "democracy" upon the "liberalism" rather than driving the two wings apart.

Iskra carefully followed and pointed out the fluctuations of liberal "extremism." When the April zemstvo congress adopted a demand for Four-Tail suffrage, *Iskra* hailed it as a victory for democracy even though it was weakened by support of a two-house legislature.[7] It was recalled that this marked a significant advance over the November 1904 congress's demand for simply a "people's" instead of an "all-people's" representative body. The proletariat, however, recognizing the liberals' advance toward democracy, was warned not to be deceived and to realize always that "only its own revolutionary pressure, only its independent class struggle converts liberals by nature into democrats in spite of themselves."

This journalistic grin was followed by a frown. The 6 June deputation to the Tsar was scornfully hailed as an event marking an "historic day" in the bourgeois sense: "there was no blood shed, no convulsions took place, much was said, many words." Could the zemstvists, who even watered down, en route to the palace, the pungency of the petition they were commissioned to present, forget that what was permitted them on 6 June was denied to the proletariat of St. Petersburg on 9 January? The conduct of this delegation proved "all the nonsensicalness and reactionariness of efforts of the liberal constitutionalist party to *lead* the all-people's movement." Fortunately this was no new discovery to the Mensheviks. They had never believed the liberals could lead. Their role was to play second fiddle to the worker vanguard, and in doing so they were bound to waver, wobble, and hobble in the rear, as Lenin said. Nevertheless, under constant Marxist prodding, they were still capable of material aid to the proletariat.

3.

All in all, the Mensheviks' chosen bourgeois ally had not disappointed expectations in the first few months of the Revolution. More prodding was of course necessary, and how to impart it was one of the most pressing problems for the April Conference of Mensheviks in Geneva. This meeting represented the party committees of St. Petersburg, Moscow, Vilna, and several cities of the South and the Caucasus where the Mensheviks were especially strong. They decided to recognize the party split and deal with it realistically while at the same time setting about systematically to re-unify the party. The Conference declared *Iskra* to be not officially the party organ, but only that of the enumerated organizations. Refusing to name a Central Committee, it set up an Organization Committee to serve as executive. Plekhanov withdrew from the Menshevik faction in protest at the overt recognition of the schism which he had sought to avert and close. But otherwise the Mensheviks managed to strengthen their hand, while acting in such a way as to usurp no prerogatives reserved for the united party which they sought.

The Menshevik Conference stated its prescription for a "decisive victory over Tsarism" in dual form: it was to come either by establishment of a provisional government through a popular uprising, or "by the revolutionary initiative of one or another representative institution, which under direct revolutionary pressure of the people decides to set up a people's Constituent Assembly." Either event would inaugurate a "new phase" of "mutual struggle among the elements of politically emancipated bourgeois society for the satisfaction of their social interests and for the direct acquisition of power." By its objective nature, the provisional government would have to fight against those "factors which threaten the foundations of the capitalist system"— factors which included, commented Lenin bitterly, the proletariat itself.[8] Social Democracy must not, the Conference decided, tie its own hands in its fight against the "self-seeking policy" of the bourgeois parties by setting itself "the aim of seizing power or sharing power in the provisional government, but must remain the party of extreme revolutionary opposition." Partial, episodic, and local seizures of powers, indeed, were not ruled out. But only if the revolution spread to Western Europe could Social Democracy think of holding power and immediately "entering the path of socialist overturn."

We see that the Mensheviks thought that the workers must lead the bourgeois revolution, but leave to the middle class the fruits of power, unless the revolution spread to the West. This was an inverted statement of Trotsky's basic proposition, that the Russian proletariat would be able to keep power alone, by means of the assistance of the proletariat of the West. The Mensheviks said that this was indeed the condition of the Russian proletariat's taking power, but they regarded it as most unlikely that that condition would be realized. What they assumed was that the Western proletariat ought not to be a critical factor in the practical calculations of a Russian party. Failing its help, Russian Social Democrats must relinquish power in the moment of victory because by trying to retain it, they would simply disillusion the workers in themselves, since they could not realize socialism at once. Furthermore, by trying to share the power they would "cause the bourgeois classes to recoil from the revolution and thereby diminish its sweep."[9] They should therefore stay outside the government and apply "pressure" on it.

Martov, Axelrod, and their comrades thus followed to its logical conclusion the inconvenient theory of "bourgeois revolution" in a semi-feudal state. The objective nature of such an overturn made the only possible ally of the proletariat the liberal bourgeoisie, but that ally was one which was bound to hold power alone. Since the bourgeoisie might not be willing to follow through an armed uprising, the peaceful establishment of a Constituent Assembly was envisaged as an alternative. Plekhanov had long ago declared that the Social Democrats must not brandish the "red phantom" in a bourgeois revolution, and the Mensheviks had followed his advice faithfully.

The Conference resolution accordingly appeared to yield the supremacy of the proletariat rather readily. The Mensheviks, however, did not believe the matter was subject to their own will. The determining factor was "the objective conditions of social development," which "spontaneously raise" the problems to be solved. Events would be too strong for conspiratorial schemes, no matter how passionately advanced. They might be too strong for the Geneva blueprint itself. The matter on which the Mensheviks focused their attention was not so much the exact course of the revolutionary government as the overthrow of Tsarism and tactics directed to that end. They were taking the miler's stride next to the sure and constant pace of history; Lenin, they might have said, was unleashing a sprint he could not possibly maintain. The Mensheviks did not fear a bourgeois government. Lenin, on the other hand, was engaged in a desperate race with the middle class for power.

Notwithstanding all this, the Mensheviks might have seemed to the liberals to be offering them power of their own free will. Perhaps as a *quid pro quo* for their involuntary gift, they once more laid down a series of conditions under which they would support the middle class, sharpening the terms of the Potresov resolution of 1903. Not only Four-Tail suffrage must be demanded, but the liberals must demonstrate "energetic and unequivocal support of every determined action of the organized proletariat," even "active participation in the self-armament of the people." This was as close to mention of "armed uprising" as the Menshevik conference came. Lenin demanded scornfully why the Mensheviks did not require the liberals to fight for a republic, but as we have already tried to show, that would not have altered his own refusal to support them, and the Conference seems to have recognized that the "monarchy" issue in itself was of little importance—what mattered was whether the monarch or anyone else had any power. Lenin had declaimed that the monarchy was unacceptable because free elections could not be held while it lasted, but it is unlikely that he would have had greater sympathy toward elections held under a republican government controlled by treacherous bourgeois. It was true, as he pointed out, that the Conference did not mention the word "republic" anywhere in its resolution. The Mensheviks did in fact favor a democratic republic as the alternative to be supported in the Constituent Assembly. If they said so too pointedly, however, it might have accentuated a latent disagreement within the Kadet party which could serve no purpose at the moment. About the "democracy," the Mensheviks did not equivocate. It was the masses who in the final analysis would give form to the bourgeois revolution, and it was they alone who could give strength to any political group.

It was as a successful attempt to organize mass support that *Iskra* regarded the "professional unions" which were growing fast in the spring of 1905.[10] Since the authors of this attempt were bourgeois democrats, *Iskra* declared Social Democrats must stand aside from the "unions," meanwhile redoubling their own efforts to organize the much broader masses under the Marxist banner. Time was, mused the writer, when Russian bourgeois democracy was "pale" and "weak" and could offer the workers' party no competition. Lenin shared the analysis of the "union" problem presented thus far by *Iskra*. The effect of the facts as both saw them on their tactics was, however, diametrically opposite. Lenin foresaw the liberal competition and feared it; the Mensheviks welcomed it, because the liberals and they were working for the same immediate ends. All the help that could be obtained in organizing the masses was welcome. Breaking decisively with the old underground traditions, Social Democracy, said *Iskra,* must "enter the path of converting a *party for the masses* into a *party of the masses themselves."*

With one eye on the liberals, the Mensheviks thus hailed the growth of the mass movement in the cities. In the same fashion they approached that of the countryside. *Iskra* had devoted little attention to the question of the doctrine that should guide peasant agitation, though the Menshevik conference had recognized the "revolutionary significance" of the peasants' efforts to seize the land. Peasant action would also be instructive to the liberals. *Iskra* declared that the more active were the Social Democrats in the village, the faster bourgeois society would fully understand the true situation in agrarian affairs, and "the more radical will be that agrarian revolution which it must support." [11]

The Mensheviks were also active in the armed forces, and their southern members vigorously supported the Potiomkin mutiny, which was, according to the party organ, an example of those unsuccessful uprisings of history which had more revolutionary significance than some successful ones.

4.

Commissioning Menshevik agents in the field to arouse mass support, *Iskra* concentrated its own literary efforts mainly on the liberals. The July zemstvo congress evoked praise of a sort its predecessor congresses had not received. [12] For the first time, declared *Iskra,* zemstvo liberalism had found the courage "to break with traditions of gentry pre-reform opposition and to attempt to play a political role on the *European*-bourgeois level." Of course stones had to speak and cruisers threaten Tsarist fortresses (a reference to the Potiomkin mutiny) before Russian liberalism had been induced to ask a minimum of that which above all its own political interest demanded! Much earlier it might have decided boldly "to stand irrevocably on the ground of constitutionalism and show even a small desire to rely on the people," but in any case this had been done at last. Above all was an ideological victory of the proletariat discernible in the zemstvists' decision to reject unconditionally the Bulygin Duma. True, they had determined to participate in elections, in order to "wreck from within," but this was not necessarily an opportunist tactic. Its actual success would depend upon the confidence and support of the people, which could be gained only in the course of the mass struggle. However, previously the zemstvists had had nothing in common with the people and showed only the most reactionary attitude to its revolutionary independence. True, still lacking popular confidence, the congress dared not speak openly for participation in elections.

Nevertheless, the decisions of the July congress represented the beginning of the liquidation of Russian constitutionalism as a largely landlordist tendency and marked the beginning of the founding of a real "liberal-democratic party." *Iskra* had already pointed out the presence of two groups in the liberal movement, the landlord opposition and the *raznochintsy* democrats, and had declared that severing the links between them was the first prerequisite for the latter to become the "backbone" of a broad popular, though nonproletarian, movement. Social Democracy was faced with the problem of breaking off the liberal-Left, so that the Third Element could embark upon a course of independent action side by side with the revolutionary proletariat.

The program of the May congress, for a monarchy and a two-house parliament, must be exposed by the workers as reactionary. If one day the constitutionalists demanded the arming of the populace and a Constituent Assembly, the proletariat would support them, but only in order to "open the epoch of revolution." [13]

5.

The decision of the zemstvists to take part in elections for the Bulygin Duma was answered by *Iskra* with a definite Menshevik plan to spur on the middle class.[14] This was a legitimate heir of the earlier "plan of a zemstvo campaign" which Lenin had attacked so bitterly. The Bulygin Duma, wrote *Iskra*, abhorrent as it was, would "deliver into the hands of the revolution great material for agitation" and help to concentrate the attention of the masses on one concrete problem.[15] Boycottism would not suffice to utilize the situation in a positive manner. The Union of Unions, in resolving upon a boycott, was in reality taking a passive attitude. True, the workers should refrain from taking part in the elections. They must, however, simultaneously with the elections carry on electoral agitation, founding "workers' committees" to demand Four-Tail suffrage, and finally endeavoring to convene an illegal assembly which would show up the impotence of the Duma. Insofar as this plan worked, it would cover the nation with "a network of organs of revolutionary self-government." This was a slogan which the Mensheviks used forcefully. "Organization of revolutionary self-government" was essential to the preparation of a popular uprising. Anyone who rejected this method [16] must prefer either no uprising at all or one of separate classes or circles—a sally aimed, of course, at Lenin. The workers must drive onward the liberals. This is what the Mensheviks had been saying, and now they urged their proletarian followers to do it. Those who would not be driven, would (and should) fall by the wayside.

In other words, Martov and his friends were driving for a split in the liberal camp which would create a purified democratic ally for themselves and ditch the crudely-class-conscious moderates who would only drag the revolution back anyway. Such a split they now thought they saw coming. In consequence of the Treaty of Portsmouth ending the war with Japan, and of the law of 6 August on the Bulygin Duma, "weakening the hopes of liberalism for the swift capitulation of the government," *Iskra*[17] discerned deep cracks appearing in moderate ranks. For example, there was the conflict between university students and professors over the popular agitation which had found a haven in the schools since the grant of university autonomy. While some professors, led by the historian Maxim Kovalevskii, talked of the "risk to the existence of the universities" and in effect took the side of Autocracy, many students were calling for the conversion of institutions of self-government into "revolutionary tribunes."

Lenin, thought the Mensheviks, incorrectly interpreted the effect of the law of 6 August. The Bulygin law did not at all represent a victory of the moderate bourgeoisie, through collusion with the monarchy, over the people. Not even the minimum bourgeois demands were thereby conceded; the middle class was victimized along with the rest of the nation. What both the peace with Japan and the August law were doing was to drive the democrats towards ever more radical action, while inducing the moderates to consider "premature betrayals" of a kind native to their class character.

Finally, on the eve of the October Manifesto, *Iskra* cheered [18] as it saw the complete break between liberal camps it had long awaited. This was made possible by the collapse of the moderate leadership of the zemstvo movement. The September zemstvo congress hesitated at placing its full trust in the people; it sought only the people's sympathy, not their freedom. The zemstvo men had forgotten their resolve to subvert the Duma and now spoke only of "perfecting" it. The liberal bloc was dying and its body splitting in two.It was on the threshold of dividing into two parts, one reactionary, one in union with the *raznochintsy*. The latter half would doubtless continue the struggle until it too "exhausted its progressiveness" as the zemstvo liberals had done. Now the *raznochintsy* could assume the leadership of peasant and petty-bourgeois democracy. Through "revolutionary self-government," said *Iskra,* Social Democrats would complete the separation of "perfectionist" liberals from revolutionary democrats.

In the autumn of 1905 Martov believed that events had fully justified Menshevik tactics. The Mensheviks, as the ideologues of the proletariat, together with the Kadets,[19] ideologues of the petty bourgeoisie, were thought to be in a position to carry to the end the "bourgeois revolution." Together they would succeed in mobilizing the masses. Using the Duma and "revolutionary self-government" as levers, they would shatter the power of Tsarism and summon a Constituent Assembly. Lenin and the Bolsheviks (as well as the Socialist Revolutionaries) , since they seemed to base their conduct on a different sort of tactics, would surely yield when they found that their simpler, directer methods could not be realized. A bourgeois government would replace the disintegrating Tsarist fabric. The proletariat would play an heroic part in leading the middle class to victory, and then step aside. In a bourgeois revolution, the workers could not do otherwise.

MILIUKOV: AN INSTALMENT ON REVOLUTION

According to Basil Maklakov, "in 1905 there was organized one common front, from the revolutionaries to the conservative sections of our society."[1] It was indeed true that by that time the entire educated Russian public whole-heartedly despised the Tsardom, if not the Tsar himself. Gurko, the bureaucrat historian, substantiates this with unconscious humor[2] when he writes that every public meeting was "convinced of its superiority to the bureaucracy." There was no one who did not think that he could do better —in fact, that almost anyone could do better than the government was doing. The few ultra-conservatives despised its inability to maintain order, the overwhelming majority of vocal people deemed it unfit to introduce the changes needed to satisfy popular clamor. Maklakov adds correctly, however, that the unanimity of his broad front was limited to one point: "to continue as before was impossible." Unanimity was in fact broken by the summer of 1905 by the industrialists and Rightist gentry[3] who showed readiness to settle with Autocracy on the basis of a consultative assembly. The older current of moderate opinion, represented by the Slavophiles, found itself completely isolated, since it shared neither the belief of the liberal-Left in constitutional democracy nor the "legaistic" views of the Maklakovite liberal-Right which was seeking a "strong government" as the way out of the impasse. To Shipov, for example, the law of 6 August for the Bulygin Duma[4] represented merely another demonstration of the government's "complete lack of comprehension" of the "essence" of Autocracy and Russia's historical past, since it strove to appease discontent on a legal instead of a "moral" basis. The Slavophiles could only limp along behind the more radical zemstvists of Left and Right, without influence or support.

As for Miliukov and the Left-liberals, throughout 1905 they

moved ever closer to sympathy with the general idea of "revolution." When the zemstvists were deliberating as to what their attitude to the Bulygin Duma should be, Miliukov cautioned them sharply[5] that they represented "only a small part of that wave which is irresistibly rushing on to its culmination, and that before this culmination is reached, no kind of 'pacification' is conceivable." What Miliukov meant was that the common end of democratic change which all the opposition parties shared must claim the united efforts of all the public bodies which transcended party bounds. His constant loyalty to the extreme Left, to which his friend and executor, B. I. Elkin, testifies, was the keynote of his tactics in 1905.

Some of the Right liberals taunted him with precisely this. Kuzmin-Karavaev declared that the extreme Left was simply utilizing the Liberation movement for the purpose of social revolution and thus tried to obstruct the swift accomplishment of reform —just as did the reactionary Right. Miliukov rushed to the defense of his allies. This was not true, he said, since, "not one 'Leftist' party believes in an *immediate* social overturn" and since "all parties" welcomed "swift reform" as broadening the possible means of further action. Did not Kuzmin-Karavaev himself constantly refer to Leftist activity as the strongest argument in favor of quick reform, retorted Miliukov wryly. One thing, declared Miliukov, the liberals must not do: "treat allies like enemies" as does Kuzmin.

Now Miliukov was fully aware of his differences with the revolutionaries, Social Democrats and Socialist Revolutionaries alike. He was no more eager to attempt a union of the three groups than were the socialists. Starting with a rationalist conception of the political change he desired, he was no more willing to abandon or compromise it than Lenin or Chernov. His conception of even the "first phase" of revolution was not identical with that of the socialists, nor did he believe it to be so. The Liberationists were too good students of Marxism to be so deluded; among their ranks they numbered several ex-Social Democrats who had learned by intimate experience in the 90's quite precisely what Marxist expectations were. Nevertheless, Miliukov believed that the features of his own concept of "revolution" (which had one, not two phases) was basically similar *enough* to the "first phase" of the socialists so that all three groups could work together until it was achieved. Whether the first phase was called "democratic," "toilers'," or "bourgeois," it at least was to have nothing socialist about it, and was to be concerned with liberty and democratic government. Since the precise form of government was to be determined by a Constituent Assembly or at any rate some freely elected popular representative body, the Russian people and not any one opposition party would have the final voice in any case. Therefore, differences between liberals and socialists as to "monarchy" or "two chambers" and so forth were of little importance. After democracy was reached in Russia, all could speak freely, breathe freely, work for the changes and reforms they desired. There would be no need for a "socialist" revolution. Miliukov hoped that "the actual practice of general suffrage will do more than anything else" [6] to wean the socialists away from Utopianism—and he had abundant evidence to support those hopes from the recent history of Western European socialism.

It is of course not true that the Liberationists chose the revolutionaries as allies simply because their rational patterns for the future closely resembled each other. They did so with a careful eye on the masses. As self-proclaimed democrats, the Left-liberals sought the support of the workers and peasants who would, under a regime of universal suffrage, control Russia's destiny. In the existing stage of Russian political consciousness, however, the Liberationists alone could not gain sufficient results from a direct appeal to the mass of the people. The Social Democrats and Socialist Revolutionaries, who had not only proclaimed themselves to be spokemen of the workers and peasants, but had gained a certain amount of influence among them through popular agitation and propaganda, could be of great assistance in bringing mass support to bear behind the Liberation Movement. This was a prime necessity for success. Just as the Tsar *would* not, so "society" *could* not achieve constitutional democracy alone against the forces of the bureaucracy, the army, the church, and reaction in general. The liberal gentry and intelligentsia, from whom the Liberationists drew for their own strength as a party, were not enough. They had to have allies, and the only possible ones were the two revolutionary parties. The Liberationists advanced no "conditions" which the socialists must meet to merit their support. The wooing was chiefly from the Liberal side. As Struve had said, the liberals could only criticize "the inexpediency and insufficiency" of the revolutionists' methods, and otherwise must take them as they were.

The obvious paradox in this policy was, of course, that the idea of "revolution" as commonly understood was itself repugnant to the liberals. It appears that they never expected even the "first phase" to develop to the point of mass uprising or armed insurrection.

It was rather expected that as discontent grew and the threat of overwhelming popular force became great enough, the Tsar would yield in order to save his throne—for the Kadets left the "monarchy" in their program for this and other purposes, as bait for the time when the imperial fish became hungry enough. There would be an "October" situation, when there would be mass action which would compel Autocracy to end its existence. There would follow a constitution and the creation of a popular representative body which would decide the fate of the Russian state. What the liberals did not envisage, as clearly as Lenin did, was that an "October Manifesto" might follow instead.

2.

During most of 1905 the Liberationists and Zemstvo-Constitutionalists devoted their attention not so much to the attempt to form a political party as to the effort to organize support among public bodies, the zemstvo and municipal congresses and "professional unions."[7] The Union of Liberation had decided in October 1904 to undertake the formation of "professional unions." By May 1905 this process was far enough advanced for a Union of Unions to be set up, and in this Miliukov took a prominent part. The Union of Unions embraced 14 member bodies: academicians, lawyers, agronomists, physicians, veterinarians, pharmacists, railway workers, writers, Zemstvo-Constitutionalists, engineers and technicians, teachers, accountants, and unions for the Equality of Women and the Equality of Jews. Soon, according to Marc, more than 50 "unions" had sprung up, most of them affiliated to the central body. Naturally there were differences between such groups as the railway employees and the academicians. However, enough unanimity could be reached for the Union of Unions,[8] at its July conference, to declare an active boycott of the Duma and to resolve that terrorism was justified by the pernicious conduct of the government. It was after this conference that Miliukov, concluding that these groups were proving too radical to provide a suitable foundation for Liberationist action, decided to found the Constitutional Democratic party. According to Martynov,[9] the isolation felt by the Zemstvo-Constitutionalists owing to the Righting of the zemstvo congresses and the Liberationists owing to the Lefting of the "unions" was the cause of the Kadets' decision to form a party of their own. It was true that Miliukov had not yet been able to find the mass footing he sought for Liberationism, but the word "isolation" implies pessimism and impotence, and these feelings were absent. It was with confidence and great expectations for the future that Miliukov and his cohorts advanced to the building of the first great open political party in Russia, and many men and women who came from both zemstvos and "unions" joined in this enterprise.

3.

The future Kadets fought hardest for the allegiance of the zemstvo congresses. These public meetings from the congress of November 1904 managed to take and keep the spotlight in the Liberation Movement until the great strikes of the autumn of 1905. Here was a prize worth winning.

In February, just after the Tsar directed his interior minister to draw up a scheme for a consultative assembly, the II Congress of zemstvists took place. It was intended to represent for the first time all the gubernias which enjoyed zemstvos. Although delegates from only three-quarters of them arrived, Maklakov writes that they "felt representative" at any rate. They proceeded to define the character of the "legislative assembly" which they had demanded the previous November as one elected by Four-Tail suffrage.

The III Congress, which followed at Moscow in April, did actually represent all the zemstvo provinces. Here the zemstvo men went so far as to adopt in only slightly differing language the revolutionists' demand for a Four-Tail Constituent Assembly. By a 71-37 vote, they resolved that the first meeting of the legislative body, based on Four-Tail suffrage, should have the task of "determination of the state order of the Russian Empire."[10] That is to say, it would be a Duma which would "assume the rights of a Constituent Assembly." Shipov and his cohorts, who a few weeks earlier had published a brochure[11] setting forth their own reform program, declared at the III Congress for a legislature which would be elected by universal though indirect suffrage, by way of reorganized and democratized zemstvo institutions. Separate votes were taken on the individual parts of the "Four-Tail" slogan, showing how great an importance it had assumed in the public mind. The vote on universal suffrage was 127-8, on equal 133-3, on secret 136-0, on direct 86-49. Shipov, shocked by the radical tone of the congress, led the "minority" in a walkout. One liberal journalist commented simply that if they had not walked out, it would have been necessary to exclude them anyway.[12] The majority of the delegates, writes Maklakov with evident disapproval, were at open war with Autocracy. "The Revolution did not frighten them."[13] Chermenskii, the Soviet historian, asserts the exact reverse. He charges that this effort to "hobble after the growing revolutionary movement" was conditioned by the fear of a break with the masses. For whatever reasons, open and radical opposition was the keynote of the III Congress.

There followed the news of the naval defeat of Tsushima, which climaxed the incongruous voyage of the rickety Baltic fleet halfway around the world in order to be promptly sunk by the Japanese. "Society" winced and started. Another meeting was summoned, and through the mediation of the Moscow zemstvist, F. A. Golovin, the Shipovite group was persuaded to join in a "coalition congress" which met on 24 May. Though the radicals were still in the ascendant, it was agreed to try "for the last time" to reach an agreement with the Tsar, and only 36 delegates objected to the unprecedented step of sending a deputation to see him personally. By a 104-90 vote the congress narrowly rejected the idea of sending a mass deputation. This was regarded as being too offensive to the Emperor, though the congress included on the small panel which actually went, two men who were known to be personally anathema to him, I. I. Petrunkevich and F. I. Rodichev. The loyal words of Prince S. N. Trubetskoi, who led the deputation, were violently condemned by the Russian opposition as far Right as the Liberationists,[14] but there were many voices, including the liberal *Russkie Vedomosti,* who approved the step as designed to secure the "union of the Tsar with *all* the people." The Tsar did reassure the zemstvists who visited him on 6 June of his "immutable will" to act in the sense of his reform promises made earlier, but these assurances soon appeared empty of meaning. When the next zemstvo congress was forbidden by the police, disillusionment was open and bitter.

The IV Congress which had met despite police warnings on 6 July "abandoned the loyal path," as Maklakov says.[15] Even Chermenskii admits that the Right was "not noticeable." Count Heyden, though he had long been a "loyalist," declared that the only result of the 6 June deputation had been that the July congress had been declared illegal. The tone of this meeting was sounded well by I. I. Petrunkevich, who declared that the liberals must abandon hope for reform from above; "from now on our only hope is the people . . . Now we must boldly go to the people, and not to the Tsar." And the congress adopted a proclamation addressed "to the people" by a 200-8 vote. Although the question of taking part in the Duma to come was left open, dissatisfaction with the Bulygin project was almost universal.[16] N. Shchepkin declared that for the sake of obtaining liberty "we must penetrate into the camp of the enemy, that is, into the Duma . . . the first session of the Duma will become Constituent." Rodichev talked of the Duma as an "ambush" for the enemy. The congress was not uniformly radical, however; the minority, led in the absence of Shipov by Count Heyden and others, mostly kept quiet.

At the July Congress, delegates from the city councils were admitted on a footing of equality with the zemstvists. Some of them had been present in May, but only on 16 June had a city-council congress met to arrange systematic representation, and the IV Congress recognized the 16 June meeting, along with the zemstvo congresses of 6 November and 22 April, as its official predecessors. The association of the industrialists (chiefly from the two capitals) which had taken steps to organize in the spring, also endeavored to gain admission to the IV Congress, but was refused as being openly a "class" body. By September the issue of cooperation with the industrialists was dead, as they were taking a line independent of the zemstvists.

The final meeting of the zemstvists and city councillors took place on 12 September. As their political program was now complete, they turned to consider the question of social reform. They approved compensated expropriation of private lands (with certain reservations), the eight-hour day, universal free education, and autonomy for the border regions. Participation in the Duma, although apparently it had been on the verge of being condemned by the July congress, was now recognized as a "painful duty," though few expressed satisfaction with the terms of the law of 6 June. In general, however, the "minority" was much more in evidence again.

In accepting the principle of expropriation of land, the September zemstvo congress adopted a demand the Group of Zemstvo-Constitutionalists had advanced in February 1905. The Group met again in May immediately following the zemstvo congress of that month, and was almost convinced that it could abandon its meetings separate from the larger zemstvo body. It discussed the joint formation of a party together with the Liberationists. Count Heyden disapproved this as likely to "frighten" moderates, while Tugan-Baranovskii thought such a union would include groups too divergent in opinion. On 9 July the Group met again in order to disavow the zemstvist deputation to the Tsar and now resolved to undertake at once the organization of a Constitutional Democratic party. The Group appointed a committee for that purpose which joined with an analogous one set up by the IV Congress of the Union of Liberation, held at the end of August, and together they convened the I Congress of the Kadet party on 12 October. In so doing, the Kadet intelligentsia abandoned hope of basing their party on a broader nucleus (the whole "professional union" movement and/or the whole zemstvo congress membership) than had hitherto followed their banner. They substituted for this hope the more substantial one of winning a mass following among the common people, and after the election campaign in the spring of 1906 it looked as if their optimism had been fully justified.

4.

The fight of the liberal-Left for hegemony in the moderate camp was reflected in the pages of *Liberation* as Struve exerted every effort to prevent a split in the movement. Following "Bloody Sunday" the newspaper had at once blasted the Tsar as "the executioner of the people" and renounced any effort to speak of him or with him any further.[17] This was a curious statement from an organ which remained "monarchist," but only illustrates the essential indifference of the radicals to the issue of monarchy as such, coupled with deep hostility to Nicholas II.

Struve welcomed the final publication of the program of the Union of Liberation[18] in March as a long step towards building a constitutional democratic party. The program emphasized strongly that before a Constituent Assembly could be convened, a regime of legally assured liberties was necessary. The Union, like Lenin, was concerned at the possibility that the Assembly might be corrupted by Tsarist meddling with elections, though of course it did not subscribe to Lenin's belief that only a "revolutionary dictatorship of proletariat and peasantry" could assure a fair vote. Yet here as all during 1905 there was evident the radical desire to keep common front with the revolutionaries even if they could not capture the moderate camp.

The Slavophiles who criticized the revolutionary allies in principle were silenced by this time, but the empiricist Maklakovite Right was not. One contributor of this stripe declared he recognized the "moral resources" of the Left and did not desire to enter into polemics with it, but criticized it for lacking "a sense of political reality." True, the liberals must go to the people; but in the village, for instance, would their promises not look pale indeed beside those of the Socialist Revolutionaries? "We are always afraid of being insufficiently Leftist, we fear being accused of opportunism, bourgeoisness." Liberals should declare that a clear line of demarcation separates them from SD's and SR's, and refuse to cross it. The liberal problem was, how to wait till the "tomorrow" which would bring constitutional democracy to Russia without "losing themselves" in the swift current of revolution.

Struve quickly took up the radical cudgel in retort.[19] Instead of worrying about inability to outbid the revolutionaries, the liberals must realize that the program of the socialists was their greatest weakness and hampered their approach to the masses. Look how the republicanism of the German Social Democrats had the contrary effect of strengthening the monarchy! The masses distrusted extremist doctrines, and in both village and factory, the appeals of gradualists had had most success. The failure of the 1 May celebrations should suggest that to the revolutionaries. The Liberationists' moderate program, "foreign to doctrinaire demands which are not understood by the mass of the people, makes our task easier." We must work with a will among the masses, especially in the village where "our main job" lies. The two forces which go to make up the Liberationists, the socially privileged gentry intelligentsia and the propertyless intelligentsia, could only through complete unity with each other secure the adhesion of the third decisive force, the people, to Russian democracy.

Struve here sounds almost as if he is interested in competing rather than cooperating with the far Left. However, he was at the same time approaching the least hostile section of the revolutionary camp with hand outstretched. He was wooing the Mensheviks. It is ironic that while the Mensheviks were trying to deepen schism among the liberals in their search for a reliable ally, the Liberationists were trying to do the same thing to the Social Democrats. While *Iskra* was doing its best to split the Liberationists from the rest of the moderates, *Liberation* was encouraging the Mensheviks to move farther from the Bolsheviks. Struve used great caution in his overtures to *Iskra;* he was fully aware that too open bourgeois support was the kiss of death to a Marxist. His restraint did not save *Iskra* from savage attacks by Lenin, but perhaps left the Mensheviks in a better position to defend themselves. Generally he was content to use harsh words about Lenin without praising his opponents overmuch. The basic trait of Bolshevism,[20] wrote a contributor to *Liberation* after the April Marxist conferences, was "abstract revolutionism, insurrectionism, the attempt by any means whatsoever to arouse an uprising among the popular masses and in their name to seize immediate power; this to a certain extent brings the 'Leninists' close to the SR's and in their mind confuses the idea of class struggle with the idea of an all-people's Russian revolution." Struve pursued this point by comparing the Bolshevik and SR land programs. As for the resolutions on relations with liberals, Struve said that of the Bolsheviks displayed "almost comic" contradictions, while he noted that the Mensheviks' one was a good deal milder.

In an even sharper attack on the decisions of Lenin's III Congress,[21] Struve took care to speak of "Social Democrats" rather than "Bolsheviks," taking Lenin's claims for the congress at face value, though he then proceeded to make some criticisms which Mensheviks might well approve. The Social Democrats, he observed, were bound by their own doctrine to support the bourgeoisie insofar as it was revolutionary or only oppositional, yet they must simultaneously attempt to prove its antiproletarian nature to the workers. How, he wondered, was one to interpret their real attitude? It appeared by this time that the sole use of the Union of Liberation to the Marxists was as the address to which their charges against the "bourgeoisie" were delivered. The Union was regarded as the agent of the expected bourgeois "treachery." "It is difficult and useless to argue with these book prophecies, which so clearly foresee what will be, and so absolutely fail to understand what is." Struve disclaimed any desire to discredit Social Democracy; he merely intended to show how great an area of political struggle remained entirely outside its sphere of activity, "thanks to its rejection of any kind of contact with 'bourgeois' reality" in an effort to preserve its "unity" of tactics and "purity" of theory.

Miliukov likewise showed growing impatience[22] with the socialists in connection with the "union" movement on which he was setting so much store in the spring. "It is not treachery and pusillanimity that together with the voices of extremists and theoreticians there begin to be heard more moderate and practical ones: this is only the result of the consciousness that vital questions causing distress for decades at last draw near their—if not final, at least proximate and urgent—decision . . . to impede a good [decision] in expectation of a better is to risk being deprived of all influence on the march of events, since it is already impossible to stop it anyway."

Here Miliukov showed some of the confidence that the Mensheviks displayed in the inexorable movement of history as bound to lead the democratic current to victory. All parties were to advance on the shoulders of the mass movement to their common end of democracy. He knew that the Mensheviks were still talking in these terms, although it is not clear that he understood the different road that Lenin and Chernov were taking. His misunderstanding of Lenin's attitude toward the future provisional government, his bewilderment over SR conduct towards the I Duma, tend to indicate that he did not comprehend how these two groups had altered their notion of "democratic revolution." He continued to speak of the revolutionaries as some kind of unanimous whole not only at the I Kadet Congress, but throughout the First Revolution. Nevertheless, his faith in history and the mass movement, like that of Martov, seems to have led him to take little account of how anyone—even Lenin—could hope to "swerve" the march of events by will. His policy of solidarity with the revolutionaries (rather than with the Right-liberals) was one that he did not regard as depending on verbal agreements, but on the predetermined force of the people's struggle. That Lenin could rely also on the masses to bring about a different result, and adjust his tactics thereto, seems to have eluded Miliukov.

5.

As the Tsar was finally compelled to make his first constitutional concessions from the Bulygin Duma onwards, the spotlight was thrown onto the Kadet reaction to these measures. The socialists examined the Kadet response with close attention and suspicion. The Liberationists were consistently critical of these concessions, but equally determined to utilize them—against their Imperial author. "Between what the Duma gives society and what society wants," Miliukov wrote, "is a great abyss." [23] Nonetheless, "the act of 6 August is not simply a piece of paper. From it there can be no turning back." Struve, in the pages of *Liberation*, first wavered [24] as to the usefulness of the Bulygin law, then declared that Russia "had wrenched from the hands of Nicholas II" a new instrument in the struggle with Autocracy which should be used to the fullest. A more radical contributor emphasized that the Duma could be a "weapon" but nothing more, and said flatly, "there must be no talk of compromises." Struve agreed, but said the chance of using the Duma as a weapon depended on the oppositional attitude of society. Boycotting the elections would simply be "political suicide by the opposition," while nothing could be risked by taking part. Moreover, the results would silence reactionary newspapers which were sure that the country would repudiate the constitutionalists in favor of Autocracy.

The radical line was best stated by a contributor signing himself "A Democrat."[25] Some were trying to overestimate the importance of the Duma, others, terming it harmful, to underestimate it. "The Duma of itself will have no significance." Its power will depend entirely on the forces outside it—the people and "society." The focus of the activity of all the parties must be attracting, organizing, leading mass forces to the struggle, and to this task the problem of the Duma must be decisively subordinated.

6.

At last, five days before the October Manifesto was published, Miliukov and the Kadets met in Moscow to form a constitutional democratic party. The questions of program had been settled, for the most part, long before. What now stood before the congress was the problem of the next move. The immediate task was the recruitment of mass support, but there must be some focal point at which to direct it. The socialists might concentrate on the "revolution" proper, that is, demonstrations, strikes, and so forth. The Kadets had no objection to these methods, they were important and useful to them. They were quite willing, for example, to support the first general strike of October 1905.[26] Its "illegality" was of little consequence to a party which strove for a rule of law for the precise reason that in their opinion one did not yet exist. The Kadet party itself was "illegal" and remained so throughout the First Revolution. Nevertheless, the methods of direct revolution were not theirs. The party was "parliamentary" by nature (again, precisely because there was as yet no parliament), as its leaders repeatedly stated, and therefore the Duma, however bad, was the logical instrument for the Kadets. Inevitably the difference of chosen means, between Miliukov and the socialists, contributed to the obstruction of the common end.

For this difference was not mere "division of labor." The Kadets, though accepting "revolution" insofar as that meant illegal action and alliance with the revolutionaries, rejected violence in principle. The socialists were naturally suspicious of this position. Struve referred to their assertion that only those rights are solid which are conquered by society itself, and declared that acceptance of the argument did not require one to reject peaceful methods.[27] This did not satisfy the extremists; the bourgeoisie had itself used violence in the past and rejection of violence in the popular cause could only mean a hint of some sort of "treachery." They had no patience for explanations. To them, fear of violence was merely an expression of the narrow self-interest of property-owners.

No doubt the liberal-Left feared destruction of property by violence, but they no less distrusted the deliberate preparation of mass insurrection as likely to unleash what Berdyaev[28] called "irrational forces," to lead to a dictatorship instead of democracy—and they found confirmation of this in Lenin's own prescription for revolution. That Lenin's was not to be a personal dictatorship, but that of a "class and a half," did not alter the fact that it was to be some kind of dictatorship, under which the Kadets could not see any place for a Constituent Assembly or any other kind of elected body. The rule of legality they hoped to institute negated the very idea of dictatorship. Of course their idea of "legality" was a "bourgeois" one, but was this not to be a "bourgeois" revolution? Obviously the problem of violence was related to much broader considerations than the desirability of bloodshed. The liberal-revolutionary differences about violence stemmed from their divergent conceptions of the whole character of the overturn in prospect. Struve no doubt realized the signi,cance of this difference when he declared that while it had been resolved there should be no compromise with the Right, it was not yet clear enough to the Kadets that similarly there must be no yielding to the Left, for the idea of "law" which inspired liberals was foreign to the extremists.

Even if he realized the difference which Miliukov saw less clearly, Struve was by this time far out of touch with the attitude of the Kadets as a whole. He had never, since coming over to the liberal camp, been as consistently radical as the history professor who led the Kadets. It was the liberal-Right whose consistent spokesman was Maklakov (not Struve, who constantly wavered between the two wings) for whom Struve now spoke. It was they who talked about "peaceful methods" and "law"—and, occasionally, about "strong government" which was an Octobrist rather than a Kadet slogan. It was they who looked to experience as the test of correct politics, rather than the reason, the apriorist schemata, which drove Miliukov on. Looking to experience, they used the words "reality" and "compromise" which were not in good standing in radical circles. But if the radicals were apriorist, they were not necessarily bad or wrong apriorists. They saw in advance where differing rational schemata ("program demands") might lead to trouble. They were not deluded into thinking they shared all of the demands of the revolutionaries; they perhaps did fail to see the *extent* to which they did not share them.

So it was that in his vital opening speech to the Kadet Congress,[29] Miliukov referred not to "violence" as offering possible difficulties with the revolutionaries, but two "program demands": for a republic and for socialization of the means of production. These points, if the revolutionaries emphasized them too strongly, might lead to a schism with the Kadets—though Miliukov expressed confidence that such a break would be avoided in the immediate future. Of course, a break was inevitable—all parties recognized that—but it need not come before the victory of democracy. Miliukov declared that the boundary to the Right of the Kadets lay "where they come out in the name of the narrow class interests of the Russian gentry and industrialists. Our party will never stand in awe of these interests to the damage of the interests of the working classes! Between us and our—we would like to say not opponents but allies of the Left" lay another kind of boundary, concerned with the program demands just mentioned. It was not that Kadets rejected them in principle, however, some did not share them because they considered them unacceptable in general, but others, according to Miliukov, simply considered them as lying outside the realm of practical politics.

What, then, were the Kadets? Miliukov declared they approached the group known in the West as "social reformers," although their program was farther Left than any other analogous party in Europe. As Vinaver writes,[30] they bore in their minds an apriorist "image of a state with noble features," a state after the pattern of Western constitutional states, but not identical with them. Russia could profit by western experience and move directly to realize a better, more rational pattern of state order. They need not retrace the tortuous paths which the West had traversed. As Miliukov told Sir Bernard Pares[31] sharply, he should not expect Russia to follow in the path of England's four Georges. One typical Kadet, F. F. Kokoshkin, declares that three ideas motivated all his political activity; the inviolable reign of freedom and equality, the complete sovereignty of the people's will, and the realization of social justice for the working classes. These ideals, nurtured in the liberalism of the West, inspired the Kadets with confidence and determination to combat the dying principles of Muscovite Autocracy. A party dedicated to such ideals could not reject "revolution" as an expression of the democratic will.

Just after the Congress, Miliukov wrote,[32] "We will understand and fully recognize the supreme law of revolution as a factor creating the law of the future in open struggle with the historical law of the already outmoded political order. But we do not deify revolution, we do not make of it a fetish and remember as well that revolution is only a method, a means of struggle, and not an end in itself." It is good if it attains the desired end, bad if it harms that objective. "Yes, we are for the people—but we reject the pretensions of those who wish alone to speak in the name of the people and limit their conception of the people to the book concept of 'conscious proletariat.'" The Kadets say to the government, make way for popular representation; every day you remain in power doing nothing you only "increase the destructive forces of revolution and paralyze its creative forces." To the Leftist parties they say, "Do not forget that we have common aims with you, and then you will have us on your side." But you isolate yourselves and lay a trap for yourselves by declaring the revolution to be "permanent," unleashing its elemental forces, giving it unattainable ends.

The vital question was the ends to be sought. In relation to these ends, and accordingly in their concept of the method of "revolution," Miliukov was not far from Martov in the short run. However, it was not yet so clear that a great gap lay between them both and Lenin and Chernov, not only in relation to means, but ends as well. Miliukov had been right in concentrating his attention on ends in his speech to the Kadet congress. He was also right in the passage just quoted when he wrote that by declaring the revolution "permanent" (that is, by talking about social revolution before the political phase was over) the Leftists might "isolate themselves" (that is, bring about a break with the Kadets).

How different these ends were, it was not easy to see in 1905. A "dictatorship of proletariat and peasantry" had not yet existed on the earth's surface. Therefore the Kadets simply deemed such an aim "bookish" and impossible to reach; therefore setting forth such an aim would only defeat all concerned. Miliukov believed such an aim would be lost in the march of history toward Russian democracy. In relation to 1905, he was right that mixing phases of revolution would defeat the whole Russian opposition. In 1905, no one foresaw as clearly as Lenin that this "bookish" aim would be realized, that the most consistent and ruthless, the most rationalist group would secure its ends *if* all groups were not to fight together for a common goal.

When the news of the October Manifesto, promising a legislative assembly, was announced at the Kadet Congress, Miliukov at once growled, "Nothing has changed; the struggle goes on."[33] If Chermenskii alludes to the Kadets when he writes, "The liberals were satisfied with the concessions and promises" of the Manifesto, he is in error. They had resolved to enter the Bulygin Duma "with the exclusive aim of fighting for political freedom and a just representation," and they would go to the new Duma in the same spirit.[34] They had sympathized with the October strike; now it was the turn of the revolutionaries, they thought, to support their fight in the Duma. Their expectations in more respects than this were to be bitterly disappointed.

Part Four

THE CALM

XI

THE SR's IN A QUANDARY

When the news of the October Manifesto was received in Geneva, according to Zenzinov,[1] the reactions of the emigre Socialist Revolutionaries there were conflicting. Some believed it meant the coming of liberty to Russia, others not. The very existence of a group which was willing to give the Tsarist Manifesto a trial, indicates that the SR's did not completely share Lenin's conception of the manner in which the revolution would be realized. The Bolsheviks rejected the sensational new law in principle, simply because it was promulgated by the Tsar and not by a revolutionary government. Of course the Manifesto, even if faithfully executed, would not have satisfied neo-populist wishes. Nevertheless, it was thought, it might inaugurate the political freedom which the revolutionary parties needed in order to begin work for their next objective, a Constituent Assembly, and their ultimate end, socialism.

Rubanovich,[2] for example, objected not to the form of the Manifesto so much as its manner of execution by the Witte government, which he termed a "caricature" of the promises of 17 October. These promises might, however, approach realization through co-operation with the liberals. If the zemstvists, for example, could "surround" Witte, cut off his ties with reaction, and induce him to grant full amnesty and genuine liberty, the revolutionaries might show them temporary confidence.

This optimism was not shared by many of Rubanovich's colleagues, but still the emigre leaders rushed back to their homeland during the "Days of Freedom" to face the future with hope which the beginning of the counterrevolution had not stifled. The Central Committee set to work in the city Soviets, as well as in the villages and among the soldiers, to bring the pressure to bear which should compel Nicholas II to honor his promises. In almost every Soviet in Russia they acquired an important influence, and in that of

Belostok, for example, they even had a majority. In the St. Petersburg Soviet, where their leaders were Chernov himself and Avksentiev, they had several delegates, and their relative strength was even greater in Moscow.

When the chairman of the St. Petersburg Soviet, Khrustaliov, was arrested, Chernov proposed to the other delegates that each measure of repression be answered by a terrorist act. Nevertheless, the party had suspended the activity of its own Battle Organization immediately after 17 October and the further justification of terrorism suddenly became a question which divided the SR's themselves. Gotz had wished to disavow terrorism entirely. Even Azef had declared that terror was a suitable weapon only against absolutism and that the chief task had now become the mass social struggle.[3] There were others, however, who clung to the old method of political murder. Chernov therefore exercised his talents for compromise by engineering a temporary suspension of terror. During the rest of the Revolution terrorism in the party underwent many vicissitudes. It was formally renewed by the new party Central Committee in January 1906. Among the victims of this period of activity was Father Gapon, leader of the Bloody Sunday procession, who appears to have been unable to abandon his double role as police agent and popular leader, and was assassinated for the charge of betraying several socialists. When the First Duma opened, terror was once more discontinued, then revived after the dismissal in July. Understandably enough, the local party groups were unable to respond to these undulating instructions as quickly as the centralized Battle Organization, and they continued spontaneous terrorist acts in many regions. The presence of treachery in the Battle Organization itself had been suspected more and more strongly, and the culprit was thought to have been found when the police agent Tatarov was exposed and "executed" in May 1906. Incredibly enough, the much more important spy, Azef, was not exposed until 1909.[4] The effects of the exposure itself were to be infinitely more destructive to the unity and prestige of the party than all the provocation achieved by Azef up till this time. The secrecy and organizational autonomy which the use of terrorism necessitated were thus to exact a fearful price from their originators.

2.

Some of the conspiratorial energies of the neo-populists, as of the

Marxists, were channeled off into the formation of *druzhiny*, small armed bands originally organized to fight the pogroms of Black Hundred mobs, but retained for possible use in an armed uprising. The Socialist Revolutionaries mobilized about three hundred *druzhinniki* to fight in the Moscow insurrection of December, more than either the Bolsheviks or Mensheviks could muster. The party's terrorists were also active in the Moscow uprising; Zenzinov, for example, blew up the office of the Moscow *Okhrana*, the state secret police. Altogether the SR's played a more important role in the Moscow rising[5] than in the St. Petersburg strikes, and Chernov declared that if the failure of the rising signified the failure of the revolution, then the blame[6] must be laid at the door of the St. Petersburg Social Democrats who could offer no aid to their Moscow revolutionary brethren.

In fact, the Socialist Revolutionaries had attempted to restrain the St. Petersburg Soviet from "forcing" events by declaring the second general political strike in November. They traced the reason for this mistaken decision in turn to the failure of the erroneous tactic of trying to achieve the eight-hour day by direct action. Nevertheless, the party felt bound to support the second strike when it was declared and helped to organize village uprisings in Saratov and elsewhere to assist St. Petersburg. By this time, however, they retained little hope of immediate success. They believed it would be necessary to wait for the help of the peasants, presumably to be available in the spring. The counterrevolution had proved too strong for the proletariat alone. The SR's felt they could have predicted this and that the Marxists had by their "narrowness" helped to court disaster. The newspaper *Son Of the Fatherland* shrilled, "The counterrevolution is madness incarnate.[7] It is a wild beast, which strains ever harder to break its chains. And the citizens must meet it like a wild beast." But the bayonets, in the hands of peasant-soldiers, were on the side of the beast, and the revolutionaries had to give way.

As the turmoil of December ground to a halt, the party attempted to pick up the pieces. Its press was still weak. *Revolutionary Russia* had been discontinued, and only in mid-November had the *Russian Wealth* group, close to the Socialist Revolutionaries, obtained control of *Son of the Fatherland*. When this paper published the "financial manifesto"[8] issued on 2 December by SD's, SR's, and other groups jointly, it was closed. It was not until May that the party obtained another journal.

3.

Even more pressing than the problem of propaganda outlets was the long-deferred matter of a party Congress. One was finally convened at Imatra, Finland, on 29 December. All significant neo-populist tendencies were represented here: that which was to become "Popular Socialist," by Annenskii, Miakotin, and Peshekhonov; the future Maximalists, by only a few delegates; and the orthodox SR current by the chief party leaders.

Rubanovich opened the meeting with a speech[9] which strongly emphasized the party's adherence to and acceptance by the organized forces of international (that is, Western) socialism. At the Amsterdam congress of the Second International in 1904, the party had in fact been admitted to that wider body. Rubanovich was even prouder of the fact that only a few days before the Congress, Kautsky in *Die Neue Zeit* had recognized the right of the Russian people to "all the land"—which was taken to mean at least qualified approval of the neo-populist agrarian program. A month earlier Rubanovich had cited Western theory and practice as justification for SR revision of Marxism as regards agriculture. He had pointed out that certain Western socialists, like the Russian SR's, had recognized the fact that concentration was not proceeding in land ownership in the same fashion as in industrial production, and were altering their doctrines accordingly. Furthermore, French and Italian socialists, he remarked, had been much more successful in spreading socialism among smallholders than among landless rural workers—and this was cited as justification of SR practice.

The party's acceptance of Western socialism and the political struggle, Rubanovich continued, "separates us in a decisive and explicit manner from all bourgeois parties, however radical their program from the social and political standpoint," and of course on the other side from the anarchists as well. The congress thereupon resolved to boycott both the Duma and the elections thereto, continuing the tactics of mass agitation accompanied by terrorism —though the "agrarian terror" which the Maximalists preached was specifically condemned. It was further decided to forbid relations with the bourgeois parties and treat them with intransigence "since the tasks which the moment presents us are precisely those which our divergence of views affirms in the most absolute fashion." To execute these policies, a new Central Committee consisting of Azef, Argunov, M. A. Natanson, Rakitnikov, and Chernov was chosen. Chernov was singled out for special praise by the Congress for his efforts over the past five years towards theoretical elaboration of the party program. It was he, after all, who almost single-handed had led the SR's into the intellectualized, Westernized paths where they could meet (and perhaps someday master) the Social Democrats.

4.

The orthodox doctrinal position of Chernov and the old party leaders, however, was by no means acceptable to all of the Congress. Both the Maximalist Left and the Popular-Socialist Right were outspoken in their criticism. The latter group, mainly writers and journalists who followed Mikhailovsky, had from the first stood aside from the actual work of building a party and had continued to concentrate on the publication of *Russian Wealth* and literary work in general. It was they, rather than the "orthodox" leaders, who had obtained control of *Son of the Fatherland* in November, and they had not delayed to state their desire to create "one great army . . . a true *people's* socialist party."[10] A secret organization, they declared, could not embrace the masses. At the Congress, they raised the question of legalizing the party, for they asserted "it is impossible to drive the masses of the people underground." They were persuaded to shelve this issue, but there were other points of disagreement. They criticized the leaders for yielding to Marxist influences, thus introducing "eclecticism." On the score of the agrarian program they denounced as "inadmissible" "compulsory measures against wage labor"—by which they meant, forcible "socialization" of peasant lands, as well as those of state, church, and gentry. They also were suspicious of the boycott of the Duma, and thought terrorism superfluous.

The Popular Socialists remained in the Socialist Revolutionary party only a short time. In the spring of 1906 the group split off and decided to organize an independent party under the "Popular Socialist" label.[11] It set up a political organ at once, but did not attempt effective organization until September. Though it participated vigorously in the elections for the II Duma and elected several deputies, it never became the "mass party" it sought to be, and did not get beyond unifying the old readers of *Russian Wealth,* some dissatisfied SR's, and small student groups. After the dismissal of the II Duma, the party disappeared for good.

The Maximalists were scantily represented at the December 1905 Congress, so were ineffectual in their protests that if the land was to be "socialized," so should factories as well. They demanded the elimination of a "program-minimum" entirely: that is, they demanded immediate social revolution. Such voices had first been raised by the Geneva group of "agrarian terrorists" which had sent N. N. Sokolov to Russia in the fall of 1904. Despite his arrest in the spring of 1905, Maximalist ideas continued to be preached by the Geneva *Leaflet for Free Discussion,* which was in partial agreement with the circle of Ustinov which preferred a federation of workers' communes to a republic. While the Ustinovists later joined the anti-intellectualist Makhaevists, however, the other Maximalists during 1905 remained in the SR fold and gained a certain following in Russia, especially in the Northwest around Belostok. Only a month after the party Congress they met in separate conference and decided to leave the party. As the Union of SR Maximalists, they set up their own Battle Organization. The circle gained notoriety by the attempt on Stolypin in August 1906 and the "expropriation" in Fonarnyi Street in October which netted them 400,000 rubles, enough to finance their activities for some time. Their doctrines were simple: they believed a social revolution would end in establishment of a "labor republic," a dictatorship of the masses in which all necessary measures would be enacted into law, so that even the right to strike could be dispensed with. They were bitterly denounced by orthodox SR's, who took fright, sneered a Menshevik writer,[12] at "their own reflection in the Maximalist mirror." The Maximalists disappeared in mid-1907 and their remnants joined the anarchists—where, Chernov might have said, they belonged all along. The Maximalist tendency among SR's was not finally dead, however; the Left SR's of 1917 were to revive it—but were to gravitate towards Lenin rather than Chernov.

5.

Thus the I Congress led to immediate schism of the party's extreme Left and extreme Right. Still another neo-populist group soon made its appearance, that of the Trudoviks. It had much greater importance than either of the two splinter bodies and temporarily overshadowed the main party altogether. To declare a boycott of the Duma was a great deal easier than to keep a boycottist party alive when other political activity was impossible. The Social Democrats managed to perform this feat more successfully than the Socialist Revolutionaries, though indeed the Mensheviks abandoned the boycott early enough to send some delegates to the

I Duma. Had the SD's maintained the boycott, however, probably they still could have held the party together more easily than the SR's. For it was a great deal simpler to explain the boycott to the largely organized, politically conscious urban workers than to the scattered peasants, who usually retained a good deal of respect for central governmental institutions no matter how much they desired the land of the neighborhood gentry.

Considering these factors, SR boycottism was bound to do great damage to the party, and the rise of such a group as the Trudoviks was inevitable. With the SR's standing aside from the elections, it was natural that a proposal should be made as early as January 1906, in an appeal to "electors" published in *Our Life,* for all nonparty "democrats" to unite "in the interests of toil." In Saratov a Union of Toilers (*Soiuz Trudiashchikhsia*) was formed, but the Trudoviks arose as a group of national significance only after peasant deputies started arriving in St. Petersburg for the Duma session in April.

The representatives chosen by the peasant curia were chiefly nonparty, though they had often used the label "Left Kadet" in the electoral campaign. On the initiative of Aladin and others, several of these "Left Kadets" formed a club. This establishment at first had to compete with a hostel set up by the Interior Ministry in order to try to attract peasant deputies into Rightist parties. "Thank God," Witte had said on receipt of the first election returns in the Council of Ministers, "the Duma will be peasant." Only gradually did it dawn on the government that this meant a radical, not a loyal Duma, but the bureaucracy did not give up trying to win peasant support. It was not long, however, before the design behind the hostel became clear, and most of the Interior Ministry's "Eroginist" group joined the Trudoviks. The new grouping of deputies was ludicrously heterogeneous. It at first included 2 SR's, 10 SD's, 9 Peasant Unionists, 7 "non-party socialists," 1 Radical, 2 Freethinkers, 18 "Left Kadets," 8 "autonomists," 21 "nonparty," 27 "undefined." Their common purpose was chiefly to bring about land reform in the interest of their peasant constituents, but in deference to their worker members they also demanded the eight-hour day. Their general political goal was defined as the use of the Duma in order to "create the conditions for the right disclosure of the people's will" in a real parliament, thus to avoid civil war. And to the vexation and confusion of Socialist Revolutionaries and Bolsheviks alike, the Trudoviks concluded what was in effect a working alliance with the Kadet plurality in the I Duma.

6.

The SR's were deeply disturbed by the appearance in the new legislature of a large-sized bloc of peasant deputies which followed the Kadet lead instead of their own. As a matter of fact they themselves had been forced to take part in the electoral campaign in order to agitate for boycottism, and it now appeared that this action had been in direct contravention of their own best interests. There was considerable discontent with the whole boycott policy. At the party council of May 1906 there was a partial reversal. It was proclaimed that in spite of governmental pressure, the Duma had proved itself oppositional, that the Duma did contain deputies from the working classes, and that conflict between Duma and government would increase the revolutionary consciousness of the masses. At the II Congress in February 1907 boycottism was formally abandoned (only to be renewed after the coup d'etat of 3 June 1907 when Stolypin drastically modified the electoral law). Gershuni silenced objectors at this meeting by inquiring why, if the peasants desired only an armed uprising and no delegates in the Duma, did the latter exist and not the former? He courageously tried to dispel the illusion of an imminent mass outbreak, and traced this dream to an intellectual confusion of the will of thousands of propagandized peasants with that of tens of millions yet untouched. By going to the Duma, the SR's might hope to capture the Trudoviks from Miliukov. Too much ground had been lost, however, in the I Duma to be regained instantly. If the SR's had been able to do better in the II Duma, they might have been willing to try again in the III and IV Duma, however "bad" they deemed those to be.

7.

When the government relaxed repressive measures at the opening of the I Duma, the SR press revived. Chernov started a great daily in St. Petersburg entitled *The Cause of the People,* and throughout Russia during the first half of the year 20 party dailies appeared. Chernov waged a journalistic campaign for SR orthodoxy, attacking the Maximalists as "vulgar socialists." Lenin notes[13] that he paid less attention to the Popular Socialists, those "SR Mensheviks." Since Chernov was already planning to enter the II Duma, perhaps he felt it would be inexpedient to attack "legalism" at that point.

As he faced the uncertain future in early 1906, Chernov posed an alternative[14] similar to that which some party members thought existed in October 1905. Should the SR's push ahead at all costs, or utilize the new "freedoms" to consolidate their position first? The decision depended upon an evaluation of the forces involved in the first autumn battle. In Chernov's opinion, those were in fact the ranks of the urban proletariat alone, though acting in an atmosphere of universal popular sympathy. It was evident from the very structure of the opposition that it was inevitable for portions of it to fall away from the proletariat. The problem was, how much of it would 17 October detach? It was to the interest of the vanguard to retain the sympathy of a large part of "society" and certainly to utilize the latter's influence on the army. Still, the more pressing task was to bring to bear the "army" of peasants behind the urban vanguard, and that could not be done till the spring freed the peasants from constant farm duties. To attempt to force the struggle by relying on industrial workers alone was a seductive policy, very flattering to the workers, but not one which could achieve complete victory.

Summing up the battle of November-December, Chernov regarded its effect as of great value in accelerating mass organization by way of Soviets and unions. The tight little Social Democratic worker circles had been exposed to the "quality" of Socialist Revolutionary ideas which had made much headway especially among the younger generation. While the SD's had managed to cling to their control of the Soviets, neo-populists had increased their representation in them considerably and prevented their being proclaimed Marxist bodies. Even the rise of the counterrevolution had had its uses in compelling the workers to arm themselves, thus leading to the Moscow uprising. Indeed the government itself had temporarily proved to be an "ally," since its every act merely stimulated a new revolutionary outbreak. Still, bitter experience had shown that without the mass support of the peasants, the working classes could not win through, and the revolutionaries must bide their time—using the boycott and new opportunities for direct action to maximum advantage—until, in a few months, conditions would be ripe for the final blow. Thus Chernov, like Lenin, clung to the hope that the Revolution was not over, and would recover from its temporary setback, by the participation of the as yet quiescent peasantry.

The intelligentsia and the people came face to face in 1905. But this was the beginning, not the completion, of organizing the masses. As *La Tribune Russe* put it, the parties were now crystallized,[15] the chief social forces more or less determined, but the grouping of the masses into the parties had scarcely begun. This aim remained to be achieved, and the effects would be tremendous. The revolution, breaking out of the "Procrustean bed of dogmatism" in which Social Democrats expected it to lie confined in "bourgeois" limits, would soon rise again to continue towards the final victory of socialism.

8.

By the eve of the Duma, the Socialist Revolutionaries had maintained fairly effective solidarity with the Bolsheviks. At the same time they had demonstrated the limitations of the alliance. Both still believed in armed uprising as the means of achieving the democratic revolution: an uprising of workers supported by peasants, leading to a Constituent Assembly. Chernov's hostility to the bourgeoisie, however, was less absolute than that of Lenin's, and this was bound to have some effect. Before October, the SR's had declared that the Liberationists might still be of assistance; in the "Days of Freedom," they had hopefully called on the zemstvists to frustrate reaction. Although they despised the Kadets, especially in their management of the I Duma, the SR's continued to believe that they might serve to weaken Autocracy. The SR's of course could not any longer expect the Kadets to approve of their own objectives—since these included armed uprising and "socialization" of land. They foresaw for the Kadets a sad end; a party exclusively parliamentary in a non-parliamentary country unavoidably must become a "diplomatizing party, a politicking party in the worst sense of the word." [16]

The Left-liberals were worthy of contempt—but not of fear, in SR eyes. Chernov, unlike Lenin, did not speak of Kadet "treachery." Treachery could only be perpetrated by a party with strength; only power could inspire fear. Lenin always accused the neo-populists of failing to see the strength of bourgeois liberalism in Russia. The truth was rather that, while indeed evaluating liberal strength at a low level, the SR's still believed its forces might be thrown into the balance for, and not against, the "first phase" of revolution· Although the SR's refused to have any relations with the Kadets—perhaps remembering their embarrassing position at the October 1904 Paris conference—they recognized clearly that the Kadet Duma was struggling against Autocracy in its own way with all its might. Support for the Duma did not become a major factor in SR tactics, because they believed it to be essentially impotent. But they still encouraged it to do what it could, convinced not that the Kadet deputies were "betraying"the people, but that they were bumbling along in a well-intentioned fashion which did some harm to Tsarism.

9.

In the Duma itself the Socialist Revolutionaries could play no role as such. Their deputies were too few even to form a pigmy fraction as the Social Democrats finally managed to do. Their sole act of any significance was to bring about the introduction of a draft land reform law, called the "Project of the 33."[17] The draft opened with a declaration that only a Duma elected on the basis of Four-Tail suffrage could enact real agrarian reform, so its authors had no expectation that the I Duma would accept this law. The text itself provided for abolition of all private property in land, including peasant allotments, and establishment of a "consumption norm"[18] as the basis for redistribution of holdings. Since the Trudoviks had already introduced a "Project of the 104"[19] which would leave peasant property intact, it was a notable achievement to secure thirty Trudovik signatures to a measure which would abolish peasant ownership, a measure which provoked some peasants to grumble, "We were sent to get the land, and not to give it up."

Although the "33" Project had no chance of adoption, its very introduction evoked alarm. Petrunkevich demanded that it be debated immediately before being sent to committee, since it envisaged a "fundamental social overturn," not just land reform. Aladin, the Trudovik spokesman, retorted that "once we touch the agrarian question in Russia, thereby we touch the whole system of social relations." Therefore, continued Aladin, why should a proposal which simply concerned two or three additional aspects of the problem, not be discussed along with the two previously introduced drafts? The Kadets could hardly oppose the project on principle, since their own draft provided for confiscation. However, the Kadets remained confident that the peasants wanted not the "loss" of their own property, but simply the acquisition of that of the landlords.

When the Duma was dissolved, the Socialist Revolutionaries, like the rest of the opposition, hoped for some sort of popular rising. They took some part in the Kronstadt mutiny,[20] and together

217

with the Social Democrats declared an abortive general strike in St. Petersburg on 20 July. *La Tribune Russe* declared that the dissolution of the Duma destroyed the "illusions" [21] of the people in a possible peaceful outcome, but added that the elections for the II Duma could be converted into a means of organizing for the revolutionary struggle. The boycott was abandoned. Rosy hopes died slowly; but the Revolution was over.

XII

THE ENEMY OF THE WORKING CLASS

> *"We asked Bronsky to find out whether it
> would not be possible to get to Russia through
> Germany . . . Ilyich did not sleep nights on end.
> One night he said to me, 'You know, I could
> travel with the passport of a dumb Swede.' I
> laughed and said, 'It won't work, you might give
> yourself away in your sleep. You might dream of
> the Kadets and exclaim in your sleep, "Scoun-
> drels, scoundrels!" And they would find out you
> are not a Swede!'"* N. K. KRUPSKAIA, writing of
> 1917.[1]

During the "Days of Freedom" which followed the October Manifesto, the Marxists had reason to ponder de Tocqueville's maxim,
"Pour un mauvais gouvernement, le moment le plus dangereux est
ordinairement celui où il commence à se transformer." [2] For the
moment was not only dangerous to Tsarism, but to the Social
Democratic leadership of the strike movement as well. It proved
to be one thing to strive to lead a united nation to demand liberty,
but quite another to decide what to do when Autocracy had
granted something which purported to be but was not quite that.

When the Manifesto was published, the St. Petersburg Soviet
of Workers Deputies was only four days old. It had been formed
when the political strike was already under way, on the basis of
numerical representation of factory workers irrespective of political
affiliation, although the Mensheviks had a more or less effective
ascendancy. The publication of the Manifesto caught them off
guard. Rallying, they announced that they would continue the
fight for a Constituent Assembly, amnesty, a people's militia, and
abolition of martial law. Although the new law did not appease
the Soviet, it was however plain that it had satisfied some part of

the population—though perhaps through misunderstanding—and on 19 October it was decided to call off the first strike until the situation cleared a little.

The pro-Menshevik leaders of the Soviet, Khrustaliov and Trotsky, might alter their tactics abruptly, but they had their strategy clearly in mind. They had not forgotten the Marxist prescription for a "bourgeois revolution." When they sent a deputation to the St. Petersburg city council requesting aid for the strike, one delegate declaimed: "We come to you in order to learn whose side you are on:[3] with the people against Asiatism or with absolutism against freedom. We did not come to ask you to accept our militant watchwords, or to struggle side by side with us. . . . The change which is taking place in Russia is a bourgeois change; it is also in the interests of the bourgeoisie. It is to your interest that it should be over soon, and . . . if you really understand the interest of your class, you should with all your power assist the people in the conquest of absolutism . . ."

Despite these words, the Mensheviks did not expect really active support from the middle class, although the "petty-bourgeois intellectuals" of the Union of Unions did participate vigorously in the general strike. The Soviet leaders were primarily concerned with organizing the maximum number of workers for economic and political struggle, rather than serving as a revolutionary general staff. Trotsky termed the St. Petersburg Soviet a "parliament of the working class." The Bolshevik historian Chernomordik[4] is willing to agree, but regards this as nothing to boast about. The Soviet, he writes, "accomplished and organized little, and talked and declaimed too much;" it failed in the real task, that of organizing an uprising.

The first strike had been political in character, and as such had obtained almost universal sympathy. However, when the Mensheviks turned to economic objectives the employers balked. Whereas they had often actually continued to pay (in whole or part) the strikers up till now, when the Soviet attempted on 29 October to "proclaim" the eight-hour day, they answered by widespread lockouts. The Soviet leaders hoped that the second political strike, declared a week later, would enable them to gloss over their obvious "economic" mistake. However, the fundamental weakness of the St. Petersburg Soviet was becoming more and more apparent. The second strike lasted only three days, and soon afterward the eight-hour day campaign had to be abandoned. On 26 November the enigmatic figure who had presided over the Soviet, Khrustaliov,[5] was arrested. The following day Trotsky took over the post, and there was a dramatic scene when he, as new Soviet chairman, shook hands with the president of the Peasant Union amid tumultuous applause. But this merely symbolized Social Democratic hopes for peasant aid, hopes which a handshake could not realize. On 3 December Witte arrested the entire St. Petersburg Soviet, and initiative passed to the Moscow body.

The Moscow Soviet, declares Chernomordik, was no workers' parliament but a "fighting union of socialist and revolutionary democrats" largely dominated by Bolsheviks.[6] It had been formed late, and remained insufficiently prepared when it was induced to declare a third political strike on 7 December. Three days later the strike had developed into armed insurrection in Moscow and a few cities of the South. The Moscow garrison systematically squeezed off the rising into the Presnia district, and when crack guards regiments arrived from St. Petersburg and Warsaw on 15 December, the insurrectionists were mopped up in three or four days. For whatever reasons, pro-Bolshevik tactics in Moscow had failed quite as miserably as the pro-Menshevik tactics in St. Petersburg. Not only had the peasantry failed to rise to help the urban workers, but the peasant army, despite scattered mutinies,[7] had remained loyal.

This is not to say that the countryside remained peaceful. By the end of 1905 local risings, growing in momentum from the spring onwards, had involved a third of all Russian uezds, and in the spring this proportion rose to one half.[8] In the South and East, especially Saratov province, hundreds of manors were destroyed, land was seized and turned over to the communes, and almost thirty million rubles' worth of damage was done. At the II Congress of the Peasant Union on 6 November, a "general strike of the land" was threatened if "land and liberty" were not granted forthwith. Nevertheless neither the Peasant Union nor any other organization could speak for the whole peasantry or lead it to revolt. The rural risings remained spontaneous, disconnected, and therefore powerless to affect the immediate course of events. The fate of the revolution was decided in the cities, mainly in the two capitals.

2.

The two factions of Social Democrats, while continuing to differ sharply on tactics, fought together in the autumn strikes, and as a result the two party organizations moved closer to reunion. At first the new legal party press which mushroomed in November remained split between the Bolshevik *New Life* and the Menshevik *Beginning,* with Trotsky's *Russian Gazette* maintaining a mid-position between them. When several papers were closed for printing the "financial manifesto" of 2 December, however, the first united Social Democratic organ since 1903, *Northern Voice,* appeared briefly.

In November the factions met in separate conference, Bolsheviks at Tammerfors, Mensheviks in St. Petersburg, to plan reunion of the party. In both factions, writes Martov, democratization was proceeding[9] and the workers felt the burden of intellectual domination lifting. The principal point which separated the two groups in terms of the immediate situation was the party's relation to the Duma. The question of armed uprising, it was reasonably plain, would no longer depend on written resolutions but on the course of rapidly moving events, and there was little use of spending more time in discussing the matter. As for the Duma, the Bolsheviks remained firm in support of complete and active boycott, while the Mensheviks advanced various plans[10] for utilizing the elections or the Duma itself to hasten "revolutionary self-government."

The great, unspoken question which confronted all was not the Duma, not insurrection, but this: what effect had 17 October had upon the revolution? Had the bourgeoisie been "satisfied"? Would it immediately "betray" the revolution? Lenin, of course, believed the betrayal had already begun, but would its sweep increase? As for the Mensheviks, in whose tactics "bourgeois treachery" was a much more central factor (since Lenin intended to bypass the bourgeoisie no matter how they behaved), would they have to abandon any reliance on the moderates? In a word, was the balance-sheet of social forces the same as before, or if it had changed, how?

Lenin had termed 17 October simply "the first victory of the revolution." [11] There would be more victories to come, since Autocracy had not capitulated but merely retreated. The revolutionary proletariat, he recognized, had achieved the first success. But now it was necessary to broaden and deepen the base of the revolution, spreading it to the village allies on whom he had counted so strongly. Looking at the Kadets, he found them talking hopefully about freedom and a Constituent Assembly to come; but these good things remained empty phrases without guarantees. "The *only* serious guarantee," he declared, "can be a victorious uprising." [12] The Kadets' effort to play the role of a "White" party between Red and Black was a sham; "Whoever is not a revolutionary, is a Black Hundredist."

And, Lenin believed, the Red camp was still growing in strength. The army itself—he boldly asserted—on which so much depended, was even now splitting into the army of freedom and the army of Black Hundredism. The Sevastopol mutiny[13] was "neither unique nor accidental;" it was a symptom of this increasing division in the armed forces. While the uprising in the Crimea had been beaten down, the uprising in all Russia was unbeatable.

And the leader was to be, as before, a tightly organized Social Democratic party. Only the party remained capable of leading to victory the Russian proletariat, hand in hand with the Social Democratic proletariat of the whole world. Did this mean that Lenin was ready to give up reliance on the peasants and turn to the workers of the West as the only hope for aid? Indeed not. Lenin thundered: let there be union between the government and the reactionary bourgeoisie; let the liberal bourgeoisie vote confidence in Witte. "Against the union of Autocracy and bourgeoisie we must put union of Social Democracy and all revolutionary bourgeois democracy"—that is, union of the parties of worker and peasant.

Into this formula, on which Lenin based all his 1905 tactics, the new Soviets fitted perfectly.[14] Before he reached Russia in the autumn, he wrote that these new bodies had emerged naturally from the general strikes in which all the proletariat including non-Social Democrats had taken part. The composition of the Soviets was not, as some asserted, too broad, but too narrow. Into them must also go deputies from soldiers and sailors, the revolutionary peasants, and the revolutionary bourgeois intellectuals. The non-proletarian views of Socialist Revolutionaries and so forth were unsuitable for proletarian tasks. Yet Marxists ought not to try to expel them from the Soviets, any more than they should drive out workers who still believed in God, or intellectuals who were on the side of mysticism—"Pooh! Pooh!" Lenin could apparently more readily excuse workers than intellectuals for "unscientific" beliefs.

The Marxists, he said, must use these democratic bodies as forums in which to preach the correct proletarian viewpoint. As unions of Marxist and non-Marxist democrats, the Soviets "must be regarded as the embryo of a *provisional revolutionary government*," and they ought as soon as possible either to proclaim themselves to be one or to set up one. This did not at all mean, Lenin thought, that Social Democrats must accept "nonpartiness."[15] That was always and everywhere a weapon and slogan of the bourgeoisie, and the workers' party should combat it mercilessly, even though it was but a natural phenomenon arising from the bourgeois character of the revolution. In other words, Social Democracy, clinging firmly to Marxist doctrine and the Leninist conception of party, should strike out boldly as the leader of the mass democratic movement, no matter how confused, erroneous, and misguided were the petty bourgeois allies of the proletariat.

3.

The urban workers and peasants could and must continue to victory, said the Bolsheviks. What, then, of the bourgeoisie? When the Bolshevik *New Life*[16] had begun to appear, before Lenin arrived in Russia, it had seemed to waver in regard to the liberals, even citing Plekhanov's old formula, "March apart, strike together," as the proper tactics toward the bourgeois opposition. A few days after this article, however, the old intransigence reappeared. N. Minskii wrote, "between bourgeois and Social Democratic policy there is not and cannot be even external and formal points of contact," and Galerka expressed fears of an imminent agreement between the zemstvists and the bureaucracy.

Lenin soon reinforced *New Life's* hostility to the moderates. He was willing to envisage[17] the possibility that Witte might consent the next day to the calling of a Constituent Assembly. The only important question was, what *kind* of a Constituent Assembly would be called under a bourgeois regime? The zemstvists wanted a parliament which would simply protect the dominance of capital instead of that of bureaucracy, retaining the monarchy and standing army so they could prevent the revolution from being carried to the end. When *Our Life* and the Union of Unions gave serious attention to paper "projects" for convening a Constituent Assembly, they simply fostered illusions which weakened the revolutionary energy of the masses and followed behind the Kadets, "who have betrayed the revolution." When the newspaper *Rus'* urged the zemstvists to form their own provisional government, Lenin saw in this merely another bourgeois step induced by revolutionary pressure.[18] It was "an undoubted sign of the strength of the revolution," but did not alter in the slightest his attitude toward liberals. These gentlemen, according to Lenin, talked of a provisional government merely as a threat to Autocracy in order to hasten the "deal" which was their real and hidden desire.

By March Lenin believed [19] he discerned a definite switch in the position of the middle class. The gentry, he said, had gone over from the Kadets to the Octobrists. The Marxists now had two alternatives: if they decided the revolution was now impossible, then they must reject an uprising as an immediate objective and give "support to these or those strata of liberal democracy as a real opposition force under a constitutional regime." They must then regard the Duma as a parliament, although a bad one, and take part in its deliberations as well as in the elections to it. If, on the other hand, they recognized revolution to be still possible and necessary, they must continue unflinchingly as before. Lenin unhesitatingly chose the second alternative. Plekhanov's "new methods," [20] including organization of unions, legalization of the party, and so on, belonged to the first alternative and had to be rejected.

Even though the gentry had moved Right,[21] thought Lenin, the bourgeois party lineup remained essentially the same. The Octobrists and other Rightist parties were openly counterrevolutionary; the Kadets and the Party of Democratic Reforms, not being definite class organizations, continued to waver between the Right and the Left; only with the revolutionary bourgeois democrats, i.e., the Socialist Revolutionaries and the Peasant Union, did fighting agreements remain possible.

The Kadets, in Lenin's eyes, had betrayed the revolution as they had been expected to do all along. This did not occur at a given instant. Neither did it consist in "personal treachery, of course. Such a crude view is at the root foreign to Marxism." [22] The bourgeois treason consisted of the fact that the Kadets connived at the retention of power by the old regime, obeyed its orders, and were preparing to "divide" power between the Autocracy and bourgeoisie. Plekhanov had written that the Kadets had not yet betrayed the revolution, though they would in the future. This was simply a failure to understand the meaning of words: already the Kadets had betrayed liberty "a thousand times." Their very program was composed of demands which depended on "deals" with bureaucracy for their realization. Thus Lenin evaluated his most hated, most feared enemy.

However despicable the Kadets were to Lenin, notwithstanding, he never underestimated their strength and the damage they might do to his plans. The SR's and Mensheviks might be guilty of doing so, but never the Bolsheviks. The victory of the Kadets in the elections came as no surprise. They won, said Lenin in his brochure *The Kadet Victory and the Tasks of the Workers' Party,* simply because as a result of the boycott they were the farthest Left party in the field. Their democratic noises, their appeal to the people—which had so far succeeded that Struve was probably right when he contended that the peasant deputies in the Duma would be Kadet—were quite comprehensible. It was necessary to rely on the masses for support. "Without this, the bourgeoisie will not achieve power and never did achieve power." Kadet tactics were both "harmless and advantageous" to their authors—harmless, because their blunted weapon of pseudo-revolution could not destroy Autocracy, but would only shake it enough to permit Kadet victory; advantageous, because they gave the appearance of revolutionariness and attracted sympathy from some elements which desired a real revolution.

Kadet behavior was determined by the economic position of the petty bourgeoisie. Their two-faced wavering between capital and labor, their readiness to take a scrap of paper for a constitution, all showed the Kadets to be not a party but a symptom, not a political force but "a scum" on the waters of revolution. It could not govern, since the real masters of bourgeois society (the Shipovs and the Guchkovs) stood aside from it. The Kadets would fall together with the "constitutional illusions" which they foster, "fertilizing the ground"—perhaps for the triumph of the Shipovs and Guchkovs, perhaps for a revolutionary dictatorship of proletariat and peasantry.

What then of Kadet strength in the Duma to come? Their numbers would be immaterial to the course of the revolutionary crisis. If they had a minority, this would retard the collapse of the party and of the people's fascination with the Kadets. If they had preponderance, they would either have to fulfil their grandiose promises or stand self-exposed before the nation.

Must Social Democrats support the Kadet Duma? Some said yes, surely, since they were committed to support of the revolutionary and oppositional bourgeoisie. Still, this was not a question of the bourgeoisie in the general and abstract, but of the Kadets concretely. Plekhanov advocated support of the Kadets on the ground that this would isolate reaction. Were the Kadets then against reaction? The moderate newspaper *Report (Molva)* claimed they would settle for a Shipov ministry. Others might deny this, but to support their denial they must quote Kadet *utterances*. Lenin declared that not words, but deeds, were needed to prove the point to him. "And whoever examines the entire political conduct of the Kadets in general and as a whole, must recognize that what is said by *Report* is fundamentally true." [23] Therefore the Kadets were not against reaction, and Marxists could not support them or their Duma.

If there was a real parliament, established as the chief form of ruling class domination, where revolutionary utterances could evoke no revolution, then Marxists must support Kadets, or even Shipovists, against reactionaries. But there was no parliamentary regime. Marxists must use the Duma to the fullest extent—but only for the purpose of employing its internal conflicts in order to choose the best moment for renewing the attack on Autocracy. The Kadets, Lenin, concluded, were a parliamentary party in the absence of a parliament. Such a party at the moment could be more harmful than a reactionary party, by diverting the masses from the main task, which consisted of extra-parliamentary struggle for real parliamentarism. Whoever did not understand this, did not understand dialectics.

Plekhanov had told Marxists to imagine two men caged with a lion. Lenin embellished this parable: suppose one man fights, while the other notices a tablet on the lion's breast inscribed "constitution" and forthwith announces, "I am against force from Right or Left." What then is the other to do? The answer is that he (the SD party) must strain every nerve to expose the sham fighter in the eyes of the people. When "constitutional illusions" vanish, the peasantry will split into different parts, and one will go over to the revolution. The Kadet ephemera will disappear for good.

Thus Lenin, on the eve of the First Duma, renounced any sort of common action with the Kadet plurality. The nature of the Kadets was to betray, and no Marxist could support them. Lenin had made perfectly clear that if the revolution was really over, no matter how bad a Duma existed, he would support any kind of bourgeois party against Tsarism. However, he believed the revolution would continue. Therefore the crime of the Kadets in the spring of 1906 was that they were diverting the attention of the people towards parliamentary struggle when an uprising—the only sufficient means of achieving democracy—was still possible.

The meaning of the slogan "constitutional illusions" becomes plain. It meant not illusions that constitutions bring beneficial re-

sults, not illusions that a constitution existed in Russia, but simply
illusions that any "constitution" at all which Tsarism might grant
could take the place of armed worker-peasant insurrection. No
amount of "improvement" of the Duma, the electoral law of 11
December, or the Fundamental Laws of 23 April could satisfy
Lenin, any more than the Kadets could ever alter their words
enough to merit Lenin's support, however limited or temporary.
If the situation changed enough to make support of bourgeois
groups necessary once more, the Kadets were no worthier of cooperation than the Octobrists—Lenin had written, "even the most
villainous" bourgeoisie. Bourgeois democracy, as distinguished
from petty-bourgeois (i.e., peasant) democracy, was unalterably a
sham and a delusion.

Thus the Bolsheviks based their tactics in early 1906 on the
clear assumption that the situation was basically the same as the
previous autumn. The country was ripe for revolution, and anything which diverted the masses from that objective was evil. Like
Chernov, Lenin expected the spring would bring the peasant army
out in support of the urban vanguard, and carry both to victory.

4.

The Mensheviks, who had placed their hopes in the democracy
of the liberal-Left, were at first more puzzled than Lenin about
the effect of 17 October. *Beginning* first predicted [24] the bourgeoisie would go over to reaction "and back." Its fear of the
proletariat would send it in one direction, its own class interests
in reverse. Since the middle class, for which the revolution was
preparing dominance, was least fitted to lead, the proletariat would
continue to take the decisive role. "We will push forward the bourgeoisie," not fearing its victories, for "they are conditions of our
further successes."

Three days later, however, the tone changed. E. Smirnov,[25] suspicious of the zemstvists' relations with Witte, wrote, "We should
foresee that our party alone will fight against the united reaction
of liberals and the Autocratic-police regime." Another contributor
asserted that at the November zemstvo congress "Messieurs the
bourgeois have finally thrown off the mask of 'friends of the
people'." The editors of *Beginning* declared flatly,[26] "the revolution
has completed its first phase. The zemstvo opposition has detached
itself and has become a counterrevolutionary force."

Was the "first phase" over? If it was, the middle class should be in power, and it was not. Consequently the Mensheviks, on second thought, renewed their appeals to the liberals to "choose" [27] between revolution and counterrevolution, though Trotsky's presence among the editors of *Beginning* served to weaken further their already shaken confidence in the liberals. Trotsky wrote, "Our liberal bourgeoisie appears as counterrevolutionary already before the revolutionary culmination;" the intellectuals were weak, the peasantry simply a mutinous element which "can be put to the use of the revolution only by that force which seizes state power. There remains the proletariat" alone. Here Trotsky's exclusive trust in the urban workers appears in sharp focus.

The real Mensheviks of the Martov stripe were, on the other hand, not so optimistic about the chances of an independent proletarian attack. As their hope in the liberals waned, they looked hopefully, if rather tardily, in the direction of the peasantry. The Saratov uprising showed, said one writer, that the rural worker could be drawn to the proletariat as a temporary ally. It was not true, he insisted, that Social Democracy was new to the peasant problem. Marxist doctrine envisaged the active participation of the rural masses as a whole, as an "oppressed class," in the democratic revolution. Even if this writer could speak for all Menshevism, it was rather late to bring the word to the peasants that Marxism had always counted on them.

There was a last desperate blast at the liberals at the height of the Moscow rising. "Bourgeois "society," declared *Our Voice*,[28] had betrayed proletariat, peasantry, army, and fleet. "It betrayed itself in refusing to assist the people in the task of self-armament, giving up without a fight to the attack of reaction the freedom . . . won in October." But it was too late to change tactics. The peasants had not come to the workers' aid, while the Kadets, on the other hand, were still in outspoken opposition to the government. The Mensheviks were compelled to return to their pre-October position. The liberals might be a poor thing, but they were the Mensheviks' own, and there seemed to be no alternative.

5.

Having already declared for qualified participation in the elections to the proposed Bulygin Duma, the Mensheviks likewise decided to use the Witte Duma. This tactic was confirmed at the Menshevik St. Petersburg conference of November 1905, which agreed to reunite the party at a spring Congress. Martov and Dan fought in the reunited St. Petersburg organization for participation in the elections, but the Leninists defeated them by a 36-28 vote. Plekhanov, from abroad,[29] urged maximum use of the Duma for party objectives and criticized the wisdom of the Moscow uprising: "We ought not to have taken up arms." The Mensheviks had never been enthusiastic about the idea of *organizing* (i.e., deliberately planning) an insurrection. They believed, like the Socialist Revolutionaries, that the Bolsheviks had been responsible for "forcing" events instead of waiting for a fuller awakening of the masses and a united assault on Tsarism by all groups. They did not believe, unlike Lenin and Chernov, that the "spring" was bound to bring an uprising which could continue where the Muscovites had left off in December. The only practical weapon left was the Duma, and they thought it suicidal for the revolutionaries to ignore a tangible public forum in favor of some kind of transcendental riot.

When the IV Congress of the Social Democratic party met in Stockholm in April, the two factions were in fact farther apart than they had been in the winter, although they now came to "reunite." The elections were almost over and had given victory to the Kadets by default (whether *because* of default can never be definitely known.) The boycott had failed to accomplish anything except reduction of worker representation in the Duma to the vanishing point. The decision of the Congress to take part in the Caucasian elections, still pending, was justified by resounding Marxist successes which ensued there, but this capture of the peelings only made more bitter the contemplation of the rest of the apple which had been cast away. To the failure of the boycott and their own success in leading the Soviets of October, the Mensheviks attributed the majority they had won of the delegates at the Stockholm Congress.[30]

The Menshevik majority did not delay to push through a series of resolutions sanctioning their position. The first problem discussed was the revision of the humble "cut-offs" agrarian plank of the platform of 1903. All believed drastic revision of this was necessary, but there was not even unanimity within each faction as to what changes there should be. Plekhanov denounced Lenin's "nationalization" plank as being of a piece with his defense of "seizure of power," and defended Maslov's "municipalization" plan. The latter was adopted by a 61-46 vote.

The notion of "municipalization" of land [31] was conceived by Maslov as a counterweight to a bourgeois, possibly reactionary central government which might remain after the end of the "first phase." It meant the passage of large private holdings into the hands of local organs of self-government (reorganized zemstvos), and might be accomplished either by force or by legislation in the form of a "tax." At the same time church, state, and imperial lands were to be nationalized—not "municipalized"—by the "democratic" state, and all semi-feudal obligations and class restrictions on the peasantry were to be abolished. As with all such schemes for some kind of land expropriation, the land taken over by local zemstvos or the central government would then be available for lease to the peasants, in return for which they would pay a "tax" instead of rent, depending on the yield of the land in question.

Under Maslov's plan the peasant allotments were left intact. Like the Popular Socialists in the neo-populist camp, the Mensheviks believed the peasants would never "give up" their own lands voluntarily.

To this plan Lenin opposed his own for "nationalization" of all lands. He was not able to obtain acceptance of this plank by even the Bolsheviks without a struggle. B. Avilov had opposed it in the party press as strengthening a bourgeois state, and N. Rozhkov agreed.[32] Finn and Borisov leaned simply toward division of gentry land among the peasants. Lenin agreed with Maslov in condemning land division schemes as petty-bourgeois utopianism. He based his own plan, however, on expectations very different from Maslov's as to the nature of the "bourgeois" state which would be created by the "first phase." Maslov believed it would be a state dominated by the middle class, whether by its more or less democratic segments. Lenin envisaged [33] a "peasant-democratic" state, governed by his "revolutionary dictatorship of proletariat and peasantry." Both, we must remind ourselves, would be "bourgeois."

"Nationalization," Lenin wrote, was definitely "a *bourgeois* measure," but it involved "the maximum of bourgeois-democratic reform in the realm of agrarian relations." If a *"completely democratic state"* was created, the bureaucracy would be destroyed and thus there would be no danger of its being propped up or saved by nationalization. It could thus do no harm, in this event. Would the peasants "give up" their lands, in any case? Of course not, if to the Trepovs of Tsarism;[34] nor to the Petrunkeviches and Rodichevs who might sit in the Maslov-approved zemstvos. But under "nationalization" the peasants would not give up the *land* to anyone—they would merely yield the right to receive rent, which would accrue to the people's state.

6.

We may pause here for a moment to compare Lenin's and Chernov's schemes for agrarian reform. They agreed on the need for legislation which would destroy the power of the gentry, give the land to the poor peasants without compensation payments, and by radical alteration of the whole system of land tenure provide a better stepping-stone to full socialism. Lenin said his proposal would be a "bourgeois" measure; Chernov as always refused to use this word but was explicit in showing that "socialization" did not mean socialism. The difference between the plans of Lenin and Chernov, from the standpoint of the stated intent of the authors, was that under "nationalization" (likewise under the Mensheviks' "municipalization") the growth of capitalism in agriculture would continue, while under "socialization" it would come to a halt. Yet private landed property was to be abolished under both plans. How could capitalism continue under the first and not the second?

To understand this point, we must see that the "capitalism" envisaged by Lenin to follow "nationalization," would be as little like previous capitalism as the peasantry was like the gentry. He selected this mode of land reform because it would benefit most his chosen class ally. The fault of the Menshevik plan,[35] he said plainly, was that Maslov "failed to understand that only a 'coalition between proletariat and peasantry' " could guarantee the victory of the bourgeois revolution in Russia. In other words, just as Lenin chose a peasant rather than gentry partner in the fight for freedom, he chose a peasant type of capitalism instead of the admittedly progressive type of agricultural capitalism prevailing on many great estates. This nascent capitalism, he wrote in a striking anticipation of the New Economic Policy, "must be sacrificed"[36] to the broad and free development of capitalism on the basis of the rejuvenated *small producer* system. Yet "capitalistic" this new system would certainly be, simply because the "despotism of capital" would not be eliminated. Only the man who possessed capital, in liquid form or in machinery, would be independent. The man who did not would be the slave of capital, even under "nationalization." (*Much* capital, to be sure, would probably not be accumulated by anyone under a sharply progressive land tax.)

How, then, could some kind of capitalism continue under one plan, and not the other, if both would abolish private property? The answer, to Lenin, was simple: it *would* continue[37] under

Chernov's scheme (as well as his own) whether Chernov liked it or not. To believe that land could be "socialized" without socializing capital, said Lenin, was a mere delusion. This was a verbal muddle. Chernov did not believe land "socialization" meant socialism. If someone wanted passionately to call the transition system "capitalism," weakened and stifled as it might be, Chernov would probably have shaken his head, but would perhaps have recognized the unimportance of the semantic difference. In the same way, he objected to the Marxists' use of the term "bourgeois" revolution, yet meant nothing essentially different by his own term "toilers'" revolution.

As for the physical mechanics of the two programs, so far as can be seen, they differed in two respects. Chernov would openly aim at equalizing land *holding* on the basis of a "consumption norm," whereas Lenin, though renouncing equal holding as "Utopian," would, by giving the land only to the poor peasants and by using a progressive land tax, approach the same goal by a different route. Second, Lenin would give land *title* to the state, Chernov to the communes. Lenin had always believed the commune in theory to be a reactionary institution, and since he disputed Chernov's contention that peasants would prefer to yield their land to the communes rather than to the state, he refused to change his mind about them on practical grounds either. He thought that the state, although being preponderantly "peasant," would be less likely to reflect the peasants' reactionary tendencies than the separate communes. There were, after all, no urban workers in the mir to apply any corrective measures which might be needed.

In either case, actual production would continue on the basis of extended small holding. Thus, in practice, Lenin had approached the SR agrarian program closely enough so that he had to emphasize strongly his different theoretical foundation in order to prove that the Socialist Revolutionaries were still petty-bourgeois Utopians, while he was a scientific socialist. Even though he refused to admit that the specific programs were similar, he did confess that in general Russian Marxists, even after the Revolution had begun, had failed to apply the theory of Marx to "the peculiar conditions prevailing in Russia," [38] and had repeated conclusions drawn from foreign conditions in a different epoch. "The agrarian revolution is the basis of the bourgeois revolution in Russia, and determines the national peculiarity of this revolution." Substitute "toilers'" for "bourgeois," and Chernov could have written the words himself.

7.

The IV Congress adopted Maslov's agrarian plank, designed to avoid the counterrevolution which "nationalization" might arouse among peasants irate at losing their land, and to counteract the power of the bourgeois state to follow the "first phase." The Congress also adopted Axelrod's resolution for participation in the Duma in order to use it as an instrument of struggle. Plekhanov declared, "The Duma stands on the highroad to revolution." By a 63-40 vote, it approved the resolution of Plekhanov and Cherevanin which declared that the struggle for power could be effective only if large segments of both bourgeoisie and peasantry took part. Finally, the Polish and Lithuanian Social Democrats were admitted to the party, the Latvian Social Democrats and the Jewish Bund "recognized," and a Menshevik-dominated Central Committee set up.

Unity had been proclaimed, but not achieved. The ink on the resolutions of the Congress was scarcely dry when Lenin appealed to the Bolsheviks to fight with all their might for their repeal—which could only be accomplished if Lenin's supporters regained their majority in the party. At the V Congress at London in 1907 they were to be successful in doing so, but the majority was precarious and it was not long afterward that the party fell into many small fragments. The Social Democrats were never really reunited, at Stockholm or subsequently.

The tactics of the Menshevik-dominated "party" towards other political groups had been laid down by the Plekhanov-Cherevanin resolution which declared bourgeois and peasant support to be a prerequisite of any uprising. These two groups were both acceptable to the Mensheviks; but to them the middle class was simply a more important political force in the existing situation than the peasantry. "The peasant movement is in essence petty bourgeois"— said the Maslov resolution—although it could have revolutionary significance. As for bourgeois democracy, it had not so far played a central role because "the disintegration of absolutism proceeded much faster than the political organization of the forces of 'society' ";[39] their mobilization lay in the future, to be accomplished in connection with the Duma. Bourgeois liberalism, in a word, would still play a progressive role, so not only any idea of a radical break with it, but also the boycottist policy, must be rejected.

Officially, Social Democracy thus assumed a favorable attitude toward the Kadet Duma. The Menshevik *Neva Gazette* called for a popular demonstration to celebrate its opening. When the Bolshevik *Wave* disparaged this as a festival of the "counterrevolutionary bourgeoisie," Plekhanov warned the workers against such an attitude and exhorted them not to strengthen the position of reaction by ill-considered attacks on the liberal opposition.[40]

Although supporting the attacks of the Kadet plurality on the government, the Central Committee desired an independent voice, however small, for Social Democracy. After the Menshevik deputies, elected mostly from the Caucasus as a result of the renunciation of the boycott at Stockholm, finally arrived, on 12 June a Social Democratic Duma fraction was organized, consisting of 18 members. The bulk of them had belonged to the "Workers' Group" which three weeks earlier had published an appeal "to all the workers of Russia."

The new fraction sponsored a declaration,[41] presented by S. Dzhaparidze on 16 June, which declared the Duma to be "the center of the all-people's movement against the police Autocracy," as well as a possible stage in the struggle of the people for a Constituent Assembly and for power. The Menshevik *Voice of Labor* echoed [42] that the Duma was an organ "which combined the struggle of the classes into a unit," an "organ of pan-national opposition." Despite these declarations of solidarity with the Duma, equivalent to support of the Kadet leadership, the Social Democratic fraction maintained an independent line. It opposed the Kadet grant of 15,000,000 rubles to the government for aid to famine victims, and voted against the Kadet appeal to the people on the land question as too moderate. In the matter of the various projects for agrarian reform presented to the Duma, however, the Mensheviks favored the Kadet draft as more progressive than those of the Trudoviks. If the Social Democrats could not enact their own agrarian plank, wrote Martov,[43] "the proletariat must 'support' the program of bourgeois democracy against the program of reactionary peasant 'socialism.'" The old Menshevik tactics had not changed.

8.

Lenin maintained uncompromising hostility to the Kadet Duma throughout. The Kadets, he wrote, "dream of peaceful parliamentarism. They have taken the dreams for reality." [44] To those who said, "They fight, let us support them," Lenin replied, "Think instead of the significance of the dismissal of the Duma in terms of the future." Martynov and Plekhanov had been wrong when they said that the Kadets as a party were more important than the Socialist Revolutionaries, for the latter, though in themselves a nullity, were "reflectors of the spontaneous tendencies of the peasantry;" they were part of that revolutionary democracy without which the proletariat could not hope for full victory.

In the Duma, Lenin noted, SR strength was negligible, but they had concluded a rapprochement with the Trudoviks—which was no accident. Both groups represented the "small, laboring peasant, unspeakably oppressed, dreaming of equal division of land, fit for the most decisive, unlimited struggle, pushed toward this struggle by the entire march of events and all the conduct of the government." [45] It was they, and not the Kadets, whom Social Democrats must support.

Lenin urged not only that his party should support the Trudoviks, but should put maximum pressure on them to oppose the Kadets. They ought to be shown that the bourgeois democrats sought only to subordinate the peasant movement to their own control, leaving partially intact the big landholdings while satisfying the property instincts of the peasants in order to weaken the revolutionary movement. Marxists must warn the Trudoviks against the whole Kadet program, and make clear to the peasants that in order to be successful in their fight for land and liberty, they "must act entirely separate and independent of the Kadets."

The old fear of Lenin that the liberals would seduce the workers from Marxist control was thus transferred to fears for the political virtue of the peasants. The enemy of the working class was still the Kadets, and their preponderance in the Duma had justified his predictions of an important role which the liberals would play, just as it confirmed his worst fears and concentrated all his antipathies. When he would fall asleep and dream of "scoundrels," as Krupskaia said, he would have in mind not Tsarists, but Kadets. Lenin fought the Kadets as bitterly as he could from outside the Duma; for he was not fighting for control of the Duma—what he was contending for was the bodies of the Trudoviks, and behind them, the peasants.

The proposal for a Kadet ministry, which the Mensheviks supported as a progressive demand, provoked Lenin to the literary grimaces of one who had foreseen this calamity. "Again and again, it behooves us to beg Messieurs the Kadets the same thing: what you do, do quickly." [46] To say a Kadet ministry would tear power from the court camarilla was a "bourgeois lie;" for it would be only a new liberal camouflage for the camarilla. It would not convert a false constitution into a real one, it would simply clothe the old one in a new costume. The Mensheviks, Lenin charged, had first supported the idea of a Kadet ministry without qualification, but then had added the condition that the Kadets demand an amnesty, real "freedoms," and the end of martial law before assuming office. Lenin sneered, "Before supporting the Kadets, it is necessary for them to demand and require that the Kadets cease to be Kadets."

9.

The Bolshevik leader thus found no word of praise for the Kadets in the Duma, or the Duma in general. Even serious support for the Trudoviks, he wrote, could only be exerted outside the Duma, and depended not on "us" but the trend of events. A new spontaneous wave was rising, he said on 6 May, and Social Democrats must strain every nerve to prepare for the new battle.[47]

Nevertheless, "we must not force events . . . this lesson we must draw from the experience at the end of 1905 . . . Not on our will does the choice of forms of this struggle depend—the historical development of the Russian revolution determines them with iron necessity." [48] And because of historical conditions independent of Marxist wills, the chief form of the liberation movement "cannot become the parliamentary struggle." The Duma, despite the use which could be made of it, was guilty above all of being simply a Duma instead of an insurrection. As long as an insurrection remained possible—as Lenin believed it did—a Duma of whatever variety served merely to divert the people from the real task, whose achievement necessitated violence.

When the Tsar dissolved the Duma,[49] Lenin observed cynically that it was done on "strictly constitutional grounds." The Kadets were driven to the adoption of the Vyborg manifesto, which "infringes the law." The hopes of the Kadets were thus transferred from constitutionalism to revolution by a single strictly constitutional act of the supreme power! What was important about the dismissal was that the people would lose their "constitutional illusions;" especially was this true of the "most backward" peasants and therefore the army, both of which set such a store by the Duma.

The dismissal marked "a complete return to Autocracy." Therefore an uprising was now more possible than ever, and Social Democrats must agitate with all their might for an insurrection to bring about a Constituent Assembly. Just in time for Lenin to add a postscript to his brochure on the dismissal of the Duma, came the news of the Sveaborg mutiny, but it was not followed by an insurrection. A month passed, and Lenin wrote hopefully, "An explosion is inevitable and may be near at hand." [50] At any rate, "the dissolution of the Duma marks the end of the liberal hegemony, which was retarding and degrading the revolution."

Lenin was right in asserting that the liberal hegemony was at an end; but with its termination came the end of the revolution itself. The "Duma of people's hopes" was replaced by a "Duma of people's wrath" in which the liberals were weaker, and the revolutionaries were stronger—but so was the Right. This time the Tsardom, not fearing the united action of the Duma, felt strong enough not only to disperse the Duma—which was legal—but simultaneously to reduce the Duma opposition by drastically altering the suffrage—which was illegal. The Kadets had fallen, as Lenin had predicted, but no "extraparliamentary" struggle replaced the parliamentary one. Ascendancy passed not to a dictatorship of proletariat and peasantry, but to the "Guchkovs." The Russian liberals, whom Lenin had fought hardest, were beaten.

XIII

WHAT KIND OF PARLIAMENT?

Maurice Baring, traveling from the Far East, arrived in Moscow
the day after the October Manifesto. Paying a visit to a public
bath, he was convinced a new order had come to Russia when he
heard a ten-year-old bath assistant direct, "Give the *citizen* some
soap." [1] Whether Russia's urchins and vagabonds were consciously
reviving the "spirit of 1793" or not, they were behaving in a manner which convinced the opposition leaders that they were riding
the crest of a "revolution" in the tradition of its classic predecessors.

A revolution had one essential feature: it must take power. As
Miliukov noted in December, in the great revolutions of the past,
power had passed from the old regime to a popular assembly called
by it, upon which the revolution could lean. "Popular representation was that stalk on which the revolutionary idea grew up and
emerged into the light and air," Miliukov wrote, but in Russia the
shoots of the revolutionary idea lay on the ground because they
found no firm support, no power. The extremists sought such a
support in a provisional revolutionary government, but this was
a charmed circle.[2] Without such a government, there could be no
revolution, and vice versa.

Miliukov had well expressed the Kadets' conception of revolution. An assembly called by the old regime, preserving a semblance
of authority, would serve as the means of transfer of power to the
people. Even if that assembly were unrepresentative, the Russian
opposition ought to be able to dominate it and crush the old
order by the aid of mass popular support. The setting up of a
"revolutionary government," on the other hand, would be an erroneous tactic. It would have the effect of provoking civil war
between the old legal power, which would still control the army,
and the leaders of the uprising. In this conflict, the old regime
would be bound to win through superior military force, and in

self-defense would probably set up a military dictatorship. Now the Kadets did not condemn violence during the revolution. During the period when the new assembly, the Duma, was expected to wrest power from Autocracy, it was thought that violence probably could not be avoided, in any case. Nevertheless, Lenin's tactic of an armed uprising aimed at the seizure of power was quite another matter, and must be avoided for the reasons cited.

This idea of revolution may or may not have corresponded to what actually happened in England in 1642 or France in 1789. The important point was that it was based on an unqualified hostility to the old order and a determination to destroy it—whether the Tsar retained a crown or not would not matter if the state were controlled by popular sovereignty. Power had to pass to the people; this was the prerequisite of a settlement. This position separated the Kadets in a decisive manner from the parties of the Right which desired to reform the old regime gradually and to leave its foundations intact.

2.

The long-standing quarrel inside the liberal camp between the advocates of "reform" and "revolution" had been shelved temporarily due to the prudent silence of the Minority of the zemstvo congresses in the summer of 1905. In the November congress, however, the debate broke into the open again, and resulted in final schism between Right and Left liberals. Petrunkevich exhorted the zemstvists to fight on: "To renounce the revolution means to renounce ourselves." Shchepkin, another Kadet, declared, "For us . . . [the Manifesto] might be enough, but behind us is the people, and we cannot rest before we satisfy its pressing needs."

According to Martynov,[3] the mass of Great Russian delegates at this congress moved sharply to the Right, especially when news came of the Sevastopol mutiny, and they could point to the flood of telegrams from local bodies (especially city councils) demanding that the zemstvists stand behind the government. Certain delegates from the border regions, however, still stood firm in opposition. As a result the congress declared once more for a Duma with Constituent functions (that is, a qualified Constituent Assembly) and announced that their confidence in Witte's government would be determined by the extent to which it realized the promises of 17 October. However, a sizeable group of delegates favored outright support of Witte, and while the zemstvo congress was still in session, they took steps to form a Union of 17 October,[4] under the guidance of Count Heyden, Shipov, A. I. Guchkov, and others. The "Octobrists" thus finally split from the Kadets, and there was no further attempt to unite them in a zemstvo congress even for purposes of discussion.

The Octobrists at least temporarily swallowed up the outstanding Slavophiles. On 17 October they became, in the phrase of N. A. Khomiakov, "constitutionalists by imperial decree." If the Tsar had granted a constitution, it was their obligation to receive one loyally. Yet the dominant tendency in the new party was represented not by the Slavophiles but by Guchkov. Its strength lay in the richer gentry and even more in the industrialists of the capitals and larger cities. Earlier there had been attempts to form openly "capitalist" parties (such as the conservative Progressive-Economic Party of St. Petersburg and the Commercial-Industrial Party of Moscow, and the more moderate Commercial-Industrial Union of St. Petersburg and Moderate-Progressive Party of Moscow).[5] But the industrialists had decided a broader political grouping was the only way to make an effective bid for electoral support, and by the end of the I Duma most of these parties were absorbed into Octobrism.

By the summer of 1906 it was clear that the Octobrist leadership, especially Guchkov himself, was willing to make its peace with Stolypin and support harsh measures against the Left. At this point many of the ex-Slavophiles left the Union of 17 October to form the small Party of Peaceful Renovation.[6] This new party demarcated itself "from extreme Leftist parties, considering it possible to change the social order by forcible realization of abstract theories, as well as from Rightist elements, which are satisfied only by partial improvements," and demanded "radical and immediate reconstruction of the state." Octobrism continued to signify the recognition of the Manifesto as implying a constitution, the "unity" (that is, no local autonomy) of Russia, and a "strong government." Certain "social reforms" were indeed called for, but even the most reactionary parties, such as the Party of Legal Order, did not dare disavow the need for reform, and the pressure of Octobrist demands was for internal order, not new legislation.

3.

Meeting at the height of the strike movement, the I Kadet Congress had carried non-socialist democracy to the furthest point of radicalism reached during the Revolution. It left the question of monarchy open, repeated the demand for compulsory alienation of land, with compensation at "just price" (which, said Herzenstein, would be "lower than market price"),[7] and decisively rejected the idea of reaching party objectives through talks with the government.

The Kadets, like their Liberationist predecessors, aimed at uniting all democrats outside of socialism, but did not entirely succeed. Right after the Congress, their extreme Left elements broke off to form the Radical Party and Party of Freethinkers, and later the additional group of "critical socialists" under Kuskova, Prokopovich, and Bogucharskii, which published *Without a Title* and *Comrade*. In the autumn of 1905 the Kadets, despite their radical position, lost practically none of their Right wing. This took place later when Prince Eugene Trubetskoi and others went over to the Party of Peaceful Renovation in the spring. Just before the elections, the *Messenger of Europe* board, along with a few professors like Kuzmin-Karavaev and M. M. Kovalevskii, organized a Party of Democratic Reforms. It was hoped that this party would attract some Right Kadets. Its reformist demands differed little from those of the Peaceful Renovators, and the two groups were united in their distrust of Kadet sympathy with the revolutionaries. These two parties remained minuscule. Maklakov, with much of the "empirical Right" (as we earlier termed his following), entered the Kadet party and remained there, although more or less dissatisfied with the radical, rationalist party leadership.

In the main, however, the empiricists of Russian political life had now grouped in the Rightist parties. They did not bother to justify empiricism, to make it into an "ideology;" they merely practiced it. They would in general do what seemed best to them at the time. They would bring about faster or slower reform, depending on whether they belonged to the Union of 17 October or the Union of the Russian People, but they would not try to create a new type of political order in conformity with an apriorist scheme. But though they did not share the rationalism which we have attempted to show was one prominent feature of the Russian political opposition, they showed signs of the other feature, Western influence. The industrialists, for example, leaned heavily on the experience of German business men in organizing and setting forth their demands. More broadly, the Octobrists in particular supported a program of nationalism and imperialism patterned closely after the German and other Western models. And for the immediate task of suppressing the revolution, which was uppermost in all Rightist minds in 1906, there was Western precedent enough.

4.

The Kadets shared with the rest of the opposition the task of defining their attitude toward the Duma. Having begun their I Congress determined to consider how best to convert a Bulygin Duma into an assembly which would terminate the old regime, they ended it with at least the Tsar's promise of a Witte Duma. As a representative institution, in principle the latter was regarded as scarcely better than the former. In practice, the Kadets might hope for a much larger delegation in the assembly to be called on the basis of the electoral law of 11 December.

They were faced, however, with not only a new legislature, but also something which purported to be a constitution. If this was not the culmination of the "bourgeois revolution," at least the Right immediately decided that it was. The Kadets saw evidence that the extreme Left agreed with the Right's appraisal. Miliukov wrote bitterly, "of course, the role of a 'bourgeoisie' in a revolutionary overturn, according to theory, is a base one. The 'bourgeoisie' must conquer and on the day after victory 'betray' the people. But why does the 'bourgeoisie' nevertheless not fulfil its assigned, base role? How will the bourgeoisie risk holding back from victory and thereby slowing up the progressive march of revolution?" [8] More than the ordinary bitterness of political polemics had crept into Miliukov's tone. It was somewhat frustrating for him to hear grave discussions in Leftist circles as to whether the "bourgeoisie," whose most advanced spokesman they agreed the Kadets to be, had committed treason against the revolution— discussions in which nobody bothered to consult the Kadets as to their position. In the passage just quoted, Miliukov tried to make clear to his Leftist allies why the bourgeois "victory" *could not* have occurred and *could not* possibly occur yet. He argued thus: first, there was no "bourgeois" government; the prime minister was a Tsarist bureaucrat. Second, the only immediate prospect for a bourgeois government was the plan then current for declaring a zemstvo congress to be a Provisional Government; and the Kadets could not accept this, for the result would be a zemstvist cabal. The revolution must remain a movement of *all* the people. The "bourgeoisie" could not afford any sham victory; the only real victory could be by way of a Duma of the Russian nation, even though at first not a fully representative one.

The next step, therefore, was to exert every effort to make the Duma an opposition body, and the organization of the Kadet party was pointed squarely at that objective. In October, 7 local committees[9] were organized; in November, 28; in December, 13; in January, 13. Their party workers were active chiefly among the middle classes, but also among the students of the capitals and to some extent in the provincial villages. They made the fullest use of their many gifted writers in their growing party press: in St. Petersburg, *Birzhevye Vedomosti* (Exchange News) and *Law,* and from February the chief party organ, *Rech'* (Speech), and *Messenger of the People's Freedom;* in Moscow, where the party agrarian committee and the *People's Law* publishing house was located, the newspaper *The People's Cause;* in the provinces some two dozen journals. In December Struve started a weekly, *Polar Star,* which reflected the quasi-Octobrist position at which he had arrived by a steady movement to the Right ever since his Marxist days (although certain contributors like S. Frank [10] defended the orthodox democratic point of view of the Kadets in its pages.) All this intensive organizational and journalistic activity was to bear startling fruit when the Duma elections were held in the spring.

5.

By January 1906, when the II Congress met, the Kadets had not quite recovered from the shocks of revolution and counterrevolution of the preceding months. Nevertheless, the leaders saw signs that "society" was getting over its fright at the Sevastopol and Moscow uprisings. Miliukov declared at the Congress,[11] "The chaos which should have instilled in the citizen horror at revolutionary terrorism instilled in him to a much greater extent fear of governmental terrorism . . . Frightened by the revolutionists, the citizen still did not trust the government."

In other words, counterrevolution had objectively served the democratic cause, and the Kadets could advance to fight the elections with determination. Even though the absence of the necessary guarantees of liberty might make participation difficult, it would offer great opportunities for agitation and would give a better representation to the toiling classes than the existing "unions," thought Miliukov. Above all, since the Kadet party was a "preeminently parliamentary" one, the elections would facilitate its own organization. The Duma itself, however, was a separate question, and tactics in regard to it must depend on the outcome of the elections—if only two or three Kadet deputies could be elected, for example, a boycott of the Duma might be desirable.

The January Congress moved slightly to the Right. It altered the Kadet program to include a demand for a "constitutional and parliamentary monarchy." The tactical plan was also changed, by rejecting talks with the government (of Witte) not in principle, as in October, but because there existed "no basis for confidence in the *present* government." Nevertheless, the congress declared that despite their determination to use the Duma, the party "puts all its strength into the broadest organization of social consciousness by all means, excluding armed uprising," and once more there was a call for "unity among the opposition parties." Martynov notes that the party kept solidarity with the proletariat in connection with the celebration of the first anniversary of 9 January, and that it had thrown off "the Octobrist infection." [12] However, he writes critically, it felt its own hegemony of the opposition movement and tried to take an independent lead.

This contention of Martynov is borne out by Miliukov himself. He replied to criticism of the Kadets for moving to the Right,[13] that it was true that the II Congress "thought more about itself than others." Still it said nothing really new, and the party lost some of its membership on the Right, not the Left, as a consequence of its composition. "In spite of all that movement to the Right which manifested itself in the attitude of society as a reflection—we hope temporary—of the recent mishaps of the 'Liberation Movement'" and attempts of the Right to reinforce itself by weaning away Kadet members, the Kadets remained "an *opposition* party," ready to call to account the enemies of democratic constitutionalism and social reforms. "Opponents of the Kadet party seek entirely in vain . . . for any kind of evidence of 'treachery' or change of position."

In general Miliukov was correct. The Kadets had maintained their old Liberationist position through a difficult period. They had remained democrats. Even the Moscow uprising had not alienated them from the revolutionaries. It had only proved, said Miliukov,[14] that a government which "was forced to consider all the people its enemy" could not exist, even when sustained by "bayonets and bullets." Yet while the extremist parties became no less acceptable to the Kadets as allies, their use of insurrectionist tactics was severely criticized. At the II Congress, Miliukov attributed the weakening of the revolutionary mood of "society" to "certain mistakes of the revolutionary parties"— a paradoxical statement only if the Kadet conception of "revolution" is not understood. The leaders of the party realized that Lenin would try again, if he could (though it is not so clear that they understood that Lenin aimed at destroying them as a political force quite as much as overthrowing Tsarism.) Nevertheless, Plekhanov and other Menshevik leaders were supporting Kadet efforts to end Autocracy through use of the Duma; and the Kadets remembered orthodox Marxist teachings of a "bourgeois revolution."

Miliukov still believed, in a word, that it was possible to continue the old tactic of common front with the Left, for the good reason that the common objective of destruction of Autocracy was yet unrealized. It was the Left which he felt was deserting him, not the opposite. It was the revolutionaries who were forgetting their old apriorist scheme on which the common front of opposition parties had been based. He wrote sharply, "We accept the political jargon of our opponents and remind them that the political victory of the bourgeoisie, by their own teaching, is all that can be achieved in the present moment." Let Kadet aims be represented as a struggle for precisely this goal; let their limitation to proximate tasks be called the "classic 'treachery' of the bourgeoisie;" let their struggle against revolutionary Blanquism and "active measures" be called organization of counterrevolution. But, said Miliukov, "we ourselves know quite well that the 'bourgeoisie' is 90% of the population of Russia," and that real counterrevolution involves precisely those "active measures" we seek to avoid.[15]

The attitude of the Left to the Duma, of course, provoked among the Kadets the greatest alarm. Talk of a different popular assembly which would be convened instead of, or simultaneously with, the Duma, wrote Miliukov, though "more fantastic than dangerous," did a disservice to the Liberation Movement. He quoted with approval P. Blank's accusations[16] against certain Russian socialists of "an extremely superficial understanding of the principles of scientific socialism, a striking lack of feeling for the needs of Russian reality and a complete contempt for the lessons of Russian history of the past few months in particular." The viewpoint of the extreme Left, wrote Miliukov, was based on a denial in principle of the parliamentary means of struggle—and in this respect he showed that he understood Lenin thoroughly. "Combatting 'parliamentary illusions,'" the extremists clung to "archaic revolutionary illusions," believing they would organize a victorious revolution by "conspiracy," "spontaneity," "Blanquism," and so forth, concepts the force of which stemmed not from logic, but from "unconscious, instinctive" attitudes of mind.

It was true, continued the Kadet leader, that a "one to one" struggle between the revolutionists and Tsarism was inevitable (even though hopeless) if no other means were available—but in this case there was a better alternative: the Duma. The Kadets, Miliukov recognized, faced a serious difficulty in summoning the Leftist parties to go over to parliamentary forms of struggle, when the Kadets themselves realized these forms were at present "insufficient and unstable." Yet the opposition had to do its best with the unsatisfactory circumstances that existed. The ambiguity of which the Kadets were accused in relation to revolution, charged Miliukov, lay not in the will of liberals, but "in the situation itself, reflecting . . . all the contradictions of a moment of transition."

6.

The Kadets thus appealed to the Left to abandon its expectations of an uprising and to assist them in their efforts to make of the Duma a real parliament, if not a Constituent Assembly. Nevertheless the socialists boycotted the elections. This boycott left the Kadets, alone of the three opposition parties, in the field. They won the elections, securing an impressive plurality, and they did so through their own efforts. This victory generated a great wave of optimism in the party; only retrospect can prove it to have been overconfidence. The situation in April was highly uncertain. The government was wary, the Left was expecting a new uprising, the Kadets had, as they hoped but scarcely dared expect, captured the Duma for their own use. The party, wrote Miliukov—"we say boldly, perhaps it alone"—can bring Russia out of its fatal impasse.[17] "But for that, it is necessary that it remain by itself, that it remain that which attracted to it universal confidence."

The party met only a week before the Duma in the III Congress to work out its legislative tactics and program. Miliukov presented four "theses," including the determination to realize democratic goals "not flinching even before the possibility of a break with the government." [18] By this time, however, the rank and file of the party, moving Left, was in some respects more radical that Miliukov. His thesis was changed to read, "not flinching before a complete break." There was other radical criticism by Friedman of

St. Petersburg and de Roberti of Tver on the score of the draft
laws prepared by the Central Committee, but the party leaders
carried the congress behind their tactics of caution in the Duma
until the new assembly could entrench itself firmly.

7.

In the I Duma, out of 449 members counted, there were at first
153 Kadets, 107 Trudoviks, 63 "autonomists" (Poles, Lithuanians,
Latvians, Ukrainians, Moslems), 4 Democratic Reformists, 13 Octobrists, 3 from the industrialist parties and 105 "non-party." Two-
thirds of the Kadet deputies had received higher education,[19] as
against 42% of all the Duma, and their knowledge of Western parliamentary procedure and organization made their preponderance
far more impressive than their numerical proportion. It was also
bolstered by support they were able to draw from other groups.
When the question of a Kadet ministry arose, Miliukov com-
puted [20] that when, to the 177 who by now had identified themselves as Kadets, there were added 25 non-party men and 26 Trudoviks who supported them, plus 18 Democratic Reformists, an absolute majority of 240 was at their disposal not counting 31 Poles
and 34 Moslems who might often be relied on for aid. Therefore
a Kadet ministry could be organized without coalition with any
other faction.

In fact the Kadets were indeed able to exert effective control
over the operation of the Duma from the first session up to the
Vyborg Manifesto, although Maklakov declares that the "real
hero" [21] of the Duma was the Trudoviks, whom the Kadets treated
with condescension, and he goes on to assert that they had "more
unity than the Kadets" in viewpoint, if not in discipline and program. The Trudoviks did indeed regard the Duma only as an organ for carrying the Revolution to the end, while the Kadets, once
they realized that they had gained the ascendancy and "responsibility" for Russia's first legislative assembly, tasted just enough of
the heady wine of power to become a little confused as to precisely what they were attempting to achieve in and with the Duma.

The Duma, after being welcomed by a short address by the Tsar
at the Winter Palace, began its formal sessions on 27 April. Petrunkevich started proceedings with a sharp speech demanding an
amnesty, the subject of almost universal popular outcry ever since
October. This demand and others went into the Duma's Answer
to the "Speech from the Throne," as the deputies chose to style

Nicholas' brief address to them. The Answer provoked Maklakov to lament that it contained no thanks to the monarch, although the Kadets were supposed to be monarchists. "The new order," he writes sadly, "had strong enemies and few defenders."[22]

Expropriation of land was mentioned in the Answer, but compensation, in deference to the extremist viewpoint, was not.[23] But compensation or not, the Duma's agrarian program was "unconditionally unacceptable" to the government, as the new Prime Minister, Goremykin, declared in his reply to the Answer on 13 May. His speech provoked the first open clash between the Kadets and the government. The Duma retaliated by a vote of no confidence—which neither surprised nor disconcerted the bureaucrat ministry. Maklakov declared that the I Duma was never able to recover from the self-administered blow of 13 May, but one may suspect other reasons for its failure.

Its legislative accomplishments included only one law actually passed by Duma, State Council, and signed by the Tsar, one granting 15 million rubles to the government for famine relief. The Duma also passed a law abolishing capital punishment, but the measure got no further. Naturally this might be thought a poor record indeed, if it were not that several sweeping laws were under consideration at the moment of the dismissal of the Duma. These included laws securing the various "freedoms," reforming the judiciary, and guaranteeing equality of classes and citizens, an extensive inquiry into the Belostok pogrom, and above all, a law for land reform.

The Kadets had introduced their own land law on 8 May as the "Project of the 42."[24] It was based on the principle of compensated expropriation, excluding only certain cases of exceptionally intensive cultivation, with a "labor norm" as the determinant of maximum holdings. The draft had been extensively discussed at the III Congress, where there had been demands to go further yet and advance as a slogan "nationalization"[25] of all the land, though this was not intended even by its supporters to affect peasant holdings immediately.

The slogan of "nationalization," Miliukov noted, originated in America and England, where its purpose would be to take land from the control of "market speculation or aristocratic immobility" and give it into the hands of the smallholder. In those countries, the idea had an undoubtedly progressive significance. On the other hand, in Russia it was true that not only had the idea of private property never sunk deep roots, especially in the purely Russian provinces, but the idea of "nationalization" (the primacy of the state over land) could be traced to old Muscovite principles, with traces of Byzantine and Moslem influence. However, said Miliukov, judging from the experience of "nationalization" in Bosnia, the unwillingness of administrators to make necessary readjustments had not made the idea "prove especially attractive for small producers." Miliukov implied that the same could be expected in Russia. Of course, continued the Kadet leader, if one believed that small holding was doomed anyway, one naturally would support "socialization," "municipalization," or "nationalization." However, recent specialist researches by no means indicated the immediate ruin of small producers and the old Marxist scheme was in this connection contradicted by reality. Even though some of the peasant deputies seemed fascinated by the slogan *qua* slogan, concluded Miliukov, the attempt to apply it without exception would surely bring a clash with the wishes of the peasants when they found "nationalization" involved not only meddling with the gentry land, but their own as well.

The Kadet land law, like the Trudovik "Project of the 104," envisaged leaving the peasant holdings untouched but placing gentry, state, and church lands in a national land fund for apportionment to smallholders. It is reasonable to suppose that, if the I Duma had been allowed to continue, a law with those features would have been passed, just as it is not to be doubted that the Tsar would have vetoed it. The effect of such a veto on the peasants might have been striking, and might conceivably have rallied popular support to the Kadets and the Duma in general in a manner sufficient to throw the government on the defensive—in a way it had not been since October. But the Goremykin government, perhaps foreseeing such a possibility, on 20 June reiterated its refusal to accept any form of land expropriation.[26] From then on it was a race between the Duma to arouse the people to support its land law and the government to prevent the Duma leaders from presenting them with a direct challenge on the matter. The Trudovik, Zhilkin, declared, "When there is unrest in the broad revolutionary sense, when there is organized support, when the people rallies round the Duma, it will obtain the present land law and other laws."[27] With roughly these calculations in mind, the Kadets framed an appeal to the country to support the Duma's land law while it awaited a "peaceful" solution of the problem. Using this appeal as a pretext, the Tsar dissolved the Duma on 8 July.

8.

The dismissal followed on the heels of the second of what Miliukov calls the "three attempts" to form a nonbureaucratic ministry.[28] The first had been immediately after the October Manifesto, when Shipov had been invited to take a minor post under Witte as Prime Minister. Then Shipov had declined unless talks were conducted with the zemstvo Bureau. When in late June he was summoned again by Stolypin, he repeated the same demand, now in reference to the Kadet party instead of the zemstvists. Shipov was not a Kadet himself, but he believed it impossible to constitute a stable coalition cabinet without Kadet approval.

There was an attempt to compromise on a Kadet coalition (with the bureaucrats, not any other party) cabinet, but Miliukov would accept only a ministry based on a Duma majority. Trepov was meanwhile carrying on talks of his own, with a straight Kadet ministry in mind, as the only means of pacifying the country. Trepov told an interviewer,[29] just as Shipov told Muromtsev, that such a ministry would break the link between the Kadets and the Trudoviks, and make the former presumably more "responsible." Trepov however refused to accept certain features of the Kadet program: land expropriation, an amnesty, and others. The attempt to create Russia's first parliamentary ministry thus failed. The reason, wrote Miliukov later, was that "there could be no question not only of parliamentarism, but of constitutionalism," because for the gentry faction not only Kutler (a Kadet identified with the land program) but even Witte was regarded as a revolutionary.[30] Thus, asserts Chermenskii, the Duma was dismissed at the very moment when, as a result of these talks with the government, the Kadets were breaking with their Leftist allies, and therefore he asserts the error of those Rightist critics of the Kadets who say that the Kadets brought on dissolution by "not severing the revolutionary tail."

Did the Kadet talks with the government in June prove the long-standing accusations of "treachery" flung at them by their Leftist friends? From the beginning of the Duma the Kadets had made it quite clear that they would keep their own identity and think of themselves first. When the Trudovik Zhilkin had declared the intention of his group to march together with the Kadets in relation to the Duma presidency and to avoid mutual misunderstandings, Miliukov had warmly welcomed this statement.[31] The two groups had maintained a generally effective sort of collaboration throughout the session. Nevertheless, Miliukov observed in June that the Trudoviks, while performing the valuable service of arousing popular sympathy for the Duma and becoming heroes to the peasantry, were in a weak position from the standpoint of internal unity. They had, he contended, fluctuated between Socialist Revolutionary, Social Democratic, and Kadet influences in a manner that had deprived them of much of their force inside as well as outside the Duma. What separated the Kadets from the Trudoviks, said Miliukov, was not only that their views differed slightly, but that the Kadets did not believe the Trudoviks were yet in a position to demand the prerogatives of a real political party. After all, the Kadet deputies had been elected because they were Kadets; the Trudovik deputies became Trudoviks because they had been elected.

Lenin and Miliukov thus shared one opinion at least regarding the Trudoviks: they were, at their current stage of development, fit not to lead but to follow the more conscious parties. The Kadets had never made any kind of formal undertaking with the Trudoviks, nor had they promised formally or otherwise to include them in any coalition ministry. If the Kadets could not maintain a supporting Duma majority (though they thought they could), they might have to think about coalition. Until that time, they would remain alone.

9.

There was no "treachery," then, involving Kadet betrayal of the Trudoviks or any other Leftist deputies in the Duma. In Lenin's view, of course, "treachery" was present in every step the Kadets had taken and were bound to take. Thus the repetition of the charge in connection with the June talks is devoid of meaning unless it is contended that a Kadet ministry would have behaved in a counterrevolutionary manner toward their Leftist allies. The mere fact that the Kadets might attempt to govern alone, however, was not criticized either by the Mensheviks, who themselves insisted on remaining separate from Trudoviks as well as Kadets since they were "part of bourgeois democracy," or by the Bolsheviks, who never believed the Kadets belonged in any coalition with the Left anyway.

It is true that the Kadets at the I Congress bound themselves not to seek their ends "by means of conversations with the representatives of the government," and although they later qualified this, they still violated the letter of their pledge in the June talks. Did this bear out Lenin's contention that they aimed only at peaceful "agreement" with the government in order to end the Revolution? In a certain sense, Lenin was quite right. Miliukov repeated over and over that "the whole Liberation Movement must be induced to change its method and ways of struggle," that is, to engage in parliamentary warfare, not violence. (At one point he even wrote that if the Left was determined to drown the Liberation Movement in blood,[32] threatening the whole nation with chaos which could end only in military dictatorship, then the Kadets would not assist it.) Given peaceful, parliamentary tactics, there could be only one way of finally ending the Revolution, through an accord with the government.

The question, nevertheless, remains, what kind of agreement would be acceptable to the Kadets? Did they envisage Nicholas II —like Louis XVI or Charles I—giving way to an all-powerful parliament which he himself should have summoned, or simply consenting to admit Kadet leaders into the favored bureaucratic circle in order to deceive the people? All the evidence at hand supports the first alternative. The Kadets would accept agreement only on the basis of constitutional democracy. Miliukov himself wrote later that not a Constituent Assembly, but the very idea of a real constitution, was the factor that prevented an accord.[33] Lenin and Miliukov shared the belief that neither the October Manifesto nor the Fundamental Laws were a real constitution. The difference between the two men was that a real constitution would have made Miliukov ready to end the Revolution, while it would have made no difference to Lenin in his immediate tactics—he was willing to take part in a parliament as opposition when no chance of a successful uprising remained, whether there was a real constitution or a pure sham. A real constitution would have satisfied Miliukov, not Lenin. "Peaceful agreement" in Miliukov's thinking was almost analogous to Lenin's "victorious uprising"; it was to be the means of achieving his stated ends, not of abandoning them.

In Miliukov's view, "peaceful agreement" did not imply retreat by the Kadets, but rather by the Tsardom. The seventeenth of October had been an example of such "peaceful agreement"; frightened by popular discontent, the Tsar had been forced to yield. If the country had made clear that it supported the Duma land law, Nicholas II might have had to take another step back, and a Duma thereby strengthened might have compelled the Trepovs to admit the Kadet program along with Kadet ministers. Neither Miliukov's "agreement" nor Lenin's "victorious uprising" occurred. Both depended for their realization on the clear manifestation of mass popular support which was not forthcoming. In a sense, both were "revolutionary" in that they aimed directly at a transfer of power.

It was thus no accident that the Kadets resorted to the Vyborg Manifesto, revolutionary in essence as even Lenin admitted, to appeal to the people to take measures of passive resistance in support of the Duma. At that moment, writes Miliukov, the great majority of Kadet deputies stood by "the line of coalition with the Left, taken in the I Duma."[34] Vyborg, however, was the last attempt of the Kadets to realize constitutional democracy through alliance with the Left. From the time of organizing the Union of Liberation, the liberal-Left had based their tactics firmly on alliance with the revolutionaries. That this was true both Miliukov, who approved these tactics, and Maklakov, who opposed them, agree completely. But when the Vyborg Manifesto failed to arouse any manifestations of mass discontent, the Kadets were at last ready to admit that this alliance could not achieve their objectives—partly because their allies were too weak, partly because the alliance was no longer, if indeed it had ever been, in existence.

CONCLUSION

THE FIRST POPULAR FRONT

> *"Instead of being opposed to the ideas of state and patriotism, the intelligentsia must become creatively and constructively oriented towards the state . . . Instead of being anti-religious and fanatically atheistic, the intelligentsia must be converted into a group of people who are truly cultured . . .Instead of being spiritually proud and impatient, it must become truly human, rejecting every kind of terror, physical as well as moral. Instead of being a closed, narrow group of theoretical fantasists, the intelligentsia must become a broad, open national society of intellectually developed people."* A. S. IZGOEV, 1910.[1]

In 1896 there was no group in Russia which claimed or deserved the title of political party; ten years later there were a dozen or more. Only three of these parties had a history of more than a few months at the time of the first elections, in March 1906, and only these three (or four, if one counts both Social Democratic factions) survived to have any important influence during the Revolution of 1917. For years prior to 1905 these three had remained mere circles of intellectuals, beset by endless internal polemics and schisms. Yet in the First Revolution they emerged from these difficulties with sufficient likemindedness and determination to seek to organize the universal Russian discontent with the government, and to become the only important political parties in the country.

All three parties had been built up by men who were strongly influenced by the political doctrines and models of Western Europe, where a definite grouping of parties had been slowly worked out after some sort of parliamentary system had been established. Lenin and his rivals managed to create a spectrum of political parties in Russia, however, years before a Duma came into existence. Unhindered by the necessity of making compromises in order to win elections or pass bills, unaffected by the confusing traditions which often attracted Western sons to their fathers' parties whether or not by political belief or economic interest they belonged there, Russian intellectuals created three major parties which were intended to express, more or less, the interests of the three chief social components of Western and Russian society alike: the peasantry, the urban workers, and the middle class. These parties were created by men who were consciously preparing in advance for the time when mass support could be brought to provide the foundations for the already existing political superstructures.

2.

The socialist party leaders—Lenin, Martov, and Chernov—had a definite notion of the economic groups they were supposed to represent, and clear ideas as to how their own parties and competitors were expected to behave, especially in time of revolution. The liberal leader, Miliukov, while endeavoring to avoid identifying his party with any class, was willing to accept the label "bourgeois" for purposes of adjusting his tactics to the patterns the socialists had constructed. These patterns were those of Marxism. Lenin and Martov were orthodox Marxists; Chernov accepted much of Marxism; Miliukov made his peace with it. It is this phenomenon which Lenin evaluated to Bolshevik advantage when he wrote, "The dialectic of history is of such a kind that the theoretical victory of Marxism compels its enemies to reclothe themselves as Marxists."[2] An opponent of Lenin might interpret the same phenomenon by asserting that it is next to impossible to oppose or compete successfully with Marxism unless one has clearly worked out his own position in advance; that is, it is next to impossible to do so in the struggle for the allegiance of *intellectuals.* Half a century of politics in Europe, Africa, Asia, and America has provided overwhelming evidence that this remains true. The intellectuals of four continents have bitterly disputed the origins, nature, and destiny of various social groups, and the societies which they constituted. They have most often done so by employing categories derived from or influenced by Marxism. Marxism has not been universally accepted, of course, by intellectuals, but too often those who rejected it did not provide any successful alternative analysis of recent history, and were thus often influenced by Marxism in spite of their own intentions. The success of Marxism for a time made men who were partially influenced by Marxism advertise the fact, as Lenin noted; more recently some such men have found it best to conceal it, sometimes even from themselves.

The consequences of the apparent "theoretical victory of Marxism" have been twofold. First, the intellectuals of the world underemphasized and denigrated the importance and value of peasants, who had no coherent place in the Marxian theoretical framework. Second, these intellectuals underemphasized the importance of *themselves.* They often refused to accept the intelligentsia as a proper object of study, denying, like Marx, that it made up a separate social category, and retorting in hot and hostile fashion to those men like A. S. Izgoev who examined it, drew conclusions, and made recommendations.

Both of these consequences were dramatically exemplified in the course of the events analyzed in this book. In Russia first of all did it become clear, for those who were willing to see, that these consequences were latent in the thinking of intellectuals not only in Russia. Of course it is not true that Russia was unique, or different from the rest of Europe, in possessing either peasantry or intelligentsia. There were peasants, both smallholders and tenants, to the West of Russia, and there were also intellectuals. Much of the ink spilt over the peculiarity of the Russian intelligentsia could have been saved by a closer examination of the similar group of political-minded intellectuals in the West. The difference was that in the West these intellectuals were fairly closely linked with middle-class urban elements, and could think in urban terms, without the grotesque incongruity of doing so in nearly wholly rural Russia. A Marxist can and does talk about anything he chooses, including peasants and intellectuals, as this book has shown. That is not the same thing as saying that the theory of Marxism has a place for either group.

It was Marxist and other western social scientific thought that distorted the Russian intelligentsia's view of the Russian people, and of itself. The same distortion occurred in Western Europe, but it was not so important in its effects. Hostility to national feeling and religious sentiments, on which Izgoev commented, was present in the Russian intelligentsia, but even more fundamental was its inability to understand the peasant ideal, the desire of the Russian people, which had been formulated by the early populists in the slogan "Land and Liberty." If the intelligentsia had gone "to the people," as Herzen advised, with a sufficiently objective willing-

ness to understand what they wanted, and if they had simultaneously investigated themselves carefully enough to understand what
it was *they* really wanted, their historical analysis and their political action might possibly have avoided the calamity of the Revolution of 1905 and its failure. By 1905 it seemed clear enough that
Tsarism would be too late to act with sufficient foresight and states-
manship to determine the future of Russia. What was far from clear
was whether the people would find expression of their desires
through the intelligentsia.

The intelligentsia devoted itself to constructing almost mathema-
tically formal patterns of the course of future events. They then
undertook to translate these patterns into reality with the utmost
vigor and unlimited confidence. They failed, however, to inquire
what land and liberty meant to the Russian people. Those who
probably understood that meaning best were the Trudoviks, who
were intellectually too unsophisticated to undertake any practical
steps to translate it into successful political action, but in addition
to that were incapable of competing with the articulateness and
effectiveness which the established parties possessed, owing to their
highly developed ideological frameworks. The peasant in Russian
history has been forever in search of an ideology and a leadership
which would permit him to realize his goals. The failure of the
intelligentsia to provide him with those things proved to be disas-
trous for peasant and intellectual alike.

3.

Those who did endeavor, in their untutored and spontaneous
way, to speak for the people directly, encountered resistance within the parties with which they were powerless to deal. Khrustaliov,
the president of the St. Petersburg Soviet, writes that that body had
to contend not only with the police, "but also with the revolutionary parties, and in particular with the Social Democrats, who
saw in the projected organization a possibly dangerous competitor." [3] The members of the Peasant Union, to an even greater extent,
experienced the same sort of frustration. The leaders of the parties
did not start the revolution or any particular uprising, riot, strike,
or mutiny, but when it had begun, its aims had to be expressed
in the revolutionary jargon of the parties, which flowed in turn
from their historical analyses. As Chernov had observed in the
90's, one could not shout down a Marxist by decrying "all this

THE FIRST POPULAR FRONT

talk," even in a turbulent revolutionary assemblage. One had to be able to operate on his opponent's level of intellectual sophistication in order to get a hearing.

Since the intelligentsia so easily carried the field of revolutionary leadership, it was natural for its various segments to look to each other. The problem, as these leaders posed it, was always how to maintain the unity of the opposition parties, or of a given portion of them. The unity of the people with the parties was taken for granted; if it failed, the disaster was attributed either to the cleverness of the regime or the tactical error of some party. Unity with the people was surely a gratuitous assumption. As Kuskova wrote of the extremist parties in 1906, "there are no such parties . . . there are circles of propaganda and agitation, and there are broad mass tendencies more or less coinciding with the outlines of the circles."[4] They coincided less rather than more, but there was no time nor inclination to examine the reasons for this phenomenon.

It was equally taken for granted that disaster was certain if the unity of the parties failed. Precisely such failure did occur in 1905. Mavor writes[5] that it was the fact that opposition groups acted simultaneously for a time but could not unite for positive action "which brought the Revolution of 1905-07 'to dust,' and gave time for the Autocracy to collect its demoralized forces and to overcome the extreme factions." It is indeed possible that success might have been achieved if the unity of the parties had been maintained.

Why did the unity of the parties fail? The Soviet historians of course explain the failure in class terms, since they assume the parties to have "represented" classes. Chermenskii asserts[6] that "the liberals were satisfied by the concessions and promises" of the October Manifesto, the bourgeoisie thereupon going over to the counterrevolution and helping the government to crush the revolutionaries. Similarly, A. Sidorov declares that during the First Revolution "the bourgeoisie decisively came out against the idea of democracy."[7] These assertions cannot be maintained even within the framework of Marxist assumptions. The Kadets, supported by professional men and part of the gentry whom Lenin regarded as "bourgeois," remained in opposition to the government and based their whole tactics in the I Duma on their complete dissatisfaction with the Manifesto and the Fundamental Laws. Not even a Marxist can deny that it is in the interest of the "bourgeoisie" to seek "bourgeois democracy." The failure of the unity of the parties must be ascribed not to the satisfaction of the economic interests of the groups "represented" by the liberal intellectuals, but to a schism within the intelligentsia. The schism may be described symbolically as one between Lenin and Miliukov.

4.

Socialist Revolutionaries, Bolshevik and Menshevik Social Democrats, and Constitutional Democrats approached the Revolution of 1905 with objectives related to a striking degree with their apriorist analysis of its expected course. The socialist parties actually separated their demands into two sets which were to be realized in turn as the revolution proceeded by certain definite steps. The liberals distinguished no program-maximum from program-minimum, simply because they expected the revolution to stop after the "first phase." The leaders then sought for step-by-step empirical confirmation of their analysis by revolutionary events, each of which would be followed by a tactical move appropriate to the next step.

Lenin carried apriorist analysis furthest[8] by this list of the stages of revolution, written at the end of 1905:

(1) the workers' movement rouses the proletariat and awakens the liberal bourgeoisie, 1895-1901-2

(2) the workers' movement passes to open struggle and carries the latter along with it, 1902-5

(3) the workers' movement is in direct revolution, while the liberal bourgeoisie is thinking about compromise, but its radical elements are inclined to enter an alliance with the proletariat in order to go farther, 1905

(4) the workers' movement is victorious in the democratic revolution, the liberals temporize, the peasants as well as the radical republican intelligentsia actively assist. The uprising of the peasants is successful, the power of the landlords is broken (Revolutionary democratic dictatorship of proletariat and peasantry)

(5) the liberal bourgeoisie becomes counterrevolutionary, along with the rich and much of the middle peasantry

(6) the Russian proletariat and the European proletariat organize the revolution.

Of course Lenin elsewhere gives slightly different predictions, of simply a dual revolution (bourgeois and socialist), or of three stages (the "democratic revolution" being separated into two parts, "bourgeois"—limited monarchy, and "democratic"—republic).

These prognoses are not, however, contradictory. They all deal with the expected transition from capitalism to socialism and a corresponding shift in political forms appropriate thereto.

Lenin's list of six steps is phrased in terms of economic groups, but one can easily substitute party names by interpolation based on his other writings. In (4), for example, clearly he expects SR's to support him, the KD's to "temporize"; in (5), the KD's become "counterrevolutionary." In other writings of 1905 he puts it more bluntly. The liberals were expected to seek an accord with Tsarism in order to betray the revolution. This would not for a time involve armed counterrevolution—rather because the liberals pusillanimously shrank before real action than because they lacked hostility to the revolutionaries. Lenin's immediate expectations for 1905 can be summarized; the proletariat, supported by the peasantry, not needing or capable of getting the aid of the liberals, would overthrow Autocracy by force. This would bring about a "bourgeois-democratic revolution."

The Mensheviks interpreted the classic Marxist schema of dual revolution in a semi-feudal state in a less complex fashion. The "first phase" would mark a united onslaught of the masses on Tsarism. In this, the proletariat would lead, supported by the liberal bourgeoisie, utilizing to the best advantage the peasants' revolutionism directed chiefly towards land seizure. Autocracy would be destroyed; the bourgeosie must and would come to power. The proletarian party would go into opposition, utilizing the newly-won freedom to organize the workers for the socialist phase of the struggle.

The Socialist Revolutionaries believed, in contrast to some Marxists, that the Russian bourgeoisie was already in a favored position under Tsarism. Therefore the "first phase" would not be "bourgeois," but rather simply a "political" or "toilers'" revolution, although the bourgeoisie, especially its radical elements, would assist the proletarian vanguard, aided by the mass army of the peasantry, in overthrowing the Tsardom by means of an uprising. A democratic republic would then be established, land would be "socialized," and workers and peasants together would begin to fight for real socialism.

The Kadets foresaw a united onslaught of all classes on Autocracy. The proletariat and peasantry would follow the political lead of the better educated liberal bourgeoisie in massed popular demonstrations and action calculated to compel the surrender of Tsarism. A constitutional democracy (whether monarchy or republic) would then be set up. A ministry responsible to a freely elected parliament would govern the nation, aiming at the creation of an ideal state under which liberty and social justice would be the means for weaning the masses away from the Marxist teachings of violence and seizure. Being deprived of mass backing for their insurrectionism, the socialists might then take honorable places as parliamentary representatives of the laboring classes in Russia's legislature, as they had done already in France and Germany.

5.

Thus ran the expectations of Lenin, Martov, Chernov, and Miliukov. The analyses were similar enough so that all could and did say that they shared a common objective, that of a bourgeois/toilers'/democratic revolution which would destroy Tsarism and introduce liberty and democracy, although afterwards they would tread different paths.

In 1905, however, their very apriorism forced them apart in their tactics before the "first phase" was over. Lenin, dragging the Socialist Revolutionaries with him, declared that although the Constituent Assembly must be the instrument for bringing about democracy (which all the opposition believed), such an assembly if convened by the old regime would be a mockery and a sham. It could only be summoned by a revolutionary government which must have seized power by force. Autocracy could not consent peacefully to abolish itself; it must be destroyed by violence. One may suggest, on the basis of the evidence presented, that even more important to Lenin was another consideration. An uprising was necessary not only to root out Autocracy, but to prevent peaceful passage of the power into the hands of the liberals. If this should occur anyway, said Lenin, "bourgeois democracy," not real democracy, would be introduced. His tactics of uprising were directed against Miliukov as much or more than against Nicholas II.

Miliukov, on the contrary, believed the Constituent Assembly would and ought to develop naturally out of a Duma summoned by the old regime, as in the case of the French Revolution. An uprising was not necessary in order to compel the summoning of a Constituent Assembly. More important, it would be intrinsically harmful, because it would precipitate an armed clash in which the whole opposition—not only the revolutionaries—would be crushed swiftly by superior force, leaving Tsarism more firmly entrenched than ever. The Kadets remembered the Paris Commune of 1871. Force, moreover, did not create a propitious atmosphere for democracy to develop. A military dictatorship either by the Tsar's ministers or by a revolutionary junta (for a class or a "class and a half" could not dictate, whatever the intention of Lenin's slogan) would bring only suffering and destruction. With this reasoning the Mensheviks agreed to some extent, though they admitted one possibility was that an armed uprising would lead to a Constituent Assembly. The other possibility, they said, was that it would be summoned by the old regime. In this they agreed with Miliukov.

Thus, in the very midst of the "bourgeois" revolution, a fundamental conflict arose within the ranks of the opposition as to the revolution's nature and objectives. Not the question of a Constituent Assembly or freedom or social reform divided Lenin and Chernov from Miliukov and Martov. It was overtly the problem of the means by which these good things were to be attained: armed uprising or parliamentary struggle. The choice of method resulted directly from the conflicting sociology of the two sides. It depended on the desire of each to permit or prevent the liberals from coming to power, and thereby to prevent or permit swift transition from "bourgeois" to "socialist," from political to social, revolution.

6.

The Socialist Revolutionaries were quite open about their desire to use the first phase for the purpose of gaining "commanding heights," to use a phrase of the 1920's, from which to advance directly to socialism. Ever since the old populist days they had fixed their eyes firmly to the final goal of social revolution. Lenin wrote of swift passage from the bourgeois to socialist phase, but he never mentioned making the bourgeois phase semi-socialist in order to facilitate the transition. It has remained for Soviet historians to assert openly that Pokrovskii was wrong when he called 1905 a "purely bourgeois" revolution. E. Iaroslavskii writes[9] that in it "bourgeois revolution developed into socialist revolution," and that the proletariat fought with all its might to achieve that conversion. He continues, "Lenin did not attack and could not attack the defenders of conversion of the bourgeois-democratic revolution into a socialist one, because Lenin himself considered possible and inevitable the passage into socialist revolution." Iaroslavskii is in general right. By 1905 the "Chinese wall" separating the two phases in the old Marxist scheme of Plekhanov had vanished from Lenin's mind. He was bent on what Trotsky had called "uninterrupted revolution" (though his calculation of the social forces involved differed from Trotsky's.) The bourgeois would not be allowed to nourish themselves on the fruits of revolution. They were not even to be left to a hungry isolation. They were to be destroyed along with Autocracy.

In other words, the doctrine of "dual revolution," on which united action of the opposition leaders depended, had by 1905 lost its original meaning. There was no longer any question, practically speaking, of two successive phases, but of two simultaneous assaults. These assaults, moreover, had incompatible objectives. This was apparently not fully understood by many of the intellectuals in 1905, for the old phraseology ("march apart, strike together," et cetera) often continued to be used, and this served to conceal the divergent goals.

The opposition leaders, however, cannot be accused of entirely failing to see the real situation. As 1905 wore on, there were ever more signs that Lenin and Miliukov were seeking different things. If we may use the names of the two leaders as shorthand for the forces of the intelligentsia involved, the situation was the following: Lenin and Miliukov both saw their differences. Yet at the same time Lenin could not afford to see that he could not win without Miliukov, since he had already decided to do without him and had in so doing doomed the efforts of both. More than that, however, Lenin and Miliukov each believed himself to be right. Each relied on the course of history, which he believed he had accurately estimated to bring victory to his own strategy and compel anything from unwilling acquiescence to grudging support of the inevitable outcome. The Kadets did not seriously fear the prospect of socialist revolution. Since an event was unknown to modern European history, they believed it simply Utopian, and as such a disruptive influence on the attempt to deal successfully with reality. Since 90 per cent of the Russian people belonged to the "bourgeoisie," as Miliukov wrote, why should they worry about the triumph of the proletariat? It was, in the democratic era to come, simply a dream which reality was bound to shatter.

Lenin, on the other hand, was firmly convinced that the armed victory of the proletariat, supported by the peasantry, was a foregone conclusion. He believed that this victory was in sight by the end of 1905, and that the Kadets' alternative was the one which was absurd, impossible, and therefore only a means of sabotaging and delaying the predetermined outcome. The "constitutional illusions" of the Kadets must soon be exposed by events as false, and the exposure would inexorably lead to Bolshevik success. He did not underestimate the harm they could do in the short run, however, to his theoretical patterns. So he concentrated his wrath upon the Kadets. In his own mind Tsarism was already beaten—and in this the whole opposition more or less concurred. The triumph would be his, unless Miliukov, not Nicholas II, was able to circumvent it. Thus it was the liberals who were, to his way of thinking, the greatest villains of all.

7.

Into the wheels of the rationalist machinery of the opposition leaders, already perceptibly out of gear, the Tsar unwittingly threw a tremendously effective wrench in the form of the October Manifesto.

The Manifesto was met by a moment of wild public rejoicing—in which the four parties shared for no other reason than because, as the first real step back of Tsarism, it was a good omen for the victory to come. None of the parties was satisfied by the Manifesto. It did not even lead any of them to alter tactics. The Kadets and Mensheviks had already resolved to utilize the Bulygin Duma to the best possible advantage, and they went to the Witte Duma with similar intentions. The Bolsheviks and Socialist Revolutionaries rejected the one no less than the other.

What had happened? Something important, all were convinced; but what exactly, their apriorist patterns failed to reveal. Lenin looked for the immediate retreat of the bourgeoisie, although this was not supposed to occur until a limited monarchy was attained —and he was quite certain it had not been and that there existed no constitution. The SR's at first thought liberty might be at hand, although it could not be until the "political revolution" was over— and then they decided that it was not, and boycotted the Duma. The Mensheviks immediately scented bourgeois treachery, although it was not to come until the first phase was past; they then decided that a Kadet ministry might bring the bourgeoisie to power, though that could not come before the overthrow of Autocracy. The Kadets were certain that no constitution had been granted; they repeated this over and over, and made it the basis of their tactics in the I Duma, to the intense chagrin of Maklakov and their own Right wing. And yet they gradually altered their attitude to the legislature, talking less and less about "parliamentary struggle" and more and more about "constitutionalism" and "legislative work" until they came virtually to regard the Duma as a parliament and the Fundamental Laws as a constitution, although neither was supposed to be possible while Autocracy remained.

By the odd document which Witte persuaded him to sign, Nicholas II thus disrupted the political patterns of his intellectual enemies and set off premature cries of "treachery" on the one side and premature moves toward compromise on the other. The division among the intellectuals had repercussions on the broader segments of the population whose support they could command. An armed uprising was undertaken by the extreme Left in Moscow, though denounced by both Plekhanov and Miliukov as an error in tactics. The workers in Presnia were put down by the Tsarist army. Once that was done, Plekhanov and Miliukov declared that it was not only unwise, but impossible, to try to repeat the Moscow episode. Kadets and Mensheviks then turned to the parliamentary struggle. Since the Bolsheviks and SR's would not assist the fight in the Duma while they believed an uprising still possible, the Kadets were deprived of the support of the powerful organized workers of the capitals, the most effective manifestation of popular opposition feeling in Russia. Thus they were finally obliged to seek for popular support among other social forces.

The most formidable of these, the Kadets hoped, would be the peasantry. If, as Stalin says,[10] "the history of this period is the history of the struggle of the Kadets (liberal bourgeoisie) and Bolsheviks (proletariat) for the peasantry," then the Kadets certainly bested their rivals. But they proved unable to turn the peasants' passive support into active resistance, and the sympathy of the rural masses was not enough to compel the Tsar to accept the Duma's land law. In part this was because of the difficulty of organizing the peasants at all at the "grass roots" level, in part it was due to the weakness of their Duma representatives, the Trudoviks. Arising suddenly in the vacuum created by the SR boycott, the Trudoviks proved unable to rally the kind of political influence the SR's might have done, and were able to do later. The Mensheviks in the Duma were too feeble. The Kadet leadership of the Duma hung suspended in the air.

While there was disorder in the streets, the parties had kept nominal unity. But when the disorder was suppressed and a parliament was summoned, the Bolsheviks and Socialist Revolutionaries refused to maintain unity and denounced those who still wished to struggle as best they could for "betraying" the revolutionary cause, and, through the fostering of "constitutional illusions," lessening the chances of armed uprising. It was not that Lenin and Chernov could take the mass of the proletariat and peasantry along with them in this tactic, but that the only people from those social groups who could be politically effective were those who supported the Bolshevik and SR parties—there were no other parties of significance operating, except for the Mensheviks, who did not act decisively, in part out of unwillingness to split the "working-class front." The Kadets were at first unwilling to try to summon the masses to resistance in their behalf, and when at the end of the Duma they became willing, they proved unable to do so. Thus parliamentary struggle failed in 1906 just as had armed uprising in 1905, and the First Duma was dissolved without violence.

There was summoned a Second Duma, but it was hopelessly divided between the extreme Left and the extreme Right, with the Kadets a helpless minority between them. The Second Duma had the weakness of the First but not its unity.[11] There followed, on 3 June 1907, a second dissolution and a drastic and illegal revision of the electoral law. In consequence, the opposition was cut down sufficiently so that in the Third and Fourth Dumas the government was able to work, at least part of the time, with a Duma majority. The latter two Dumas accomplished a great deal, and the Prime Minister from the time of the dissolution of the First Duma until the next to the last year of the Third, Peter Stolypin, provided a policy. This policy envisaged the attainment of a stable polity in Russia under which a constitutional monarchy supported by a small-holding peasantry would achieve reform while avoiding revolution. Stolypin accomplished a great deal toward the goal of helping the peasant to realize "land," though he seemed less interested in "liberty." He could not and did not conciliate any of the intelligentsia, who from SR's through SD's to Kadets would have opposed any Tsarist government, feared that his regime might postpone revolution, and scorned his social goal of creating an independent peasantry as impractical or pernicious.

As a result of the Revolution of 1905, the intelligentsia and the government both realized the people were not with them. But it was the government which made the headway with the peasantry; the revolutionaries made none until 1917. After 1906 Stolypin made the decision to destroy the commune and establish farms. The revolutionaries produced no new ideas at all, and thus in effect were found lamenting the weakening of the commune, though many of them decried its influence. If the fate of Russia could have been settled by reference to the peasantry alone, Stolypin might have succeeded. It is probably true that he realized how important the intelligentsia in Russia were and might be, but he certainly was unable to influence them. Men like Izgoev, who evaluated the experience of 1905 in terms of the shortcomings of the intellectuals, were widely regarded by their fellows as renegades and reactionaries. During the interval between revolutions, the government changed some, and succeeded in changing the peasantry still more. The intelligentsia did not change. They remained as a whole positivist and rationalist, committed not only to the root-and-branch destruction of the Old Regime, but also to some kind of socialist order for the people. Herzen had written long ago, "If thought once masters a man, he ceases to discuss whether the thing is practicable, and whether the enterprise is hard or easy."[12] The Russian intelligentsia found their chosen enterprise as easy in 1917 as it was hard in 1905. There was a third chapter to this revolutionary story, however, which began to loom on the horizon during the summer of 1917 and began to be written from October of that year.

8.

In retrospect the story of 1905 appears as the story of the first Popular Front. Of course there had been earlier cases when various opposition groups cooperated against a government before and during a Revolution and fell out in its course. Such is the history of most revolutions. The difference was the presence for the first time of Communism (at that time called Bolshevism) as an organized force in a political struggle. The Popular Front idea was the one formulated by the Seventh Congress of the Comintern in 1935 as a means of securing Communist objectives through participation with non-Communist parties and groups in governments.[13] There was never any doubt about the significance of the Popular Front device. It was intended to facilitate the attainment of Communist hegemony, and never to entail any sort of friendly cooperation. It was aimed at exposing the false claims of rival parties to represent the interests of the people or some segment thereof. The Popular Front idea of 1935, which was either originated by or sanctioned by Stalin, went further in the direction of association with non-Communists than Lenin was willing to go in 1905. As has been noted, Lenin was unwilling to consider any sort of cooperation with the Kadets, although he appeared willing to cooperate with the Socialist Revolutionaries or Trudoviks as junior partners—and indeed the

Mensheviks themselves were similarly regarded. Nevertheless Lenin recognized that the liberals, or some of them, perhaps in spite of themselves, might have an effect from time to time in bringing closer the sort of end result which he sought. Lenin's attitude was not clear enough to the liberals in 1905 so that they were able to recognize that a "Popular Front" with Communists was fundamentally impossible over any period of time. It was the dogma of the time, however, that for the opposition parties there was "no enemy on the Left." The corollary was that it was the duty of all opposition parties to do all possible to maintain unity, without compromising any essentials of their positions. In retrospect it can be observed that the Kadets' mistake, if they were to assure any possibility of liberal survival in a future democratic Russia, was not in the extent to which they compromised their fidelity to the revolutionaries, but in the degree to which they maintained it. This not only alienated some of their own members and capable people to their immediate Right, but made impossible their securing a position in the government. Unity with the immediate Right, after years of experience in the Dumas, was accepted in the Progressive Bloc of 1915, but it was too late for the Kadets to carry with them any sizeable number of the intelligentsia. Their identification of themselves with the political forces of the Fourth Duma at this late date may have played a significant role in enabling their opponents to attack them successfully in 1917, and to deprive them of any opportunity to achieve broad popular support in the final struggle. The Kadets, in rejecting the overtures of bureaucrats in 1905 and 1906, saw themselves as poised unhappily between the intelligentsia and the government. They did not consider the possibility of relying on the Russian people to the extent of identifying themselves with the peasant's, rather than the intellectual's, interpretation of "land and liberty." It ought to have been the pride of the Russian liberal party to lead Russia toward the solution of Western European—or American—type smallholding. But the spell of the commune,[14] praised by Westernizers and Slavophiles alike and their successors ever since, even when they decided that the commune must be changed, hung over the Kadets as well as the other opposition parties.

This is not to say that the voice of the muzhik was raised in 1905 in favor of the freedom to farm, liberated from the impedimenta of commune and bureaucracy alike. He usually knew only the way of extensive agriculture, and under such conditions the sole conceivable solution was to his mind more land. Thus tremendous peasant support was given to the Kadets in the First Duma. It can be said that the Kadets in the substance of their draft land law did not go beyond the agricultural comprehension of the peasant, in concentrating their efforts upon enlarging the land held by the peasants at the expense of the gentry, and failing to bring about any reform because they insisted upon that particular one and yet were not strong enough to carry it into force. The Kadets adhered to the idea of confiscation, however, not primarily because the peasant clamored for it, but because the idea remained the touchstone of their "revolutionariness." It was with an eye not so much on the village as on the rest of the intelligentsia, in and out of the Duma, that the Kadets clung to their original land program and were crushed along with that program when the First Duma was dismissed. As Brutzkus says, all "the democratic elements regarded compulsory alienation of land as the sole correct method for the resolution of the agrarian problem, and took upon themselves the defense of the commune . . ." [15] The Kadets were not orthodox socialists, of course, but their agrarian program, in Brutzkus's words, "though softening certain details of the populist program which were especially harmful to the economy, in essence held to the same basis." [16] They were thus too much influenced by socialism to be content with a French-Revolutionary type of land settlement. Their agricultural spokesmen, such as Manuilov, were found during the Stolypin era to be emphasizing the vitality of the commune and criticizing the conception of small-holding, although their liberal principles should have led them to attack the former and support the latter.

The task of leading the peasant toward the better life which intensive and diversified agriculture might secure him, was accordingly left to Stolypin, who was no supporter of political democracy, and whom the Kadets distrusted in principle as a bureaucrat.[17] They themselves were left with little to say to the peasant in 1917, and the job of solving the "land question" was left to the Socialist Revolutionaries. Their program, like that of the Kadets, was more often than not interpreted by the peasants as implying individual cultivation if not ownership, despite its socialist coloration. The Bolshevik program did not have that advantage, and Lenin recognized as much when he was finally constrained to steal the Socialist Revolutionary thunder and enact their land program into law in order to secure his seizure of power in October 1917. One cannot say that a genuinely liberal program of land reform was rejected by the Russian people, but rather that one was never offered them.

9.

It was the Kadets who first discovered, to their dismay, that co-operation with the Bolsheviks was impossible. The remainder of the opposition retained their illusions until 1917, believing that the liberals had been proved to be "bourgeois" and that it was therefore all the easier to maintain a common socialist front. In March 1917 even the Bolsheviks seemed to agree. Then Lenin returned, and showed by the "April Theses" where he stood and would soon persuade the Bolsheviks to stand, in opposition to "bourgeois democracy" and in favor of its overthrow. The method of "armed uprising" which he fruitlessly proposed against Tsarism in 1905 was successfully employed against the Provisional Government in October 1917. If more attention had been paid to what his intentions in 1905 were, less confusion might have been occasioned by his utterances in 1917. The moderate socialists, Mensheviks and Socialist Revolutionaries, now found themselves in the company of the Bolsheviks in the Soviets, but deprived of that company within the Provisional Government. After October 1917 the Bolsheviks removed them from the government and the Soviets alike. The full meaning of "Popular Front" became clear to all but the stubborn Left Socialist Revolutionaries,[18] and the bitter experience of a few short months was to teach them the lesson as well. This was not yet the end, and twenty years later the Old Bolsheviks were to go the way of the non-Bolsheviks. The difference was that the latter had been allowed to escape the executioner.

All of this was not inevitable in 1905. The potentiality clearly was present, but that fact is clear in retrospect as it could not have been clear to the men who were fully taken up with the practical tasks of the First Revolution. If the lesson of 1905 could have been learned in time, it surely was that liberalism in Russia depended for its survival less on the unity of the opposition parties than on its responsiveness to the needs of the people. Miliukov, Martov, and Chernov lived to see their mistake according to their different lights.

The year 1905 saw the first entry of Communism into the political arena of any nation. In fact, it was during 1905 that Communism as it has since developed first took any sort of recognizable shape. The year 1905 also saw the first attempt at a "Popular Front" with the Communists on the part of liberals and socialists. In a peasant nation whose political leaders were intellectuals, a struggle was waged some of whose features have recurred in many countries since that time. If Russia's intellectuals had studied its

CONCLUSION

own peasants and themselves more carefully, they might conceivably have been able to avoid the cataclysm which overtook them. Many peasant nations have fallen into Communist hands since the Communists learned to represent themselves as nationalists and partisans of smallholding in agriculture—that is, "land reform." It was in 1905 that Lenin learned he might have to do so in order to win, and it was in 1917 that he learned how to do so with success. The Communists have been able to "go to the people" with the message they wish to hear, although their own real message they reserve until their power is solid enough. This message is destruction of national independence and agricultural smallholding. Since they believe that extension of their power represents the attainment of the supreme good for mankind, it is not surprising that they do what is ideologically required to make possible the spread of their power, just as they continue to employ "armed uprising" and other useful devices directed toward that goal. What is surprising is that the liberals and socialists of other nations, among them peasant nations, have been so slow to study and learn the lesson of the fate of Lenin's rivals in 1905, in 1917, and since.

NOTES

I

"TO THE PEOPLE"

1 *My Past and Thoughts* (trans. by Constance Garnett; Berlin, 1921), Vol. V. pp. 330-1.

2 *Kolokol*, London, Geneva, 1857-67.

3 See N. Berdyaev, *The Origin of Russian Communism* (London, 1948), ch. 1; article by M. Tugan-Baranovsky, in *Intelligentsiia v Rossii* (St. Petersburg, 1910).

4 *Ulozhenie* of 1649, which set no time-limit for the recovery of runaway peasants.

5 Petrunkevich, *Vospominaniia, Arkhiv russkoi revoliutsii*, XII (Berlin, 1934), p. 101.

6 G. T. Robinson, *Rural Russia under the Old Regime* (New York, 1949), chs. V and VI.

7 George Pavlovsky, *Agricultural Russia on the Eve of the Revolution* (London, 1930), p. 194. Figures following from P. I. Liashchenko, *Istoriia narodnogo khoziaistva SSSR* (Moscow, 1949), Vol. II, p. 83.

8 Robinson, *op. cit.*, p. 106.

9 Liashchenko, *Ibid.*, Vol. II, pp. 168-9.

10 V. Gorn, "Krest'ianskoe dvizhenie do 1905 g." in Martov, Maslov, Potresov, eds., *Obshchestvennoe dvizhenie v Rossii v nachale XX-go veka* (St. Petersburg, 1909-14), Vol. I, p. 257.

11 Liashchenko, *Ibid.*, Vol. II, pp. 152-4.

II

TSARISM IS TOO LATE

1 *Polnoe sobranie rechei Imperatora Nikolaia II. 1894-1906* (St. Petersburg, 1906).

2 See Michael T. Florinsky, *Russia: a History and an Interpretation* (New York, 1953), Vol. II, pp. 1163-6.

3 S. Iu. Witte, *Samoderzhavie i zemstvo*, with foreword by R. N. S. (P. B. Struve) (Stuttgart, 1901).

4 "Dnevnik A. A. Polovtseva," *Krasnyi Arkhiv*, No. 3, 1923, p. 109.

5 See D. N. Shipov, *Vospominaniia i dumy o perezhitom* (Moscow, 1918), ch. 7.

6 P. N. Miliukov, *Constitutional Government for Russia* (New York, 1908), p. 7.

7 V. A. Maklakov, *Vlast' i obshchestvennost' na zakatie staroi Rossii* (Paris, 1928), Vol. II, p. 360.

8 James Mavor, *An Economic History of Russia* (London, 1925), Vol. II, pp. 475-6.

9 *Stenograficheskie otchety. 1906 god. Sessiia pervaia.* Vol. I (St. Petersburg, 1906).

10 See P. N. Miliukov, *Tri popytki* (Paris, 1921).

III

THE YEAR 1898

1 Axelrod, *Bor'ba sotsialisticheskikh i burzhuaznykh tendentsii v russkom revolutsionnom dvizhenii* (Geneva, n.d.), p. 13.

2 Miliukov, *Russia and its Crisis*, p. 284.

3 See Franco Venturi, *Il populismo russo* (Torino, 1952).

NOTES

4 Quoted in Potresov, "Evoliutsiia obshchestvenno-politicheskoi mysli v pred-revoliutsionnuiu epokhu," in Martov, etc., eds., *op. cit.*, Vol. I, p. 553.
5 Burtsev, *Bor'ba za svobodnuiu Rossiiu. Moi vospominaniia. 1882-1922.* Vol. I (Berlin, 1923), p. 73.
6 See Gen. Alexandre Spiridovitch, *Histoire du Terrorisme Russe 1886-1917* (trans. from Russian by V. Lazarevski) (Paris, 1930).
7 Nicholas Rusanov, article on "Petr Lavrovich Lavrov" in *Encyclopedia of Social Sciences* (New York, 1949), Vols. 9-10, p. 201.
8 Plekhanov, Preface to *Sotsializm i politicheskaia bor'ba*, in *Sochineniia*, Vol. I (Geneva, 1905), p. 141.
9 See his *Zapiski Sotsialdemokrata* (Berlin, 1922).
10 Lenin, in *Chto delat'?* in *Sochineniia* (4th ed.) Vol. 5, p. 350; Martov, *Zapiski*, 315.
11 Quoted in E. D. Chermenskii, *Burzhuaziia i tsarizm v revoliutsii 1905-1907 gg.* (Moscow, 1939), p. 5.
12 Plekhanov, *In Defense of Marxism* (trans. by Andrew Rothstein of *K voprosu razvitiia monisticheskogo vzgliada istorii*, London, 1947), p. 297.
13 See N. Angarskii, *Legal'nyi Marksizm*, Pt. I, 1876-97 (Moscow, 1925).
14 *Chto delat'?* in *Soch.* Vol. 5, p. 334.
15 Martov, *Zapiski*, p. 328.
16 Leon Trotsky, *My Life* (London, 1930), p. 113.
17 Martov, *Zapiski*, p. 407.
18 The contention of A. S. Izgoev, *Russkoe obshchestvo i revoliutsiia* (Moscow, 1910), p. 4.
19 "Osnovnaia oshibka abstraktnoi teorii kapitalizma Marksa," *Nauchnoe obozrenie*, May 1899; Struve "Protiv ortodoksii," *Zhizn'*, Oct. 1899, and "Die Marxistische Theorie der sozialen Entwicklung," *Brauns Archiv*, 1899.
20 Letter of May 19, 1899, in Potresov and Nikolaevskii, eds., *Sotsial-demokraticheskoi dvizhenie v Rossii. Materialy.* Vol. I (Moscow, Leningrad, 1927), p. 44.
21 See his own remarks in preface to *Ot marksizma k idealizmu* (1903).
22 Plekhanov retort to article by "Old Narodovolist" in *Letuchii listok:* in *Novyi pokhod protiv russkoi sotsial-demokratii* (Geneva, 1897).
23 Letter to Potresov, Jan. 26, 1899, *Letters of Lenin* (trans. by E. Hill and D. Mudie, London, 1937) p. 72.
24 Lenin in *Ot kakogo nasledstva my otkazyvaemsia?* in *Soch.* Vol. II.
25 *Russia and its Crisis*, p. 224.
26 A. A. Kizevetter, *Na rubezhe dvukh stoletii* (*Vospominaniia 1881-1914*) (Prague, 1929), p. 89.
27 *Blizhaishie zadachi zemstva*, text in *Iz zapisok*, p. 453.
28 See Maklakov, *Vlast' i obshchestvennost'*, Vol. II, p. 287 ff.
29 See I. P. Belokonskii, *Zemskoe dvizhenie* (2nd ed., Moscow, 1914).
30 Maklakov, *Vlast' i obshchestvennost'*, Vol. I, p. 140.
31 According to Belokonskii, used first in speech by Vice-Governor Kondoidi of Samara in 1899.
32 See note II/3 above.

IV

THE POPULISTS REFURBISHED

1 From *Protokoly I S"ezda Partii Sotsialistov-Revoliutsionerov* (1906), p. 136.
2 O. Radkey, *The Party of the Socialist-Revolutionaries and the Russian Revolution of 1917* (unpublished dissertation for Harvard University, 1939), Ch. 4.
3 V. Chernov, *Zapiski Sotsialista-Revoliutsionera* (Berlin, 1922), p. 163.
4 Chernov, *Ibid.*, p. 275.
5 *Sozialismus und Landwirtschaft*, 1903.
6 D. Mitrany, "Marx v. the Peasant," *London Essays in Economics: in Honor of Edwin Cannan*, ed. by T. E. Gregory (London, 1927), p. 344.
7 Chernov, *Konstruktivnyi sotsializm* (Prague, 1925), p. 111.
8 Mitrany, *op. cit.*, p. 356.
9 In *Konstruktivnyi sotsializm*, p. 128.
10 Chernov, *Zapiski*, p. 169.
11 *Ibid.*, p. 276.
12 *Ibid.*, p. 336.

274

13 Chernov, *Konstruktivnyi sotsializm,* p. 111.
14 Maslov, "Narodnicheskie partii," in Mattov, etc., eds., *op. cit.,* Vol. III, p. 102.
15 "Three Who Made a Revolution; a Review Essay," (of Bertram D. Wolfe, *Three Who Made a Revolution* (New York, 1948) , *American Historical Review,* Vol. LV, No. 1 (Oct., 1949) , pp. 87-9.
16 Editorial, *Revoliutsionnaia Rossiia,* No. 3, Jan. 1902; "Stikhiinaia revoliutsiia i soznatel'nye revoliutsionery," and "Otvet 'Zare' " in No. 4, Feb. 1902.
17 "Terroristicheskii element v nashei programme," *Rev. Ros.,* Nov. 7, June 1902.
18 "Krest'ianskoe dvizhenie," *Rev. Ros.* No. 8, June 25, 1902, which replies to *Iskra,* No. 21.
19 *Iskra,* No. 24, *Rev. Ros.* replies in "Programmnye Voprosy, I," No. 11, Sept. 1902.
20 "Sel'skie rabochie v iugo-vostochnykh guberniiakh evropeiskoi Rossii," *Rabotnik,* No. 6, 1899.
21 "Programmnye voprosy, III," in *Rev. Ros.,* No. 13, Nov. 1902.
22 No. 2 *Krasnoe Znamia;* reply by *Rev. Ros.* in "Sotsial'-demokraty i sotsialisty-revoliutsionery," No. 16, 15 Jan. 1903.
23 "Po povodu rostovskikh sobytii," *Rev. Ros.* No. 15, Jan. 1903.
24 For discussion of SR agrarian program see Chapter VII.
25 "Osnovnye voprosy russkoi revoliutsionnoi programmy," *Rev. Ros.,* Nos. 32 and 33, 15 Sept. and 1 Oct. 1903.
26 "Novoe vystuplenie russkikh liberalov," *Rev. Ros.,* No. 9, July 1902.
27 "Oppozitsiia ego Velichestva i g. von-Plehve," *Rev. Ros.,* No. 13, Nov. 1902.
28 Reply to No. 3 *Ozvobozhdenie,* in "Russkii liberalizm i dvoriantsvo, kak soslovie," *Rev. Ros.,* No. 11, Sept. 1902.
29 "Sostav liberal 'noi partii," *Rev. Ros.,* No. 33, 1 Oct. 1903.
30 "Iz dnevnika chitatelia," *Rev. Ros.,* No. 38, 15 Dec. 1903.
31 "Agrarnaia programma russkoi sotsial'-demokratii," *Rev. Ros.,* No. 38, 15 Dec. 1903.
32 "Proekt programmy partii S-Rov," *Rev. Ros.,* No. 46, 5 May 1904.
33 Documents published in *Rev. Ros.,* No. 56, 5 Dec. 1904.
34 According to article, "Sotsialisty-revoliutsionery i nesotsialisticheskaia demokratiia," same issue of *Rev. Ros.*
35 Konni Zilliacus, *The Russian Revolutionary Movement* (trans.; London, 1905) , p. 346.

V

TWO KINDS OF MARXISTS

1 Bertram D. Wolfe, *Three Who Made a Revolution* (New York, 1948), p. 248.
2 Martov, *Zapiski,* p. 398.
3 *Rabochaia Mysl', Otdel'noe Prilozhenie,* Sept. 1899.
4 Refers to the orthodox Marxist emigre Group for the Emancipation of Labor.
5 *Popiatnoe napravlenie v russkoi S-Dii,*" *Soch.,* Vol. 4.
6 *Protest rossiiskikh S-Dov* (which also contains text of *Credo*), *Soch.,* Vol. 4.
7 Proposed by Lenin in letter to Potresov, 27 June 1899, in *Letters* (Hill and Mudie trans.)
8 From *Zadachi russkikh S-Dov,* in *Soch.,* Vol. 2, p. 303 etc.
9 P. B. Axelrod, *K voprosu o sovremennykh zadachakh i taktike russkikh S-Dov* (Geneva, 1898) .
10 The I Congress of Russian Social Democratic Labor Party, March 1898.
11 F. I. Dan, *Proiskhozhdenie bol'shevizma* (New York, 1946) , p. 308.
12 *Kak chut' ne potukhla "Iskra"?* in *Soch.,* Vol. 4, p. 316.
13 Quoted by Potresov in *op. cit.* from Martov, etc., eds., *op. cit.,* Vol. I, pp. 615-6.
14 Letter of 30 Jan. 1901, in *Letters* (Hill and Mudie trans.) .
15 Called the Group "Social-Democrat."
16 Editorial, *Rabochee Delo,* No. 1, April 1899.
17 *"Vademecum" dlia redaktsii "Rabochego Dela"* (Geneva, 1900) . Lenin's praise of it in letter to Krupskaia, Sept. 1900, *Letters* (Hill and Mudie trans.) .
18 *Chto delat'?* in *Soch.,* Vol. 5.

19 Preface to *Der deutsche Bauernkrieg* (3rd ed., 1875), cited in Lenin, Vol. 5, p. 343.

20 Letter to Krupskaia, Sept. 1900, in *Letters*. "Struve-freundliche Partei" mentioned in Krupskaia, *Memories of Lenin 1893-1917* (trans. of 2d. Russian ed., 1930, London, 1942).

21 "Na poroge dvadtsatogo veka," *Iskra*, No. 2, Feb. 1901.

22 "Chego ne delat' ", *Iskra*, No. 52, 7 Nov. 1903.

23 "Burnyi mesiats," No. 3, April 1901; on the new demonstrations: "Nachalo demonstratsii," No. 13, 2 Jan. 1902; on the " revolutionary year" in "Revoliutsionnyi god," No. 40, 15 May 1903.

24 See his articles in Nos. 2-3 and 4 of *Zaria* against Bulgakov, Chernov, and other critics in agrarian theory.

25 Lenin, *Razvitie kapitalizma v Rossii* in *Soch.*, Vol. 3, p. 145.

26 "Rabochaia partiia i krest'ianstvo," No. 3, April 1901.

27 "Pochemu S-Dia dolzhna ob"iavit' reshitel'nuiu i besposhchadnuiu voinu S-Ram?", in *Soch.*, Vol. 6, p. 151.

28 "Revoliutsionnyi avantiurizm," *Iskra* Nos. 23 and 24, 1 Aug. and 1 Sept. 1902.

29 "Vul'garnyi sotsializm i narodnichestvo," *Iskra* No. 27, 1 Nov. 1902. Plekhanov's reply to SR's in "Proletariat i krest'ianstvo,' *Iskra*, Nos. 32, 33, 34, 35, 15 Jan., 1 Feb., 15 Feb., 1 Mar. 1903.

30 *K derevenskoi bednote*, *Soch.*, Vol. 6.

31 "Samoderzhavie i zemstvo" in Nos. 2 and 4, Feb and May 1901. Lenin's reply: "Goniteli zemstva i Annibaly liberalizma," *Zaria*, No. 2-3, Dec. 1901.

32 Refers to the "oath" liberals were spoken of as taking to overthrow Autocracy, as Hannibal had sworn not to rest until Rome was destroyed. The use of this phrase in the Russian situation apparently dates from Herzen.

33 "Politicheskaia agitatsiia i 'Klassovaia tochka zreniia,' " *Iskra* No. 16, 1 Feb. 1902.

34 "Programma russkikh liberalov," No. 23, 1 Aug. 1902.

35 "Nasushchnye zadachi nashego dvizheniia," No. 1, Dec. 1900.

36 According to Martov *Iskra* began publishing 4,000 copies an issue but by 1903 was turning out 13-15,000, the greater proportion of which went to Russia.

37 See accounts by Lenin in first part of *Soch.*, Vol. 7; *Shag vpered, dva shaga nazad*, in same volume; and Wolfe, *Three Who Made a Revolution*, Ch. 14.

38 "Ob agitatsionnykh zadachakh nashei partii," *Iskra* No. 43, 1 July 1903.

39 Only to return at the IV Congress at Stockholm in 1906.

40 From *Bor'ba s osadnym polozheniem*, 1904.

41 "Chego ne delat' " in *Iskra*, No. 52, 7 Nov. 1903.

42 "Pochemu ia vyshel iz redaktsii "Iskry"?, *Soch.*, Vol. 7.

43 *Istoricheskoe polozhenie i vzaimnoe otnoshenie liberal'noi i sotsialisticheskoi demokratii v Rossii* (Geneva, 1898).

44 Martov, *Zapiski*, p. 399; Lenin, in letter to Potresov of 26 Jan. 1899 in *Letters*, wrote, "In my opinion 'utilize' is much more accurate and suitable than support and union" with the liberal opposition.

45 *My Life*, p. 142. His brochure of 1904: *Nashi politicheskie zadachi* (Geneva, 1904).

46 In *My Life* he recounts his arguments with leading Mensheviks, especially Zasulich, who were placing great hopes in the liberals; but he called for "uncompromising resistance" to liberal attempts at gaining mass support.

47 "Ob"edinenie rossiiskoi S-Dii i ee zadachi," Nos. 55 and 57, Dec. 1903 and 15 Jan. 1904; "Tsentralizm ili Bonapartizm?" No. 65, 1 May 1904. Axelrod quote is from article in No. 55 cited.

48 "O kruzhkovom Marksizm i ob intelligentskoi S-Dii," *Iskra*, No. 78, 20 Nov. 1904.

49 "Probuzhdenie demokratii i nashi zadachi," No. 58, 25 Jan. 1904.

50 "Chto sluchilos'?" in *Zaria*, No. 1, April 1901.

51 "Vsegda v men'shinstve," *Zaria* No. 2-3, Dec. 1901.

52 See, for example, "Novye soiuzniki 'S-Rov,' " *Iskra* No. 67, 1 June 1904.

53 "S narodom ili protiv naroda?" in *Iskra* No. 55, 15 Dec. 1903. After 1904 zemstvo congress: "Itogi 'Zemskogo parlamenta,' " *Iskra* No. 78, 20 Nov. 1904. *Iskra* on story of Nov. 22: "Rabochii klass i burzhuaznaia revoliutsiia," No. 79, 1 Dec. 1904.

NOTES

54 "Chto zhe dal'she?" in *Zaria*, No. 2-3, Dec. 1901.
55 "Ob"edinenie burzhuaznoi demokratii," No. 79, 1 Dec. 1904.
56 Letter to Central Committee of 10 Dec. 1903 and letter to Rakhnitov, Zemliachka, Papa, 3 Dec. 1904, both in *Letters*.
57 In Zinoviev, *Lenin* (Leningrad, 1924), p. 21.
58 *Zemskaia kampaniia i plan "Iskry", Soch.*, Vol. 7. For a Menshevik discussion of this "plan," see P. A. Garvi, *Vospominaniia Sotsialdemokrata* (New York, 1946), p. 411 ff.
59 "Voina i burokratiia" in *Pravo*, No. 39, 1904.
60 Letter to M. M. Essen, 24 Dec. 1904, *Letters*.

VI

RUSSIA GETS A LIBERAL PARTY

1 P. N. Miliukov, *God bor'by* (St. Petersburg, 1907), p. 366.
2 Translation of a Russian term (*obshchestvennye deiateli*) meaning not officials, but members of the educated class with a public interest and, usually, on good terms with the highest officials personally.
3 D. N. Shipov, *Vospominaniia i dumy* (Moscow, 1918), p. 145 ff.
4 *Ibid.*, p. 153.
5 V. A. Maklakov, *Vlast' i obshchestvennost' na zakatie staroi Rossii* (Paris, 1928), Vol. 1, p. 12.
6 Maklakov, *op. cit.*, Vol. I, p. 243.
7 I. P. Belokonskii, *Zemskoe dvizhenie* (2nd ed., Moscow, 1914), p. 92 ff.
8 See S. Smirnov, "P. N. Miliukov," in *P. N. Miliukov. Sbornik materialov po chestvovaniiu ego semidesiatiletiia. 1859-1929* (Paris, n.d.)
9 *Russia and its Crisis* (Chicago, 1905) contains these, the Crane Lectures for 1903, with some additions: see esp. pp. 521-2.
10 *God bor'by*, p. 26.
11 Quoted by Chermenskii, *Burzhuaziia i tsarism v revoliutsii 1905-1907 gg.* (Moscow, 1939), p. 42, from D. I. Shakhovskoi, "Soiuz Osvobozhdeniia," *Zarnitsy* No. 2, 1909, p. 119. "Novosiltsevian" meetings: see Belokonskii, *op. cit.*, p. 174.
12 See Shipov, *op. cit.*, p. 159-168. Maklakov's reaction: *op. cit.*, Pt. 3.
13 See text of conversations in Gurko, *op. cit.*, 691-703.
14 Shipov, *op. cit.*, p. 205.
15 "Ot russkikh konstitutsionalistov," *Osvobozhdenie* No. 1, 18 June 1902; "Ot zemskikh deiatelei," same issue.
16 "Mirnaia oppozitsiia ili revoliutsionnaia bor'ba?" *Osvob.* No. 7, 18 Sept. 1902. Anton Staritskii: "Lozhnii shag," same issue.
17 "Nedodumannoe i nedoskazannoe," *Osvob.* No. 11, 18 Nov. 1902. "Old Zemstvist": "Chto-zhe nam delat?" No. 13, 19 Dec. 1902.
18 Edit., *Osvob.* No. 15, 19 Jan. 1903.
19 "K ocherednym voprosam, I" *Osvob.* No. 17, 16 Feb. 1903. Struve's comment in Pt. II of same article.
20 Edit., *Osvob.* No. 2, 2 July 1902.
21 "Po povodu odnogo uprioka," *Osvob.* No. 7, 18 Sept. 1902; addressed revolutionaries: "Liberalizm i t.n. 'revoliutsionnye' napravleniia," same issue.
22 See chapter III.
23 "Germanskie vybory," *Osvob.* No. 1 (25), 18 June 1903.
24 "K agrarnomu voprosu," *Osvob.* No. 9 (33), 19 Oct. 1903.
25 In his *Pis'ma iz derevni*, 1885.
26 "Znamenatel'nyi povorot," *Osvob.* No. 13 (37), 2 Dec. 1903, commenting on Plekhanov's article in *Iskra* No. 52.
27 "Voina," *Osvob.* No. 17 (41), 5 Feb. 1904; "Voina i patriotizm," No. 18 (42), 19 Feb. 1904. "Another writer likewise accusing": "Liberal'naia partiia i vneshniaia politika Rossii," same issue. Struve's open letter to students: in *Listok Osvobozhdeniia*, No. 1, 11 Feb. 1904.
28 "Voina i russkaia oppozitsiia, I" *Osvob.* No. 19 (43), 7 Mar. 1904. Struve's reply in Pt. II of same article.
29 "Voina i samoderzhavie," *Osvob.* No. 21 (45), 2 Apr. 1904. Maklakov's reaction: in his *op. cit.*, Vol. I, p. 240.
30 Curiously forgotten by Stalin in his comment on victory over Japan in World War II: "For forty years we, the men of the older generation, have

NOTES

waited for this day."
  [31] "Politika liberal'noi partii," *Osvob.* No. 20 (44), 19 Mar. 1904.
  [32] Criticism of editors in "Zadachi konst. partii v nastoiashchii moment," *Osvob.* No. 50, 25 June 1904; editors' reply in "Ocherednye zadachi russkikh konstitutsionalistov," No. 52, 19 July 1904.
  [33] "Otkrytoe pis'mo k Prof. Kn. E. N. Trubetskomu," *Osvob.* No. 58, 14 Oct. 1904.
  [34] "Novyi kurs," *Osvob.* No. 57, 2 Oct. 1904; following comment from "Fiasko 'novogo kursa,'", No. 60, 10 Nov. 1904.
  [35] Letter of "Nemo" in *Osvob.* No. 58, 14 Oct. 1904.
  [36] *Proiskhozhdenie bol'shevizma*, p. 319.
  [37] See Section 3 above.
  [38] Text of Union of Liberation program in *Osvob.* No. 69/70, 7 May 1905.
  [39] Maklakov, *op. cit.*, Vol. II, p. 332.
  [40] Specified consideration of "the general conditions unfavorable to the correct development of the political life of our land, which require change."
  [41] Shipov, *op. cit.*, p. 249.
  [42] See chapter III.
  [43] Maklakov, *op. cit.*, Vol. II, p. 327.
  [44] In summary the 11 Points were: (1) the present state order led to absence of the necessary trust between govt. and society; (2) govt. prevents society from considering state problems; (3) arbitrary bureaucracy destroys faith in govt.; (4) necessity of unity between Autocracy and people; (5) demand: inviolability of person and home; (6) freedom of conscience and religion, speech and press, assembly and organization; (7) equality of rights of all citizens in Empire; (8) equality of peasants with other classes before law; (9) a non-class, all-Empire organization of zemstvos; (10) a legislative assembly; (11) a plea to use 10 as means for bringing about cooperation between govt. and people.
  [45] According to Chermenskii, *op. cit.*, p. 43.
  [46] See chapter V.
  [47] At this time Mirskii told the Tsar there might be a constitution in "10 or 20 years." Compare Plehve on the same subject, in section 6 above. See Mirskii's narrative to Shipov in Shipov, *op. cit.*, p. 286.
  [48] Maklakov, *op. cit.*, Vol. II, p. 332.
  [49] See Belokonskii, *op. cit.*, p. 212; M. N. Pokrovsky, *A Brief History of Russia* (trans. by D. S. Mirsky; London, 1933), Vol. II, p. 115.
  [50] Maklakov, *op. cit.*, Vol. II, p. 332.
  [51] See Shipov, *op. cit.*, p. 266.
  [52] *Russia and its Crisis*, p. 527.
  [53] Article in *Liberation* Miliukov refers to was in No. 9 (33); cited above in note 24.
  [54] *Inter alia* by demanding a Constituent Assembly; see section 10 above.

VII

CHERNOV: A TOILER'S REVOLUTION

  [1] Cited by V. Chernov in *Rozhdenie revoliutsionnoi Rossii* (Paris, 1934), p. 239.
  [2] See B. Nikolaevskii, *Aseff: the Spy* (trans. by George Reavey; New York, 1934).
  [3] See Maslov, "Narodnicheskie partii," in Martov, etc., ed., *op. cit.*, Vol. III.
  [4] "Preddverie revoliutsii," in *Rev. Ros.* No. 58, 20 Jan. 1905. Shishko article: "La Question Agraire en Russie, VIII," *La Tribune Russe* No. 30, 20 May 1905.
  [5] "La Crise de l'Autocratie et les Coalitions Politiques," *La Tribune Russe* Nos. 22 and 23, 20 Nov. and 5 Dec. 1904. See chapter V.
  [6] *Protokoly I S"ezda Partii S-Rov* (1906), pp. 220-1.
  [7] See his *Soch.*, Vol. 6, p. 181.
  [8] Chernov, *Konstruktivnyi sotsialism* (Prague, 1925), p. 128. See also Chernov, "La Lutte de Classe dans les Campagnes," *La Tribune Russe* No. 1, 31 Jan. 1907. Chernov citing Kautsky on nationalization: in latter article, cites Kautsky, *Die Agrarfrage* (1899).
  [9] Chernov, "La Lutte de Classe dans les Campagnes," *Service de Renseignements Rapides de la Tribune Russe* No. 73-88, 30 Sept. 1906.

278

NOTES

[10] "Nekotorye itogi parizhskoi konferentsii," *Rev. Ros.* No. 61, 15 Mar. 1905. See also *Rev. Ros.* No. 56, 5 Dec. 1904. Struve article replied to is in *Osvobozhdenie*, No. 65.

[11] Chermenskii, *Burzhuaziia i tsarizm v revoliutsii 1905-1907 gg.* (Moscow, Leningrad, 1939), p. 53. SR on *Iskra's* "Plan": in article cited in *Rev. Ros.* No. 61.

[12] "Konstitutsionnoe tvorchestvo russkikh liberalov," *Rev. Ros.* No. 64, 15 April 1905; also, Party of SR's, *Gosudarstvennye idealy liberalizma* (n.p., n.d.)

[13] Supplement to *Rev. Ros.*, No. 67, 15 May 1905.

[14] "Agrarnaia programma liberalov," *Rev. Ros.*, No. 70, 1 July 1905. Compare Miliukov's article (No. 78 in *God bor'by*) on Kadet agrarian program.

[15] "La Douma et la Revolution," *La Tribune Russe*, No. 33, 10 Oct. 1905.

[16] "Eshcho o gos. Dume," *Rev. Ros.*, No. 76, 15 Oct. 1905.

[17] "Po povodu novykh podvigov 'Iskry'", Supplement to *Rev. Ros.* No. 72, 1 Aug. 1905.

[18] At the Gapon conference there were represented most of the small nationalist-socialist groups which had taken party in the October Paris Conference in addition to the SR's—but not the Union of Liberation. The conference issued a declaration similar to that adopted at Paris.

[19] "Ortodoksal'nye marksisty i krest'ianskii vopros," *Rev. Ros.*, No. 75, 15 Sept. 1905.

[20] "Novye sobytiia i starye voprosy," *Rev. Ros.*, No. 74, 1 Sept. 1905.

[21] See I. N. Steinberg, *In the Workshop of the Revolution*, New York, 1953.

VIII

LENIN: A DEMOCRATIC REVOLUTION

[1] From *Pervaia russkaia revoliutsiia 1905-1907 gg.* (Moscow, 1940), p. 4.

[2] 440,000 as against 430,000.

[3] Martow, *Geschichte der russischen Sozialdemokratie* (trans. by Alexander Stein; Berlin, 1926), p. 133.

[4] Chermenskii, *op. cit.*, p. 119.

[5] Kautsky, Jaures, and others. See "Kautskii o nashikh partiinykh raznoglasiiakh," *Iskra* No. 66, 15 May 1904.

[6] See Berlin's review of Rothstein's edition of Plekhanov, *In Defense of Materialism*, in the *Slavonic Review*, Vol. XXIII, p. 261.

[7] See especially his *1905* (trans. by Parijanine; Paris, 1923). Quotations which follow from p. 211, 55, of this book; Speech at London Congress, 12 May 1907, printed as appendix to edition cited, p. 372; and p. 894. See Wolfe, *Three Who Made a Revolution*, p. 191 ff., for a discussion of Trotsky's rationalism.

[8] Parvus first expounded a similar theory in a pamphlet, *Do 9 ianvaria*, in early 1905; see articles by both F. Mehring (reprint from *Die Neue Zeit*, No. 6) and Trotsky in *Nachalo*, No. 10, 25 Nov. 1905. Compare Trotsky, *Permanent Revolution* (Calcutta, 1947), esp. p. 28, for his retrospective remarks on the theory.

[9] Lenin, "Samoderzhavie i proletariat," *Vperiod*, No. 1, 22 Dec. 1904.

[10] "Rabochaia i burzhuaznaia demokratiia," *Vperiod*, No. 3, 11 Jan. 1905.

[11] A reference to the Potresov resolution adopted by the II Congress of 1903, as modified by the Menshevik Conference of April 1905.

[12] "Osvobozhdentsy i novoiskrovtsy, monarkhisty i Zhirondisty," *Vperiod* No. 9, 23 Feb. 1905.

[13] "Otnoshenie Ros. S.-D. Rabocheii Partii k liberalam," *Vperiod* No. 10, 2 Mar. 1905.

[14] See chapter VI.

[15] "Proletariat i burzhuaznaia demokratiia," *Vperiod* No. 10. See also Lenin, "Novyi revoliutsionnyi rabochii soiuz," *Proletarii* No. 4, 3 June 1905.

[16] "Agrarnaia programma liberalov," *Vperiod* No. 15, 7 April 1905.

[17] See note X/16.

[18] "Politicheskie sofizmy," *Vperiod* No. 18, 5 May 1905. Comment on April congress: "Sovety konservativnoi burzhuazii," *Proletarii* No. 2, 21 May 1905. On the deputation to the Tsar: "Pervye shagi burzhuaznogo predatel'stva," *Proletarii* No. 5, 13 June 1905; and "Bor'ba proletariata i kholopstvo burzhuazii," *Proletarii* No. 6, 20 June 1905.

NOTES

19 "Proletariat boretsia, burzhuaziia kradetsia k vlasti," *Proletarii* No. 10, 20 July 1905. "As a trader, a broker": "Revoliutsionnaia bor'ba i liberalnoe maklerstvo,"*Proletarii* No. 3, 27 May 1905. Reaction to September congress: "Zemskii s"ezd," *Proletarii* No. 19, 20 Sept. 1905.

20 Lenin refers to Struve's preface to Witte's memoir, *Samoderzhavie i zemstvo.*

21 "Demokraticheskie zadachi revoliutsionnogo proletariata," *Proletarii* No. 4, 3 June 1905.

22 "Proletariat i krest'ianstvo," *Vperiod* No. 11, 10 Mar. 1905.

23 "Ot narodnichestva k marksizmu," *Vperiod* No. 3, 11 Jan. 1905.

24 "Nachalo revoliutsii v Rossii," *Vperiod* No. 4, 18 Jan. 1905.

25 "O boevom soglashenii dlia vosstaniia," *Vperiod* No. 7, 8 Feb. 1905. Lenin's speech to III Congress explaining reasons: text in *Soch.*, Vol. 8, p. 384. For Menshevik attitude to the Gapon conference, see *Iskra*, No. 98, 23 April 1905.

26 Stated in 'Rev. armiia i rev. pravitel'stvo," *Proletarii* No. 7, 27 June 1905. For slogan, "rev. demo . . . ": "Rev. Demo. diktatura proletariata i krest'ianstva," *Vperiod* No. 14, 30 Mar. 1905.

27 "S-Diia i Vremennoe Revoliutsionnoe Pravitel'stvo," *Vperiod* No. 13 and 14, 23 and 30 Mar. 1905.

28 Lenin's draft of resolution in *Soch.*, Vol. 8, p. 373.

29 According to Martov, in Martov, etc., eds., *op. cit.*, Vol. III, p. 558.

30 Lenin meant, of course, the Bolsheviks.

31 Lenin used this phrase to underline the contrast between the Menshevik position and his own of consciously planned uprising, and to emphasize the alleged similarity of this conception to the "tactics-as-a-process" theory defended by the Economists of a few years earlier.

32 *Soch.*, Vol. 9, p. 29.

33 *Ibid.*, p. 30.

34 *Ibid.*, p. 79.

35 *Ibid.*, p. 94.

36 As Struve did in *Osvobozhdenie* No. 72, 8 June 1905.

37 In *God bor'by*, Article 3. Wolfe's mistake: *op. cit.*, p. 292.

38 "Burzhuaziia torguetsia s samoderzhaviem, samoderzhavie torguetsiia s burzhuaziei," *Proletarii* No. 7, 27 June 1905.

39 (Refers to the character in Gogol, *Dead Souls.*) "Boikot bulyginskoi Dumy i vosstanie," *Proletarii* No. 12, 3 Aug. 1905. Reaction to Bulygin law: "Edinenie tsaria s narodom i naroda s tsariom," *Proletarii* No. 14, 16 Aug. 1905. Approval for Union of Unions: "V khvoste u monarkhicheskoi burzhuazii ili vo glave revoliutsionnogo proletariata i krest'ianstva?" *Proletarii* No. 15, 23 Aug. 1905.

40 "Chego khotiat i chego boiatsiia nashi liberal'nye burzhua?" *Proletarii* No. 16, 1 Sept. 1905.

41 "Vstrecha druzei," *Proletarii* No. 18, 13 Sept. 1905.

42 "Uroki moskovskikh sobytii," *Proletarii* No. 22, 11 Oct. 1905.

43 *Proletarii* No. 16.

44 "Burzhuaziia spavshaia i burzhuaziia prosnuvshaiasia," *Soch.*, Vol. 9.

45 "Ravnovesie sil," *Soch.*, Vol. 9, p. 382.

IX

MARTOV: A BOURGEOIS REVOLUTION

1 "'Deviatoe ianvaria," *Iskra* No. 85, 27 Jan. 1905.

2 "V vodovorote revoliutsii," *Iskra* No. 86, 3 Feb. 1905. For discussion of Menshevik conception of role of party in 1905, by a Menshevik, see Garvi, *Vospominaniia S-Da*, p. 447 ff.

3 See *Soch.*, Vol. 9, p. 26.

4 B. I. Gorev, 'Apoliticheskie i antiparlamentskie gruppy," in Martov, etc., eds., *op. cit.*, Vol. III, p. 534.

5 "Vroz' idti, vmeste bit'," *Iskra* No. 87, 10 Feb. 1905.

6 "Narozhdenie novoi Rossii," *Iskra* No. 89, 24 Feb. 1905. "Borne on the crest": "Dvoinaia igra," *Iskra* No. 92, 10 Mar. 1905. "Liberal spirit" divided: "Tragediia liberal'noi dushi," *Iskra* No. 93, 17 Mar. 1905.

7 "Demokraty po nevole," *Iskra* No. 99, 1 May 1905. To June deputation: "Istoricheskii den'," *Iskra* No. 102, 15 June 1905.

8 Resolution of Menshevik April Conference may be reconstructed in full

NOTES

from Lenin's *Dve taktiki* in *Soch.*, Vol. 9, beginning with p. 17. Lenin's comment cited: *Ibid.*, p. 27.

9 From resolution of the Caucasian Menshevik Conference, quoted by Lenin in *Soch.*, Vol. 9, p. 75.

10 "Organizatsiia burzhuaznoi demokratii," *Iskra* No. 103, 21 June 1905.

11 "Tsarskoe popechenie o krest'ianakh," *Iskra* No. 98, 23 April 1905. On Potiomkin mutiny: "Chernomorskoe vosstanie," *Iskra* No. 104, 1 July 1905.

12 "Ne nachalo-li povorota?" *Iskra* No. 105, 15 July 1905.

13 The April zemstvo congress had already demanded the calling of a body equivalent to a Constituent Assembly, as Lenin had been willing to recognize, but the phrasing was vague. The Mensheviks attached much more importance than Lenin did to the exact terms of the liberal program, in accordance with what Lenin scornfully dubbed the "litmus-paper" theory.

14 This plan was expounded by Axelrod in the brochure *Narodnaia Duma i Rabochii S"ezd*, and further developed by a South Russian Menshevik conference in Aug. 1905. See Garvi, *op. cit.*, p. 508 ff.

15 "Oborona ili nastuplenie?" *Iskra* No. 106, 18 July 1905.

16 "Nasha taktika i Gosudarstvennaia Duma," *Iskra* No. 108, 13 July (misprint for Aug.) 1905.

17 "Liberal'nye izmeny," *Iskra* No. 111, 24 Sept. 1905.

18 "Krakh liberal'nogo bloka," *Iskra* No. 112, 8 Oct. 1905.

19 The Mensheviks preferred to talk of the *"raznochintsy"* or democrats rather than mention the Kadets by name, somewhat as Lenin was reticent about mentioning the Socialist Revolutionaries outright instead of "revolutionaries of bourgeois democracy," etc.

X
MILIUKOV: AN INSTALMENT ON REVOLUTION

1 Maklakov, *Vlast' i obshchestvennost'* Vol. II, p. 352.

2 *Features and Figures of the Past* (trans. by L. Matveev; Stanford, 1939), p. 375.

3 Although the July 4 congress of industrialists had a majority which declared a consultative assembly insufficient, this group expressed general satisfaction with the law of 6 August.

4 Shipov, *Vospominaniia*, p. 329.

5 Miliukov, *God bor'by*, p. 32. In reply to Kuzmin-Karavaev in *Rus'* No. 152.

6 *Russia and its Crisis*, p. 522.

7 Accounts of the 1905 zemstvo congresses, see Belokonskii, *Zemskoe dvizhenie*, and King, "The Liberal Movement in Russia, 1904-5," *Slavonic Review*, July 1935.

8 See P. Marc, *Au seuil du 17 octobre 1905* (Leipzig, 1914), p. 70; also Cherevanin, "Dvizhenie intelligentsii," in Martov, etc., eds., *op. cit.*, Vol. II, Pt. 2.

9 His article, "Konstitutsionno-demokraticheskaia Partiia," in Martov, etc., eds., *op. cit.*, Vol. III, p. 9.

10 Text in full in Shipov, *op. cit.*, p. 311. "Assume the rights of a Constituent Assembly": King, *loc. cit.*

11 *K mneniiu men'shinstva chastnogo soveshchaniia zemskikh deiatelei 6-8 noiabria 1904 goda*, 1905, cited in Shipov, *op. cit.*

12 G. Landau in *Syn Otechestva*, No. 51, 15 Apr. 1905.

13 "Did not frighten them": *op. cit.*, Vol. II, p. 373. Chermenskii's comment: *op. cit.*, p. 76.

14 See article by "Independent." *Osvob.* No. 74, 13 July 1905. *Russkie vedomosti* editorial referred to in No. 152, 8 June 1905.

15 Maklakov, *op. cit.*, Vol. II, p. 386; Chermenskii, *op. cit.*, p. 108.

16 The July Congress' own desires regarding the content of a constitution were shown by the adoption of the draft "Basic Law of the Russian Empire," first published in *Russkie vedomosti* No. 180, 6 July 1905; text is reprinted in Belokonskii, *op. cit.*

17 "Palach naroda," *Osvob.* No. 64, 12 Jan. 1905.

18 Text in *Osvob.* No. 69/70, 7 May 1905.

19 "Kak ne poteriat' sebia?" *Osvob.* No. 69/70; Struve reply in "Kak naiti sebia?" in No. 71, 18 May 1905.

NOTES

20 "Raskol v russkoi sotsialdemokratii," *Osvob.* No. 72, 8 June 1905.
21 " 'Soiuz osvob.' i drugie politicheskie partii," *Osvob.* No. 74, 13 July 1905.
22 *God bor'by,* p. 48 ff.
23 *Ibid.,* p. 67-8.
24 "Itti ili ne itti v Gos. Dumu?" *Osvob.* No. 75, 6 Aug. 1905: "Iz ruk tsaria iz ruk Mikado i Anglii," No. 76, 2 Sept. 1905. Contributor cited: "Lzhe-konstitutsiia i forma dal'neishei bor'by," same issue. Struve's reply: "O Gos. Duma," No. 77, 13 Sept. 1905.
25 "Gos. Duma i zadachi demokraticheskoi partii," *Osvob.* No. 78/79, 5 Oct. 1905.
26 The Kadet Congress formally declared its solidarity with the strike on 14 October.
27 "K obrazovaniiu K-D Partii," *Osvob.* No. 78/79.
28 See *The Origin of Russian Communism* (London, 1948), p. 129.
29 Text in *God bor'by,* p. 97 ff.
30 Vinaver, *Nedavnee. Vospominaniia i Kharakteristiki* (3rd ed.; Paris, 1926), p. 137.
31 Pares, *My Russian Memoirs* (London, 1931), p. 91. Kokoshkin: his *Respublika,* p. 5-6, cited in Vinaver, op. cit., p. 139.
32 *God bor'by,* p. 165.
33 Quoted by Maklakov, *op. cit.,* Vol. III, p. 431. Chermenskii: *op. cit.,* p. 142.
34 Miliukov so declared at the I Congress. *God bor'by,* p. 101.

XI

THE SR'S IN A QUANDARY

1 Vladimir Zenzinov, *Iz zhizni revoliutsionera* (Paris, 1919), p. 16.
2 In interview in *Rus'* No. 22, 17 Nov. 1905.
3 Nikolaevskii, *Aseff: the Spy,* p. 128.
4 See Burtsev, *Bor'ba za svobodnuiu Rossiiu.*
5 S. Chernomordik, *Moskovskoe vooruzhennoe vosstanie v dekabre 1905 goda* (Moscow, Leningrad, 1926), p. 199. Zenzinov's activities: see his *op. cit.,* Ch. 6.
6 Chernov, *Proshloe i nastoiashchee* (St. Petersburg, 1906), p. 28.
7 Editorial, *Syn Otechestva,* No. 240, 27 Nov. 1905.
8 Exhorting the people to demand coin payments, withdraw bank deposits in gold, and refuse to pay taxes or redemption payments.
9 *Protokoly,* pp. 1-4. A month earlier Rubanovich: in *Rus'* interview cited above.
10 In first issue of *Syn Otechestva* under the new editorship, 15 Nov. 1905.
11 See Maslov, "Narodnicheskie partii," in Martov, etc., eds., *op. cit.,* Vol. III, p. 151 ff. For Makhaevists, see Gorev, "Apoliticheskie i antiparliamentskie gruppy," *Ibid.*
12 Gorev article, p. 523.
13 Lenin, "Es-erovskie men'sheviki," *Soch.,* Vol. 11.
14 In *Proshloe i nastoiashchee.*
15 *Service de Renseignements Rapides de la Tribune Russe,* No. 3-14, 3 April 1906.
16 "Konstitutsionalisty-li nashi 'konstitutsionalisty'?" *Znamia truda,* No. 1, 1 July 1907.
17 Text in *Gos. Duma. Stenograficheskie Otchety. Sessiia Pervaia.* Vol. I, p. 1153 ff.
18 In contrast to the Trudovik project, which was based on a "labor norm." That is, the SR project aimed at enough land to yield each family the income needed for a "healthy life," although it also set as a maximum to be held the area of land workable by a single family—the "labor norm" idea.
19 Text in *Steno. Otchety,* Vol. I, p. 560 ff. Petrunkevich demanded: *Ibid.,* p. 1142.
20 See Spiridovitch. *Histoire du Terrorisme Russe,* Ch. 12, based on Zubelevitch. *Cronstadt en 1906.*
21 *Service de Renseignements Rapides de la Tribune Russe.* No. 99-118, Nov.-Dec. 1906.

NOTES

XII

THE ENEMY OF THE WORKING CLASS

1 Krupskaia, *Memories of Lenin.*
2 Cited in this connection by Trotsky, *1905*, p. 180.
3 Quoted by James Mavor, *An Economic History of Russia* (London, 1925), Vol. II p. 490.
4 Chernomordik, *op. cit.*, p. 48.
5 Pseudonym of Nosar. This singular figure, not long a Social Democrat, was elected president of the Soviet at an early session.
6 Chernomordik, *op. cit.*, p. 52. See Garvi, *Vospominaniia*, p. 624 ff., for an account of the Moscow rising by a prominent Menshevik participant.
7 Mavor in Vol. II, p. 508, says the mutinies "were in no case determined by political motives," which may well be an overstatement.
8 A. Shestakov, *Krest'ianskaia revoliutsiia 1905-1907 gg. v Rossii* (Moscow, 1926), table, p. 27. Damage done: according to Maslov in article, "Krest'ianskoe dvizhenie," in Martov, etc., eds., *op. cit.*, Vol. II, Pt. 2, p. 260.
9 Martow, *Geschichte der russischen Sozialdemokratie*, p. 154.
10 M. Pavlov, *Dumskaia taktika bol'shevikov v revoliutsiiu 1905-1907 gg.* (Leningrad, 1947)), Ch. 1.
11 "Pervaia pobeda revoliutsii," *Proletarii* No. 24, 25 Oct. 1905.
12 "Mezhdu dvukh bitv," *Proletarii* No. 26, 12 Nov. 1905.
13 "Voisko i revoliutsiia,' *Novaia zhizn'* No. 13, 15 Nov. 1905 (Vol. 10, p. 35).
14 *Nashi zadachi i Sovet Rabochikh Deputatov, Soch.*, Vol. 10, p. 1. Bertram D. Wolfe comments on the curious fact that this document was not published until 1940 in *Three Who Made a Revolution*, p. 316-7.
15 "Uchites' u vragov," *Novaia Zhizn'* No. 16, 18 Nov. 1905 (Vol. 10, p. 43). Natural phenomenon arising from bourgeois character: "Sotsialisticheskaia partiia i bespartiinaia revoliutsionnost'," *Novaia zhizn'* No. 22 and 27, 26 Nov. and 2 Dec. 1905 (Vol. 10, p. 57).
16 Articles as cited in Martov, etc., eds., *op. cit.*, Vol. III, p. 591; from *Novaia Zhizn'* Nos. 1 (27 Oct.), 7, 13.
17 Lenin, "Rev. kantseliarshchina i rev. demokratiia," *Novaia Zhizn'* No. 18, 20 Nov. 1905 (Vol. 10, p. 44).
18 "Umiraiushchee samoderzhavie i novye organy narodnoi vlasti," *Novaia Zhizn'* No. 19, 23 Nov. 1905 (Vol. 10, p. 48).
19 "Russkaia revoliutsiia i zadachi proletariata," *Partiinye Izvestiia* No. 2, 20 Mar. 1906 (Vol. 10, p. 119).
20 "Sovremennoe polozhenie Rossii i taktika rabochei partii," *Partiinye Izvestiia* No. 1, 7 Feb. 1906 (Vol. 10, p. 94).
21 *Takticheskaia platforma k ob"edin. S"ezdu RSDRP, Soch.* Vol. 10, p. 127.
22 "Rabochaia gruppa v Gos. Dume," *Volna* No. 13, 10 May 1906 (Vol. 10, p. 372). See also "Kak rassuzhdaet T. Plekhanov o taktike S-Dii?" in *Vpeod* No. 1, 26 May 1906 (Vol. 10, p. 438).
23 *Pobeda kadetov i zadachi rabochei partii, Soch.*, Vol. 10, Lenin's footnote to p. 208.
24 Editorial in *Nachalo* No. 1, 13 Nov. 1905.
25 "Ili svoboda s revoliutsiei-ili reaktsiia s G. Vitte." *Nachalo No. 3*, 16 Nov. 1906. Another contributor asserted: V. Zvezdin, "Gospoda burzhua i 'Syn Otechestva'," same issue.
26 In *Nachalo* No. 8, 23 Nov. 1905.
27 F. Dan, "Pered novoi bitvoi," *Nachalo* No. 4. 17 Nov. 1905. Trotsky wrote: "Sotsialdemokratiia i revoliutsiia," *Nachalo* No. 10, 25 Nov. 1905. Saratov uprising showed: "Krest'ianskii vopros i revoliutsiia," *Nachalo* No. 7, 20 Nov. 1905.
28 No. 1 *Nash Golos*, 18 Dec. 1905.
29 In *Dnevnik Sotsialdemokrata*, esp. Nos. 3 & 4.
30 Martow, *Geschichte der russischen Sozialdemokratie*, Ch. 9.
31 Maslov, *Kritika agrarnykh programm i proekt programmy* (Moscow, 1905).
32 In *Novaia Zhizn'* Nos. 11 and 16, cited in Martov, etc., eds., *op. cit.*, Vol. III, p. 590.
33 Lenin, *Peresmotr agrarnoi programmy, Soch.*. Vol. 10, p. 161.
34 Lenin's speech to IV Congress. Vol. 10, p. 261.

NOTES

³⁵ Lenin, *Agrarnaia programma S-Dii v pervoi russkoi rev., Soch.*, Vol. 13, p. 392.
³⁶ *Ibid.*, p. 265.
³⁷ "No laws in the world" could prevent it, said Lenin in "Vopros o zemle i bor'ba za svobodu," in *Volna* No. 22, 20 May 1906 (*Soch.* Vol. 10, p. 404).
³⁸ *Agrarnaia programma*, Vol. 13, p. 392.
³⁹ Martynov speech at Stockholm Congress. *Protokoly s"ezdov i konferentsii V.K.P. (b)*; *Chetviortyi (Ob"edinitel'nyi) S"ezd R.S.D.R.P.* (Moscow, 1934), pp. 163-5.
⁴⁰ In *Kur'er* No. 4, as quoted in Martov, etc., eds., *op. cit.*, Vol. III, p. 622.
⁴¹ In *Steno. Otchety*, Vol. II, p. 1404.
⁴² *Golos Truda* No. 8, 29 June 1906, as quoted in Pavlov, *Dumskaia taktika*, p. 118.
⁴³ *Otkliki sovremennosti* No. 4, 25 May 1906, as quoted in Pavlov, *op. cit.*, p. 128.
⁴⁴ Lenin, "Duma i narod," *Volna* No. 12, 9 May 1906 (*Soch.* Vol. 10, p. 366). Martynov and Plekhanov were wrong: "Krest'ianskaia ili 'Trudovaia' Gruppa i R.S.D.R.P.," *Volna* No. 14, 11 May 1906 (Vol. 10, p. 380).
⁴⁵ "Plokhie sovety," *Volna* No. 23, 21 May 1906 (Vol. 10, p. 413).
⁴⁶ "Sredi gazet i zhurnalov," *Vperiod* No. 4, 31 May 1906 (Vol. 10, p. 462). "Bourgeois lie": "Bor'ba za vlast' i 'bor'ba' za podachki," *Vperiod* No. 17, 14 June 1906 (Vol. 11, p. 15). "Before supporting the Kadets . . .": "Eshcho o dumskom ministerstve," *Ekho* No. 6, 28 June 1906 (Vol. 11, p. 56).
⁴⁷ "Novyi pod"iom," *Volna* No. 10, 6 May 1906 (Vol. 10, p. 358).
⁴⁸ " 'Ne kverkhu nuzhno gladet', a knizu,' " *Vperiod* No. 7, 2 June 1906 (Vol. 10, p. 469).
⁴⁹ Lenin, *Rospusk Dumy i zadachi proletariata*, Vol. 11, p. 91.
⁵⁰ "Pered burei," *Proletarii* No. 1, 21 Aug. 1906 (Vol. 11, p. 113).

XIII

WHAT KIND OF PARLIAMENT?

1 Baring, *A Year in Russia* (London, 1907), p. 27.
2 Miliukov, article of 15 Dec. 1905 in *God bor'by*, p. 80.
3 Article, "K-D Partiia," Martov, etc., eds., *op. cit.*, Vol. III, p. 20.
4 Dan and Cherevanin, "Soiuz 17 okt." in *Ibid.*
5 The Progressive-Economic Party was led by M. N. Tripolitov; the Commercial-Industrial Party by G. A. Krestovnikov; the Moderate-Progressive Party by P. P. Riabushinskii (all individuals named were themselves industrial figures); the Commercial-Industrial Union represented the middle merchants of the Apraxin market and *Gostiinyi Dvor*. Riabushinskii and his friends left the Octobrists to join the ex-Slavophiles mentioned below in forming the Party of Peaceful Renovation.
6 *Partiia Mirnogo Obnovleniia. Postanovleniia* (1906), p. 13. See excellent diagram of party platforms in *Molva* No. 18, 26 Dec. 1905.
7 See Maklakov, *Vlast' i obshchestvennost'*, Vol. I, p. 218.
8 Miliukov, *God bor'by*, p. 14, written 2 Dec. 1905.
9 See Chermenskii, *op. cit.*, p. 201 ff.
10 See for example Frank's articles in *Poliarnaia Zvezda* Nos. 1 and 2, 15 and 22 Dec. 1905.
11 Text in Miliukov, *op. cit.*, p. 109.
12 In "K-D Partiia," p. 28.
13 Miliukov, *op. cit.*, p. 116.
14 *Ibid.*, p. 178. "certain mistakes of the rev. parties": *Ibid.*, p. 108.
15 *Ibid.*, p. 366.
16 Quoted by Miliukov from *Nasha Zhizn'* in *op. cit.*, p. 348.
17 *Ibid.*, p. 247.
18 Article 77 in *Ibid.*
19 Martynov, *loc. cit.*, p. 36.
20 Miliukov, *op. cit.*, p. 492. written 18 June 1906.
21 Maklakov, *Pervaia Gosudarstvennaia Duma* (Paris, 1939), p. 41. The remark undoubtedly reflected as much Maklakov's irritation with his own Kadet party

NOTES

as his admiration for the Trudoviks.

[22] *Ibid.*, p. 73. By "new order" he intends the "constitutional monarchy" created by the October Manifesto and the Fundamental Laws of 1906.

[23] *Steno. Otchety*, Vol. I, p. 322.

[24] Text in *Ibid.*, Vol. I, p. 248.

[25] *God bor'by*, p. 338.

[26] In the state-controlled newspaper, *Pravitel'stvennyi Vestnik*, 20 June 1906.

[27] *Steno. Otchety*, Vol. II, p. 1974.

[28] *Tri popytki* (Paris, 1921).

[29] Story first published by Reuters in London and reprinted by *Novoe Vremia*. See Article 128 in *God bor'by*. Shipov told Muromtsev: Shipov, *op. cit.*, p. 449. Shipov was trying to persuade Muromtsev himself to take the chairmanship of the council of ministers.

[30] *Tri popytki*, p. 60. Chermenskii asserts: in *op. cit.*, p. 288.

[31] *God bor'by*, p. 384, written 29 April 1906. He observed in June: "Evoliutsiia trudovoi gruppy," *Rech'* No. 109, 25 June 1906.

[32] *God bor'by*, p. 394 ff. written 24 June 1906.

[33] *Tri popytki*, p. 12.

[34] *Tri popytki*, p. 61.

CONCLUSION

THE FIRST POPULAR FRONT

[1] Izgoev, *Russkoe obshchestvo i revoliutsiia*, Moscow, 1910, p. 11.

[2] "Istoricheskie sud'by ucheniia Karla Marksa," in *Soch.*, Vol. 18, p. 546. This quotation is also found on the title page.

[3] "The Council of Workmen Deputies," *Russian Review*, London, Vol. II, No. 1, Feb. 1913, p. 91.

[4] Kuskova, "Otvet na vopros—kto my?" *Bez zaglaviia*, No. 3, 5 Feb. 1906.

[5] Mavor, *An Economic History of Russia*, Vol. II, p. 598.

[6] Chermenskii, *op. cit.*, p. 142.

[7] Sidorov, "Nachalo pervoi burzhuazno-demokraticheskoi revoliutsii v Rossii," *Istorik Marksist*, No. 2 (78), 1940, p. 23.

[8] "Etapi, napravleniia i perspektivy revoliutsii," *Soch.*, Vol. 10, p. 73. For a variant, see "O vremennom rev. pravitel'stve," *Proletarii*, No. 2, 21 May 1905.

[9] Iaroslavskii, "Ob odnoi nevernoi otsenke rev. 1905 goda," *Istorik Marksist*, No. 2 (54), 1936.

[10] Stalin, *Voprosy Leninizma* (11th ed.). Ogiz, 1945, p. 37.

[11] Its membership was the following: SD's 66; Trudoviks 104; SR's 37; Popular Socialists 16; Kadets 98; Right 55; Nonparty 50; Poles 46; Moslems 30; Cossack group 17.

[12] *My Past and Thoughts*, Vol. I, Pt. I. This quotation is also found on the title page.

[13] See Franz Borkenau, *World Communism: a History of the Communist International*, New York, 1939.

[14] See, for example, A. Manuilov, "Agrarian Reform in Russia," *Russian Review*, London, Vol. I, No. 4, Nov. 1912.

[15] B. D. Brutzkus, *Agrarnyi vopros i agrarnaia politika*, 1922, p. 90.

[16] *Ibid.*, 106.

[17] See my article, "Was Stolypin in Favor of Kulaks?" forthcoming in the *American Slavic and East European Review*.

[18] See I. N. Steinberg, *In the Workshop of the Revolution*, New York, 1953.

APPENDIX: CHRONOLOGY OF PRINCIPAL
CONFERENCES OF POLITICAL ORGANIZATIONS

Socialist Revolutionary Party

    I Congress: 29 Dec. 1905—4 Jan. 1906. Finland.

    II Congress: Feb. 1907.

Social Democratic Party

    I Congress: 1 March 1898. Minsk.

    II Congress: 17 July - 10 Aug. 1903. Brussels, London.

    III Congress: 12-27 April 1905. London. (Bolshevik; Mensheviks held a Conference in Geneva simultaneously).

    IV ("Unification") Congress: 10-25 April 1906. Stockholm.

    V Congress: 30 April—13 May 1907. London.

Union of Liberation

    Conference: July 1903. Near Constance.

    Conference: Sept. 1903. Kharkov.

    I Congress: 3-5 Jan. 1905. St. Petersburg.

    II Congress: 20 Oct. 1904.

    III Congress: 25-28 Mar. 1905.

    IV Congress: Aug. 1905.

Group of Zemstvo-Constitutionalists

    Conference: 8 Nov. 1903. Moscow.

    Congress: 23 Feb. 1905.

    Congress: 27 (?) May 1905.

    Congress: 9-10 July 1905.

Constitutional Democratic Party

    I Congress: 12-18 Oct. 1905. Moscow.

    II Congress: 11-15 Jan. 1906. St. Petersburg.

    III Congress: 25-28 April 1906.

    IV Congress: 24-28 Sept. 1906. Helsingfors.

    Conference: 30 Jan. 1907.

    Conference: 18-20 Aug. 1907.

Union of Unions

    I Congress: 8-9 May 1905. Moscow.
    II Congress: 24-26 May 1905. Moscow.
    III Congress: 1-3 July 1905. St. Petersburg, Terioki.
    IV Congress: 16 Jan. 1906.

Pan-Russian Peasant Union

    I Congress: 31 July - 1 Aug. 1905.
    II Congress: 6-10 Nov. 1905.
    III Congress: Mar. 1906.

Zemstvo Representatives

    Congress: May 1896.
    Congress (Zemstvo Union formed); 8 Aug. 1896. Nizhnii Novgorod.
    Conference: Aug. 1898. Moscow.
    Congress: 23-25 May 1902. Moscow.
    Conference: 25 April 1903. St. Petersburg.
    I Congress: 6-9 Nov. 1904. Moscow.
    Conference: 22-26 Feb. 1905.
    II Congress: 22-26 April 1905.
    III Congress: 24-26 May 1905.
    IV Congress: 6-8 July 1905. (Joined officially by city council delegates, who had met 15-16 June 1905, and who participated also in V and VI Congresses.)
    V Congress: 12-15 Sept. 1905.
    VI Congress: 6-13 Nov. 1905.

Congress of Trade and Industry

    Conferences: Jan., April 1906.
    I Congress: Oct. 1906.
    II Congress: 22-24 May 1907.

Union of October 17

    I Congress: 8-12 Feb. 1906.
    II Congress: 6 May 1907.

INDEX

Parentheses contain pseudonyms; brackets, real names.

Author's Note

In the research for this book I gratefully acknowledge the assistance of the librarians at the following institutions: the Bibliothèque Internationale Contemporaine and the Bibliothèque Nationale, Paris; the British Museum, the Colindale Newspaper Library, and the Library of the School of Slavonic Studies, London; and the Bodleian Library, Oxford.

The system of transliteration used is that of the Library of Congress, except when prevailing usage is otherwise. Direct citations are given in the footnotes; lack of space prevents inclusion of a complete bibliography.

Special thanks is due Professor Michael Karpovich, who read the manuscript and gave constant encouragement; Mr. Isaiah Berlin, Mr. B. I. Elkin, and Mr. V. A. Maklakov, whose observations were invaluable; and my wife, whose insight and patience were indispensable. I am obliged to Professor Karpovich for allowing me to see, just before this book went to press, the manuscript of the first volume of the memoirs of Paul Miliukov, to be published shortly by the Chekhov Publishing House.

I cannot fully express my debt to Mr. B. H. Sumner, to whose memory this book is dedicated in the consciousness of the example of character, scholarship, and devotion he left forever in the minds of his students.